Materials and Meaning in Contemporary Japanese Architecture

Tradition and Today

Dana Buntrock

Materials and Meaning in Contemporary Japanese Architecture

Tradition and Today

LONDON AND NEW YORK

First published 2010
by Routledge
2 Park Square, Milton Park, Abingdon, Oxon OX14 4RN

Simultaneously published in the USA and Canada
by Routledge
270 Madison Avenue, New York, NY 10016, USA

Routledge is an imprint of the Taylor & Francis Group,
an informa business

Designed and typeset in Rotis
by Chuck Byrne / Design, Oakland, Ca, USA

Printed and bound
by The Replika Press Pvt. Ltd., Sonepat, Haryana, India

British Library Cataloguing in Publication Data
A catalogue record for this book is available from the British Library

Library of Congress Cataloging in Publication Data

Buntrock, Dana, 1958-

Materials and meaning in contemporary Japanese architecture :
tradition and today / Dana Buntrock.
p. cm.
Includes bibliographical references and index.

1. Architecture—Social aspects—Japan—History—21st century. I.
Title. II. Title: Tradition and today.

NA1555.6.B86 2010

720.952'0905—dc22

2009036832

ISBN10: 0-415-77890-5 (hbk)

ISBN10: 0-415-77891-3 (pbk)

ISBN13: 978-0-415-77890-9 (hbk)

ISBN13: 978-0-415-77891-6 (pbk)

Contents

Acknowledgements

The research for this book was supported by a Fulbright Fellowship, the timing of which was particularly ideal. I was in Japan from July of 2006 through December of 2007: Terunobu Fujimori was featured at the 2006 Venice Biennale, a show reprised in Tokyo in 2007; his work also extensively discussed in journals and pamphlets published around the same time and in public talks and other events; Jun Aoki's Aomori Museum of Art opened in 2006 to similar fanfare; Ryoji Suzuki's buildings at Kotohira Shrine were completed in 2004, but they were the subject of a book published in 2007 and two related book talks.

I owe an enormous debt to Dr. Terunobu Fujimori of the University of Tokyo. As I wrote the opening chapters to this book, I could not help but recall the earliest days of our acquaintance. Jackie Kestenbaum (then a promising architectural historian) introduced me to Dr. Fujimori after a 1994 lecture he gave on Bruno Taut. He generously invited us to his hometown soon after, so that I could photograph the Jinchokan Moriya Museum early in the morning. Throughout that day, we three spoke of Takamasa Yoshizaka, of flowering crepe myrtles, of Fujimori's childhood and his love of rural Japan. At the end of a full day, Fujimori offered us tea, and I even now recall my surprise at his lack of concern for rotating bowls or choreographing the ritual. Afterwards, Fujimori's mother insisted that we all go off to a popular hot springs. It took me 12 years to start the book embedded in that day.

Dr. Fujimori has generously accommodated me in his research lab twice over the years, first while I was on a National Science Foundation/Japan Society for the Promotion of Science post-doctoral fellowship in 1998, and then again in 2006-2007, while on the Fulbright. I am not an architectural historian, and there are many ways that my opinions on these pages diverge from those of my colleagues and friends in the Fujimori lab and from Dr. Fujimori's own. But I am thankful for the privilege of countless hours hearing each student in the lab struggle with the waves of change that have occurred in Asia over the last 150 years.

As will become clear, this book relies heavily on Fujimori's simple structuring of the architectural community in Japan as "Red" or "White." Yet while I link the term "regionalism" to Red, Fujimori himself, in a country where the word suggests only regressive nostalgia, would not have done so. I hope that in the end he and others in Japan will reconsider the problems for the profession that result as they avoid openly acknowledging regionalism is also open to innovation. Fujimori has taught me that the particularities of place, when not valued and maintained, are far too easily rendered obsolete.

I am also deeply grateful to Fumihiko Maki for his influence. I often feared my interest in the role tradition plays today would be too easy to romanticize. Maki, who deftly acknowledges the weight of history in his writings and his works, was an inspiration that allowed me to believe I could avoid Orientalism. He was also the only one of my subjects who demanded I be very clear about the political and social influences on many of these structures I discuss. I knew that I had accomplished something when I received a note from Professor Maki one Christmas Eve, telling me of the pleasure he took in my piece on his work in Shimane. I wish more people I research in Japan were as assertive; I consider Professor Maki's ongoing mentorship both a gift and a call to responsibility.

Each of the other architects I discuss has been unsparingly supportive. Kengo Kuma, who became a key figure in this text, met with me always with great hospitality. He made his staff and his library

A screen of soft oya stone at Kengo Kuma's 2006 Chokkura Plaza seems almost woven, showing the architect's interest in Gottfried Semper.

available, assisting my efforts to understand odd details; in the process, I discovered a side to him that I had not known before. Most Westerners, in fact, are likely unaware of his wit and intelligence as an insightful author. Jun Aoki was not only a cordial subject of my scrutiny, but also, quite by accident, my immediate neighbor. In years ahead we will warmly recall the charming artwork his son exhibited on their window for my husband and I, and the many convivial dinners we all enjoyed together. Ryoji Suzuki and Masato Araya, too, have been unfailingly accommodating and indulgent, assisting in my investigation of works not easily accessible to the public. Each of these men are not merely research subjects, but also people I have come to know with great gratitude and fondness. It is a privilege to know them all.

Clients, too, are almost always a delight to meet, generous with their time and thoughtful responses to in-depth queries. Even within an unusually hospitable group, Itsuko Murai stands out in the extreme, making me early morning feasts and (far more delightful for an academic) offering a comprehensive clipping service on the museum she commissioned.

Other architects have an unseen but important presence on these pages. Hajime Yatsuka has been an unfailing and central influence in my life; as I completed this text, I re-discovered his essay "Internationalism vs. Regionalism" in my files and realized to my chagrin that I essentially set out to rediscover much of what he has argued over the years. I am lucky to have as a friend someone with both a towering intellect and infinite patience.

Itsuko Hasegawa may be surprised to find herself thanked on these pages, but a casual comment she made midway through this work did much to shape its final form. Toyo Ito, too, while playing only a modest role in the text, has been an active stimulant throughout, also offering exciting digressions from this path during my time in Japan. I am looking forward to more opportunities to survey his work.

And finally, my thanks to Kay Itoi, who took the time to be both a check on my translations and a careful Japanese-language copyeditor. Of course, any mistakes in my translations should only be blamed on me – but they are fewer thanks to Kay.

My Berkeley colleagues have been supportive in ways both visible and invisible; I simply do not believe I would have written this book had I remained in the Midwest. I find traces of the long conversation we at Berkeley have on regionalism, linked to the work of others once associated with my department, some quoted in these pages: Marc Treib, Philip Theil, and E. Michael Czaja. My colleagues have been unquestioningly open to the fact that I took nineteen months away from campus to research and write this book, even though I teach core courses. Some, like Susan Ubbelohde and Mary Comerio in my department and T.J. Pempel in the Institute of East Asian Studies, have gone further, offering unstinting and always timely advice. Lauren Mallas, my student, friend, and colleague, covered classes for me while I was gone and made my return far easier than it could have been.

Colleagues at other institutions who should not be overlooked include Bill Coaldrake, Deb Barnstone and George Wagner, each of whom offered support at timely junctions on the path to completing this manuscript. Deb deserves credit for starting this book by asking me to speak at a symposium in London – when my paper provoked passionate argument amongst all there, I realized this might be a project to take further. Bill Coaldrake has been unsparing in his insights and advice; George Wagner tends to just take a moment to scare the socks off of me. In the final days of writing this book, Clover Lee gave me a refuge far from home to quietly and calmly complete my work. I am fortunate to be amongst an international network of scholars.

Finally, there are those who inspire in print, as I hope I might. I have yet to meet Gregory Clancey, but I would like to. His book, *Earthquake Nation: The Cultural Politics of Japanese Seismicity, 1868-1930* (Berkeley: University of California Press, 2006), is one of the few I know that attempts to understand Japanese architecture and its history through materials and construction. I am grateful for the way his work influenced and informed mine.

The team at Routledge has been tremendously accommodating, especially Francesca Ford, who surely found me a demanding and insistent author. Chuck Byrne was brought in as a designer at my request and – with what turned out to be a remarkable level of difficulty – he incorporated footnotes and Japanese text on each page (in spite of not knowing Japanese!). I know from my earlier book with the same publishing family that the firm makes a commitment to scholarship that will be valued for a long time, but it is thanks to Chuck, and the time he took to mentor me, that this book is an attractive one. Many times, he brought a richer and more nuanced way of understanding what architects expressed simply in his insightful arrangement of illustrations and text.

It seems odd to thank disembodied, digital organizations (especially in a book that is inclined to the visceral), but I am also grateful to the people at Berkeley's Baker service, who collected materials on my behalf, sending them to me electronically while I was in Japan. Such support is a luxury; no research assistant could have been as attentive and untiring. In addition, I have no idea why services like DropSend exist or where they make their money, but allowing me to store materials on-line in a trouble-free and cost-free way offered me peace of mind as I shuttled between the two territories I love, each waiting for an enormous earthquake. Thank you to both of you.

And finally, arriving at the heart and in the hopes that its impression most endures, I want to thank the man I adore, often dubbed "Saint LeRoy" by those who know him well. It is he who taught me to take time for pleasure and be open to the many kinds of indulgences embodied in this book. If I had never met LeRoy, I would likely never have lifted a camera, never ventured to Japan. I would have spent little time, if any, luxuriating in *onsen* waters and eating feasts set on short tables on *tatami* floors. He was with me in Japan each day this book emerged, listening as I tried out ideas, distracting contractors, sharing *sake*. Without my husband, without his unfailing support and sustenance, without his absurdly enormous camera and good cheer, there simply would be no book at all – and life would be far less fun.

Introduction

Japan is a sort of accordion of history: a long compressed concertina where the past is very close to the present.
—Philip Thiel[1]

Temples and teahouses, shrines and sliding *shoji* screens, cascading cherry blossoms and solitary stones; perhaps this is what comes to mind when you think of Japan. Tokyoites carrying the tiniest, technologically sophisticated telephones insist they are unaware of tradition, yet all around them vestiges remain: small Buddhist cabinets at home, *sake* offerings sitting on the shelf of a delicate Shinto shrine in a favorite *sushi* restaurant. Craftsmen split bamboo with old instruments or shave ribbons of cedar by hand, using oddly beautiful planes. Many still employ their grandfathers' tools – then ship completed work to distant nations or install it on the highest floors of soaring skyscrapers not even possible a few years ago.

Art historians Julia Moore Converse and Ann Bermingham recently observed, "Despite the tremendous social, political, and economic upheavals of the twentieth century, Japan continues to inspire the world as a culture at once ultra-modern and profoundly traditional, international and yet intensely local."[2] One cannot help but wonder: how does an architect address the conflicting and concurrent demands of tradition and today?

Adopted from outside Japan in the mid-nineteenth century, architecture from the first expressed its modernity. Professor C. Douglas Lummis wrote:

> ... after the Meiji Restoration the Japanese government labored to remake Japanese society politically, economically, technologically, and culturally. Eric Hobsbawm and Terence Ranger's *The Invention of Tradition* included no analysis of Japan, but surely Japan ought to be considered as a paradigmatic case.[3]

Architecture and engineering emphasized the Japanese Empire's innovation, introducing rail lines and train stations, post offices and schools, offices and art museums – all new building types, constructed in all-new materials, and often inhabited by people in oddly innovative attire. The entire character of public space in society changed in a short time.

Everything added in the late nineteenth century emphasized the importance of the capital, the new seat of the Emperor – Tokyo – underscoring its centrality. That primacy – in architecture, infrastructure and education – is still evident today. Most of the nation's leading designers are based in Tokyo, for practical reasons if nothing else. All rail lines express their direction in relation to the megalopolis: going "up" to Tokyo, or moving "downwards" when headed away, whether north, south or westward, uphill or downriver. The web of speedy *shinkansen* bullet trains, also initially following the *Tokaido* shore, only extended farther nearly forty years after the first lines were built, but all still ultimately end in Tokyo. Likewise, few domestic flights connect cities on the periphery, yet many link the urban areas of the *Tokaido* belt – especially Tokyo, Yokohama, and Osaka – to the rest of the nation.

Japan's leading universities, too, cluster in the capital: Tokyo Uni-

Age expressed in bamboo lath, crumbling plaster and bits of straw.

1. Thiel (1962) p. 107.
2. Converse and Bermingham (2007) p. 6.
3. Lummis (2007).

versity, Waseda, Keio. A few other important ones exist – most, like Kyoto University, remnants of the Imperial University system started in the Meiji era. Universities rapidly injected Western scientific and professional knowledge into what was until the mid-nineteenth century essentially a pre-modern society separate from international exchange. Writing of the flagship, Tokyo University, historian Stefan Tanaka points out "... article one of the Imperial ordinance outlining the organization of the university stated, 'It shall be the purpose of the [Tokyo] Imperial University to teach the sciences and the arts ... in accordance with the needs of the State.'"[4] Unlike today, when architecture students explore the private territories of houses and housing, those initial undergraduates studied models for modernization; they went on to design and supervise the construction of schools, post offices and train stations, brick banks and bridges, factories and furnaces. They also became the first generation of long-term faculty, replacing the forefront of foreign hires.

Looking back almost one hundred years later, the influential architect Kenzo Tange argued:

> At the time [of the Meiji era], of the persons who had received training as Western-style architects, practically all had to connect themselves to the State or else to state influence and power ... some became supervisors of architectural administration or else architectural engineers of the government offices, some became professors in universities ...

He continued, "It may be said that the existence of an architect as a free citizen was permitted only as an exception."[5]

In those early years of the Meiji era, Japanese architects earnestly studied European eclecticism, articulating their ideas in an entirely alien language, English.[6] They were concerned not with their nation's history and traditions, initially almost entirely ignored (understandable as those first faculty, all foreign, would have little known or appreciated the intricate systems embedded in Japan's indigenous architecture). Instead, students delved into the Romanesque and Renaissance, European antiquity an endorsement of the newly elite establishment, as it was abroad. But by the time these students progressed to professorships, Japan's enthusiasm for all things Western had weakened.

Anthropologist Marilyn Ivy explained, "The state became increasingly aware of the destabilizing social forces that modernization could unleash, and came to temper its calls for advancement with appeals for time-honored 'tradition.'"[7] The Meiji government continued to embrace engineering and scientific innovation, but also began to employ religious rites to assert legitimacy. Among the earliest and most influential native-born teachers at what is today Tokyo University, architect and architectural historian Chuta Ito accordingly argued for an evolutionary architecture, adopting elements from ancient Asia in novel architectural works like his 1895 Heian Shrine in Kyoto. He drew the past into the present, asserting through his architecture that Japan would never be Western – it was of and in the Orient.

Efforts to affirm tradition were also emphasized in pavilions at international expositions in far-flung Vienna and Chicago, illustrating the argument that Japan, too, enjoyed a distinguished and cultured pedigree. An authority on Japanese architecture with an interest in these artifacts, William Coaldrake, pointed out, "... a long and rich tradition of architecture became for Japan a vital tool for countering Western perceptions of Asian inferiority."[8]

4. Tanaka (1993) p. 41.
5. Tange (1956) p. 10.
6. I am indebted to Don Choi for this important point.
7. Ivy (1995) p. 70.
8. Coaldrake (2008) p. 200.

Thus, in the opening years of the twentieth century, Japan nurtured two distinctly different poles of architectural practice: it built structures underscoring modernity and a new social fabric, internationally up to date, and yet also offered ongoing allusions to an older Asia, to Japan's religious roots or residential realms. Discourse divided into technology and science versus culture and arts, the latter often (but not always) indigenous. By the 1920s, architecture also offered a solution that straddled both: the *Teikan Yoshiki* style, concrete buildings capped with sweeping roofs recalling religious structures. Arata Isozaki asserted:

> Beginning in the late 1920s, the Japanese nationalist "decorated shed" became popular as an easy, practical way of representing Japan-ness ... Many thought that the *teikan* style was the most direct way of realizing that purpose, and accordingly a number of public buildings of the prewar era showed such ideology.[9]

Others isolated these two territories of ancient and innovative, embracing both in separate realms. Tokyo-based Czech architect Antonin Raymond, once an employee of Frank Lloyd Wright, is best known in Japan for exposed concrete structures of Perret-like lacy screens and Corbusian purity, designed and built contemporaneously with their more widely known European exemplars. But concurrently and with no sense of contradiction, Raymond designed playfully artless retreats, summer villas beyond the city. Inspired by the folkcrafts movement in Japan, Raymond used hand-hewn chestnut logs and cedar planks at these homey hideaways, buildings shingled in bark, shaggy beds of larch branches laid over metal roofing.[10]

Japan's early twentieth-century architects also used abstraction to unify past and present, an architecture of achromatism achieved by unpainted natural materials, modularity in a clearly articulated and simple structure, all inspired by the history of *shoin* and *sukiya*. The approach reached its finest expression in Junzo Sakakura's Modernist 1937 pavilion in Paris – but Sakakura's design, notably, was accomplished only through cunning; his bureaucratic clients intended something more conventional, the architect arguing its impossibility abroad. Even at the moment of Japanese architecture's greatest prewar expression, Isozaki asserts, "... because of its internationalist associations, modern architecture was oppressed and persecuted in Japan during the 1930s."[11] Orientalizing texts from this era, such as Jun'ichiro Tanizaki's 1933 *In Praise of Shadows*, remain in print abroad, seemingly washed of the implications in this shift from international to inward-turning.

Two years after Sakakura's Paris pavilion, things had changed considerably. As Akiko Takenaka-O'Brien argued in her dissertation, "In the New York World's Fair of 1939, amidst the pavilions of streamlined, futuristic design ... Japan constructed a national pavilion modeled on a traditional Shinto shrine."[12] With war unfolding, international modernism became impossible; even its strongest advocate, Kunio Maekawa, capitulated in the end. Others, especially Sutemi Horiguchi, adopted artfully collaged compositions of vernacular and modern materials, relying on the aesthetics of the teahouse, but retreating to the private realm of the residence. He looked inward, to the residential *sukiya* style.

Kenzo Tange's earliest unbuilt works, executed in the waning days of World War II, also blended past and present, drawing on Japanese archetypal architecture. His award-winning proposals in key compe-

9. Isozaki (2006) p. 9.

10. Raymond's 1933 summer retreat so closely resembled Le Corbusier's 1930 Errazuriz House (proposed for a site in Chile) that the two architects had a brief falling out. I discuss the Errazuriz House further in the next chapter. See also Helfrich and Whitaker (2006), p. 332. Dr. Terunobu Fujimori, discussed in the next chapter, continues to draw on the model offered by the Raymond house in Karuizawa, which served as a basis for the 1997 Nira House and the 2007 Yakisugi House. See "*Doukutsu Juutaku – Yakisugi House*" 洞窟住宅 – 焼杉ハウス [Cave Living – Charred Cedar House], in *Shinkenchiku* 新建築 [New Architecture], vol. 82, no. 6 (June, 2007) pp. 62–63.

11. Isozaki (2006) p. 14.

12. Takenaka-O'Brien (2004) p. 1.

titions alluded to the Grand Shrines of Ise, the Kyoto *Gosho* Imperial Palace and Katsura *Rikyu*, an Imperial retreat. Tange wrote books on two of these sites in the postwar era, published both at home and abroad and read even now. More importantly, Tange taught many architects who are still influential: Arata Isozaki, Fumihiko Maki, the late Kisho Kurokawa, and Hajime Yatsuka. Architectural historian Jonathan Reynolds rightly insists that "... [mid-century] discourse successfully shaped a consensus that modern architectural practices in Japan [were] inexorably bound up with and could not be understood outside the context of pre-modern architecture ..."[13]

Noticeably, in these three periods – the initially modernizing Meiji, the early twentieth-century before World War II, and the initial postwar years – architects drew on different pasts. In the nineteenth century, Asian allusions drew a line demarcating East from West; in the early twentieth century, Japan invaded Asia and asserted its own distinctiveness in opposition to the Orient, illustrated by archetypes on its own soil. Defeated in World War II, surrounded by little but what was leveled, architects and artists advocated a re-evaluation so thorough and complete that they returned to the past of the Japan's Neolithic *Jomon* era. Tange wrote of the *Jomon* people as powerful peasants: dark, Dionysian, brutal, strong-willed, spirited, and solid; the primitive period was a perfect paradigm for the impoverished and almost annihilated nation. Even today for older architects the word is an allusion to freedom from hierarchy, to raw strength and spirit. But Tange also acknowledged that Japan rose above this privation, presenting in his discourse an aesthetic struggle between the nomadic *Jomon* and the subsequent culture of the *Yayoi* people, primogenitors for the present, who were Apollonian and elegant aristocratic elites, ultimately eclipsing the *Jomon* people through agricultural abundance.

Tange was not alone in offering these analogies of ancient eras struggling for expression in Modern architecture, though he is perhaps best known abroad. The artist Taro Okamoto studied ethnography in Paris with Marcel Mauss and Georges Bataille before turning to painting; he first framed these ideas, and architects such as Sei'ichi Shirai advocated them as well. Shirai wrote, "To us who create, to use tradition – which is at the same time an image of the future – as a moment for creation is ... to recognize in our reality the potential as an *a priori* force connected in its history."[14] And here is where Horiguchi's *sukiya* seeds took root: enlarging on the Arcadian teahouse and the primitive power of the *Jomon* period, postwar architects underscored affinity to a populace with political power (not the Imperial elites of earlier eras); they used rustic references to celebrate commonality and community.[15] Shortly after the end of the U.S. Occupation of Japan, Ryuichi Hamaguchi wrote of, "... the spirit of 'resistance' as shown in the *sukiya*. The *sukiya* must always have a certain link of sympathy with the lives of the poor ..." Hamaguchi linked the architecture of private retreats to the political tenor of the times: "when one speaks of *wabi* or *sabi*, there are (1) resistance to authority, (2) a feeling of solidarity with the poorer classes ..."[16] tellingly continuing,

> at least in a sentimental sense. For that reason, in modern *sukiya*, no matter how much money has been spent on it, and no matter how luxurious it may be, it must not give the impression that it is different from the way of life and characteristics of the general multitude.[17]

13. Reynolds (2001) p. 316.
14. Shirai (1956) p. 4. Shirai also links Rikyu to the *Jomon* era on the same page.
15. See, for example, Ito (1956) p. 37.
16. Hamaguchi (1956) p. 57.
17. Ibid., p. 59.

In those initial years of the postwar era, Japan thus reframed an international understanding of what it offered by proffering gentle arts: flower arranging and fine kimono, pottery and handmade paper. The nation emphasized modest rustic retreats, thatched farmhouses and small shrines demanding regular reconstruction – not the robust architectures of monumental temples or of castles set on tall curving walls of huge, hand-cut stone.

Japan roared back to life, its economic recovery a new sort of war, white-collar workers encouraged to undertake aggressive innovation. Only decades after its thoroughgoing devastation, Japan's economy ranked second internationally, thanks in part to technological innovation. At the first Olympics in Asia, held in Tokyo in 1964 (and then again at the first International Exposition in Asia, held in Osaka in 1970), visitors from abroad boarded high-speed trains traveling 200 kilometers an hour, bound for Kyoto's gardens and shrines. The nation felt no need for tradition to tell its tale to any but tourists; it used technology to state its strengths. Tange's sophisticated stadia sheltered them in Tokyo, his sprawling steel space frame in Osaka. There were robots and prefabricated capsule hotels; architects offered audacious proposals to urbanize in Tokyo Bay. Scientific civilization supplanted the cultural arts. That trend continues today, with Buck Rogers elevators zipping through trellis-like tubes at Toyo Ito's Sendai Mediatheque and spare, 16-millimeter thick (5/8 of an inch) structural sheets all that enfold Kazuyo Sejima's Plum Grove House. Architects' explorations in shipyard steel, curving concrete and extruded aluminum annihilate expectations of what is unbuildable.

And so today, the leading Tokyo University architectural historian Hiroyuki Suzuki understandably objects, "... the fiction is that Japanese architecture has been created in the spirit of ideas such as *mono no aware, wabi, sabi, shibui, iki* ... generated by the traditions of Shinto, the philosophy of Zen, and the way of tea."[18] To evade such threadbare thinking, many simply avoid talking of tradition today. Science is instead embraced.

While architects enthusiastically accepted commercialism and cutting-edge technology, ignoring antiquity, society was drawn to "Discover Japan." In the aftermath of the 1964 Olympics and the 1970 Expo, the nation exploited its extensive new infrastructure to explore its past.[19] The domestic tourism industry offered excursions to leafy shrines and stone gardens, ending the day immersed in *onsen* hot springs or on a futon laid on a *tatami* floor. The two territories of tradition and today each grew, one romantic and provincial, the other international and innovative; regional richness was pitted against representations of national know-how.

A few hardy postwar *machi-tsukuri* ("town-building") pioneers developed districts around the scattered remains of earlier eras, often in service to tourism. Their ability to offer a critical examination of local character, however, was hampered by the clientele they served, who desired familiar counterfeits and cleverly concealed modern comforts. When challenged to acknowledge the past, industry fell back on stereotypical symbols, nationalized traditions derived from shared sources, the selections shifting with time, but remaining remarkably united. (Coaldrake points out that even a model of a farmhouse shipped to an 1873 exposition in Vienna, one "which would normally display distinct regional characteristics, is a strangely generic building rather than one that can be identified with a specific part of Japan."[20]) An undercurrent of interest in the past only

18. Suzuki (1996) p. 9.
19. See Ivy (1995).
20. Coaldrake (2008) p. 204.

smoldered until Kisho Kurokawa tried to revive the ornamental excess of Toshogu Shrine as part of his postmodern pastiche, arguing for a revived respect for Japan's Edo era (1603 – 1867) as early as the 1960s. Perhaps it is only evident in retrospect why his effort died, irrelevant in moments of extreme economic vigor, the Toshogu too Chinese at a time when Japan as yet felt superior to Asia. Had he lived a bit longer, Kurokawa might have had better luck: Japan today cannot help but acknowledge the economic impact of its larger next-door neighbor.

In the Japanese countryside today, economic optimism is no longer evident. Small city centers are in decay; silent, shuttered shops separated by open urban lots. In the wake of Japan's burst Bubble era of economic speculation, municipalities merge and villages are vanishing.[21] To towns beyond Tokyo, tourism is often the only industry. Just as the Meiji government once used architecture to draw a distinction between East and West and the nation subsequently used architecture to emphasize its autonomy in Asia, now rural clients insist architects underscore the unique nature of each outpost. This is uncomfortable territory for architects. Accustomed to short daytrips to distant sites, unschooled in Japanese architectural history (a legacy of those early days of education offered by foreign faculty), almost all today remain ignorant of the past, unaware of the subtleties of place. Clients commodify their heritage with no awareness of complications, but architects fear that acknowledging custom and local culture may move them uncomfortably close to convention and *kitsch*. They grapple with how to accommodate history.

In a book entitled *The Future of Nostalgia*, Russian émigré Svetlana Boym argues that there are not merely differences in one's comfort with the past, but also in one's construction of it. She offers two types of nostalgia, restorative and reflective: "Restorative nostalgia does not think of itself as nostalgia, but rather as truth and tradition. Reflective nostalgia ... does not shy away from the contradictions of modernity."[22] Elsewhere in the same book, she adds, "Restorative nostalgia manifests itself in total reconstruction ... of the past, while reflective nostalgia lingers on ruins, the patina of time and history"[23] and adds, "... restorative nostalgia has no use for the signs of historical time – patina, ruins, cracks, and imperfections."[24] It was exactly this acceptance of age that started me on my search for the meaning in materials, my confusion at the works illustrated in the pages ahead embracing decay, deterioration, corrosion and cracking, without in any way being conservative. In the end, I have come to see these approaches as embodying a reflective response to tradition, establishing a range of regionalisms, representing differing perspectives on the relationship between past and present.

21. See, for example, Kohara (2007) pp. 7–11. The newsletter can be accessed on-line at http://newslet.iss.u-tokyo.ac.jp/. Kohara points out that overall municipalities in Japan dropped from 3,232 in 1999 to 1,820 in 2006, and that in some prefectures the number of municipalities dropped to nearly 1/4 of earlier totals.

22. Boym (2001), p. xviii.

23. Ibid., p. 41.

24. Ibid., p. 45.

Black
Blood Red
to
Palest Pink

Neolithic Daddy

Terunobu Fujimori

1

Is pleasure not the province of architecture?—*Paul Finch*[1]

Even in Japan, Terunobu Fujimori's structures are oddities: buildings balance on crooked legs, stumps driven directly into soggy soil; lumpy plaster walls crazed in a filigree of fine cracks; weeds sprout from buildings' skins.[2] Inside his 1991 debut structure, Jinchokan Moriya Museum, is a capriciously inaccessible tower (for building storage) reached by a drawbridge. Associates, who knew Fujimori as a respected historian, assumed this first building was an architectural aberration. Emboldened, Fujimori's subsequent structures were instead odder: his second was an awkward, over-heavy lump speckled with tiny, fragile flowers and topped with a pyramidal lawn. Fujimori's designs emerge as if from illustrations in a child's book: tree-trunk columns in a forest-like interior, playful teahouses punningly close to tree houses, a valiant bush topping Camellia Castle. "Soda Pop Spa," for nude bathing, wears dapper stripes of scorched cedar and white plaster. Each architectural effort is entirely unique and idiosyncratic. Fujimori once impishly insisted, "Someday I would like to make something like Gaudi's out of wood ..."[3] Outlandish, Fujimori's architecture is also in demand, his tiny structures often published in the professional press or exhibited alongside far more complex masterpieces by Toyo Ito, Arata Isozaki and other major architects.

Fujimori himself is something of an outlier. A historian specializing in Japanese architecture of the late nineteenth century, he only began to design buildings in his middle age. He argues that today

1.2

1.1 Tucked away in Nagano Prefecture, Terunobu Fujimori's 1992 Jinchokan Moriya Historical Museum was his debut work.

1.2 Long, hand-split cedar shakes, evidence of a lost art, meet a stucco coat applied with gouged blocks of styrofoam.

1. Finch (2006) p. 27.
2. "Since ancient times, a method of sinking the pillars about three feet into the ground was widely used, but was eventually abandoned because the wood rapidly decayed" (Parent 1983) p. 2.
3. Fujimori *et al.* (2005) p. 13. Original Japanese: いつか木造ガウディをつくってみたいが無理だろう。

1.3

1.4

"... I find the act of conceiving and building ... to be immensely rewarding, since the act of practicing architecture gives life to the knowledge I have gained as a historian."[4] Managing no more than a handful of structures in any given year, Fujimori is an award-winning provocateur.

His architecture invokes built tradition without being slavish. He mixes vernacular references with inspiration from the early days of Modernism, especially its unexplored opportunities. While avant-garde architect Toyo Ito worried, "... that Fujimori-style architecture pretty much repudiates all of Modernism is vexing," Fujimori corrected Ito, arguing, "[I] collect the dregs and things that twentieth-century modernism threw off, and draw them together."[5] Alvar Aalto's architecture might be thought an exemplar for the kind of Modernism that influences Fujimori, progressive and place-specific.[6] Other heterodox Modernist examples include Mies van der Rohe's low-slung brick buildings or the postwar architecture of Louis Kahn – rough construction and modest materials making up a sensually and symbolically rich Modernism, works of wood, brick, or stone, the familiar materials of the world around us.

Fujimori says of his approach, "In my architectural vocabulary there are many ties to older farmhouses. It's like putting together an original language derived from the fragmented words of various rural nooks and niches."[7] His building blocks are playfully altered in their incorporation. Odd elements of construction are used as punctuation marks, snagging the eye and calling attention to the way his architecture quotes the commonplace, yet also challenging you to recollect their roots. In an early essay, architect Kengo Kuma called Fujimori's work "Nostalgia like nothing you've ever seen."[8]

Especially inspired by Le Corbusier, Fujimori underscores,

> ... completing the Villa Savoye served as a consummation; after that [Le Corbusier's] style made a turn: from orthogonal boxes to rugged, sculpted form, from a white, flat wall to rough unfinished concrete surfaces. No longer only steel, glass, and concrete – natural stone, red brick, timber, earth.[9]

This is the hedonic Le Corbusier, the one pictured pot-bellied and naked at a cabin, whose architecture emerged through observation and opportunities to build in India and rural France.[10] This was Le Corbusier mourning "The destruction of regional cultures ..." arguing "... what was held most sacred has fallen: tradition, the legacy of ancestors, local thinking ..."[11]

Le Corbusier – like the early twentieth-century Tokyo architect Antonin Raymond, who was once accused of stealing from Le Corbusier's sketchbooks and who in turn influenced Fujimori – dispensed a rough regionalism where geography or use demanded: at the 1930 Errazuriz House in South America, for example, or the 1935 La Palmyre-Les Mathes cottage, a summer retreat built in the impoverished inter-war era. Of Errazuriz House, scholar Christiane Crasemann Collins suggested, "... Le Corbusier chose native tree trunks, plainly notched ... In its artless simplicity, the timber of the interior is the most overt gesture toward the 'primitive hut,' more so than the rustic stones and clay tiles."[12] She goes on to quote Le Corbusier:

> Since sufficiently skilled labor was not available in this place, the composition was developed using elements existing on the site and easy to build with: walls of big blocks of stone, roof-frame of tree trunks, roof of local tiles, therefore a sloping roof.[13]

4. Isozaki *et al.* (2007) p. 78.

5. Fujimori and Ito (2007) pp. 48–49. Original Japanese:
伊東：とにかく藤森建築はモダニズム建築と全否定しちゃうようなところがあるから、それが悔しい。
藤森：20世紀が捨ててきたカスを集めて丸めたようなものなんだね。

6. Aalto was influenced through his friendship with the Japanese consul in Finland and was founder of the Finnish Japanese Society. He also possessed an extensive collection of books on Japanese architecture. Thus the ties between Fujimori's work and Aalto's may simply be similarly influenced by Japanese tradition.

7. Fujimori (2006d) p. 021. Original Japanese:
私のヴォキャブラリーは、古いタイプの民家にツナガルものが多い、さまざまな地域の異った言語に由来する断片的単語と寄せ集めてしゃべるのに近い。

8. Kuma (1992) n.p. A similar perspective is seen in Mark Swenarton's *Artisans and Architects: The Ruskinian Tradition in Architecture Thought* (1989) p. 43. Swenarton, referring to one of Ruskin's advocates, says: "At Red Barn, [Philip] Webb used elements of the local vernacular ... but not in a way that reproduced any actual vernacular building."

9. Fujimori (2002) p. [22]. Original Japanese:
…サヴォア邸の完成を端境にして、以後作風が一転した。四画な箱から凸凹のある彫塑的な造型へ、白い平らな壁から荒々しい打ちっ放しコンクリートの仕上げへ。鉄とガラスとコンクリートだけではなくて、自然石、赤い煉瓦を、木を、土を。

10. Christiane Crasemann Collins and Harris Sobin both offer interesting scholarship on this period in Le Corbusier's work. Sobin quotes Reyner Banham as calling this the period when Le Corbusier "took to the woods." See Sobin (2007) p. 143.

11. "Excerpts from [Le Corbusier's] *Precisions: On the Present State of Architectural and City Planning*," in Canizaro (2007) p. 272.

12. Crasemann Collins (1987) p. 48.

13. Ibid., p. 49; incomplete citation suggests the original is in the *Œuvre Complète de 1929–1934*.

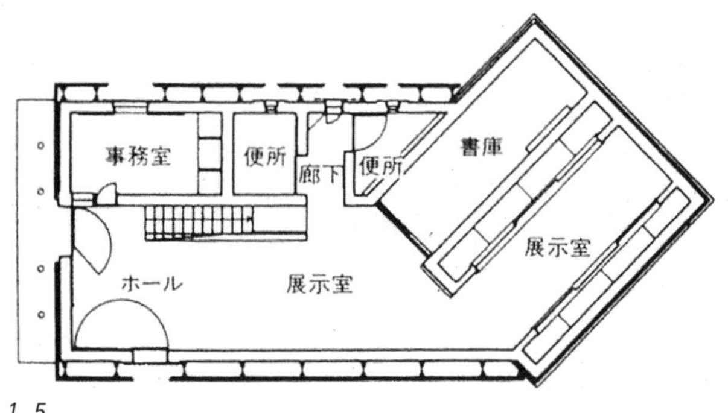

1.5

1.6

1.7

1.8

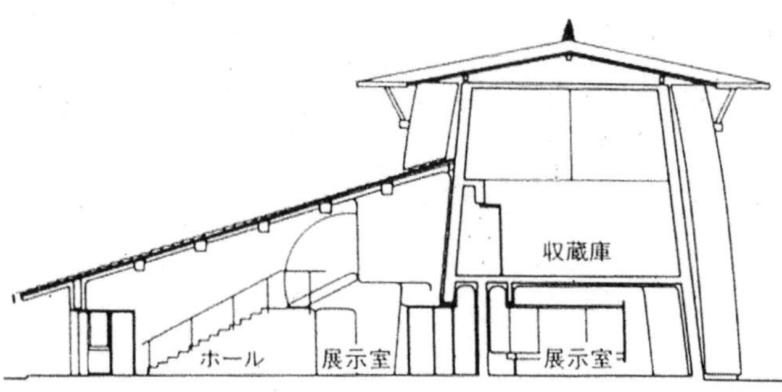

1.9

1.3-9 The entrance is framed in slender trunks culled from the slopes above the site; oddly intriguing details throughout, many reflecting Fujimori's naïveté, enliven the simple structure.

1 . 11

1 . 10–13 *Steel birds signify the tiny museum's ties to the Suwa Shrine nearby; the grain of long, hand-split shakes and the bent branches above suggest spirit yet remains in each piece of lumber.*

In these later, postwar projects, Le Corbusier's architecture is voluptuous, tactile and coarse, not the streamlined sophistication inspired by ships.

Other important architects operating outside mainstream practice in Japan also trace their education and training directly to Le Corbusier, most through Takamasa Yoshizaka, who worked in Le Corbusier's office from 1950–1952; projects on the boards at that time included Ronchamp, Chandigarh, and the Villa Shodan in Ahmadabad, India. Again at home, Yoshizaka designed the 1956 Japanese Pavilion for the Venice Biennale, unglazed openings interrupting roof and floor; the pinkish, presciently postmodern 1962 Athène Français, an exterior sporting letters incised in scalloped concrete;[14] and the 1965 University Seminar House, tiny huts scattered across a slope, an enormous inverted pyramid piercing the summit above. Yoshizaka joined Waseda, an illustrious private university, in 1959; while there, he taught many idiosyncratic architects to be discussed later in this book: Osamu Ishiyama, Hiroshi Naito, and the founders of the ateliers of Team Zoo, each embracing architectures rough and rooted. Fujimori sets his work, and theirs, in opposition to the convention of internationally-oriented architectures, which he calls a "White School" with a purist bent: spare structures, state-of-the art, smooth and swooping, scholarly and scientific.[15] Its antithesis, which Fujimori colors Red, inclines instead to rough and rugged, robust and vigorous, intending an ongoing evolution of traditional artisanship and even of artless ineptitude.

Fujimori's lively and even audacious humor distances him from a doctrinaire approach. Instead, his architecture echoes the odd peculiarities in daily life.[16] The common but quirky landscape inspires an

1 . 12

14. These letters are yet another allusion to Antonin Raymond; they are the same typeface used in a widely read book of Raymond's details.

15. While Fujimori appears to be the first to use the terms Red and White to classify architects, each term is found independently within architectural criticism. The use of "white" as a label for work by Le Corbusier and others is widely accepted; Fujimori openly acknowledges ties between his use of the term "white" and this usage. More intriguingly, I have seen Alvar Aalto referred to as a "Red Modernist" and Aalto's later work is sometimes called "white." In this case, the terms are an allusion to Aalto's materiality, not politics, but echo the historical use of "red" and "white" in early twentieth-century Finnish politics. These parallel labels are particularly provocative, as Aalto's "red" and "white" periods present a similar character to Fujimori's "Red" and "White" schools. Nonetheless, Fujimori says his references are not consciously linked to a similar use of terms regarding Aalto.

16. Tashiro (2006) p. 185. This may also be linked to Fujimori's upbringing in a relatively remote area, which would have nurtured Fujimori's avid interest in vernacular architecture as found through exploration. Using an ancient name for the region, Shinano, architectural historian William Coaldrake writes, "The rugged, uncompromising terrain of Shinano was also the matrix for local identification ... localism is evident in variations of architectural style, methods of construction and building materials" (1992) p. 12.

1 . 13

1.14

1.15

1.16

1.17

influential group of authors and artists Fujimori entered in the mid-1980s, ROJO (an abbreviation of *Rojo Kansatsugaku*, the "Roadway Observation Study [Group]"). Even now, it meets to share photographs of eccentric vignettes: a chicken caged in an obsolete television, an elaborate stair ending in an uninterrupted wall.[17] Speaking of ROJO at the Venice Biennale in 2006, another of the original members, Tetsuo Matsuda, explained:

> We go exploring ... for things that are strangely out of place, just plain odd, or mysterious. We mainly notice forms created unconsciously by city dwellers or the traces left by natural phenomena. We find new beauty in objects or structures discovered in this way ...[18]

Fujimori underscores an important distinction, one easily applied to his own architecture: "anything beautiful in the ordinary sense is excluded."[19] ROJO draws on mid-century Japanese artistic movements, on an era when performance art trumped traditions, when artists "most often chose the local and the everyday as ... terms of reference, no longer the globe or even the nation as a unit."[20] Fujimori's manifesto-like "anybody should be able to construct a temporary place to sleep in and invite friends to for meals ..." recalls artist Yoko Ono's "Art [*geijutsu*] is not a special thing. Anyone can do it. Making art does not have to be so unusual ... middle-aged men and housewives, your neighbors, can also do it."[21] ROJO's artists – especially Genpei Akasegawa – influence Fujimori more than is often understood.

Akasegawa was at the center of Japan's democratizing postwar art world: a member of the "Neo Dada" school and also one of three artists who called themselves "High Red Center," who swept the streets in absurd performance art. Akasegawa's work ultimately landed him

1.18

1.19

1.14 Inside, exhibits of animals hunted in the area in ancient times.

1.15 A tree trunk standing sentry displays its scarred surface, caused by termites and decay when it was still living.

1.16 Mortared surface meets a skin of split yew.

1.17, 18 Fujimori frankly expressed his structure's second skin.

1.19 At the eave, simple joinery ostentatiously expressed.

1.20, 21 Takamasa Yoshizaka, an architect who influenced Fujimori, offered a playful pink concrete wall at his 1962 Athène Français in Tokyo.

1.20

1.21

in the Supreme Court, a debate about his Warholian 1,000-yen note facsimiles turned into the ultimate in performance art. The artist is intellectually indebted to the painter Taro Okamoto (who first developed a Japanese postwar primitivism), and Fujimori to architect Kenzo Tange.[22] In the 1960s, Okamoto inspired Tange to argue, "... Jomon culture may be considered a product of sheer vitality, while Yayoi culture resulted from a process of thought which imposed a recognizable order ..."[23] He added, "One [the *Yayoi*] is resigned and still; the other rebellious and dynamic."[24] Tange's ersatz history of *Jomon* and *Yayoi* seems strongly paralleled in Fujimori's architectural extremes of Red and White.

Akasegawa alluded to this thinking when he dubbed Fujimori a "Neolithic Daddy" in a 1991 illustration of the academic-cum-architect awkwardly hacking at a piece of wood.[25] In 2007, Akasegawa recalled initially identifying Fujimori as *Jomon* (Neolithic) and the rest of ROJO as *Yayoi* (the agricultural period that followed the Neolithic era), playing up Fujimori's unsophisticated origins within this group of urbanites.[26] In the end, ROJO's members aligned themselves with Fujimori, evolving backwards in time, becoming the "*Jomon Kenchiku Dan*" (literally, "Neolithic Construction Crew", usually referred to in English simply as the *Jomon* Company). All but one are also in the *Jomon* Company, amateur artisans called upon to finish Fujimori's finest architectures. Some also commissioned notable structures: the *Nira* (Leek) House, Camellia Chateau, and several teahouses. Fujimori feels, "... without the [*Jomon*] Company, I don't think the tearooms that followed would exist."[27] These are, I would argue, his most important bits of architecture.

In the end, Tange abandoned *Jomon* dynamism; Fujimori positions himself as reviving Red. He jokes that initially his first work, the Jinchokan Moriya Historical Museum, mystified most architects, although a few, including Isozaki and Ando, deemed it "interesting." ROJO's artists, on the other hand, were overwhelmingly enthusiastic. Shinbo Minami recalled they worried they might hate this pioneer work; they were instead delighted to discover a building "not like something that had been made, but like something that simply was."[28] Fujimori insists even now that when Akasegawa is by his side he feels greater confidence; this may be why he was undeterred by the architecture community's initial antipathy when at first derided as an amateur architect.

Other aspects of Fujimori's architecture are even more enigmatic; the Jinchokan Moriya Historical Museum also grappled with ancient, pantheistic Shinto. A childhood friend asked Fujimori to identify an architect for a museum of reliquaries associated with the Main Upper section of Suwa Grand Shrine.[29] Instead, Fujimori decided to design the structure – evidently without entirely explaining his inexperience. The Moriya family perhaps never thought to ask; they trusted Fujimori to propose a building sympathetic to its surroundings.

Fujimori's simple, shed-like structure sports a long, sloping slate roof echoing the hills beyond, distinctly different from most modern museums. Fujimori once asserted, "The gods died, and thus the roof died. In the world of architecture, first the gods died and then nature died."[30] Elsewhere, he stated, "Nature's rain condenses drip by drip; the roof – the architecture – receives the rain drip by drip. The roof is the contact point with nature; nature permeates the roof."[31] Today, Fujimori's roofs often exaggerate their nearness to nature: landscape-like, with wood planks planted with grasses, flowers strewn across

17. Perhaps all these tiny but extremely officious organizations lovingly lampoon Japan's tendency to promote groups. ROJO is composed of five members, all of whom are also members of the larger *Jomon* Company, discussed elsewhere in this chapter. Examples of Akasegawa's ROJO photos can be seen in Munroe (1994) pp. 250–251.

18. Matsuda (2006) p. 2.

19. Fujimori (2006c) p. 07.

20. Havens (2006) p. 41.

21. "Build Your Own House." "*Maison* 4.5 Mat" exhibition pamphlet Maison Hermes Eighth Floor Forum (Spring 2007). Yoko Ono is quoted in Tomii (2007) p. 41.

22. Fujimori penned an extensive monograph on Tange, published in 2002.

23. Tange and Kawazoe (1960) p. 18.

24. Ibid.

25. Akasegawa (1991) p. 8. This is about two years before a revival of interest in the Jomon era was again seen in the Japanese art world.

26. Tokyo Opera City Recital Hall (26 April, 2007).

27. Isozaki, *et al.* (2007) p. 92.

28. Tokyo Opera City Recital Hall (26 April, 2007). Original Japanese: 作ったものではなくて、有ったもの。

29. 上諏訪大社の本宮。Gunter Nitschke points out that about 10 percent of Japan's shrines belong to the Suwa cult. See Nitschke (1993) p. 18.

30. Fujimori (2006d) p. 85. Original Japanese: 神は死に、屋根も死んだ。建築の世界では、まず神が死に、次は自然が死んだのだった。

31. Ibid., p. 84. Original Japanese: …自然は雨の一粒一粒に凝集され、屋根は建築というものを一身に代表して一粒一粒を受けとめた。屋根は自然との接点ダッタ。屋根には自然が浸みていた。One could also argue that the drawbridge is an important motif in Fujimori's work.

1.22

1.23

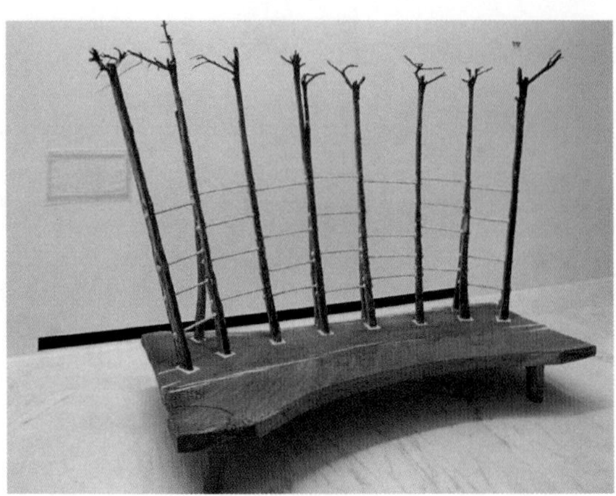

1.24

stone surfaces, tree trunks retaining valiant, bent branches and pots of perennials. These contrarian, oddly angled roofs are an important element of Fujimori's architecture and its appeal. Consciously echoing Le Corbusier's Five Points, Fujimori offers five features of his own: column, cave, soil, fire – and the roof.

Fujimori tied his first museum to nature not only in its form. He used natural materials as well: one-meter-long Japanese cypress shakes, hand blown, bubbled glass and wrought iron, under a rough roof of naturally split stone. Fujimori hoped to use rammed earth on the exterior, but settled for stucco and concealed beneath it a legally required concrete structure.[32] As the design unfolded, Fujimori observed its most powerful arguments lay in its hand-cut, natural materials. Understanding that this vitality and sensuality are often missing in the architecture around us, Fujimori committed to a consciousness of nature and the human hand.

1.25

Fujimori also recognized the religious roots of this first structure in its rituals.[33] Industrialized societies shrug off such rites, scientific know-how replacing a naïve hope that a ground-breaking or a topping-off ceremony might assure anything. But at Jinchokan Moriya Museum, Fujimori recast ritual. The Suwa Grand Shrine is rebuilt on a regular schedule; its *Onbashira* Festival is known throughout Japan, hefty logs plummeting downhill to the shrine. A small structure on land owned by Fujimori's family is rebuilt at the same time, also acknowledging these cycles.[34] He allied his Jinchokan Museum and the Grand Shrine by underscoring associations.[35]

Yet an imitation of the iconic *Onbashira* Festival would be only an absurd effort, farcical in its failure. Fujimori borrowed less obvious symbols – recognizable, but also accessible within the context of his 184-sq m (1980-sq foot) structure: he implanted notched, bird-like pieces of metal in the columns flanking his entrance.[36] In the *Onbashira* Festival, these steel wedges are embedded in sacred trees – thus these charming little birds not only recall Suwa Shrine and its famous rites, but also suggest Fujimori's structure is alive and sacred.

Fujimori culled the columnar logs flanking Jinchokan's entrance from nearby village property he and the Moriyas claim rights to. The choice was pragmatic:

> When building my debut project, the Jinchokan Moriya Historical Museum, I thought I would supply the four columns at the entrance right from the start. In this area, there are a number of varieties of yew called *minezou*, and that is what I picked. I did not really think I could get what I wanted if I left it to others.[37]

32. Fujimori's willingness to clad a concrete structure with wooden shakes, while handled with remarkable frankness, troubles many Japanese critics. He does, however, comfortably justify the approach by pointing to Semper (modern within Japan because of his Western origins) and Loos. Here, as in other points I discuss below, Fujimori can also point to Ruskin for justification; Ruskin discussed the relationship between actual and apparent construction in his *Lamp of Truth*, and, as Cornelia Baljon noted, "It is not taken for granted that the two should coincide ...rather [the two should establish] an interesting, yet intelligible, dialogue" (Baljon, 1997) pp. 401–402.

33. Although much altered here, parts of my discussion on ritual included in the following pages were first published in Japanese as Buntrock (2006a) pp. 142–145.

34. Suzuki, H (2006a) p. 89. The title offers a pun on Fujimori's name, linking him to an early influence on tea, Soujun Ikkyu. The allusion may also be due to Ikkyu's oddball reputation; one author called him a "Zen eccentric" and an "abbot-rapscallion;" see Levine (2005) pp. xl and 10. The characters in the name "Ikkyu" also suggest a moment of leisure.

35. For more on Suwa Shrine, see Nitschke (1993), especially pp.18–19 and 67–71. Nitschke points out that at the heart of Suwa Taisha's male shrine, "one is faced with a huge, naturally rooted Japanese cedar tree, immediately indicating ... that the deity's body in the shrine is a tree" (p. 19).

36. This bird-like piece is crafted from no-longer usable axe heads, and is called a *nagigama*.

37. Fujimori *et al.* (2005) p. 100.
Original Japanese:
処女作(神長官守矢史料館)の建設にあたり、正面に立てる4本の丸太柱は、最初から自分で調達するつもりだった。樹種もこの地方に多いミネゾウ(イチイ)と決めていた。市場や他人にまかせて自分の気に入るものが入手できるとはとても思えなかったからだ。

1.22 Rammed earth hearth at the center of Fujimori's 1999 The Forum, a private meeting room at a remote ski resort.

1.23 Gathering space in The Forum is sheltered under woven bamboo.

1.24 A small seat, similar to Fujimori's architectural efforts.

1.25 Bamboo lightly bound, a filigree of twigs filling in the loose lattice.

1.26 Under a vault of arcing white plaster-covered branches and charcoal twigs, a tiny tea space in a loft-like nook at The Forum.

1.27

1.28

1.29

1.30

1.31

1.27 The shaggy roof over the tiny tearoom at the 1997 Nira House.

1.28 Nira House's delicate fur of flowering potted nira – commonly (and here punningly) called a leek, but perhaps closer to Chinese chives.

1.29 The rear elevation of Genpei Akasegawa's study is surprisingly understated.

1.30 A grass-covered narrow mound separates Nira House from the street.

1.31 Seen from the narrow road it faces, Nira House's roof sloping lower than the street.

1.32 A branch topping the ridge, a purely ornamental gesture.

1.32

1.33

1.34

1.33 The tiny "crawl through" door into Fujimori's first tearoom.

1.34 Kindling is embedded in lumpy hand-set plaster walls.

1.35 The tearoom's modest tokonoma display shelf reflects in spirit the influence of the sixteenth century master Sen no Rikyu.

1.36 Thick planks wrapping the living room are frankly revealed at a window.

1.37 A tiny catwalk above the two-story living room leads to the tearoom.

1.35

Fujimori afterwards explained how this eventually became integrated in his approach to making buildings,

> ... then when I built Grass [*Tanpopo*] House, there is all this paulownia, chestnut, and Japanese oak living in the mountains of my hometown. So I provided it. I delivered the wood to the local sawmill, did everything including drying it, and supplied it to the builder. I was not actually thinking of participating in construction, just that if I picked the wood myself there were cost and design advantages over asking the builder to supply it. It was expedient.[38]

The wood on Fujimori's hillside is free to all in the community – but these trunks clearly express their humble *provenance* in knots and gnarled branches. Unlike the defect-free, precious woods used in sophisticated settings, unlike select, stockpiled lumber, the awkward angles of Fujimori's timber recall the bent, twisted beams that were all allowed to farmers and peasants in the Edo era. Fujimori's harvested trunks evolved as aesthetically distinct and spatially highlighted columns in his interiors. He keeps returning to the hillsides of his hometown, harvesting his lumber, and in this way interweaving his far-flung architecture with his ancestry and humble inspirations. When Fujimori finds this effort impractical, he'll instead choose wood available to his clients, near their construction sites. Sometimes he and his client carve a column into its final contours, bonding in its execution; a sense of impishness embodied in this ritualized reworking may lead clients to also take a more playful and open attitude toward the design of their building. Fujimori's former clients have at times joined the *Jomon* Company, participating in the construction of subsequent structures – not only strengthening and maintaining their

1.36

1.37

38. Ibid. Original Japanese: つづく、タンポポハウスのときは、桐やナラや栗の丸太は生まれ故郷の山に入って自分で調達し，村の製材所に運んで製材し、乾燥までやってから建設会社に渡している。工事に参加する気持ちはさらさらなく、建設会社に頼むより自分で選んだほうがコスト的にもデザイン上もいい。そういう材料調達の便法にすぎなかった。

1.38-42 The hip roof of Fujimori's 1995 house for his family, Tanpopo (Dandelion) House, for the dandelions and other flowers in its walls. The living room within is lined in rough lumber.

1.38

1.39

1.40

ties to Fujimori, but also tacitly encouraging a new client at a crucial moment. Sociologists argue that status and role reversal can remove reserve or reticence; the act of imitating artisans, complete with the appropriate attire, offers Fujimori's educated clients and the band of artists and *aficionados* that make up the *Jomon* Company just such a giddy role reversal. Fujimori's rewriting of ritual reflects his larger comfort with reconstructing convention.

Fujimori's ground-breaking research on the Japanese Victorian era, Meiji, is focused on a time when foreign engineers and architects changed the face of the nation. Yet in the end Fujimori repudiates the values of the Meiji era: nineteenth-century Japan embraced internationalism and was emphatically urbane, but Fujimori strives to express local differences and rural roots in his architecture. The Meiji era reshaped Shinto, Japan's indigenous faith, as rigid religion, a counterpart of Catholicism, but Fujimori accepts a romantically religious sensibility. The ancient acts of an early and intimate worship of nature, "Shrine Shinto," are too easily confused with the more recent "State Shinto," employed as a jingoist apparatus in World War II. Because of the provocative problems Shinto thus presents, most urbane architects avoid it completely. But Fujimori refutes the relatively recent reshaping of Shinto, embracing instead its ancestry, the spirit – and spirits – of place.

In the first few days of 2006, photographer LeRoy Howard and I called on Fujimori in his hometown. Abruptly our host urged, "Well, since it's the right thing to do, we should head down to the shrine." Without discussion, he shot ahead and paid for the three of us to enter the inner precincts. We were brought into its heart and prayed over, properly introduced.[39] Most Japanese I know would not comport

1.41

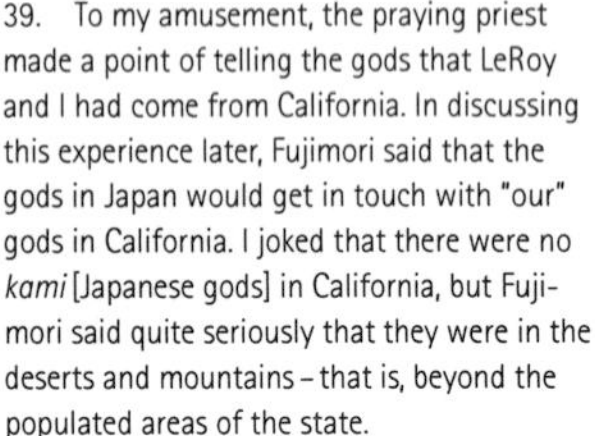

39. To my amusement, the praying priest made a point of telling the gods that LeRoy and I had come from California. In discussing this experience later, Fujimori said that the gods in Japan would get in touch with "our" gods in California. I joked that there were no *kami* [Japanese gods] in California, but Fujimori said quite seriously that they were in the deserts and mountains – that is, beyond the populated areas of the state.

1.42

1.43

1.43 Details draw the eye in this debut work. Fujimori's display shelf was so simple that he found skilled craftsmen inevitably unwilling to build it for him.

1.44 Handmade glass, bubbles of air catching the light.

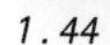

1.44

1.45

1.46

1.47

1.45 The threshold from public to private in Fujimori's home is marked with rough lumber.

1.46 A wrought iron doorknob, reflecting Fujimori's at-the-time interest in craft.

1.47 Looking from the more private kitchen to the living room, where a tree trunk marks the point separating public and private.

1.49

1.50

themselves so seriously at a shrine, would not make an effort to engage such ceremony – especially on behalf of a foreigner. In fact, at one point in our other conversations related to this book, Fumihiko Maki challenged me to identify anyone in architectural circles who took Shinto seriously as a set of beliefs.

Fujimori genuinely accepts Shinto's spirituality, musing:

> You know, in my case, the place I was raised has an extremely strong relationship to Shinto. A very special village. Afterwards I began to understand that, but you cannot really fully recognize that sort influence on you yourself. Other people, when I talk with them, I feel like – something is different. In a deep place, Shinto and its relationship, the use of materials, something is there [in my heart] ...[40]

In a talk to the International Union of Architects in Turin in 2008, Fujimori said:

> When you worship nature, you see the beauty in mountains, forests, rivers, trees, and stones. We know that spirits live in them, and these should be esteemed. The greatest spiritual weight is in the mountain itself. People, when they pray, face the mountain, and bring their hands together. There is no building, simply a fence; the place is marked as sacred. This was the way in my country – shrines like this were the only way of worshipping until the sixth century ...[41]

Possibly an element of Fujimori's comfort with being an architectural maverick stems from the other ways he is out of step with those around him, especially his acceptance of Shinto at a time when most interpret it only as lingering legend and fanciful folklore.

Unafraid to accept the past within our present, Fujimori is also inspired by tea master Sen no Rikyu, "given most credit for the *wabi* aesthetic and revolutionary, semi-democratic, Zen-inspired ideals."[42] He embedded a firepit into the living room of his second structure, the 1995 *Tanpopo*, or Grass, House.[43] At the 1997 Nira House, he offered his first explicit tearoom, an aerie above the roof, cut off from its surroundings by a tiny, crawl-through door, the interior decorated with a banana leaf as a direct acknowledgement of the influence of tea master Rikyu. Nira House is owned by artist Akasegawa, who also authored a screenplay on Rikyu (for an award-winning film directed by Hiroshi Teshigahara) and later a book that relates tales of both ROJO and Rikyu.[44]

To write of tea in Japan raises an awkward engagement with overly romanticized expectations – at odds with Fujimori's pragmatic and earthy efforts. Rhode Island School of Design Professor Yuriko Saito pointedly counsels avoiding worn-out Japanese words; instead of "*wabi*" and "*sabi*," Saito expounded on the "aesthetics of imperfection and insufficiency."[45] Fujimori, too, enthusiastically embraces these ideas, but studiously scorns the affectation implied in *wabi* and *sabi*. His teahouses, tiny structures closest to his ideals, are stingy structures, eschewing mechanical systems and ignoring human comfort; he openly embraces an aesthetic of insufficiency.

Fujimori also iconoclastically reconstructs the rituals of tea. The famed folkcraft enthusiast Souetsu Yanagi presented tea as the promulgation of perfection:

> The Way of Tea is a way of salvation through beauty. Hence the *chajin* (tea master) must make a paragon of himself so as to preach laws like a religious man. He must have a profound love of beauty, high discernment of truth, and deep experi-

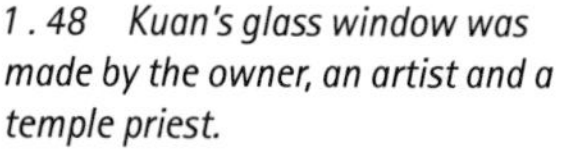

1.48 Kuan's glass window was made by the owner, an artist and a temple priest.

1.49 The handkerchief-sized garden at Kuan, completed in 2003, with a grass-covered arch that is a homage to Le Corbusier – and Salvador Dalí.

1.50 Kuan is entered, unusually, from below.

40. Interview, Tokyo (6 March, 2007).

41. Fujimori (2008) p. 12. Can be accessed at www.ilgiornaledellarchitettura.com.

42. Cadwallader (2002) p. v.

43. Although *Tanpopo* is literally translated as "dandelion," this house is sometimes called Grass House in English.

44. Akasegawa (1990). The book is a meandering meditation on Rikyu, encompassing postwar Japanese art movements and Akasegawa's arrest, ROJO, baseball, odd (and inaccurate) speculations on hand-washing in foreign cultures, Japanese wallets, and a range of other subjects.

45. Saito (1997) p. 377.

46. Pilgrim (1997) p. 286. Taken from Castle (1971) p. 82 f.

1 . 52

1 . 53

1 . 54

1 . 55

1 . 56

1 . 51-56 Completed in 2000, Camellia Chateau on the island of Izu Oshima is a shochu tasting room; its slate wall and grass roof are unusual renderings of traditional architecture in the area . At its top is a tiny, valiant camellia – at least, as long as each survives.

1.57 The older shochu brewery to the left is wrapped in a tile-and-plaster wall echoed engagingly in Fujimori's newer work.

1.58 The edge of the Camellia Castle's upstairs loft is fringed with bottle-shaped wooden wedges, made by Genpei Akasegawa, working with a hatchet.

1.59 A chestnut column in the tasting room supports the loft, but also emphatically extends further, without any obvious function.

1.57

1.58

1.59

47. See, for example, Plutschow (2003) p. 131. My parenthetical comment regarding flexibility in architectural character – as opposed to the inflexible sequence of tea actions – is based on the fact that most architects consider *sukiya* to be extremely adaptable as long as specific elements needed for the ritual are present. At a minimum, these elements include *tatami* mats outlining where people move in space and a *tokonoma* alcove to establish hierarchy. Beyond that, and in part based on specific practices, other elements may be required: a garden walk, a waiting bench, a small aperture for entry, a hearth, a column, etc. Fujimori, notably, has removed the two elements most architects consider minimally necessary, while reintroducing others.

48. Pilgrim (1997) p. 302.

49. Fujimori's retreats might also be seen as cousins to modest buildings in other societies. Barry Bergdoll, for example, describes the Italian *casino* as "... the small private pavilion for retreat into the landscape ... favored as a laboratory for exploring compositional and tectonic expressions of the greatest magnitude and potential. Despite, or perhaps because of its intimate scale, programmatic simplicity ... the *casino* simultaneously invites a freedom in interpretation and a restraint in scale and ambition." Opening line in Bergdoll (1997) p. 148.

50. The site offered an inelegant history: it was earlier the location of an outhouse. As if squeamish, Fujimori's teahouse hovers, clinging to a wall enclosing the garden and propped precariously by a bush-like branch. This is not to suggest the structure was slighted. The name "KU-an" is almost never translated, perhaps as an *homage* to the late Fuku Akino, a client Fujimori remembers with particular fondness; the "ku" character in the teahouse name is also the last character in Akino's given name, Fuku. Akino, the artist celebrated in the Fuku Akino Museum, was Kuan's client's mother.

51. One exception is the former Prime Minister Morihiro Hosokawa, owner of *Ichiya Tei* (One Night Stand]), who now makes ceramics used in the tea ceremony. The lack of a clearly indicated school of tea in his space may allow him to comfortably accommodate both major schools, which have conflicting practices. Hosokawa enjoys unusual freedom in this regard, however; he can trace his lineage to one of Sen no Rikyu's most esteemed disciples, Saisan Hosokawa, and there is even a school of tea practice in the Izumo area called the Saisan Hosokawa School. See Waraku (2003) p. 136.

1.60

1.61

1.60, 61 Archetypal storehouses finished in namako plaster and tile, the stepped structure around the window on the left expressing clearly the kura's heavy earthen walls.

ence in practice ... spiritual discipline should come first.[46]

Tea today is too often arid, its choreography only following formulae – but Rikyu himself de-emphasized prescriptions for pacing and procedures.[47] An oft-repeated quote ascribed to Rikyu is, "When master and visitor together commune direct from the heart, no ordinary measures of proportion or ceremonial rules are followed. A fire is made, water is boiled and tea is drunk – that is all!"[48]

Today tea has come a long way from such aspirations: ungainly tea bowls are breathtakingly costly, defying the original intent that these objects were to be appreciated for an offhand elegance. Tea devotees track down obscure and apparently inconsequential artifacts for their ceremonies and spaces: beautifully bundled feathers; centuries-old scrap paper; chipped, mended pottery; misshapen twigs. Instead, Fujimori advocates Sen no Rikyu's simplicity. His tea spaces are quiet resting places.[49] The *tokonoma*, for example, is usually expected to display elegant artifacts; it was legally limited to certain classes until the Meiji period. But Fujimori's *tokonoma* alcove is often so abstracted, it is unimportant – an anti-elitist, anti-consumerist choice. Fujimori's clients are unconcerned with connoisseurship; he avoids incorporating artful found objects in his works (although Red architects like Kijo Rokkaku are inclined to embrace such arrangements). His 2003 *Kuan* teahouse, in the back garden of a Kyoto temple, is an exception – but it might better be described as a collaboration between Fujimori and temple priest Hitoshi Akino, also an artist.[50] Akino hand-crafted the leaded glass window himself, adding embellishment.

But even Kuan, for all its artistry, lacks creature comforts: not even a cushioned *tatami* floor, normally needed for the choreography of tea's ceremony.[51] Fujimori instead relies on plaster at Kuan – or a rattan mat stretching uninterrupted wall to wall, a flooring with a populist personality. This may be another of Fujimori's subtle historical references – it is also found in a student lounge's tea space designed in 1950 by architect Yoshiro Taniguchi, "Banraisha."[52]

Critic Kojin Karatani argues:

> The aesthetic system ... gets pleasure not from its object but by bracketing various reactions to the object. An aesthete praises a certain object not because the object is comfortable, but rather because it is uncomfortable and possibly something to be shunned in daily life.[53]

Yuriko Saito points out that pleasure in cold, poorly lit places is an indulgence:

> ... this aesthetic celebration of the imperfect and the insufficient presupposes not only the yearning for but also the attainability of the optimum condition ... the appreciation of the imperfect was not *merely* directed toward the sensory qualities such as asymmetry, irregularity, or obscurity, or their contrast to the opposite qualities. These qualities are aesthetically appreciable *precisely because* their opposites are attainable.[54]

Citing a 1989 text by a then unknown Kengo Kuma, Saito adds, "A contemporary architectural critic points out this appreciation of impoverishment which presupposes affluence underlies the contemporary architecture of Tadao Ando."[55] In that text, Kuma argues,

> The impoverishment (*mazushisa*) of houses Ando designs is a spiritual indulgence for the rich – these are certainly not a reflection of actual poverty. For Rikyu, for Ando, for the world of tea, ... such work is an expression of ... great sur-

52. The reference may be deliberate: Banraisha also offers one of the few precedents outside of Fujimori's work where *Teppei* slate is used architecturally. (Another use of *Teppei* stone is at the house Kiyoshi Seike designed and built for his family in 1954.) Fujimori used this stone at his first two projects and at Camellia Chateau, although now he tends to avoid such unyielding finishes; 90 percent of the *Teppei* slate found in Japan is from the Suwa area in Nagano Prefecture, near Fujimori's birthplace.

53. Karatani and Kohso (1998) p. 151.

54. Saito (1997) p. 380.

55. Ibid., p. 384. Saito is discussing the chapter "Architects' Faction" in the book *Juutakuron* １０宅論 [A Theory of Ten Houses] (1989). While she cites a significant portion of this chapter, pp. 122–137, the point is most clearly made on pages 125–126 [below]. Saito writes, "Ando's residential architecture is enjoyed by its residents for the coldness during winter and the leaking roof *precisely because* they can afford more comfort." Kuma does not actually claim Ando's clients revel in the cold; it is the *nouveau riche* characters portrayed in a hugely popular Kazuhiro Watanabe illustrated novel, *KinKonKan* 金魂巻 [Scroll of a Spirit of Gold], a book Kuma says inspired his. Kuma describes an affluent resident of a fair-faced concrete home saying with pleasure, "Yech, winter is cold! Hahaha" and "This place, wow, there are a lot of leaks where the rain comes in!" Original Japanese: 『ナウなお宅はコンクリートの打放しだ、そこに住んでいる人間は友人に向かって『イヤー、冬は寒くて.....、アハハ......』と言うそうであり、こういうのってケッコウ雨モリがあるんだよネェ。とも、うれしそうに言うそうである。』 In this quote, Kuma may also be reflecting an interpretation offered by his close friend, architect Kiyoshi Takeyama, who wrote, "... the chill of Ando's concrete void spaces is symbolically similar to the ideal world Rikyu wanted to create ..." Takeyama (1983) p. 180.

56. Kuma (1986) p. 124. Original Japanese: 『それは安藤の設計した家がその貧しさによって金持に対する精神的な免罪符を与えながら、なおかつ決して貧乏くさいはないからである。利休も、安藤も、茶の湯の世界も、アーキテクト派住宅も、基本的にある余裕の上に成り立つ世界であることを、利休も安藤も見抜いていた。それが利休と安藤が成功した秘訣である。』

1.62

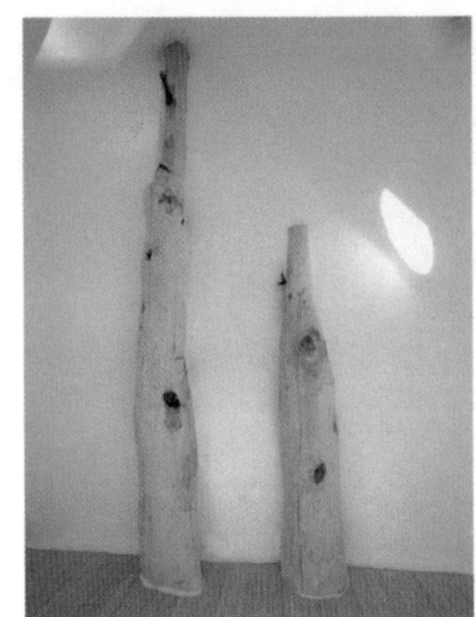

1.63

1.62 The 2005 teahouse called Tetsu, or "pierce," poised on a single tree trunk.

1.63 Within Tetsu, forking branches become fat pilasters.

> plus. Rikyu saw that. Ando saw that. It is the secret of their success.[56]

Thus, the naïve innocence expressed in Fujimori's artless architecture, walls warped and leaning inward at irregular inclinations, is enriched by an awareness of the ease with which a wall can be set plumb and a floor level. Toyo Ito once claimed:

> ... people say that I am [my architecture is] not orthogonal. I have to reject that – I am always using right angles – but it is true that I would say the non-orthogonal is, after all, interesting. But Fujimori, right from the start ... had no right angles. It was an architecture not indebted to anybody, I had the sneaking suspicion it rejected something ...[57]

While Fujimori's buildings recall an era when haphazard angularity was the norm, today this expression is harder to achieve. Odd bumps and bulges underscore a handmade character and act as *homage* to the humble landscape that inspires them, but they are simultaneously a counter-cultural gesture to be appreciated by *cognoscenti*.

Fujimori's fantastic buildings feel like children's playhouses; even his sketches maintain an unaffected artlessness. It is an awkward architecture, oddly inclined, alluding to children's dreams and imaginary places: full of face-like façades (at Single Pine Tree House, the Yoro Insects Museum and Soda Pop Spa) or tiny doors and windows low to the floor, more suited to fairies and sprites. These associations are not naïve. In the Meiji era, Westerners called the Japanese primitive and childlike; similarly scornful assertions continued into the twentieth century. Fujimori embraces the insult. He transcends it, turning instead towards innocence, using our common childhood pasts to elude intellectualism and avoid nationalism.

For Fujimori's Red architects, an interest in the idiosyncrasies of vernacular architecture almost inevitably leads to an openness to unpredictable change, especially when incorporating nature. Red architects entwine living plants in their built work – walls of bamboo, veils of vine. Fujimori, more freely experimental, goes further, incorporating vulnerable and unloved weeds: at Nira House, he planted punning leeks across the roof; for his own home, he lined the exterior with dandelions. In the end, the dandelions died, scorched by heat soaked into the stone cladding, replaced by robust flowers. The tiny pyramidal lawn topping the roof of what he called *Tanpopo* in Japanese and Grass House in English – as an homage to Bruno Taut's Glass House – requires ongoing attention or it quickly grows unkempt. Still, Fujimori sowed such roofs not only at his own home, but also on the Camellia Chateau and Single Pine House in Southern Japan. Those plants, pine and camellia, long loved in elegant Japanese gardens, are awkward in Fujimori's architectural landscape, perched too out of reach for regular pruning. His is not the calm cultivation most associate with Japan; instead, in Fujimori's work nature is untamed and iffy. He wanted "... to cover buildings with vegetation, the way the skin of the human body is covered in fine down."[58] But he allowed that in the end, "Our experiments in this domain have often ended in failure ..."[59] Fujimori, a professor at one of Japan's leading universities, should not be surprised when dandelions die, but he makes no effort to be scientific, instead encouraging instability.

Today, though, such shaggy life seems less evident in his architecture, perhaps a concession that the ongoing upkeep of this rugged rusticity is incompatible with the lifestyles of the urbane owners of his architecture.[60] In recent works, life is again expressed in leafless

57. Fujimori and Ito (2007) p. 49.
Original Japanese:
例えば、僕は直角でないということを言うのに、自分は直角ばかりやってきているから、自らを否定して、直角でないもののはやっぱり面白いんだよと言う。でも藤森さんは、最初から直角じゃないから。全然負い目がない建築だから何か全否定されちゃうというのはずるいという気もするんだけど。

58. Suzuki and Terada (2006) p. 102.

59. Ibid.

60. Several of Fujimori's clients attending an opening for his 2007 exhibition at Tokyo's Opera City Gallery noted with amusement that the lawns capping roof or wall had grown weedy and brown, in spite of irrigation systems designed to maintain them. By Spring 2007, about seven years after it was completed, the camellia topping Camellia Chateau had been replaced once and was again dead; the pine tree that gave *Ippon Matsu* [Single Pine] House its name had also died.

1.64

1.64, 65 A close-up of rough plaster textures on the outside walls of the 2003 teahouse Ichiya-tei, built for the former Prime Minister Morihiro Hosokawa, who is now a potter.

branches: a trunk piercing the 2006 *Tetsu* teahouse, a thinner shaft breaching the canopy of charred kindling arching over the tearoom at The Forum, another standing proudly isolated in the interior of the Camellia Chateau. Fujimori also numbered free-standing columns as one of his "Five Points of Architecture," drawing on Japan's rich traditions. He argues:

> ... on the dirt floor of a farmhouse, in a temple or shrine, in a *shoin* style setting, you can find many ... columns. This is not just an architectural expression, there is special meaning assigned to decorative columns like *tokonoma* poles, or the *daikokubashira*, houses' main pillar.[61]

The central *daikokubashira* column in older farmhouses is called by the name of the kitchen god; the *shinnomihashira* column worshipped within shrines.[62] Columns sometimes separated the public and private spheres of older homes. Fujimori similarly uses them as markers at important thresholds: separating a large living area from the kitchen in his own home, or defending dorm rooms in Kumamoto.

In the latter teahouses logs sometimes again retain their bark: rougher, more textured, closer to life. Scholar Herbert Pluschow wrote of such spaces:

> These small rooms coincided with the advent of the popularity of *wabi* which ... marked a return to the Buddhist essence of frugality, simplicity and ultimately to human equality ... Hence the custom, particularly prevalent in the times of Rikyu, of using only natural materials ... The *tokonoma* poles were installed with the bark still on, to give the tea room a rustic look.[63]

But today these *tokonoma* poles are often extremely expensive, even amounting to tens of thousands of dollars. To find the right trunk, architects and builders may size up the selections at numerous stockpiles and storehouses, investing extensive amounts of their time. This effort undermines the original intent.

Fujimori emphasizes, "The most overt characteristic of my tearooms is the finish of the material. I make every effort to use raw, un-

1.65

61. Fujimori *et al.* (2005) p. 165.
Original Japanese:
『...日本では、民家の土間でも寺院でも書院造りでも、たくさんの独立柱が並び，建築の印象をきめているだけではなく、床柱とか大黒柱とか特別な意味を持ってシンボリックに立つ場合も少なくない。』

62. Fujimori often incorporates an avatar-like free-standing column in his relatively tiny spaces; only with the recent *Kuan*, Too Tall Teahouse and *Tetsu* has the column again moved to the exterior.

63. Plutschow (2003) p. 52.

1.66 The living room at Fujimori's own home. Rough lumber from the hills above his childhood home was plainsawn in a small sawmill nearby, making it more willing to warp and cup with time.

1.66

worked wood, soil, and bark."[64] In Japan, there are always examples of materials plied with a minimum of processing: red, raw fish is brought to the mouth with fine-grained, unlacquered wood chopsticks; a brush and ink used to inscribe New Year's greetings on pulpy, primitive paper; the *kimono* a surprisingly simple construction, rolls of unlined cloth joined on loosely hand-sewn seams. Unprocessed materials are savored. Fujimori strives for simplicity. This is in part why he stopped using stone: it took greater effort to cut and shape.

Fujimori allows wood grain and rough edges to remain. He savors lumber's vulnerabilities in the opening lines of his book, *The Fujimori Way of Using Natural Materials*:

> When natural materials used architecturally are named, people in Japan, every one, will first think of timber. Cedar, Japanese cypress (*hinoki*), pine – the three main woods. You can continue with evergreens, *Hiba* or hemlock. Hardwood offers fewer ... choices, but types like chestnut, zelkova (*keyaki*), maple, Blume, and mulberry are common.
>
> It would be interesting to use paulownia, too. Used for boxes and ornamental screens called *ranma*, it is not really affordable [architecturally], but some that has knots, has been eaten by insects or perhaps has a bit of rot might be affordable.[65]

In a pamphlet for the 2006 Venice Biennale featuring his architecture, Fujimori lovingly listed the lumbers he had used thus far: chestnut, *paulownia*, water oak, mulberry, maple, cedar, Japanese cypress (*hinoki*), red pine, Douglas fir, and Japanese yew.[66] He prefers plebian hardwoods over aristocratic softwoods. Conrad Totman, who enjoyed an unexcelled understanding of the relationship between Japan's forestry and cultural history, argued that in Edo elites opted for conifers in architectural applications, while peasants favored hardwoods since they also supplied food and fuel.[67]

Fujimori likes lumber with ragged, untrimmed edges, planks revealing the point where branches spread from the trunk, simply barked and sliced. He has access to a small, antiquated lumber mill in his hometown, where he slices logs himself. Red School architects often incline to knotty woods, revel in wood grain and stone vein. Fujimori savors these raw flavors: flecks of straw embedded in hand-finished plaster, bumpy nodal bamboo bands, uneven wear on weak substances like straw and soil. Detailing offers a clue to architects' inclinations. Fujimori's Red School will carve or chip stone and brick, perhaps loosely stacking blocks; White School architects would rather elegantly "bookmatch" stone slabs or knowingly reveal it as thin veneer.[68] In truth, though, the internationalist White School is uninterested in stone (unless, perhaps, it is the elegant Carrara marble), inclined instead to sparkling aluminum, steel, and glass – stable, durable, and predictable. But Fujimori argues, "Steel, glass, concrete, they are not pleasant matches, never have been." He chooses common but impractical materials, celebrates that surfaces weather or wear unevenly.[69] As finishes bend, bow, and crack, his architecture comes to life.

Arizona architecture professor Fred Matter argued that:

> For a building to be understood as an expression of the time of its creation, it must provide understandable ways of recording the passage of time ... Attitudes toward permanence and durability or toward change as growth or decay are important expressions of a regionalist sensibility.[70]

For most up-to-date architects, the ideal moment in a building's life

64. Fujimori (2007) p. 80. It is quite possible this title is a direct response from Fujimori to the title of a piece I wrote somewhat earlier.

65. Fujimori *et al.* (2005) p. 8.
Original Japanese:
建築に使われる自然の素材といえば、日本の人なら誰でもすぐ思い付くように、まず木がある。
杉、檜、松を三大木材として、針葉樹ではヒバ、ツガあたりがこれに続き、広葉樹は生産量は少ないものの、栗、ケヤキ、カエデ、ミズナラ、桑などなど種類はおおい。
桐も使ってみると面白い。箱用や欄間用の高級品は手が出なくても、目が乱れたり虫喰いがあったり、一部に腐りが入っててよければ安く手に入る。

66. Fujimori (2006a) p. 8.

67. Totman (1984) p. 1 f.

68. A longer discussion of materials that mark "White School" work would point to reliance on manufactured and stable materials that are precise, flat, thin, and transparent. Low maintenance and high durability allow the building to exist independent of further attention from client or architect. Since the White School tends to reject tradition, architects avidly explore new processes and assume that technology can offer increasingly better solutions; these architects celebrate materials such as the newest alloys, no matter how rare, or technology transfer from non-construction industries, which allows application of novel technologies with some reliability and economic control. In order to attain economies in spite of unusual materials or technology, White architects hew to standard measurements and modulars; large sheets and sizes are desired to reduce overall labor costs. These architects also design for common, competitive skills available from a large pool of bidders with minimal skill, using detailing to controls variants, but minimal competence and limited supervision mean that these architects must conceal connections.

69. Interview, Tokyo (6 March, 2007).

70. Matter (1989) n.p.

1 . 67 Plaster embedded with straw; each of Fujimori's interiors sports a slightly different plaster surface.

1 . 68 A small washbasin by the entrance to the dining hall at Fujimori's Kumamoto Agricultural Dormitory, carved with a chainsaw – one of many unusual tools Fujimori employs for his rough finishes.

1 . 69 Marks of an ineptly operated adze, at Fujimori's 2009 Coal House.

1 . 67

1 . 68

1 . 69

1 . 70

1 . 71

1 . 72

1 . 70 At the 2001 Futo-an, copper sheets buttoned up with decorative round-headed nails.

1 . 71 Chestnut walls, marked by an errantly operated sander, line the living room of the 2007 Yakisugi (Charred Cedar) House.

1 . 72 The 2005 Yoro Insects Museum was finished with a final coat of wet mud.

1.73

1.74

is that fleeting instant when construction is complete, clean, the minutes or hours before relinquishing it to a client. White School structures are not designed to age but to be of their age, the occasion of perfection preserved photographically. But Fujimori himself is not inclined to call his work regionalist. In Japan, the term is associated only with a romantic replication of the past. Even as Fujimori embraces place in his building forms, engages the materials and crafts still lingering, allows his buildings to age in place, he himself would make a distinction between Red and regionalist that I, in the Western tradition, do not.

Fragility embodies another form of fleeting time: Fujimori's structures are sometimes short-lived. One teahouse was constructed for a single celebration, a short visit by Jacques Chirac. (In the end, Chirac did not make the assignation, prevented by the inauguration of the war in Iraq.) Its name, "One Night Stand," acknowledges both the speed of its assembly and the singular intention of this event. *Tetsu* sits in a grove of venerable cherry trees, occupied for the few brief days they bloom. These fugitive functions free Fujimori to accept decay and deterioration.

Yuriko Saito questioned, "Can the aged and/or damaged surface of a work of art possibly add more aesthetic appeal to its original condition?" She continues:

> ... [a] way in which the aged look of an art object contributes to its aesthetic appeal is a straight-forward increase ... [Consider] the following anecdote related by Joseph Addison. He tells of a dream in which he is viewing a row of old paintings by great masters ... being continuously touched up by an old man. This old man ... "wore off insensibly every little disagreeable gloss that hung upon a figure. He also added such a beautiful brown to the shades and mellowness to the colors that he made every picture more perfect ..." Addison then reveals the identity of this old man: Time.[71]

In the same essay, Saito writes, "[the] once smooth, uniform, simple, orderly surface gets more complex, rough and irregular with age, due to cracks, chips, soil, stain and growth of lichens and ivy."[72]

Not all believe weathering and wear enrich architecture. In their classic text, On *Weathering: The Life of Buildings in Time*, David Leatherbarrow and Mohsen Mostafavi, though striving to appreciate the architectural effects of age, repeatedly reflect contemporary unease, as in this early passage:

> Over time the natural environment acts upon the outer surface of a building in such a way that its ... materials are broken down. This breakdown, when left to proceed uninterrupted, leads to the failure of materials and the final dissolution of the building itself – ruination – hardly an outcome desired by the architect, builder or owner ...[73]

Ruination. The ornamental antler-like stumps projecting from the roof of Fujimori's *Tanpopo* House are now succumbing to decay; in the Fall of 2007, one fell out. Fujimori does not propose to replace the lost lumber or plug the empty opening. Age is something to be savored.

Missing the predictability of manufactured elements, Fujimori's materials are fat, imprecise edges meeting in ragged gaps and overlaps. The exterior shakes of Jinchokan Museum loosely lap, reminiscent of tumbledown shacks; the intervals between sliced lumber, still shaped in the outline of the tree it once was, filled with forgiving

1.73, 74 Cutting lumber for Fujimori's home in the summer of 1995, at a small sawmill in the town where he grew up, Fujimori guiding lumber for his living room through a large band saw.

71. Saito (1985) pp. 142–143.
72. Ibid., p 143.
73. Leatherbarrow and Mostafavi (1993) p. 5.

1 . 75

1 . 76, 77 & 79 An installation encrusted with small Akoya oyster shells, part of an exhibition on Fujimori at the Hermes building in Tokyo's swank Ginza shopping area. At the opening, well-dressed guests were invited to lend a hand.

1 . 78 Genpei Akasegawa, the heart of the Jomon Company.

1 . 76

1 . 77

1 . 78

plaster easily augmented as the timber shrinks. Occasionally, Fujimori creates loose screens of even lumpier wood, such as the skewered kindling that shapes the ceiling of the tearoom at Nira House, light filtering through its upper reaches while plaster fills interstices below.

Fujimori tends towards the most brutal tools to achieve his ends. He asserts,

> Unlike industrial materials, natural materials lack uniformity. In order to take advantage of this quality, I try to make the finish as rough as possible. From experience I have found that the most irregular finish on wood is produced by a jackhammer. Next to this the roughest effects can be obtained by a debarking machine, a chainsaw, a curved surface plane, an adze, a planing knife, and an ordinary plane, in that order.[74]

These inconstant finishes demand different detailing, cruder connections, plainer processes, relying on the hand and simple tools, adapted to uneven surfaces and unexpected outcomes; this open-ended attitude raises incomplete documents and late changes to a virtue.

Although craftsmen constructed his first work, there were already indications that Fujimori leaned towards a coarser touch, expressed in his naïve rendition of Japan's wood joinery. Fujimori's methods are grounded in history; initially, he unintentionally adopted Ruskin's romanticized view of labor, echoed William Morris' Arts and Crafts, filtered through the Meiji era and early twentieth-century Japanese *mingei* folkcraft philosophies which lingered as a point of national pride well into the 1970s.[75]

Fujimori found the only one person able to hand-split long wooden shakes for siding at his Jinchokan Moriya Museum; carpenter

1 . 75 Prime Minister Morihiro Hosokawa, who said he once dreamed of the life of a carpenter, applying finishes to his small pottery studio in the mountains not far from Tokyo.

74. Fujimori (2006a) p. 8.

75. Josiah Conder, one of the leading architects of the Meiji era that is Fujimori's specialty, was directly linked to Ruskin through his previous employer, British architect William Burgess. Japan tended to adopt the appreciation for handicraft, while ignoring Morris' anti-industrial stance. Both schools have a lingering influence among architects in their sixties and seventies, most of whom read William Morris in high school. Although not raised in my interviews with Fujimori, Wajiro Kon was similarly influenced by Ruskin.

1 . 79

1.81

1.82

1.80–82 The 1997 Fuku Akino Art Museum, straddling a slope.

Chuuichi Yazawa commuted to the construction site from an old-age home. Fujimori reminisced:

> ... I did not want an effect that owed its homogeneity to the Japanese saw. I tried to split wood with a hatchet, a wedge, as seen in the Kamakura era [nearly a thousand years ago] or earlier. Luckily, I met Chuuichi Yazawa, a wood splitter who learned his craft before World War II.

Red architects revive evaporating arts, cultivate construction's traditional tricks and technologies. Fujimori accedes, though, underscoring impracticality, "... But Yazawa-San died and after that I had to accept that I'll be using wood from a sawmill."[76]

For this first project, Fujimori explicitly acknowledged other artisans: Shinobu Matsuoka forged wrought iron door pulls, switch plates and handrails; Kenji Matsumoto formed bubbled, hand-blown glass.[77] They continue to contribute, but operate in anonymity. Fujimori abandoned his emphasis on artistry. A colleague contended "Most people who use natural materials respect craftsmanship, too. But you, Professor Fujimori, you use natural materials, but I do not have any sense that you hold craftsmen in high regard."[78]

Fujimori now draws a distinction between Ruskin's urbane idealism – especially the Englishman's opposition to industry – and his own pragmatism.[79] Yet the Japanese architect clearly embodies Ruskin's proposal that "The painter should grind his own colors; the architect work in the mason's yard ..."[80] – himself cutting lumber, splitting stone, and applying rough stucco. He chose an exaggerated route, embracing amateur execution, implicitly rejecting Japan's idealized, even fetishized, approach to craft.

For his own house, Fujimori asked plasterers to exclude the bonding agents that prevent cracks in order to yield novel, nubby surfaces. He seemed unaware that this was asking them to operate with exceptional inefficiency and unpredictability (an added expense), to go against the values of their trade. In an interview, Fujimori explained,

> I, of course, had interest in how things were made, but the problem was that I could not get the artisans to build what I wanted!

Regarding woodwork for the same building, he continued,

> I talked to this carpenter [about some shelves], and he said, 'I understand your taste, Professor, but you should do it yourself. We cannot make what you want.'
>
> I talked to another, and he said, 'I understand what you want. But this is not how we work. Do it yourself! You have the materials.' Well, truthfully, it was not until Nira (Leek) House that I really understood the implications of this problem ...[81]

Ruskin's oft-quoted lines from *The Stones of Venice II* summarizes issues embedded in the stance:

> You can teach a man to draw a straight line, and to cut one; to strike a curved line, and to carve it; and to copy and carve any number of given lines or forms, with admirable speed and perfect precision, and you can find his work perfect in its kind: but if you ask him to think about any of these forms, or consider if he cannot find any better in his own head, he stops; his execution becomes hesitant; he thinks, and ten to one he thinks wrong; ten to one he makes a mistake ... But you have made a man of him for all that.[82]

76. Fujimori *et al.* (2005) p. 9. Original Japanese: で、処女作ではノコギリによる均質な製剤を拒み、鎌倉時代以前のクサビとナタによる割板を試みた。幸い、戦前に割板職人だった矢沢忠一と出会い、バラバラ加減は生かされたが、矢沢さんも亡くなり，以後は製材した材を使っている.

77. See, for example, Fujimori *et al.* (2005) p. 30. In Japanese, these artisans' names are: 松岡信夫 and 松本健治.

78. Ibid., p. 187. Original Japanese: 自然素材をやるような人は職人を尊敬してる。だけど先生は、自然素材をやりながら、ちっとも職人を尊敬している感じがしない。On the same page, he quotes Nobumichi Oshima as also saying, 職人技術に対して先生が冷たい。

79. Fujimori often identifies his birthplace not as Nagano, but Shinshuu, using an ancient name for the area. People from this region are said to be pragmatic, self-sufficient, and hands-on, like Midwesterners in the U.S.

80. Quoted in Swenarton (1989) p. 29.

81. Interview, Tokyo (30 March, 2007).

82. Swenarton (1989) p. 25.

1.83

1.83 *The 2004 Too Tall Teahouse, in the town where Fujimori grew up.*

1.84 *Fujimori in a casual interview with my students, seated in the Too Tall Teahouse.*

1.85 *Unheated and with little cushion on the floor, the tea space is a simple one.*

1.84

But Ruskin, too, acknowledged, "The delight with which we look on the fretted front of Rouen Cathedral depends in no small degree on the simple perception of time employed and l abor expended in production."[83] Inevitably, Fujimori's attempts to involve workers in the experimental nature of his initial efforts led, in their minds, not to more artful architecture or elevated experience, but to economic loss. Fujimori enjoined men who spent years struggling for perfection to instead realize rough and naïve results. Understandably, the artisans opposed his ideas; Fujimori also found the fight frustrating.

Reframing Ruskin, he shifted his focus from "healthy and ennobling labour," to its results – imperfection. "Amateur artisans" he later said, "contributed to building my very first tearoom, *Shin-ken* [at Nira House], when it became apparent that technically accomplished Japanese artisans were disinclined to perform the tasks of splitting wood, laying ceiling, and hand-applying plaster."[84] While building this house for artist Genpei Akasegawa, client and architect formed the *Jomon* Company. Following Nira House,

> ... we did work for one of the old members, Eikyuu Taniguchi, he became a client.[85] This was the first time I really assumed during design that the *Jomon* Company would participate. Whatever kind of work, it should be something you can accomplish without expecting much skill, as long as enough people turn up.

But, Fujimori continues, "If I could not have called on the *Jomon* Company, the 'grass *namako*' finish [a grass and stone wall], for instance, we would not have done it. I would have thought of it and decided it was too much trouble."[86]

In a recent publication, Fujimori explained, "The name [*Jomon*, meaning Neolithic] was given to the company because of the very primitive sort of handwork it specializes in ..."[87] The corps builds badly; a magazine targeted at connoisseurs quotes Fujimori on site, admonishing the *Jomon* Company to "Work without skill! Work roughly!"[88] Construction is now a pleasure in its own right.

In articles and books, Fujimori invariably includes photographs of fabrication, highlighting this collaboration. He relies on clients and friends – even children – to achieve unschooled, unskilled outcomes. In his most personal project, Too Tall Teahouse, the *Jomon* Company was joined by Fujimori's childhood friends; he and the crane operator recall falling out of treehouses they cobbled together as kids. He lists the individuals involved in this insignificant architectural effort:

> For *Takasugian* [Too Tall Teahouse], built where I grew up, a total of ninety-six people took part in the building: seven professionals cut down and erected the tree trunks ... twenty-one amateurs built the structural framework for the floor, a group of ten pros and amateurs assembled the [structural] panels, and forty-eight people took part in the plastering, metal work and other finishing.[89]

At the Nemunoki School, mentally handicapped children shared the task of hand-crimping copper roofing for their art museum with the elite members of the *Jomon* Company. And when Fujimori was invited to exhibit at Tokyo's Hermes Gallery in 2007, a workman assisted elegantly attired guests at the opening as they donned aprons, gloves and plastic shoes, then set Akoya oyster shells in plaster.[90]

These unpretentious, unskilled efforts establish in his architecture a vitality through their spontaneity – but accidents, even when a normal part of construction, are a problem for what he calls White

1.85

83. Ruskin (2006) p. 492.

84. In this case, Fujimori's use of the term "hand-applied" is extremely precise; the *Jomon* Company used no tools, scooping plaster with their palms and pressing it in place. Fujimori (2007) p. 81.

85. 谷口英久.

86. Fujimori *et al.* (2005) p. 102.
Original Japanese:
引きつづくツバキ城は、古参メンバーの谷口英久がクライアントの仕事である。初めて縄文建築団を想定して設計をした。どんなに手間がかかっても、高度な技能でなければ、人数さえあれば何とかなる。縄文建築団の存在がなければ、"草ナマコかべ"などという、考えただけでも面倒臭い造りを実行に移そうとは思わかっただろう。

87. Fujimori (2006a) p. 08.

88. Waraku (2003) p. 142.

89. Fujimori (2007) p. 81.

90. This may be another anti-elitist reference, as the Akoya oysters are used primarily in the cultivated pearl industry.

1.86 *Too Tall Teahouse stands on two tree trunks, swaying easily in the wind – or when Fujimori stomps his feet upon the floor.*

1.87

1.88

1.89

1.87-93 The 2005 Yoro Insects Museum, its unusually thick walls suggesting mud structures that were its inspiration. Inside, Dr. Takeshi Yoro's collection lines the walls of the central space, a slender oak as a column at its heart.

1.90

1.91

1.92

1.93

School architects. Fujimori's loose approach to design and construction demonstrates an alternative to the dominant "starchitect" system, one open to shared control over aesthetic outcome, encouraging all to add their own playful flourishes. Other architects working in this way incorporate the odd rock in concrete, footprints pressed into pavers, a cloud-like fillip cut into a wooden rafter tail; through their handling of materials, architects of what Fujimori calls the Red School also draw direct, legible connections to unique characteristics of place and participation.

Instead of attachments to international modernity, Fujimori's Reds highlight local narratives – but promoting the provincial remains rare in most professional practices in Japan. An awareness of the bonds between building and place is perhaps the reason Red structures also feel physically rooted in their sites; Fujimori's 1997 Fuku Akino Museum of Art, for example, appears at one with its sloping site.

Most of what Fujimori calls Red makes up a modest collection of minor work, projects incompatible with common construction practices and corporate clients. Even the two most successful architects Fujimori sometimes claims as Red, Arata Isozaki and Tadao Ando, are at their best in small structures. Red, regionalist architects exalt in physical experience, enhanced by the scent of cedar and *tatami*, highlighting shifts in scale, light, and situation, even, in Fujimori's work, encountering new ways to enter architecture: the 1997 tearoom in Nira (Leek) House is reached circuitously on a narrow, unnerving catwalk, a low, open iron handrail offering no sense of security. This perch wraps Akasegawa's two-story-tall living room, lengthening the experience of what seemed, when stepping across it on solid ground, a small space. At the end is a tiny door no higher than your knees. Other of Fujimori's teahouses are entered on handmade, wobbly ladders, each guest popping up one at a time through the floor.[91] In tamer spaces, Fujimori fits tall volumes with balconies and lofts; he seems to love steep stairs. Fujimori thus emphasizes an awareness of the size and scale of each space; you cannot clamber unthinkingly through a tiny door or casually climb a lopsided ladder. The odd angles and artless curves of his architecture are another expression of our bodies within. Fujimori argues that rigorous training is required for straight postures and squarely bending poses; the orthogonal geometry in architecture today is a product of production – not an architecture of accommodation.

While "White" Modernism appeals to the intellect in its crisp geometry, Fujimori's Red School reaches for our fuller senses, for "the part from the neck down" – Fujimori mentions blood (and by implication, violence), sex, and physical delight. His Red School strives for a "sense of real existence."[92] Regarding his 1997 Fuku Akino Museum, where visitors remove their shoes and stand on silky marble, Fujimori joked,

> I initially thought of creating a museum in which viewers are completely naked when they look at the paintings, but I gave up on this idea because I was afraid that being undressed would actually make it more difficult for people to concentrate on the art.[93]

He argues this animal approach is more authentically architectural, that the intellectual abstraction he ascribes to the White School (or to cold commercial architecture offered up by contractors) is a product of modernization: "For those who have tasted the architectural candy from the beginning of time to the end of the twentieth

91. Fujimori calls these "*Nijiri agari guchi*" [upward crawl-through entrances].
92. Fujimori (1998) pp. 15–16. (Exhibition catalog related to a 1998 show at Gallery Ma.)
93. Fujimori (2006b) p. 12.
94. Fujimori (2006d) p. 20. Original Japanese: 原始時代から２０世紀までの建築アメ玉を味わうと、２０世紀の後はたいへんだと思う. 味というより香りしかしてかないからだ。

1 . 94

1 . 94-98 The 2009 Coal House is Fujimori's first speculative building, part of an exhibition event sponsored by Tokyo Gas, clad in charred cedar and trimmed with gold leaf. Materials within are more understated: hand-laid plaster and barely barked wood.

century, what follows today is terrible. You can no longer say you taste, but only that you breathe in a fragrance."[94]

In this way, Fujimori also challenges the orthodox conception of aesthetics accepted in both Japan and in the West: beauty, it is said, appeals to the higher senses, sight and hearing. Auditory aesthetics are unusual in architecture, so this leaves sight as the strongest source of beauty in buildings. Embracing sensuality, oddly, opens up the opportunity to eliminate beauty entirely; such experimentation emerged initially in mid-twentieth-century arts, especially painting.

But architecture is not a pure art. Obliged to satisfy clients, architects are far from free to scorn aesthetic pleasure. Fujimori, however, feels little pressure to act economically: he has no office, no office staff to keep employed, and draws a decent salary from teaching and his other pursuits. He expresses his openness to awkwardness in a child-like naïveté; Waseda Professor Osamu Ishiyama, who is briefly discussed in later chapters of this book, even more deliberately embraces ugliness. Both enjoy unusual immunity from conventional constraints. Fujimori's entire output in a single year might be under 300 square meters (roughly 3,000 square feet). He is best known for a series of structures only 5 or 6 square meters in plan – the size of a bathroom in a luxury hotel, but lacking any effort at amenities. No electric lighting, no heat, no piped in sound – thus no concern for structural or mechanical consultants.

Inevitably, Fujimori's works raise the question: "Is it architecture?" Even the most indulgent interpretation of the Vitruvian dictum "Commodity, Firmness, Delight" might be thought a poor frame for appreciating his structures. Brimming with delight, they offer only limited confidence in their construction and its durability, and frankly forgo convenient function. The aptly named "Too Tall Teahouse" demonstrates this best; Fujimori described the boundaries of the floor, 6 meters (19 feet, 8 inches) above the ground, in place – cutting it back as the structure swayed too much. As a result, the teahouse quivers in the wind – or bounces more dramatically when Fujimori gleefully stamps on the floor. My former employer, the influential architect Tei'ichi Takahashi, questioned Fujimori as to whether the structure would endure an earthquake; Fujimori simply suggested it was small enough, he could leap free of it. (I think the base will rot through long before the time that theory is tested, as water is trapped in wood.)

Is it architecture? The question appeared also in the early days of architecture in Japan, the Meiji era, the subject of Fujimori's scholarly research. Until the mid-nineteenth century, most major structures in Japan were invariably built of wood. Tenshin (Kakuzo) Okakura, writing then, lamented: "To European architects brought up on the traditions of stone and brick constructions, our Japanese method of building with wood and bamboo seems scarcely worthy to be ranked as architecture."[95] And scholar Gregory Clancey asserted that in the late nineteenth and early twentieth centuries British architects "argued over whether to apply the word 'architecture' to Japanese buildings" – even Ise Shrine, Todaiji Temple (the largest wooden structure in the world) or Horyuji Temple (the oldest). Clancey quotes Englishman H. H. Stratham defining the problem in 1912, "The word [architecture] is usually associated in our minds with monumental erections composed of solid, durable materials – granite, marble, stone, and brick."[96]

In a remarkable exegesis, *Japan-ness in Architecture*, Arata Isozaki

95. Okakura (1964) p. 30.

96. Clancey (2006) pp. 243–244.

97. Isozaki (2006) pp. 47–48. Fujimori claims that Isozaki, while a close friend, is not willing to call Fujimori's work "architecture," drawing a distinction between the amateur's output and that of professional firms such as Isozaki's.

98. As quoted in Swenarton (1989) pp. 194–195. Le Corbusier (trans. F. Etchells) *Towards a New Architecture* (Fr. original. Paris, 1923, Eng. trans. 1927) p. 23. A similar, related split occurred in art during the nineteenth century, so that today art is distinguished from craft by the presence or absence of ideas. Bruce Metcalf points out, "[Arthur] Danto thus offers a cogent explanation for the dematerialization of art. The art product can mutate into any imaginable form because art consists primarily of meaning." However, Metcalf continues, "Danto adds one proviso: art can indeed be anything, *but only if a loosely organized community of artists, arts professionals and interested bystanders, which he called the artworld, recognize it as such.*" Metcalf (1997) p. 68. My emphasis. Fujimori's work, by nature of the fact that it is regularly featured in architectural magazines and exhibitions in Japan, would also fit this kind of definition if applied to architecture.

1 . 95

1.96

1.97

discusses the problematic nature of Ise Shrine. Isozaki cites *The Problem of Style in Japanese National Architecture*, written by Ryuichi Hamaguchi in 1944, "... Ise would belong to his category of the *spatial* and *performative* – to the Japanese architectonic will – rather than the *material* and *constructive* characteristic of Western architectural will."[97] But this shift in our understanding of architecture is perhaps not so much one of East and West as one of old and new. Around the time of the debates Clancey outlines, the definition of architecture altered as architecture and building domains diverged. Architecture became associated not with material or size, but with character, while the more prosaic concerns of use and construction were delegated to the realm of mere building. Le Corbusier, for example, argued, "Architecture is a thing of art, a phenomenon of the emotions, lying outside questions of construction and beyond them. The purpose of construction is *to make things hold together*; of architecture is *to move us* ..."[98] And if one agrees that architecture is "to move us," then Fujimori is on very solid ground. His structures offer physical delight, and also appeal intellectually, reflecting and questioning major themes in architectural theory.

The most obvious theoretical connections exist between Fujimori's Red School and Critical Regionalism. Problematically, however, Fujimori never troubled himself to outline the particularities of his Red School of architecture. Japanese and Western scholarly discourse are quite different; I am taken with my Berkeley colleague Marc Treib's description of the two:

> While Western discourse tends to lead the reader, taking him or her firmly in hand from valleys to hilltops, Japanese writers tend to leap from summit to summit – leaving the reader to rely on his or her own devices for progressing from point to point.[99]

In understanding how Fujimori flirts with and confounds theory, I am obliged to parse points of difference between these two philosophies. But for Fujimori, it is sufficient to simply list architects who represent his poles of practice, allowing others to understand by implication – an approach that is also evident early on in Critical Regionalism.

Critical Regionalism is an argument of center and periphery, with Western Modernism (Fujimori's "White School") the dominant, commonly accepted context for practice. Kenneth Frampton, one of Critical Regionalism's most effective advocates, construes the center as bland and middle-brow, "Everywhere throughout the world, one finds the same bad movie, the same slot machines, the same plastic or aluminum atrocities, the same twisting of language by propaganda ..."[100] But, as the author Richard Ingersoll dryly notes, "... the distancing techniques of 'Critical' required an acquaintance with the Marxist philosophy of the Frankfurt School, which is not generally in the curricula of architectural education."[101] Advocates accommodate this problem by ignoring architects' intentions in favor of their own assessments. Academics recognizing differences between dominant forms of Modernism and an architect's output assume – sometimes erroneously – that these aberrations result from the culture of a place.

The problem is exacerbated because Critical Regionalism is defined more by what it is not – Modernism – than by what it is. In one essay, Frampton goes so far as to write, "*If* any central principle of critical regionalism can be isolated ..."[102] The theory's authors are disinclined to offer clear character or identifying attributes to be used as a yardstick; they simply list unmatched and unmatchable architects from

99. Treib (1989) pp. 304–307.
100 Frampton (1983) p. 148. Original quote in Paul Ricouer, "Universalization and National Cultures," *History and Truth* (1961).
101. Ingersoll (1991) p. 124. Although it is possible to argue that philosophy has been more common in architectural curricula than Ingersoll believes, elsewhere in the same piece, he appropriately argues that "... architects may indeed be producing an architecture of Critical Regionalism, but few would be aware of doing so."
102. Frampton (1983) p. 162. My emphasis.
103. Kelbaugh quoted in Matter (1989) Accessed on-line at http://ag.Arizona.edu/OALS?ALN/aln28.matter.html on 20 July, 2005. A more recent version of the Kelbaugh piece can be found in Kelbaugh (2002) pp. 78–89.

1.98

1 . 100

1 . 101

1 . 102

1 . 99-103 Fujimori's 2001 Futo-an, shortly after its completion, the copper skin and fat, rounded nail heads still sparkling.

1 . 103

1 . 104–106 Fujimori and his client, Morihiro Hosokawa, at a potter's wheel, a filigree of bamboo arching over the workspace.

1 . 104

1 . 105

around the world, designers who offer something different. Under the circumstances, the authors of Critical Regionalism might have done better to simply rely on a more ambiguously open term such as "alternative modernism." Yet in their broadest strokes, Frampton's form of Critical Regionalism and Fujimori's Reds appear to have more in common than imprecision. Douglas Kelbaugh once summarized Critical Regionalism as "Love of Place, Love of Nature, Love of History, Love of Craft, and Love of Limits."[103] Here, the echoes of Critical Regionalism in Fujimori's Red School emerge: architecture invested in the unique attributes of a site, stretching in scale from local practices within a tiny territory to an all-inclusive reflection of a country or a region.

But Fujimori walks a fine line, ambiguously evoking tradition in an environment trapped in a rigid reflection of the past. He does so by emphasizing something older than nationhood, saying:

> You might say that in human history there are two kinds of internationalism. One is our twentieth century idea of internationalism, and the other is an internationalism that is older than the pyramids. In the history of human structures, you might say the world was once international, then after the pyramids were built, we passed through a time when nations and regions each had their own architectures, and then we arrived at a twentieth-century form of internationalism. My architecture is not based on twentieth century "internationalism." I do not think there is a [separate] tradition for Japan, for Asia, for this country. I do not know whether mine is a critical position or not, but I have no interest in the history of a specific region. My architecture is based on an internationalism that is older than the pyramids.[104]

Fujimori objects to my use of the term regionalism, and yet his approach is deeply rooted not only in the places he designs but in the traditions that have enfolded him his whole life. Japan retains both modern and timeworn construction practices, applying one or the other routinely by a building's use; museums and hotels comfortably Modern and commercial, cheek-to-jowl with brand-new but traditionally built temples, homes or hot springs resorts. Frampton

104. Prepared text, speech to the UIA in Turin (3 July, 2008).

105. Frampton (1983) p. 149.

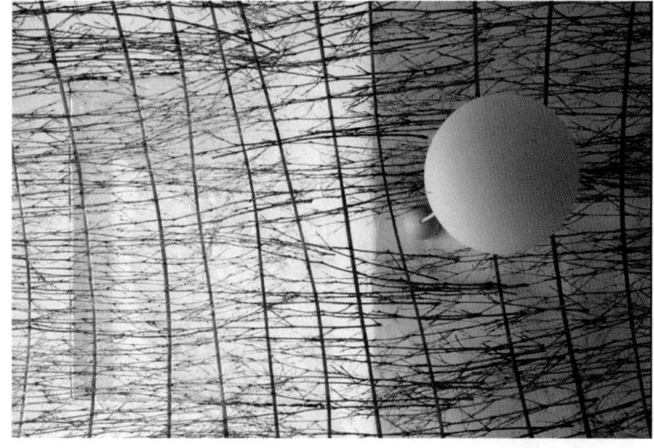

1 . 106

called for "the necessity to distinguish ... between critical regionalism and the simplistic evocation of a sentimental or ironic vernacular ... nostalgia for the vernacular ..."[105] More than one critic has struggled with this point, called Fujimori's structures nostalgic – but they must always, in the end, carefully bracket the term. My favorite is Shouichi Inoue's; an architectural historian and professor, he refers to Fujimori's architecture as a "surreal nostalgia."[106]

Fujimori claims:

> I have no interest in the past – past technology. Absolutely no interest. That's – it may sound odd to say I have absolutely no interest, but I have no special place in my heart for Japanese tradition. I care about it in exactly the same way I care about European or American wood tradition. I have no particular interest in Japanese tradition. For example, if you think about earth walls, African earthen construction is the most interesting – far more interesting than Japan's. For wood, if you consider it, the place where wood was really used it was in the British Tudor era. Boy, they used it! But I do not have a particular sensibility for Japanese traditions.[107]

His is not a conservative approach to the past, but an interpretive one; not restorative, but reflective.

Why look closely at the work of an obscure architect, little known abroad? Fujimori proposes a way of thinking about architecture and its role that others anywhere intuitively understand. While he is not concerned with establishing a universal theory, I find my students in Berkeley easily identify themselves with his schools, instinctively reacting by asking themselves, "Am I a Red School designer? Or White?" In one of his few essays on the topic, Fujimori concedes, "The present-day world of architecture in Japan, or rather Japanese society and sensitivity, is without a doubt directed toward a white, transparent world. The degree of abstraction is accelerating. As an architectural historian, I recognize this fact ..." [108] Yet in the same essay, Fujimori points to a pivotal moment when battle lines are drawn. He invited Toyo Ito, Kazuhiro Ishii and Osamu Ishiyama to join him on the grass-covered roof of his recently completed *Tanpopo* House in 1995. Fujimori explained, "... in a state of shock, nobody said a word. After a long silence, Ishii urged the other two, 'Somebody say something.' And Ito replied 'From now on, the Red School is going to be tough [competition] ...'"[109] The regionalism of the Red School has indeed gained a foothold in Japan, and this book sets out to explore its implications.

But it is a mistake to divide these two schools as if they battle for supremacy; an aware opposition to internationalism gives Fujimori's Red School its power. Kojin Karatani once noted that while

> Walter Benjamin maintained that the aura of artwork disappeared in the age of mechanical reproduction ... the truth is the opposite: It was mechanical reproduction that prompted an aura to emanate from artworks of the past. And this can be amplified further: It is the mechanization of production that endows many handmade products with auras and changes them into art.[110]

In just such a way, Fujimori's rough structures derive their zest from our almost universal interdependency between industry and architecture today.

106. Fujimori (2006d) p. 15.
Original Japanese:シュールなノスタルジー.

107. Interview, Tokyo (6 March, 2007).

108. Fujimori (1998) p. 17.

109. Fujimori (1998) Japanese p. 10, original English translation, p. 17. I retranslated the text from Japanese; the original translation misses the point of Ito's response, instead suggesting that with the completion of this second project it is the Red School that faces a challenge.
Original Japanese:
『タンポポハウスができた時、伊東豊雄と石山修武と石井和弘が見に来た。一巡して東側の屋上に上がったが、あきれはてて誰も何も言わない. しばらくの沈黙の後、石井が"何か言えヨ"と他の二人にうながすと伊東が言った。これからの赤派はたいへんだsナア。』

110. Karatani and Kohso (1998) p. 152.

Soda Pop Spa

Terunobu Fujimori

2

... shaggy and bristling, humorous and grotesque, uncanny and vaguely obscene – and at times surreally beautiful ... This is a wet, hairy architecture, ruffled by gusts of wind, shedding and sprouting with the seasons.—*Thomas Daniell*[1]

Meiji-era buildings are often charmingly diminutive, a point I have never noted in essays on Japan's architectural history. The leading authority on this era, Terunobu Fujimori, thinks the point is widely understood but nowhere articulated. Perhaps this smaller scale was due to the cramped sites in Japan's dense city fabrics, or perhaps it was because these banks and train stations were embryonic efforts, economically uncertain in those early years. Maybe the reason was related to the great difficulty involved in producing unusual building materials like brick and glass, too precious for full-scale construction. At any rate, many Meiji buildings seem shrunk to seven-eighths, establishing a Disney-esque effect.

At times, there is a fairyland character about their embellishment; this is especially true for the *giyofu* (pseudo-Western) style produced by untutored Japanese carpenters naively imitating the academic eclecticism popular with architects at the time. Attempting to reflect new styles imported from the West, carpenters added an abundance of ornament (often, oddly, inspired by Japan's Edo era – gaudy groups of phoenixes and dragons, spiky pine boughs and rolling clouds). They appended almost random oddities, like the two cherubs found framing a banner on an 1876 primary school in Matsumoto, thought to emanate from a newspaper masthead. Turrets and cupolas are far from uncommon.

For years, while most of the academic community ignored the era, Fujimori hammered away at Meiji. He wrote stacks of academic tomes, expensive volumes outfitted in stiff, silk-finished slipcovers, and impudent paperbacks clearly intended to be slipped into a jacket pocket. He discovered many unknown but still extant examples of the era in humble neighborhoods where academics rarely ventured. (In 1987, architectural historian David Stewart claimed there were only 33 such buildings in Tokyo, where Fujimori hunted.[2]) He traveled abroad to odd, out-of-the-way places to gain insight into the emergence of an almost-Westernized practice at home. A hallmark of Fujimori's research has been the even-handed way he addresses amateur and professional architect alike. He loves the unschooled exuberance of early architectural efforts; it frustrates Fujimori that he lost the trail of Thomas Waters at the point when the influential English engineer-cum-architect left Japan.

Of Fujimori's 2005 Lamune *Onsenkan*, "Soda Pop Spa," writer Kozaburo Arashiyama remarked:

> For the hot springs building Fujimori designed, he used scorched cedar and white plaster, the roof is covered in hand-crimped copper sheet, and at the tip of each peak is a tiny, living pine tree, yielding an original effect. This is "Fujimori World" at its best. It looks from the outside like a hideaway for mountain brigands, but in you go, and you find the interior is a space fit for the tea ceremony.[3]

2.1 Two tiny towers topped with scrawny pines at the heart of Fujimori's 2005 Soda Pop Spa.

1. Daniell (2001) p. 33. Daniell's remarks (as will become evident in this chapter) are remarkably prescient, but he wrote these words in relation to three early projects.
2. Stewart (1987) p. 15.
3. Arashiyama (2006). Original Japanese: 藤森さんが設計した温泉家屋は、焼き杉と漆喰を使い、屋根に手捻りの銅板が張られ、屋根の上に松の木が生える斬新な造りで、藤森ワールドてんこ盛りであった。外から見ると山賊の隠れ家みたいで、なかに入ると茶室を思わせる。

2.2 Walls around the spa's gardens are made up only of charred cedar planks.

2.3 A Disney-esque brick building, which once housed the Imperial Guards, is an example of the era central to Fujimori's research.

2.4 Kyushu's bucolic fields.

2.5 The dapper charred cedar stripes of the main buildings at Soda Pop Spa.

2.2

That flip "Fujimori World" recalls the exoticism that Meiji-era architecture must have once afforded, and explains how the two poles of his work, Fujimori's academic research and his oddball architecture, come together today. It is not that you can point to some feature of Fujimori's buildings and hazard its provenance the way he once did for chubby, Matsumoto masthead *putti*. On the contrary, Fujimori's buildings are put together in a way unlikely to be pedigreed. Critic Taro Igarashi pointed out, "Fujimori's architecture expresses strong indigenous qualities but makes us think of places that do not exist. It arouses nostalgia, but does not point to a specific region ..."[4] Fujimori's output is an update of those Japanese carpenters' *giyofu* style; the Soda Pop Spa is perhaps his most charming effort, a surprising 426 square meters (4,585 square feet) within, but broken up into a complex of tiny structures sporting turrets and trees, scaled small enough one can reach up to the roof.

2.3

Soda Pop Spa is nestled in the village of Nagayu (literally, "long, hot water"), a place uninteresting in the way many small towns often are today: much of Main Street is underutilized, and little remains of the area's earlier industries: forestry, farming or other local institutions that thrived fifty years ago. But Nagayu has one resource that remains: tourism. The popular hot springs resort is tucked away in a narrow green valley; the setting for Fujimori's baths is along a burbling river tucked between lush hillsides and just down the street from a quaint little Dutch-gabled structure that dates from the 1930s, the era when the waters of Nagayu first became an attraction, even drawing German tourists, who continue to come to this isolated area even today. Around the time Soda Pop Spa was completed in 2005, Fujimori ruminated, "How can one approach the relationship between

2.4

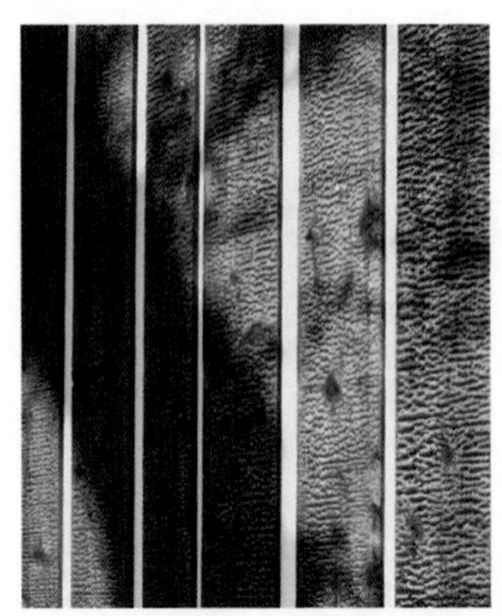

2.5

2.6 *Fujimori's sketches are sweetly unprofessional, more like a child's charming creation.*

2.6

2.7

2.7 Soda Pop Spa is nestled in a lush and rolling landscape.

mountains, rivers, rocks, earth, trees, grass, in a word, nature, self-perpetuating since the beginning of the world, and architecture, a major work of modern humanity …?"[5]

The landscape of the Soda Pop Spa roof breaks up into six ungainly pyramidal points of varying heights, each brandishing its tuft of valiant pine – giving the overall complex a sense that it is not so much one building as a tiny village itself, or that the roof is the ragged profile of a midget mountain range. The tallest point is just a bit over 10 meters high, on a relatively wide and monumental hip roof over an open porch, signaling the public entrance.

Writing of another pine, one that topped his 1997 Single Pine House, Fujimori said the tree was "… the first example where I used greenery symbolically … The single pine is like a *chonmage* [the ponytail worn by Edo-era samurai], and it is, well, you might say it is an absurdity."[6] Elsewhere, he speaks of grass sprouting from the same façade as "whiskers."[7] Fujimori links the down-like plants sprouting from the skin of his structures to Salvador Dali, yet I cannot help but also hear echoes of older Shinto legends when looking at Fujimori's structure, clad in charred cedar and topped with living pines:

> [The god Susanowo] pulled out the hairs of his beard and scattered them over the land, where each hair immediately changed into a cedar tree (sugi). In the same way, the hairs from Susanowo's chest turned into cypress trees (hino-ki), the hairs from his buttocks into black pines (maki-no-ki) and the hairs from his eyebrows into camphor trees (busu-no-ki). …Susanowo announced: "Use cedar and camphor wood when building ships; use cypress wood when building splendid halls and palaces …"[8]

In spite of Fujimori's regular and loving listing of native woods, for a long time he used cedar only grudgingly. An architect who often collaborates with Fujimori, Nobumichi Oshima, asserted, "He calls [cedar] a vegetable. A Japanese who would publicly say that he does not like cedar, well, I would guess Professor Fujimori is the only one."[9] Architect Yoshio Uchida collaborated with Fujimori on the 1997 Fuku Akino Art Museum, and explained that this dislike presented a bit of a problem, "… Fujimori in fact hates cedar … He wanted to use hardwoods, I think. But the town of Tenryu [where the museum is located] is known for its cedar output."[10] While completing the Akino Museum, Fujimori asked a gardener to char one of the cedar columns.[11] The effect stuck with him, though not entirely successful; he returned to it in the 2005 Yoro Insects Museum, but again found the result unsatisfying. At Soda Pop Spa and the subsequent *Yakisugi* House, however, Fujimori used deeply scorched and fissured cedar planks, aligning the exterior with his increasing interest in fire, one of "Fujimori's Five Points." The siding is an odd choice for a southern hot springs resort, a finish mostly seen in farming and fishing villages in the more central Kansai area of Japan, although I have also spotted it in nearby Shimane Prefecture. The effect is openly plebian; Fujimori underscored this in an interview, perversely asserting not once but three times, "Architects do not use scorched cedar."[12] As if to assure disassociation with its connotation, Fujimori claimed he has no intention of employing this cladding in regions where it is commonly found.[13] This reappropriated vernacular is intended to be at once familiar and oddly out of place.

The "U"-shaped Soda Pop Spa frames an expanse of low *sasa* bamboo grasses, populated by an odd statue (a man with the head of a

4. Igarashi (2006) p. 13.
5. Suzuki and Terada (2006) p. 102.
6. Fujimori *et al.* (2005) p. 127.
Original Japanese:
…緑をシンボリックに使った最初の例です。線で使い、点で使い、次にシンボリックに使う。一本松はチョンマゲみたいで、何とも言えない、おかしみがあるんですよ。
7. Oshinomi, Kunihide 押野見邦英, *et al.* (2001) p. 61.
8. Sonoda (2000) p. 40.
9. Fujimori *et al.* (2005) p. 87.
Original Japanese:
野菜だと言って。日本人で杉がきらいって公言したのは、藤森先生くらいじゃないですか。
10. Fujimori *et al.* (2005) p. 136.
Original Japanese:
ところで、藤森さんは実は杉がきらいである。… 本当は広葉樹を用いたかったのだと思う. 天竜は杉の産地である。
11. Fujimori also attempted to embed blackened straw into white plaster at the Fuku Akino Museum, but found soot permeated the plaster, unattractively mottling it.
12. Interview, Tokyo (4 June, 2007). In the same conversation, Fujimori pointed out that postwar architect Kiyoshi Seike, hailing from the Kansai area, considered using scorched cedar – but only in Tokyo, far away from where it was conventional.
13. *Yakisugi* House is in western Nagano – again, not in central Kansai.

2.8

2.9

2.10

2.11

2.8–11 Each roof peak at Soda Pop Spa is topped by a tiny tree.

2.13

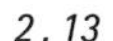

2.14

2.15

2.16

2.12 The west elevation of Fujimori's 2007 Yakisugi (Charred Cedar) House, showing similarly natty stripes.

2.13 Inside, an elegant display shelf graces the entrance foyer.

2.14 The modest master bedroom.

2.15 The fireplace at Charred Cedar House is surrounded by lumps of charcoal set in plaster, the kitchen concealed behind the curving wall.

2.17

2.18

2.16 From the garden, the main features of Charred Cedar House are easy to understand: a cave-like central space and a teahouse hanging in the air.

2.17 The tearoom, its tokonoma shelf entirely subverted.

2.18 The eroded edge of dangling charred cedar siding.

2.19 Inside Soda Pop Spa, Akoya oyster shells are embedded into the wall of the men's bath.

2.20 A web of gold leaf extends along the wall of the women's bath.

2.21 Smaller family baths allow more privacy, an innovation reflecting twenty-first century sensibilities.

2.22 The unusual hearth is intended to assure no ill effects from the high carbon dioxide content in the bathing water; the copper cup in the foreground sits above a drinking water spout.

2.19

2.20

2.21

飲用天然水

2.23

2.24

dog) and a tiny, roofed structure where waters can be collected for carrying home. Two common baths, one for men and one for women, address the public entrance across this lawn; the elevation of the bath building is rendered in a rather goofy face. Fujimori's ludic touch is at its best in this light gesture, overseeing the point where three-generation families or friends hail each other as they split into gendered groups.

A hot springs spa seems the perfect project for Fujimori, the bath deeply allusive in Japanese society, enfolding soft bodies in all their vulnerability. Scott Clark wrote an academic exegesis on the Japanese bath, arguing in his opening, "To take a bath in Japan ... is to immerse yourself in culture as well as water."[14] Isamu Noguchi insightfully related a disheartening experience when confronted with a bath near Tokyo, one in apparent ignorance of its cultural place (perhaps one of Paul Ricouer's "plastic or aluminum atrocities"[15]):

> ... caught overnight at a business hotel at Narita airport, I found myself squeezed into a pink plastic box that masqueraded as a *furo* [bath]. Throughout the room not even an illusion of time or space remained, only a crowd of things from bed to television ... Perhaps this is the logical, if ironic, result of the new architecture, with people reconciled to no time, no space ...[16]

Bathing is in most nations a private pursuit. Japanese, however, consider hopping naked into hot water an indulgence, often amiably doing so at any hour, with coworkers, friends, family and total strangers. Peter Grilli, raised in Japan, simply stated, "Bathing in Japan is best when it is communal."[17] And Scott Clark said of commercial baths, "... people usually come in groups – after all, the purpose of the visit is to associate and enjoy time together."[18] Today, the variety of establishments that offer a commercial soak is stunning: expensive resort hotels where bathing morning and night is interrupted by lavish gourmet meals, still-extant public baths in urban areas, luxury "super spas." And, of course, people bathe at home, where parents nightly

2.25

2.23 Stair to the art gallery above.

2.24 Roughly shaped logs support the crimped copper roof.

2.25 Under the loggia, husbands lounge, waiting for their wives to return from the baths.

14. Clark (1994) p. 1.

15. Frampton (1983) p. 148. Original is in Paul Ricouer, "Universalization and National Cultures," *History and Truth* (1961).

16. Grilli (1992) p. 14.

17. Ibid., p. 30. It is interesting to compare how Fujimori and Kengo Kuma accommodate bathing. Both revel in the sensuality of the bath, but Kuma, the more international of the two, tends to offer private territories that barely permit a parent and child to rinse in the same space.

18. Clark (1994) p. 82.

2.26

2.27

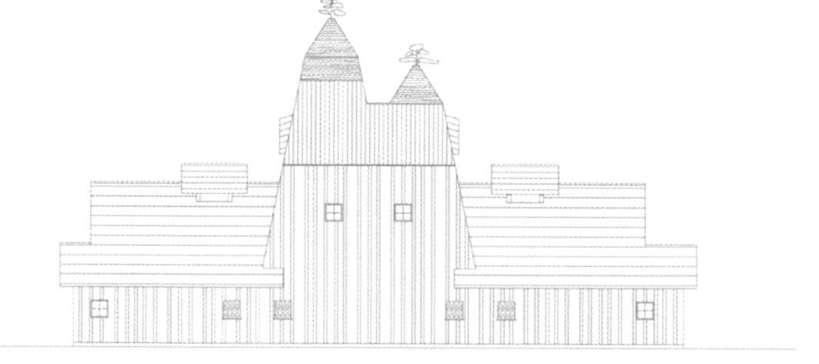

2.28

2.26 Small dormers and other elements on the roof appear only playfully ornamental, but allow light and air into the spaces below.

2.27 The family baths fall in a line, each indicated by tiny animal tracks on a signboard.

2.28 The face-like elevation fronting the two main baths, men's on the left under a slightly taller tower.

2.29

2.30

2.31

2.32

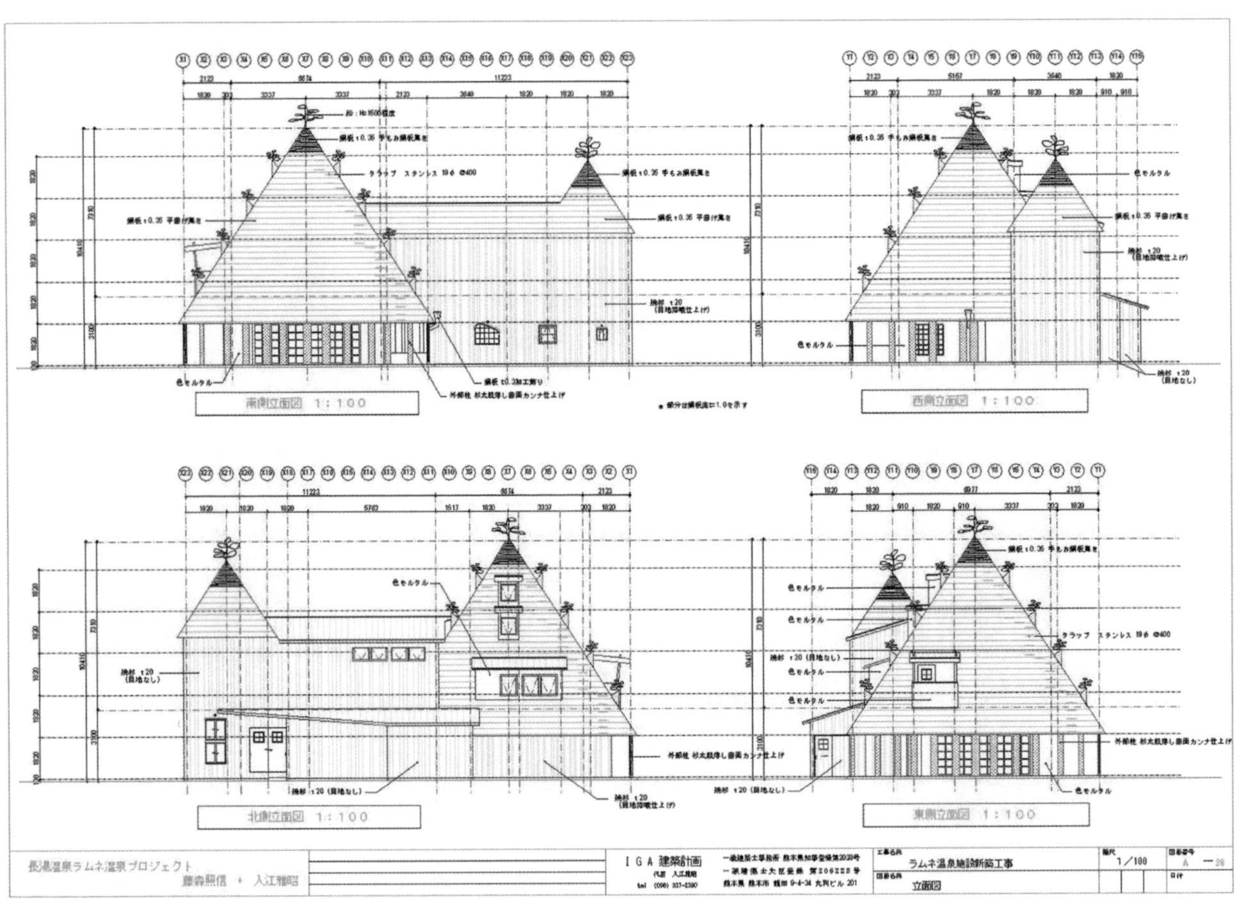

2.33

2.29 Mr. Kakudai, who owns Fujimori's favorite sawmill, assists in the simple system they have devised for charring cedar.

2.30 Fujimori watches the fire from below.

2.31 A young man from Fujimori's University of Tokyo research laboratory quenching the fire.

2.32 A garden space of white stone and black, behind one of the family baths.

2.33 Working drawings for Soda Pop Spa, by Yoshiaki Irie of IGA Projekt.

2.34 The modest landscaping around the entrance is in keeping with the rural character of the region.

2.35 The entrance and art gallery are expressed more monumentally than the intimate spaces of the baths.

2.36 Another, more lavish bath along a river nearby, by one of the early architects of Team Zoo, Reiko Tomita.

2.34

2.35

enjoy a soak with their children of either gender. In my early years in Japan, I was flummoxed when a day excursion with a group of elderly women ended in a communal dip, but in retrospect the event was unremarkable. Soda Pop Spa, which calls itself an *onsenkan* ("hot water amenity"), is a relatively modern building type, intended for just such an affable outing; Fujimori sized the baths small, to discourage the bus trade that can overwhelm the intimacy of such sites.[19] This is understandable; the exponential expansion of hot springs excursions has been going on for much of the late twentieth century. In an article on rural tourism trends, John Knight wrote, "The number of overnight stays at guesthouses in hot-springs resorts in 1987 was 122 million, equal to the total population [of Japan] and some three times the figure of thirty years earlier."[20] The popularity of communal hot baths has only swelled since.[21]

Water is of understandably obsessive interest. Signs in baths proudly proclaim the presence of radon, chloride salts, sulfuric acid or iron; brochures extol a range of hues: milky white, murky yellow, rusty brown, and even aqua blue. Establishments offer enticing baths with electrical impulses, baths with bubbles. Soda Pop Spa is called *Lamune* in Japanese, a name recalling fizzy drinks popular in the Meiji era; it offers effervescent waters. The area is, in the words of the Japan National Tourist Organization, "... home to one of the finest carbonated springs in Japan," and "Lamune Onsen in particular boasts an especially high concentration of carbonic acid."[22] Those bubbles are carbon dioxide; as a precaution, Fujimori paid more than ordinary attention to air movement. The tiny towers interspersed throughout the complex enclose chimney-like ventilation shafts, and at night candles are sometimes lit in the larger baths, naturally extinguishing if the concentration of carbon dioxide becomes excessive. (The owner jokes that in the old days people would sometimes forget their candles. With no way of monitoring the air, the first evidence of a problem would be when small children would suddenly turn bright blue.[23]) Each bath also has a high hearth embedded in the white plaster walls. Fujimori makes the point that fire is not only a way of monitoring oxygen levels, but is also emerging in his work as a way of marking human comfort:

> The inclusion of a *ro*, or ... hearth, is another crucial development ... for its presence also means the use of fire. Whether large or small, the presence of fire in a space is decisive in determining how it is equipped and given function. Architectural history begins with the temples and the dwellings of the ancients. The former served as homes for the gods, the latter as houses for people. These two functional forms developed along lines distinguished by one crucial difference: the presence or absence of fire.[24]

Oddly enough, in an essay entitled "My First Hot Springs Building," Fujimori describes how he struggled with the spa's intended use. Only when he began to see the hot water of the bath as analogous to the water used in tea, both called *yu* in Japanese, did his sense of the project emerge. Soda Pop Spa became about "Water and fire. Hot water (*yu*) and fire. The boiled water for tea and fire."[25] Of fire in the tearoom, Fujimori wrote, "... a *ro*, or hearth ... retains through the smoldering fire a connection to humankind's distant, primordial origins."[26]

Copper chimneys, quickly darkening in the iron-laden air, serve these cheery fires so oddly installed in the wet bathing areas. The lively territory of the roofscape responds here not only to rain from

2.36

19. Tiny Soda Pop Spa received 100,000 visitors in its first year of operation.

20. Knight (1994) p. 635. Kimiko Akita argues the increasing postwar popularity of bathing destinations was in part due to women's greater leisure time. See Akita (2005) p. 100. Interestingly, the Meiji era witnessed a similar bathhouse boom. Scott Clark, observed, "In the beginning of the Meiji era, [Tokyo] bathhouses began to proliferate. Indeed, the number of public bathhouses increased threefold ..." Clark (1994) p. 42.

21. In truth, this did not entirely maintain intimacy at Soda Pop Spa; the owners told me that on weekends over Golden Week (a long holiday period when many Japanese are free to travel), visitor numbers reached 1,200 a day.

22. <http://www.jnto.go.jp/tourism/en/90.html> (accessed 7 September, 2007).

23. Katsuji Shuto 首藤勝次, *X-Knowledge Home*, vol. 6, no. 1, issue 30, Special issue, no. 7: "The Fujimori" (10 August 2006) p. 71.

24. Isozaki *et al.* (2007) p. 12.

25. Fujimori (2006e) p. 125. Original Japanese: 水と火。湯と火。茶の湯と火。

26. Isozaki *et al.* (2007) p. 78.

2.37

2.38

2.37 Doors to each bath are low, a straw rope hanging over them.

2.38 The interior of the art gallery, in a forest of rough columns.

2.39 The plan of Soda Pop Spa, the two main baths to the left, family baths along the center wall, and the entrance, art museum, and offices to the right.

above. It also incorporates raised sections for ventilation along ridge lines, windowed dormers dropping light deep within the baths, a balcony and other covered outside spaces, and strongly articulated drip edges at the point where the roofs conceal soil for the pines on their peaks. The eave line is interrupted to flip slightly upward at entrances, but overall, the roofs reach low, establishing intimacy, close enough to touch; at the edge, the scale of detail shifts, smaller, denser lines of crumpled copper sheets.

The large pyramidal roof shelters the public parts of this place, a lobby and, incredibly, an art museum, fringed with an unevenly spaced set of crooked columns. Inside the lounge, where husbands invariably wait for wives, five more columns, avatar-like presences, stand guard, a gesture repeated in the museum above. The second-floor ceiling follows the roof slope, the columns here forest-like, a reverse Asplund. Within the baths at the other end of the complex, Fujimori highlights his columns' symbolic status, employing a single shaft standing sentry in the center of each space. The timber feels oddly out of place, vulnerable because of the juxtaposition of raw wood and water; the shafts stand on plaster plinths, but the effort seems unlikely to prevent decay in the steamy space.

In his book, Peter Grilli argues the importance of the bath stretches far back in time:

> The earliest myths of the Japanese people refer repeatedly to acts of bathing or ritual lustration by the gods ... the central deities of the ancient Shinto cosmos – the gods of sun, moon, and agricultural fertility – were all born out of a bath ...[27]

But Scott Clark counters, "Although the relationship between water and spiritual cleanliness remains strong, the Japanese do not customarily think of the daily bath as a religious experience."[28] I agree with Clark – but nonetheless, the Japanese bath offers a simple, everyday ritual.[29] At most such sites, any foreigner first entering a public bath is made aware of a strict sequence (although my observations tell me these steps are sometimes honored more in the breach than followed closely): completely undress before entering the room holding the bath, wash thoroughly at spigots around the edges of the space before soaking, rinse and lather again before toweling off.

More importantly, like the tea ceremony, the bath is a social leveler; the hierarchy of daily life is left in the dressing room with status symbols like clothes and jewelry. All carry the same towels, supplied by the bath; all use the same soaps. Clark opines:

> Sharing the same bath naked symbolizes removal of the social trappings and barriers of normal life. The "skinship" ... that holds significance in the parent/child bonding is also prized for its power to create close social bonds among friends and relax the normal social distance ... People feel that while naked they can obtain a closeness difficult to achieve by other means – and the only acceptable place for this communal nakedness is the bath.[30]

At Soda Pop Spa, Fujimori again readdresses ritual. The dressing rooms are essentially in the open air, enclosed only partially, but comfortingly lined in dark wood in contrast to the bath beyond, where floor, wall, and ceiling are white.[31] The path of procession is heightened and dramatized by a tiny aperture Fujimori placed between the (un)dressing area and the bath, a sort of thresholdless *nezumikido*, or "mouse-hole" opening, fringed with a rope recalling those found at shrines,

27. Grilli (1992) p. 24.
28. Clark (1994) p. 126.
29. Akita's unpublished dissertation addresses a variety of other ritual behaviors she observed.
30. Clark (1994) p. 112.

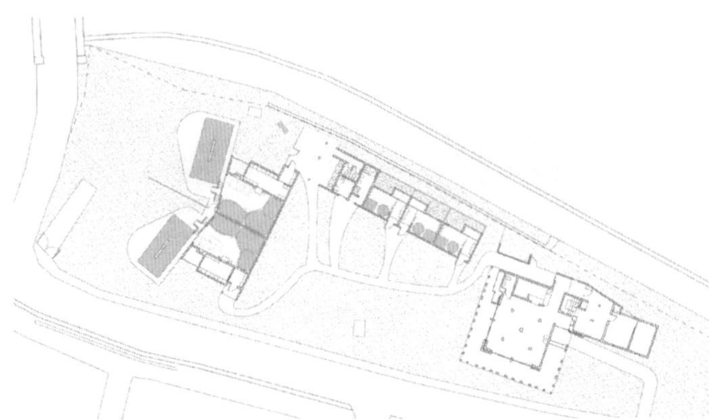

2.39

2.40

2.40 *In a clear demonstration of "skinship," the Jomon Company and essayist Kozaburo Arashiyama bathe together at Soda Pop Spa. (The outside pools were initially protected only with plastic in the winter months.) Left to right: artist Genpei Akasegawa, architectural historian Terunobu Fujimori, editor Tetsuo Matsuda, illustrator Shinbo Minami, essayist and manhole cover enthusiast Joji Hayashi, and critic Kozaburo Arashiyama.*

but with the much more prosaic intent to prevent people banging their heads. Within, all is at its most basic: gone are the spigots; gone is the shampoo. One is encouraged to simply rinse and join the bath.[32] Each common area includes an outdoor pool, which Fujimori framed in low lawns of barley. He placed a ribald grassy mound outside the women's bath, at once resembling a very large and hairy pair of testicles and yet simultaneously recalling the kind of craggy rock found in Kyoto's Zen-inspired dry gardens.

The wall surrounding the hearth in the men's bath is speckled with Akoya oyster shells, while squares of gold leaf stretch across the surface surrounding the hearth in the women's bath. Fujimori worries this gilding is perhaps too well done, left in the hands of local laborers. The plaster was once white and unembellished; elsewhere in the complex, Fujimori embedded straw, but not in the baths. An encrusted overlay of mineral deposits in the wet areas coats plaster, plumbing, even the plastic stool and bucket used before bathing. Kozaburo Arashiyama thought the resulting rusty finish recalled the rich browns of *bizenyaki*, an esteemed style of pottery dating back to Japan's Middle Ages.[33]

In addition to the two larger baths, Fujimori also created three charming family suites, strung out in a line along the third wall of the complex, protectively sited between the common bathing areas and the museum and lounge. Unusual offerings, the intimacy of these rooms is underscored by a contorted column within, marking the entrance. These suites display many of the features found elsewhere in the complex, but in a compressed and particularly effective whole. Alluding perhaps to the variations in tearoom ceilings, the height of the room is low at the entrance, reaches higher towards a window on the opposite wall (beyond which is seen a simple dry garden of white stone), and culminates at the chimney-like shafts above the baths.[34] This progression enforces the procession below: at the entrance, you shed shoes; a raised *tatami*-like mat next to the window invites you to sit as you undress, defining a dry zone in the room; a washing area and two tubs are further within. The unusual private suites are a sign of social change, fit for nuclear families, people who are embarrassed by handicaps and inclined to privacy, and those uncomfortable with the etiquette of a public bath (including foreigners), all relatively recent demographic developments.

Throughout this complex, Fujimori underscores his interests: vernacular references sourced internationally, an accessible architecture achieved through scale and playful detail, a building that will inevitably – through its vulnerable materials and living adornments – change over time. Kyoto-based architect Thomas Daniell argued Fujimori's work is "... as much straight-forward perversity as it is considered critique."[35] Yet while Fujimori is definitely engaged in tweaking expectations, this is an affectionate environment. Soda Pop Spa reflects not the staid traditions of the nation's elites, but those of family, friends, and community. The scale and organization are rooted in intimacy; the architecture is lighthearted and openly absurd, winningly naïve, the exoticism an enticement. Soda Pop Spa is willingly entertaining, but not narrowly nostalgic; its sense of place is as allusive of English Tudor as the historical roots of the tiny town of Nagayu. These baths are designed for day-trippers with time to burn, exploring a winding mountain road to discover the valiant pine trees capping the roofscape of Soda Pop Spa.

31. Clark considered this treatment common, observing, "One feature of bathhouses across the entire nation is the architectural difference between the bathing area and the dressing area. Generally the dressing area retains a Japanese style except in the most modern buildings. It tends to be done in wood or in the browns and other subdued colors associated with wood and traditional building materials. The bathing area, however, is ... bright and airy." (Clark 1994, p. 49).

32. The fact that one does not soap at Soda Pop Spa allows it to happily co-exist with other, earlier baths the community constructed, one for day trippers which offers saunas and lavish spa facilities and another that is used by locals for their daily ablutions. Locals tend to wash in the public bath across the river, then drop in to Soda Pop Spa later for a friendly soak. Signs encourage visitors, too, to try various waters at the local Japanese inns and the larger German-inspired spa. The business-savvy owner of Soda Pop Spa owns the Daimaru Ryokan, which also accommodates drop-in bathing, and helped promote the construction of both public bathing facilities.

33. Arashiyama. Accessed on-line at: <http://www.lamune-onsen.co.jp/yuumeijin.html> on 9 September, 2007.

34. There are two types of natural hot springs feeding the baths at Lamune. The earliest and more unusual are lukewarm (32 degrees Centigrade/90 degrees Fahrenheit) carbonated waters. In the postwar period, deeper wells were drilled to reach non-carbonated waters of around 42 degrees Centigrade (nearly 108 degrees Fahrenheit). Most probably prefer the hotter baths, but the carbonated water offers an unusual attraction.

35. Daniell (2001) p. 33.

From PoMo to Paulownia

Kengo Kuma

3

If you did not have the inclination for *déjà vu* or comparing subtle distinctions, the future looks pretty tedious. So for some, the only way to go forward was to look to the recent past ... You might say this for the cultured architects aware of the first half of the 20th century – Hiroyuki Suzuki or Kengo Kuma ...
—Terunobu Fujimori[1]

Kengo Kuma's early architecture was skillfully scenographic, proffering a postmodernism then popular in the United States. He created over-scaled, oddly exaggerated imitations of Western classicism – in Tokyo, which made the structures seem more knowingly ironic. His crowd-pleasing curling column capitals at the 1992 "M2" were also an expression of Kuma's overseas education; he once noted that the scrolling Ionic order is the only one of the five classical orders he discovered while a student on the Columbia University campus, used there because it expresses an academic outlook.[2] Kuma's most celebrated building in Japan's economically exuberant Bubble period was concomitantly cartoonish and pedantic.

But before M2, Kuma also indicated an appreciation of sensual delight in Japanese traditions. His first book (published when he was 32) applied Western architectural theory to Japanese house styles, but Kuma was constantly drawn into digressions on topics like tea aesthetics or ikebana, the art of flowers.[3] His earliest published architecture, too, the 1989 Izu Bathhouse, expressed an interest in Japan's past. "The shape of the joints of the bamboo rain gutters is a copy of those found at the Katsura Detached Palace," Kuma wrote at the time.[4] In a recent conversation, he said of this building:

> From the beginning, I tried to combine modern technology with a traditional material ... the main material is particleboard – for floors, the wall, the ceiling ... But I thought that particleboard was not enough for a country house. In a country house, a more natural element is necessary to get people relaxed, and so I picked bamboo as a symbol of the naturalness of the house ... I used bamboo for the gutters and drainpipe. ... I was very impressed; I thought the combination of industrial materials like particleboard with a very traditional, authentic detail ... was a meeting of two different things which can create a new kind of *wabi/sabi*.[5]

Frankly, Kuma's bamboo detailing at the Izu Bathhouse is far from beautiful. It certainly does not offer the elegance of *wabi* and *sabi*; it is closer to Fujimori's clunky choices. But the Izu Bathhouse reinforces the compelling conclusion that while it was Kuma's early postmodernist works that initially received accolades, his tendency to adopt

3.1 The sparkling white ceramic fins on the façade of Kengo Kuma's 2007 Suntory Museum in Tokyo taper to a mere six millimeters along their edge.

1. Fujimori (2006d) p. 021. Original Japanese: そういう未来が退屈そうで、概視感や微妙な差異くらべが体質にあわないとしたら、過去に向って進むしかないのではないか。...
言われるように２０世紀前半をパスした文人的建築なのかもしれない．鈴木博之と隈研吾も、閉じたサークルの中で建築という指摘をしていた。』
2. Kuma (1986) p.11. The title of this popular and accessible book is usually translated simply as *Ten Houses*, but this overlooks the punning use of homonyms: Kuma's title sounds the same as that of a well-regarded (and very difficult) text written by Kazuo Shinohara, published in 1950. In a 1997 interview, Kuma claimed his book reached a circulation of "around twenty thousand issues." See "Kengo Kuma," in Knabe and Noennig (1999) p. 36.
3. Ibid. Kuma's early and brief flirtation with postmodernism continues to dog him. In a lecture I gave in 2007, older Japanese architects discussed Kuma's current interest in Japanese history with skepticism. After a brief effort to repudiate his flirtation with postmodernism, which included writing another book in 1989 entitled *Guddobai-PosutoModan: 11 Nin no Amerika no* Kenchikuka グッドバイ・ポストモダン―11人のアメリカ建築家 [Good-bye Postmodernism: 11 American Architects] (Tokyo: Kajima Shuppan, 1989), Kuma has elected to ignore the issue.
4. Kuma (1989a) p. 41.
5. Interview, Tokyo (3 March, 2007).

3.2

3.3

and adapt Japanese tradition, better known today, was present from the start.[6]

In the end, the economic exuberance that encouraged Kuma's playful postmodernism collapsed into a long recessionary period that endures in rural regions even now. Clients and the critical press became disenchanted with the frivolous architecture of the era. Architects like Kuma then looked deeper. He began to see that site, material, and construction were at the heart of his art. This paring has taken him a long way; there is little ornamental excess left over from the days of M2 and its breezy brethren.

Kuma's inclination towards solitary, unadulterated substances originated at the 1994 Kiro-san Observatory – a project not merely rooted in its site, but embedded, a remarkably self-effacing piece of architecture. The observatory was the earliest expression of his now well-known sensitivity to site. Industrial facilities foul Shikoku Island's north coast; instead of adding to this cacophony, he dug into the earth, cleaving narrow slots into sidewalls framing slender, but surprisingly beautiful, scenes beyond. Subtlety was perhaps the only choice at such a site; as Kuma stated shortly after, "I felt that creating an object there would deal a fatal blow to the environment."[7] The observatory was entirely concrete; this employ of a single material set a strategy central in Kuma's subsequent structures.

He completed the award-winning Water/Glass in Atami, delicate as a jewel box, the following year. Kuma always argues an adjacent interior Bruno Taut completed in 1936, the Hyuga Villa immediately downslope, was his inspiration. Kuma also turned to Taut's texts, ultimately acknowledging, "Even though [Taut] stayed in Japan for only three years, his understanding of Japanese culture was surprisingly deep and I learned a good deal about my country from his books."[8] In admiration, the Japanese architect elected to make his building an *homage*.[9] Doing so through the substance of the structure was surely irresistible: the German architect's pseudonym was once "*Glas*."[10]

Taut enjoined artists and architects to eschew form, allow their own intuitive appreciation of materiality to inspire them. Water/Glass incorporates a rooftop roost that is poetically pure and startlingly single-minded: chairs and table, structure and skin – all glass, without regard for its inconvenient weight or torrid summer temperatures. The effect is a nearly surreal illustration of Taut's long-ago ideals, perched daintily above the sea. Kuma at this moment eschewed the self-conscious formalism of his earlier architecture, instead opting to express an elementary understanding of substance, whether wood or glass, steel or stone.

He learned other lessons. At Hyuga Villa, Taut – an originator of the International Style – explored Japanese staples: bamboo, tile, *tatami*, *paulownia* wood and woven sudare screens. Bamboo, once used in antiquated teahouses, is also oddly modern. Inspired by Souetsu Yanagi (the driving force behind the *mingei* folkcraft movement in Japan), Taut altered how architects apply bamboo, as did France's Charlotte Perriand.[11] Taut designed basket-like bamboo lamps and arcing umbrella handles; Perriand's bamboo *chaise lounge* echoes to her iconic work with Le Corbusier. Kuma claims:

> Taut saw modernism in the bamboo ... He recognized in the bamboo the modernism that he had aimed for and that was being abandoned in Europe. During his subsequent stay in Japan, Taut used bamboo with great enthusiasm. Bamboo is by no means easy to use as a building material. Moreover,

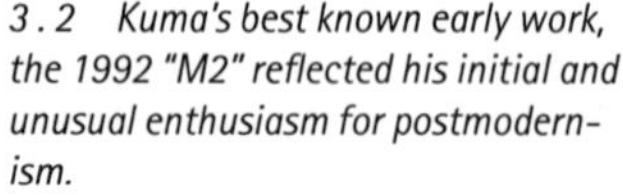

3.2 Kuma's best known early work, the 1992 "M2" reflected his initial and unusual enthusiasm for postmodernism.

6. Another minor constant is his interest in bathing. Kuma continues to take extra care in his design of baths today.

7. Kuma (1997) p. 6.

8. Kuma (2005a) p. 15.

9. This point is made, for example, in Kuma (2000) pp. 75–76.

10. For homage, see, for example, Kuma (2005a) p. 15. I also was fortunate to attend a lecture that Kuma gave on the different moments in his life when he "met" [出会った] Taut, elaborating on how these were pivotal. It is worth adding, though, that areas where glass are so used in this building are actually very limited; its role is underscored by careful selection of published photographs.

11. Kikuchi (1997) p. 354 n. 51. In Kikuchi's *Japanese Modernisation and Mingei Theory: Cultural Nationalism and Oriental Orientalism* (2004), she explicitly states, "Taut was guided and supported by Yanagi ..." (p. 100) and "Perriand was greatly inspired by Yanagi's collection ..." (p. 104).

3.3–7 For his 1995 Water / Glass, a penthouse pavilion, Kuma used glass even for the furnishings. The penthouse sits in a pool of water with an infinity edge, blending building, sea, and – on a cloudy day – even sky. Kuma's minimalist detailing here was a significant departure from his earlier efforts.

3.4

3.5

3.6

3.7

3.9 A reception room and deck on an upper floor of the Suntory Museum show Kuma's interest in connecting interior and exterior spaces.

3.8, 10 A dry garden, a modern version of an ancient art.

3.11 The 2007 Suntory Museum's strong verticals contrast with the flat landscape of the site.

3.8

3.9

3.10

> his Japanese hosts were puzzled by the fascination bamboo exercised on this international architect. Nevertheless, Taut used bamboo in furniture and architecture. He used it often inside the Hyuga Residence. The walls of the large room are lined with slender bamboo [rod]s, arranged vertically. The two or three hundred small lightbulbs on the ceiling of the social room are each hung from a bamboo chain, and the chains in turn are suspended from bamboo poles. In just three years, Taut learned practically all there is to know about the capability of bamboo.[12]

Kuma saw that he also could explore the opportunities offered in Japan's older, underappreciated materials and the crafts connected to them.

Toyo Ito explicitly inquired, "Your investigations into material and its sensibility, that theoretical stance, how do you perceive it as being related to Fujimori-San?" And Kuma replied, "Without originators like Fujimori-San, I would not have become [as I am], I think."[13] Yet there are important distinctions between the two. Fujimori rations his annual architectural output. Kuma runs a large office (employing over fifty), thus able to offer an assortment of approaches in his application of local materials and traditions, consciously and critically considered. His improvisations extend to paper, bamboo, blocks of earth, thatch, *tatami*, straw and soft stone considered unsuitable for architecture. On occasion, he alludes to historical approaches, for example, topping a Noh stage with a slate roof in a style from the Meiji era.[14] Elsewhere, Kuma adapts new forms, *kawara* tile at a recent residence in Kyoto a familiar finish, but also oddly fresh because of its unusual form. But Kuma shares with Fujimori a love of lumber, of which he

12. Kuma (2000) pp. 268–269. English from a translation by Hiroshi Watanabe, published as *AA Words Two: Anti-Object?: The Dissolution and Disintegration of Architecture* (London: AA Publications, 2008) sent by e-mail to the author, 19 September, 2007. All citations in this text are taken from the original Japanese.

13. Ito, Toyo with Kengo Kuma and Yoshio Futagawa (2006) p. 98. Original Japanese:
伊東：隈さんは、素材の質感などを追求ししつ、その論理も立てながら，藤森さんとの関係をどのように捉えているのですか？
隈：とうとう、きましたね(笑)。藤森さんみたいな原始人に、ぼくはなれないと思うし。

14. See Kuma (2000) p. 147 in Japanese; English translation (forthcoming).

3.11

3 . 12 A dramatic stair inside the Suntory only skirts the oak floor.

3 . 13 An open area on the deck.

3 . 14 The stair, an inviting gesture connecting the two gallery floors.

3 . 15 Louvers wrapped in paulownia (on the left) can be closed; the moveable walls to the right are finished in Japanese paper.

3 . 12

3 . 13

3 . 14

3 . 15

3.16

3.17

3.18

3.16 *The Suntory's café is finished in a rough banana-fiber fabric.*

3.17 *Curtains of bamboo at the Suntory's opening exhibit were Kuma's acknowledgment of the ongoing influence of Bruno Taut's Hyuga Villa.*

3.18 *The long horizontal lines of the elegant display cases are an apt match for the ancient works displayed within.*

3.19 *Public areas of the Suntory are finished in nubby hand-made Japanese paper, washed from below with light.*

3.19

3.20

3.21

argues, "… it is not exaggerating to say that not only the architectural culture of Japan but also the entire culture of Japan is grounded on the tree …"[15] and elsewhere arguing, "People choose wood because it is a material that fits their bodies. Its scale is good, its quality and essence are an exact complement for the strengths and weaknesses of the body."[16]

In an insightful essay, "Ise Shrine and a Modernist Construction of Japanese Tradition," architectural historian Jonathan Reynolds points to the chief difference between Japanese Modernism and practices elsewhere in the world: Bruno Taut, Walter Gropius and other leading Western architects, while rejecting history at home, admired what they pictured as Japan's past, the simplicity of Ise Shrine and *shoin*-style structures.[17] Reynolds argued that after Taut, Japanese Modernists identified themselves as "legitimate heirs of Japan's long cultural legacy," not in opposition to their past, but rediscovering their roots.[18] Kuma asserts this overlap of Modernism and Japanese tradition also exists in his own work: "… I now feel the need to go back to the cornerstones of traditional Japanese architecture. I think there is no fundamental difference between the basic concept of Western Modernism and that of traditional architecture of Japan."[19]

Reynolds presents an excellent and very odd example of the postwar conflation of Western Modernism and Japanese custom, a 1954 house designed by Junzo Yoshimura, built in the garden of New York's Museum of Modern Art. It followed two polemically Modernist MoMA houses, the first by Marcel Breuer, built in 1949, the second by a Los Angeles-based disciple of Neutra and Schindler, Gregory Ain, exhibited in 1950. In a clear contrast to these earlier examples, Yoshimura appropriated the style of a sixteenth-century reception hall near Kyoto.[20] Its "subtle utilization of exposed structural elements, natural materials, and meticulous craftsmanship," simultaneously suggested ancient Japanese aesthetics and Modern methods.[21] MoMA did not simply passively accept this archetypal architecture; museum director Arthur Drexler actively oversaw Yoshimura and an advisory committee including Souetsu Yanagi and leading Modernists Kunio Maekawa and Junzo Sakakura (both, notably, former employees of Le Corbusier), and Minoru Yamada. Even the building process at MoMA incorporated older customs, enacting a Shinto topping-off ceremony; almost fifty years later, in 2005, Kazuyo Sejima and Ryue Nishizawa (partners of the avant-garde firm SANAA), too, conducted a Shinto ground-breaking rite at their own New York debut, the ultra-contemporary "*New* New Museum," underscoring the way traditional Japanese practices and cutting-edge design remain interlaced even today.

Yoshimura's 1954 MoMA structure epitomizes an assimilation of tradition increasingly evident in Kuma's architecture. The contemporary architect wrote of this "Japan-flavored Modernism" in a 2005 article, citing another residence designed by Yoshimura (for Kaii Higashiyama, who painted the *fusuma* panels in the MoMA house).[22] Mid-century modernism quoted the simplicity of the *shoin* style in its asymmetry, modularity, monochromism, and overriding order established by a pronounced structural division. Layered exterior walls included painted wooden panels protecting from rain and snow, sliding aside to reveal easily removable paper *shoji* screens. These flexible, feather-weight window/walls allowed opening interiors entirely, influencing the architecture of postwar California as well.

Kuma observed:

The nature of the floor is directly linked to Japan's tradi-

15. Kuma, "Anti-Construction" (an interview with TaeHee Lim) (2007a) pp. 34–35.

16. Kuma (2005b) p. 58. Original Japanese: 人間が、自分の体にあう材料として選んだのが木。スケール感といい、その質感と存在感が、人の体の強さや弱さにちょうどよかったからでしょう。

17. Reynolds (2001) pp. 316–341.

18. Ibid., p. 316. According to Reynolds, even before Taut came to Japan, other architects, including Makino Masami (who had briefly worked for Le Corbusier), argued that Japanese tradition and pre-war Modernist practices offered notable overlap.

19. Alini (2005) p. 8. Alini frequently takes his quotes from other essays without citation, which may be the case here.

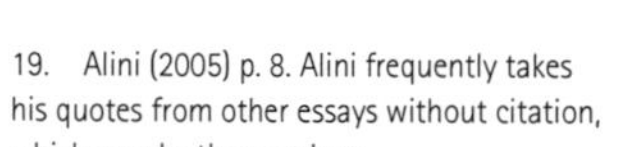

20. Arata Isozaki claims this was a full-scale reproduction of the Kyaku-den (guest house) at Koujou Temple, given the romantic name "House of Pine Breezes". Isozaki (2006) p. 34. See also an excellent summation of the story of this house at: http://www.shofuso.com/pages/HistoricalNarrative/hist_narrative_ch2.html (accessed 1 March, 2007).

21. Reynolds (2001) p. 327.

22. The house for Kaii Higashiyama is included in the article: Kuma (2005c) pp. 66–67. In a discussion on page 75 of this issue, Kuma implicitly links his own architecture to Yoshimura's.

3.20 Vines entwined through steel at the entrance lobby of the 2000 Nasu Museum of History.

3.21 Straw sliding panels at the Nasu Museum of History, developed with Akira Kusumi.

3.22

3.23

> tional architecture of post-and-beam construction and its spatial composition. Japanese people work hard to avoid the existence of walls that partition off the interior from the exterior. (The enclosed spaces of teahouses are an exception but one sometimes broken, the interior and exterior connected in a variety of ways.) Just columns and beams and in-between panel-like architectural elements that are easily opened and closed.[23]

Speaking with his mentor, Fumihiko Maki (whose work is discussed later in this book), Kuma asserted:

> I want to erase the wall, erase columns, the floor that remains becomes the architecture. At the limit of the body, underfoot, is the floor. If the floor is well designed, you have not merely made architecture, I think you have made an environment.[24]

Today, Kuma creates airy, adjustable envelopes for his architecture; he enfolds interiors with lattices of aluminum, bamboo, plastic, wood; even in his up-to-date, urbane work, the envelope is at best an ambiguous border, emphasizing openness. On occasion, Kuma's layered planes slide like *shoji*: the straw panels of the Nasu Museum of History, the bamboo panels separating space at his Great Wall (Bamboo) House in China, the paper panels used at Takayanagi Community Center. His elegant hot springs resort hotel, the 2006 Ginzan Fujiya *Ryokan*, underscores its historical nature with an immobile screen of stainless steel fretwork filled with liquescent hand-blown glass.

In the 2000 Hiroshige Ando Museum, planes of paper and a fringe of aluminum rods separate space, lightly stopping centimeters above the floor. This effect, which also appears in the long suspended aluminum rods at One Omotesando, seems to be yet another homage to Bruno Taut. In a 2007 lecture acknowledging Taut's continuing influence, Kuma remarked:

> ... at the landing of the stairs [at Hyuga], there is an element you might call a bamboo screen or lattice ... Taut layered these elements: the bamboo lattice is a layer, and beyond it is a layer defined by the [hanging line of] light fixtures, and then there is this layer beyond [which is the exterior wall]. Three thin layers, built up together, something I'm sure Taut was very aware of. In my work since I have used various screens and louvers in designs, and this is the origin of those overlapping and layered devices.[25]

Taut's bamboo curtain, with each pole loosely linked to the next by a continuous fiber cord, also had a direct descendant within Kuma's gallery at Suntory Museum during its opening exhibition – a screen of bamboo tied similarly, but overscaled. Writing of this museum, Kuma also emphasized the way he tied together form and finish,

> The walls, lit and unlit, are all large surfaces covered in *washi* Japanese paper. The screens are paulownia louvers, a simile for curtains of paulownia ... These three may be used to assemble a *tatami*-floored space (e.g., the living room) in an ordinary Japanese structure; here they are just the same, but used in a much enlarged space.[26]

The architect employed only paper at temporary structures like his portable teahouse framed in a filigree of Japanese *washi* or the "Paper Snake Pavilion[s]," shelters built from cardboard sheets in Korea.[27] Contemporary Japanese architects favor fragility, undoubtedly a result of long familiarity with paper-screen *shoji*. Atsushi Ueda, a profes-

23. Kuma (2000) p. 79.

24. Maki and Kuma (1997) p. 122.
Original Japanese:
壁や柱を消したいわけですが、床というのは建築があろうとなかろうと残るものなんです。身体がある限り、身体の下には床があるわけで、床をうまくデザインしていけば、建築物を造らなくても環境をデザインできるのではないかと思ったわけです。

25. Kuma (2007b). Original Japanese:
これは日向邸に戻りまして…竹の格子みたいなもの...お見せしたのは、レイヤーの様にショーに彼はその部分に関心があったと思うんですが、竹の格子の層の向こうに照明の層があって、更にむこうの層には、層があって、3つの薄い層が重なり合っていくところに関心があったと思うんですけど、ま、これはぼくがその後、色々なルーバーを用いて？デザインをやっていくわけですけど、その原点の一つに層が重なり合っていくということがあると思います。

26. Kuma (2007c) p. 43.

27. Frankfurt clients, concerned about the fragility of paper, resisted this proposal, which was published in Housekeeper (*sic*). "*Sekai ga Sonkei suru Nihonn no Kenchikuka Daitokushuu*" 世界が尊敬する日本の建築家大特集 a.k.a. "Architecture – Japan's New Mega Export", *Casa Brutus* vol. 85 (April, 2007) p. 91. The final version can be folded closed when not in use and uses a stronger membrane.

3.22 A sheltered area for tea at the 2002 Plastic House.

3.23 A close-up of fiber-reinforced plastic, square-shaped pipes at Plastic House, recalling natural materials like wood or bamboo.

3.24 The thatched roof and paper walls of Kuma's 2000 Takayanagi Community Center, deep in the valleys of Niigata Prefecture.

3.24

sor in Kyoto, reasoned that understanding *shoji* also allows aluminum and plastic easier acceptance: "It is not surprising that those construction materials have caught on with remarkable speed in a nation with such an ingrained tradition of the lightweight."[28] Kuma's "Plastic House," Shigeru Ban's "Naked House," and SANAA's "S House" are all wrapped in pellucid skins of polycarbonate or plastic. Some designers are squeamish about such substances, but of plastic, Kuma says simply, "It has a lightness that is natural to it, intrinsic. Light can enter the building through plastic which behaves in a similar manner to rice paper ..."[29] He also exploits films and fritted glass, Carrara marble and alabaster sliced thin – even artificial human skin, which Kuma used for the walls of another innovative, temporary teahouse. Obsessive abstraction and single-minded materiality allow Kuma and his cohorts to remain Modern and yet also echo conventions carried forward from the sixteenth-century *shoin* style in their architecture.

Today's minimalism requires meticulous craftsmanship; Yoshimura's postwar MoMA structure, first fabricated in Japan and reconstructed in New York, also relied on precise woodcraft and prefabrication.[30] The careful craft possible in Japan – where it is comparatively easy to articulate perfectly vertical or horizontal joints or to align different pieces built by differing trades – highlights the unique capabilities of the country's large general contractors.[31] Conspicuously, craft is almost never acknowledged explicitly when discussing the Western work of minimalists like John Pawson or Alvaro Siza, but invariably remarked on in relation to in Japan. Gregory Clancey, looking back to the Meiji era and the nation's engagement with Westernization and industrialization, insightfully asserts, "Conceding to Japanese superiority in the use of tools furthered the mapping of hand/mind ... dualities onto the East/West one, for by the 1870s, being good with tools was becoming a compliment reserved for non-white persons."[32]

Craft is quaint in the arsenal of a non-Japanese architect, but Kuma's work is celebrated and richly rewarded for its careful construction. He is quick to draw attention to the contributions of artisans, naming bamboo workers, papermakers, plasterers, and masons. Kuma may have been inspired by Taut; the earlier architect worked with craftsmen in Kyoto, Sendai and Takasaki, developing designs for a variety of furnishings and housewares incorporating lacquer, bamboo, and bronze. In a telling moment, Kuma's musings slipped unnoted from his own interest in craft to the German architect's:

> ... When I am considering the craftsmen to rely on in building my architecture, I tend not to want someone who is famous. After all, they will want to find ways to display their own skills, which is not my preference. To avoid that and achieve something a bit less inclined to connoisseurship – but work that was still well built and attractive – Taut, for his bamboo, worked with a Tokyo bamboo artisan, Mizuta Kuroda. [Taut's] bamboo is clearly a beautiful piece of work, but not what you might call clever. The bamboo is used frankly, with a feeling of its natural state. I think it's a good piece of work.[33]

Working with unknown artisans – not those known in the nation as "Living Treasures" – enhances an architect's control in collaborations.

Kuma could be accused of treating handwork as provincial, echoing at a smaller scale the colonial outlook often infusing architectural attitudes on artisanship. He claims craft and contemporary technology are comparable: "I listened out for and made use of everything

28. Ueda (1990) p. 67.

29. Alini (2005) p. 130.

30. Yoshimura earlier managed a similar project; in 1940, he supervised construction of a teahouse in Kyoto and its subsequent dismantling and reconstruction in New York. See Kurt Helfrich, "Antonin Raymond in America, 1938–49," in Helfrich and Whitaker (2006) pp. 50–51.

31. Japanese construction is not always reliably straight and parallel; the wood screens at Ginzan Onsen are usually arranged by the staff so that lattices are slightly slipped in relation to each other, to obscure the variable bowing of the slats. Thin steel slats that make up the ceiling of Water/Glass also bend and bow in response to temperature changes.

32. Clancey (2006) p. 44.

33. Kuma, 2 March, 2007, lecture at the Watarium Museum in Tokyo. Original Japanese: 僕が建築の職人さんの誰に仕事をやってもらおうか、と考えるときにですね、あんまり名人っぽい、要するに自分の技を「どうだ見たかみたいなものを見せる人は苦手なんですね。そうじゃなくて、もっとさりげないけど、ちゃんときれいにつくれる人と仕事をしたい、といつも思っていてタウトはこの竹のときは、東京の職人で、えーっと黒田みずたか？さんとやられるわけですね。というのが、この竹でして、確かに非常にきれいな仕事ですけれど、わざとらしいところがなくて、竹のさっぱりしたところがそのままの感じに表れているな、と。大変いい仕事だと思います。

3.26

3.25 The temple-like living area of Kuma's 2005 Lotus House sits in a pool of still water.

3.26 Private areas of Lotus House are screened in stone and steel.

3.27 Moving from the entrance to a central open patio, used for entertaining at Lotus House, one passes under exposed engineered wood joists.

3.28 Plan, showing the river.

from traditional skills of the craftsmen to the very latest technology." Yet Kuma is far more likely to acknowledge craftsmen from the countryside than the contributions of urban fabricators working in industrial materials.[34] Kuma inadvertently acknowledged, "A fundamental role in [my] process was played by the encounter and dialogue with the craftsmen who have collaborated on the realization of some of my works, especially by the ones built in the countryside"[35]

Kuma is unafraid of any taint from openly accepting history. His projects include a Noh theater, a repository for a valued Buddha, bathhouses, and a Japanese-style inn; he designed a historical museum with a replica of a large, tile-roofed gate. Most would regard such work as too romantic. But Kuma's recent projects also often comfortably co-exist with tearooms and teahouses; he took on the reconstruction of a noteworthy postwar collaboration between Modernist architect Yoshiro Taniguchi and artist Isamu Noguchi, a space called "Banraisha" (mentioned briefly earlier). His Murai Museum of Art, discussed at greater length in Chapter 4, holds at its core a room retained from the artist's shabby, architecturally insignificant studio; in "Shanghai Z58" (also called the "Zhongati Box"), as if challenging China to reconsider its wholesale destruction of architectural history, Kuma integrated an earlier warehouse. At this moment in Japan, efforts to companionably accommodate both preservation and present-day programming are mostly clumsy. Yet Kuma offers up numerous and varied exemplars of how this can be achieved; his solutions are both pragmatic and skillful, and deserve greater attention both at home and abroad.[36]

In a country best known for dainty wooden structures, Kuma is also open to highlighting heavy earthen and stone storage build-

3.27

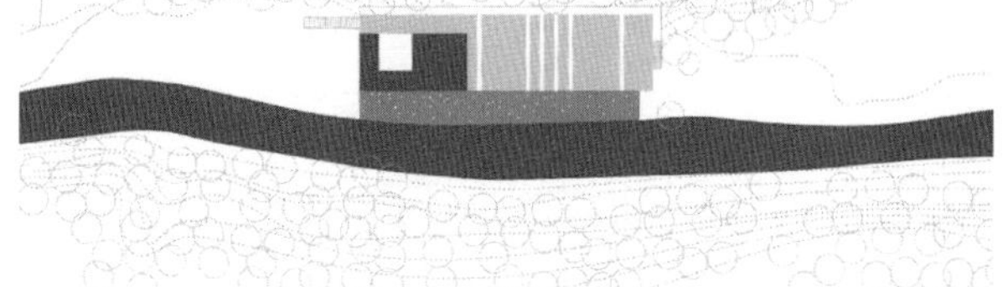

3.28

34. Kuma (2004a) p. 14. As some examples highlighting individual effort, the bamboo artisan at the Ginzan Onsen was listed in the September, 2006 issue of *Shinkenchiku* 新建築 [New Architecture] as Hideo Nakata from Kanazawa, and numerous books and articles identify the papermaker Yasuo Kobayashi, whose atelier Echigo Kadode Washi contributed to the Takayanagi Community Center and the more recent Suntory Museum. Mr. Ushida of Atelier *Ruburansu* ("Leprince") made the hand-blown glass at the 2006 Ginzan Onsen, and fondly recalls going to the area as a child. The owner of the stone museum, who employed the masons involved on the project, is Mr. Nobuo Shirai, and the stonemason for the 2006 Chokkura Plaza a Mr. Tetsuo Genmoku, who Kuma said he and engineer Masato Araya "squeezed" knowledge out of in order to make the unusual Oya stone façade. Kuma named the bamboo artisan who worked with Taut in a lecture in March, 2007: Michitaro Kuroda of Tokyo. But while the architect explains on page 102 of Kuma (2004a) that wrapping PVC around chair frames for another project "required more craftsman's skill than I imagined," that craftsman remains unnamed. Bamboo workers in China are similarly anonymous when Kuma discusses the technique for heating bamboo to 280 degrees Centigrade (536 degrees Fahrenheit), then treating it with oil, a process the workers proposed as a way to reduce insect damage.

3.29 The simple central open space of Lotus House.

3.30 The stone and steel screen delicately establishes privacy from without.

3.31 From within the screen, secluded spaces seem at one with nature.

3.29

3.30

35. Alini (2005) p. 12 f.

36. However, I should also note that Kuma made no effort to preserve buildings by Kenji Imai at the Nezu Museum. His preservation approach is pragmatic and far from pure.

37. Kuma (2000) pp. 262–263, English translation forthcoming.

38. Suzuki (2000b) p. 4.

3.31

3.32

3.33

ings at sites like the Stone Museum, Nasu Museum of History, and Chokkura Plaza. He credits his deftness to the Stone Museum, a complex that incorporated three such structures, adding others. Kuma asserted,

> There were three crumbling storehouses for rice on the site. The storehouses were made of a local stone, a plain, gray andesite called Ashino stone. Probably constructed in the Taisho era (1912–1926) or the early years of the subsequent Showa era, the storehouses are not architecturally remarkable. Nevertheless, I felt they ought to be preserved. I proposed that the overall environment be reorganized by means of a few additions to those structures.[37]

The solution was not only sensitive, but practical: the museum had a meager budget – the client, however, sold masonry, so his stonemasons contributed at no cost. Over the four years Kuma worked with these craftsmen developing details, he solved every challenge in stone. The resulting refinement is remarkably rare. I will enlarge on this issue when I write further of Jun Aoki's Aomori Museum of Art, but conventional masonry construction does poorly in earthquakes, so its art is unremembered in Japan. Kuma's handling of stone is, however, skillful, yielding novel masonry systems, solid and screen, substantial and sheer.

Often now, Kuma amplifies the effect of his architecture in his unusual handling of long-loved materials. At the thatch-roofed Takayanagi Community Center, almost invisibly integrating itself into a tiny valley village by aping the roofing materials and forms of farmhouses around it, for example, Kuma applies handmade paper in unexpected applications and odd locations: walls covered inside and out in paper; paper wrapping steel bracing, paper as a surprisingly robust floor finish.

The respected architectural historian Hiroyuki Suzuki, grumbled to Kuma about this unpredictability, "In your works, bamboo is not used as bamboo is usually used and *washi* paper is not used as it usually is."[38] But following that initial annoyance, Suzuki offered up an apt analysis of the younger architect's knack with natural materials:

> I believe Japanese architects today can be divided

3.32 An elegant and ancient standing Buddah is sheltered in a niche off the living room.

3.33 The simple detailing of the building, each plane reading as an isolated element.

3.34 The LVL and OSB ceiling of this elegant home.

3.34

3.35 Guestroom in the 2006 Ginzan Fujiya Ryokan, large lumber floating over a contemporary setting.

3.36 Guestrooms incorporate older materials in an understatedly elegant manner.

3.37 Slim strips of bamboo line the public spaces of the Fujiya.

3.38 The 1996 Noh Stage in the Forest.

3.35

3.36

3.37

into ... groups by the way they use materials.

> One group includes architects such as Osamu Ishiyama and Terunobu Fujimori, who try to retain the natural qualities of materials such as wood and earth ... The use of materials in these works may appear quite conservative and traditional, but the architects are by no means simply using traditional materials and methods. They seem to be trying to return materials to their natural condition. That is, they are trying to make a fresh start, in effect disassociating materials from the traditions that have surrounded them and restoring these materials to their natural state. Their approach might be called "noble savagery."
>
> A second group of architects that includes Kuma also uses exposed materials. However, these architects try to eliminate all traces of tradition and to turn the materials into abstract compositions ... In their hands, wood is nothing but wood and stone is nothing but stone. Their forms and methods of construction transcend tradition. The materials are not restored to nature, but instead retain a certain architectural character.[39]

3.38

Kuma repeatedly rails against construction conventions in today's Japan. He claims the finish layer is often merely graphic, so meaningless, printed wood grain or unfinished concrete wallpapers are almost acceptable.[40] He calls the round separator indentations found in fair-faced concrete "equivalent to the LV brand mark for Louis Vuitton."[41] Oft-quoted is Kuma's straightforward, "Material is not a finish. Period. If the word 'material' has already acquired the connotation of 'finish' – it may be better to quickly abandon the word 'material' and speak of 'substance' instead."[42] Despite this rhetorical stance, however, many examples of cladding can quickly be found in Kuma's work, from adobe over concrete to columns bound in bamboo slats. But unlike the scrim Kuma rails against, in his most recent, successful works, finish is isolated and articulated, an enunciated element revealing the layered nature of contemporary construction and highlighting a material's symbolic value.

Kuma revels in a rich, highly figured effect, once explaining "...the most interesting experiences of architectural space take place through contact with materials, when their texture, their depth, is revealed."[43] At times he luxuriates in the unfamiliarity of something newly on the market, as in his applications of engineered woods – exposed I-joists with OSB webs at Sea/Filter daringly thrust out beyond the roof line, squaring off against the sea, or LVL rafters running overhead at the elegant and expensive Lotus House. Kuma has won numerous inter-

39. Suzuki (2000a), p. 10. Suzuki seems to be deliberately echoing both Semper and William Morris. Mark Wigley quotes Semper as saying, "May brick appear as brick, wood as wood, iron as iron..." See Wigley (2001) p. 373 f. Morris is said to have wanted "to make woolen substances as woolen as possible, cotton as cotton as possible, and so on ..." Quoted in Olin (1986) p. 376.

40. Kuma and Fujimori (2007) p. 8. Interestingly, in this discussion Kuma misstates the name of his chapter "*A-kitekuto Ha*" アーキテクト派 [Architects' Faction] as "*Uchipanashi Ha...*" 打放し派... [Unfinished Concrete Faction]. Elsewhere, Kuma says, "...exposed concrete proved to be only one of the patterns of texture mapping. ... it is only a skin with a thickness of about 20 mm., a finish attached onto the concrete surface." See Kuma (2004a) p. 9.

41. Kuma (1986) p. 127. Original Japanese: 打放しのセパ穴はヴィトンのLVマークに相当する。

42. Kuma (2004a) p. 9.

43. Alini (2005) p. 9.

3.39

3.40

3.41

3.39–43 Kuma explains that the long years of understanding how to use ashino stone in Stone Museum, completed in 2000, marked a turning point in his work. Each façade is patterned differently, underscoring them as planar, and each corner is treated with care.

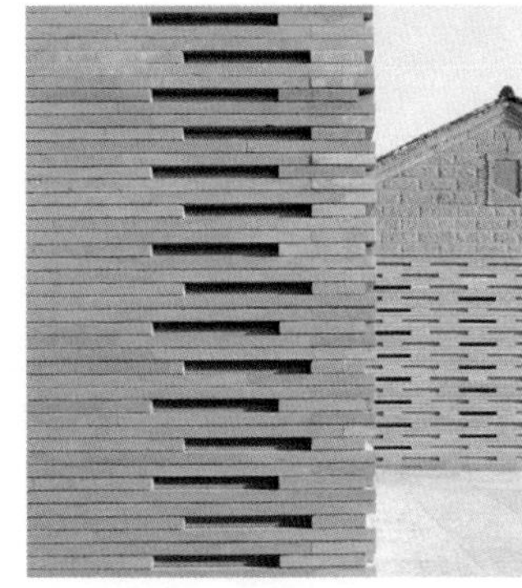

3.42

3.43

3.44 The lines of the ceiling and an interior wall at the 2007 Suntory Museum are spaced differently, underscoring their independence.

3.45 The elongated checkerboard of the exterior at Suntory Museum.

3.46 Paulownia wood, in veneers no thicker than paper, wraps the ticket counter of the Suntory Museum.

3.44

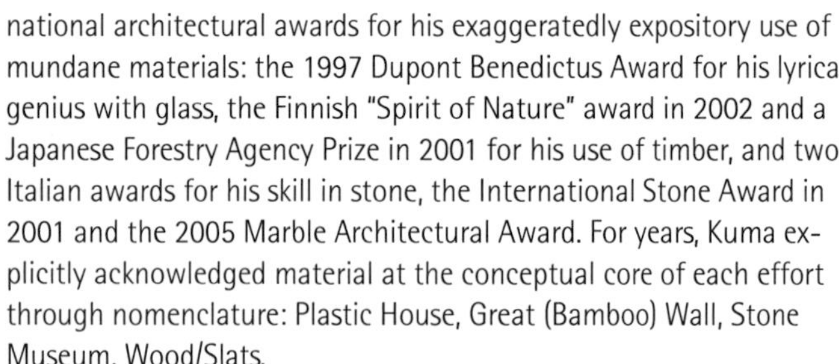

national architectural awards for his exaggeratedly expository use of mundane materials: the 1997 Dupont Benedictus Award for his lyrical genius with glass, the Finnish "Spirit of Nature" award in 2002 and a Japanese Forestry Agency Prize in 2001 for his use of timber, and two Italian awards for his skill in stone, the International Stone Award in 2001 and the 2005 Marble Architectural Award. For years, Kuma explicitly acknowledged material at the conceptual core of each effort through nomenclature: Plastic House, Great (Bamboo) Wall, Stone Museum, Wood/Slats.

For most Japanese architects, interior surfaces are likely to be orthodox, rarely ranging beyond plasterboard and concrete. Those who comfortably explore a broader assortment of finishes, architects like ADH, Hitoshi Abe, and Kuma, all worked or studied in the West. But even among this ecumenical cohort, the level of luxury in Kuma's architecture is especially exultant. He even allows himself to elevate modest and minor spaces (foyer, toilet) with a singular, exotic surface.

In an effort to enunciate each plane, Kuma is also swayed by Gottfried Semper, acknowledging, "I believe Semper was a pioneer ... I like his [idea] that architecture is a fabric; that is a very important idea. Year by year, more and more, I think of architecture as a fabric."[44] Semper partitioned architecture as platform, textile enclosure, roof, and hearth – each associated with its making: roof and carpentry; stereometric plinths, the mason's trade; woven textile walls; and inside the hearth, a ceramic construction. Of these, "The most basic enclosure was the wall of the tent, the curtain, or the plaited mat filling the carpentry frame."[45] Kuma embraces Semper's three elements enclosing architecture, establishing an unobstructed post-and-beam frame of steel or wood; interweaving solid, weighty slabs of stone or brick; and slicing off spaces with lighter, figured screens. The roof and platform, posts and planes, contend for primacy in Kuma's projects. Semper said carpentry and masonry endeavor to usurp each other; Kuma's architecture is alternately earthbound and airy – but in each project, woven screens and patterned surfaces give spaces their sensuality and soul.

Kuma's first unambiguous acknowledgement of Semper was a 2005 essay.[46] In form and detail, he invited this connection much earlier, especially in allusions to *sudare* screens. An excellent example is seen at the 1995 Noh Stage, where open slats wrap over the top of a simple scaffold-like support, simulating a screen counterbalanced like a bolt of cloth (instead of cladding, pinned or fixed on one side only). *Sudare* are also suggested in the 1996 River/Filter Restaurant façade in Fukushima and an arrangement of aluminum bars used as sun shades at the architect's Makuhari Housing; irregular rhythms induce a sense these surfaces are veiled. In a more playful gesture towards textiles, an apparently woven stone screen, at the 2006 Chokkura Plaza, appears to unravel across the building's skin.

To Kuma, there is a difference between his adaptation of traditional elements from Japanese construction and his more recent interest in woven textures:

> I had been thinking of Semper, the similarities ... when I started my louver design. But sudare and fabric are different in my mind. Sudare – the element is not woven; it is just suspended. The idea of something 'woven' is important [to me more] recently.[47]

But Kuma then went on to allow, "Sudare and woven things are – the border is not so clear, it is ambiguous, I think."[48] His emerging ap-

44. Interview, Tokyo (3 March, 2007).
45. Anderson (1982) p. 114.
46. Kuma (2005d) p. 12.
47. Interview, Tokyo (3 March, 2007).
48. Ibid.

3.45

3.46

3.47

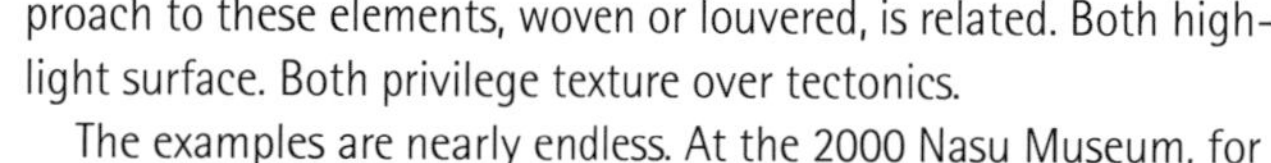

proach to these elements, woven or louvered, is related. Both highlight surface. Both privilege texture over tectonics.

The examples are nearly endless. At the 2000 Nasu Museum, for example, coarse, burlap-like straw panels line the ceiling and walls of the exhibition space. Filmy fabric wraps the reception area walls at One Omotesando, the glowing, backlit white fabric covering the furnishings as well. Kuma wrapped Plastic House in a similar fabric, and used a light, gauzy curtain to replace some of the original walls in the reconstruction of Banraisha. He seems to grow increasingly open in his exploration of textiles; in the café of his recent Suntory Museum, a banana-fiber cloth supplied by Nuno, a highly regarded Japanese fabric studio, is held taut by handmade hooks, independent of the wall behind.[49] And at the luxurious Fujiya Ryokan at the Ginzan *Onsen* Hot Springs, *tatami* mats are a particularly fine, nearly thread-like weave from Okinawa; slim bamboo slats line walls, positioned so their nodal segments rhythmically scale up and down like notes on a score, jagged lines reminiscent of the weave on nubby raw silk. Kuma pushes further in temporary structures like his 2005 KxK, where he explored the use of a spidery "Evasheet" plastic filigree.

Again, perhaps because the unusually long gestation period allowed Kuma and the craftsmen he worked with greater time, the Stone Museum is enlightening, not simply showing Kuma's walls as textile planes, but revealing his effort to render each plane individually. In *Kengo Kuma: Materials, Structures, Details*, he pointed out that, "The possible patterns for removing pieces [of stone from the wall] were infinite, thus numerous studies were made. They are reminiscent of patterns on punch cards used in early computer systems ..."[50] continuing,

3.48

3.47 One Omotesando's laminated larch fins result from the careful integration of contemporary technology.

3.48 The new 2007 Yusuhara Town Hall is built of soft, nearly non-structural cedar, requiring very large columns and beams to be spaced closely.

49. Interestingly, this is the first time Kuma worked with Nuno, a purveyor of modernist fabrics that contributes to works by many Tokyo-based architects, including Ito, Aoki and others.

50. Kuma (2004a) p. 23.

3.49 An existing stone wall laid in a herringbone predated Kuma's 2003 Horai Baths.

3.50 Louvered stone at the 2005 Nagasaki Prefectural Art Museum, designed with the larger, more corporate Nihon Sekkei.

3.51 A tiny robot rakes the sand of a contemporary dry garden in the 2004 Niwa [Garden].

3.50

> The [selected] patterns for the porous masonry were differentiated on each side. In my recent work, I have often adopted the method of changing expressions completely at ... corners. This is because I believe that things appear before us not as a mass of objects, but as a set of different planes.[51]

In earlier work, Kuma sometimes extended a finish further than its supporting surface; lately he tends to stop surfaces short of meeting. In both, he underplays turning the corner, achieving a planar effect. In his most lavish interiors, detailing gets great attention; each layer of enclosure is articulated against others – non-aligned, independent planes, wall stopping short of floor, ceiling cleanly capping wall.

In another open allusion to textiles, Kuma used an ancient Japanese pattern at the 2004 COCON Karasuma, a remodel of a historically significant structure in Kyoto. The architect wrapped the lower floors of the building with an opaque green film on glass, printed in a bold, cloud-like graphic, the "*Tenpyo Okumo*," that explicitly refers to Kyoto's Buddhist history.[52] Kuma explained that in this building,

> the theme was "superimposition of time." A sheet of glass was layered over the existing façade ... A film printed with images of clouds, a typical pattern used during the Edo period ... was sandwiched between the glass sheets. As the woodcut block for the cloud patterns, I used one that was preserved at Karacho, a long-established *karakami* manufacturer based in Kyoto. The result is a layering of three different elements over this façade: a pattern used during the Edo period, architecture dating back to 1938, and the contemporary technologies of glass and film.[53]

In a similar fashion, at a 2007 exhibition on Bruno Taut in Tokyo's Watarium Museum, Kuma used vibrant imported paints to explore a sample-book of patterns, especially bold, uneven stripes and a divided-diamond motif known in Japan as *uroko*. The latter is ambiguously employed, first used by Taut in 1912, long before he came to Japan.

Just as Japanese fabrics today rely on complex processing yielding three-dimensional pleats and corrugations, Kuma also explores how thin sheets can be given greater depth. He developed a portable paper teahouse in 2005, drawing on the structure of expanded metal. Of the fortuitous result, he accounted, "By incising into the paper and stretching it, quite by coincidence we produced a Japanese traditional wave pattern, which I found particularly interesting."[54] This pattern, called "*seikaiha* [blue sea waves]," also offered a name for the teahouse. "Basically," the architect argues,

> I try to find a new pattern, original patterns that came from some new technology or a study of materials. But sometimes along the way I suddenly find – oh! – this is similar to some old patterns. The *[Tenpyo Okumo]* cloud pattern is an exception [in my work], because that building is in Kyoto, so I tried to find a traditional, an authentic, pattern to persuade people in Kyoto "This is a traditional pattern and this building, too, is related to tradition."[55]

Many of Kuma's surfaces are screened in stripes, especially lines of louvers. Architects in other countries no longer confidently apply clean geometries, concerned that construction craft is not up to the challenge. To draw a straight line paralleling another is one thing; to expect workers on site to achieve such precision is another. Kuma can still assume the support of careful constructors; his abstraction

51. Ibid., p. 27.

52. 天平大雲.

53. Kuma (2007a) p. 51.

54. Kuma (2005b) p. 61. Original Japanese: 切れ込みを入れて広げた和紙が偶然にも日本の伝統的な波文様と一致したのは非常に面白かったですね。

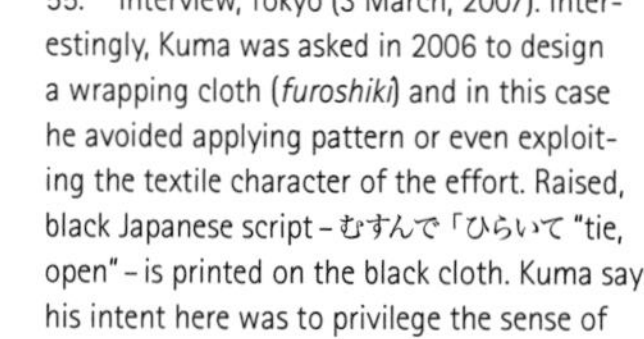

55. Interview, Tokyo (3 March, 2007). Interestingly, Kuma was asked in 2006 to design a wrapping cloth (*furoshiki*) and in this case he avoided applying pattern or even exploiting the textile character of the effort. Raised, black Japanese script – むすんで「ひらいて "tie, open" – is printed on the black cloth. Kuma says his intent here was to privilege the sense of touch over sight.

3.51

3.52

3.52 *The forms of the louvered wall of the 2003 Baisoin Temple are echoed in long wooden sotoba slats at graves in the foreground.*

3.53 *The upscale 2004 Waketokuyama Restaurant is hidden behind a screen of sliced precast planks.*

3.54 *A close-up of the entrance to Baisoin.*

3.55 *Waketokuyama from the street.*

3.56 *A closer look at the steel and precast screen at Waketokuyama.*

3.53

underscores the opportunities of Japan's construction culture. In addition, his stripes emphasize older aspects of culture, especially inspiration Kuma finds in the art of Hiroshige Ando, an early nineteenth-century *ukiyoe* woodcut artist. Whenever Kuma presents his 2000 museum housing a recently unearthed trove of Hiroshige's works, he juxtaposes Hiroshige's woodcuts with videos of this museum, arguing that the linear elements of each beat out a related rhythm.

The aesthetics of Japan's vivid geometric patterns are often associated with the *bourgeoisie* of the first half of the nineteenth century, especially in Tokyo, then known as Edo. The Japanese philosopher and *flâneur* Shuuzou Kuki, living in Paris in 1926, wrote of the same early nineteenth-century period when Hiroshige produced his art; Kuki used Western analyses to outline the structure of an understated and idealized elegance called *iki*. He explained,

> In geometric figures there is nothing which better expresses ... relational quality than parallel lines. Parallel lines, which run together forever without meeting, are the purest visual objectification of the relational. It is certainly no accident that the stripe, as design, is regarded as *iki*.[56]

Kuki continued, "... we can say it is the vertical stripe rather than the horizontal stripe which is *iki*."[57] His reasons for this distinction between level and plumb seem clearly illustrated in Kuma's work, which also tends toward upright: "In the horizontal stripe, the weight of the earth's strata rests against gravity; in vertical stripes, there is the lightness of 'willow branches' and the light rain ..."[58] While Kuma does not deliberately draw on Kuki, the same Japanese traditions influence both, underscored by Kuma's excessive use of such vertical screens.

And when his application of vertical louvers grew perhaps too routine, Kuma turned to dynamic checkerboards. As if anticipating the architect, Kuki earlier wrote, "... where the square checkerboard pattern changes into a rectangular pattern ... because of its slenderness ... it is usually more *iki*."[59] Kuma, too, seems inclined towards a vertical pattern, evident in his exterior at the Suntory Museum.

Finally, in exploring the structure of Edo aesthetics, Kuki also briefly commented on connections between *iki* and architecture: "Architecture frequently reveals a similar quality as *iki* design in that they both generally require refinement,"[60] continuing, "The *iki* coloring of architectural materials is, after all, the same as that which occurs in design. That is, all the nuances of grey, tea brown, and azure dominate ..."[61] Kuki even dangles a tantalizing comment about two of Kuma's pet finishes:

> With *iki* architecture, the relation and quality are expressed, regardless of exterior or interior, through the choice of materials and the means of compartmentalizing space. There are frequent cases where the relational is expressed in materials, as in the contrast between wood and bamboo.[62]

The 2007 Suntory Museum is an ideal expression of such an aesthetic: warm natural wood finishes inside, a white ceramic checkerboard exterior. Throughout the interior, Kuma employs louvers of precious Japanese *paulownia* wood, each plane autonomous. There is an almost odd alignment in the ceiling fins, each section acting in apparent ignorance of accidental opposition. Lines of louvers are arranged arbitrarily, and the calibration of wall and ceiling louvers contradistinct.

In a lecture in March 2007, Kuma acknowledged that he, like most Japanese, saw the soft, fleshy *paulownia* wood used throughout Suntory as better for furniture than finishes – but after observing Taut's

3.54

56. Kuki (1997) p. 87.
57. Ibid., p. 88.
58. Ibid., p. 89.
59. Ibid., p. 91.
60. Ibid., p. 103. Further, with his muted sensuality and love of fine clothes, Kuma also, it may be said, embodies Kuki's "*iki*," chic.
61. Ibid., p. 104.
62. Ibid., p. 101.

3.55

3.56

use of the wood at Hyuga Villa, Kuma changed his mind. Shortly before the Suntory opened, Kuma explained,

> … I think the *paulownia* ceiling [at Hyuga] is particularly interesting. *Paulownia* is often used in furniture, but is not taken as far as becoming a part of the architecture, as a building material. *Paulownia*, after all, part of its beauty is its softness, and I began to think about how I, too, might employ it. The fact is that I am using *paulownia* as a finish throughout a building I am currently designing, the Suntory Museum of Art … The ceilings of the galleries are all *paulownia*, and all of the walls in the foyer are finished in *paulownia*. The truth is that I faced some resistance to its use, worrying about it being damaged because it is such a soft material. But the Japanese are not so rough in their use of buildings, I believe. We will see after the building opens, because I used a good deal of *paulownia* on the Suntory Museum. Well, that was because of the influence of this [Taut's] ceiling.[63]

Suntory, a whisky distiller, also inspired Kuma to recycle white oak from its old barrels, now flooring in the galleries. The architect explains:

> Looking at it from an environmental stance, I decided to reuse the white oak from the old [whisky] tanks. The whisky tank craftsmen had once curved the wood, and we had then to find laborers who could return it to a flat state, which took some effort. It was work, but the whisky that had permeated the wood over so many years left it a mellow luster that really comes through.[64]

At the Hiroshige Ando Museum, wood was also lavishly employed, harvested from the mountain behind the museum, an expert's echo of Fujimori's own tree cutting.[65] Kuma also used logs cut from the site of the Nasu History Museum, setting them along the seams of the new metal roof to soften the visual relationship between it and a reconstructed gate and storehouse; a vine-entwined frame at the entrance is made from vines collected on site. In a similar vein, Kuma used knotty cedar glulams at the request of the mayor of Yusuhara, a tiny town tucked away in the hills of Shikoku Island, first stiffening the balsa-like wood with steel at the 1994 Yusuhara Visitors Center and then, in the 2007 Yusuhara Town Hall, compensating for its insubstantial strength with beam depths measured in meters.[66] Kuma claims using this weak wood was the only criteria he faced, and insightfully observes, "The perplexing challenge of wanting to symbolize locality – but also being asked to create a large space that could be called a factor of global culture – results in contradictions …"[67] Public clients in remote areas often request architects incorporate local production; Fujimori recalls that for the agricultural dormitory in Kumamoto, for example, the prefecture only asked him to use a lot of local wood.[68] And in the same issue of *GA Japan* picturing Kuma's town hall with its temple-like *kumiko* structure, an adjacent article featured a remarkably similar structure by Tadahiro Toh.

In interviews, Kuma admits a desire to "find the real character of each location," and "to recover the place: the place is the result of nature and time …"[69] At its best, his architecture exaggerates awareness of the particularities of place. Far too often, this has been easier for him to accomplish in rural projects, but urban examples exist. At One Omotesando, the avenue before the building – lined with

63. Kuma, 2 March, 2007, lecture at the Watarium Museum in Tokyo. Original Japanese:
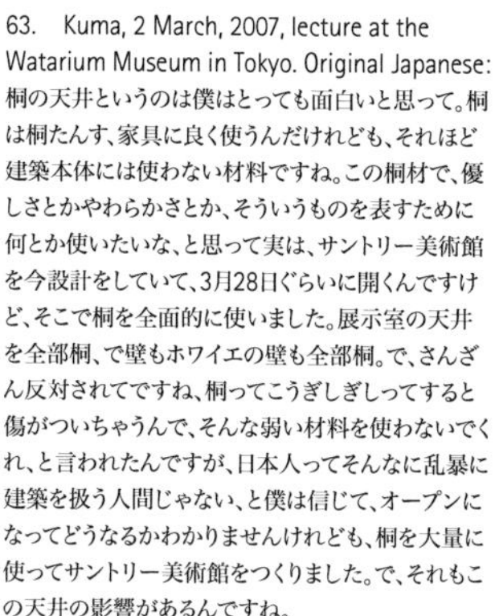
桐の天井というのは僕はとっても面白いと思って。桐は桐たんす、家具に良く使うんだけれども、それほど建築本体には使わない材料ですね。この桐材で、優しさとかやわらかさとか、そういうものを表すために何とか使いたいな、と思って実は、サントリー美術館を今設計をしていて、3月28日ぐらいに開くんですけど、そこで桐を全面的に使いました。展示室の天井を全部桐、で壁もホワイエの壁も全部桐。で、さんざん反対されてですね、桐ってこうぎしぎしってすると傷がついちゃうんで、そんな弱い材料を使わないでくれ、と言われたんですが、日本人ってそんなに乱暴に建築を扱う人間じゃない、と僕は信じて、オープンになってどうなるかわかりませんけれども、桐を大量に使ってサントリー美術館をつくりました。で、それもこの天井の影響があるんですね。

64. Kuma (2006) p. 73. Original Japanese: 「 樽のホワイトオークは、環境の観点から古い樽のリユースを試みたもの。樽職人が一度曲げた木材を、まっ直ぐに戻す作業が必要でしたので手間がかかりました。大変ではありましたが、長年使い込んだ樽の木にはウイスキーが染み込んでいて、例えようのない円熟の艶が出ています。

65. Kuma underscores this point in Kuma (2005a) p. 17.

66. These woods are generally referred to as 間伐等 (*kanbatsudai*), a term that essentially means "things like thinned trees". Windfalls are also included in this term. It is worth noting that I can easily nick these columns with my fingernail.

67. Kuma (2007d) p. 151. Original Japanese: 象徴的な難問であるローカリティという与件と, 大空間の要請という一種のグローバリズムとの矛盾・対立がこんなかたちで露呈したのである.
In fact, calling this wood "local" is also at some level problematic. Following World War II, Japan responded to excessive deforestation by promoting large-scale planting of extensive, monocultural conifer groves (which ultimately had little market value in the changing economic climate). These policies ironically both caused "overforestation" and simultaneously depleted the local resource value of forests, leading clients today to ask architects to employ such local woods. The cedar across Japan today is a manifestation of national and international political policy and economic history, not nature. See Knight (1997) pp. 711–730.

68. Fujimori *et al.* (2005) p. 185.

69. http://www.designboom.com/eng/interview/kuma.html (accessed 13 February, 2007).

3.57–59 Adobe blocks at the 2002 Adobe Repository for a Buddhist Statue are made from local muds, intended to filter not only light, but also to buffer heat and cold.

3.57

3.58

3.59

tall, vase-shaped *keiyaki* trees – led to Kuma lining his façade with wooden louvers.

Plants also offer elegant embellishment, rooting buildings to the ground, as at the ivy-covered "Z58" in Shanghai, or the honeysuckle intended to cover another recent structure. Kuma's efforts to incorporate greenery date back to the mid-1990s. Many notable unbuilt projects are collected in a 1997 special issue of the Japanese magazine *SD* [*Space Design*] entitled "Kengo Kuma: Digital Gardening." In these, he attempted to blend interactive technology with nature, in 1996 projects named "Moving Garden" or "Grass Net," the 1997 Grass/Glass Tower, and the 2000 Cubic Garden Museum. His most notable unconsummated project from this group is the 1996 proposal for the Kansai National Diet Library ("Kansai-Kan"), awarded an honorable mention in the competition; Kuma proposed almost entirely burying the huge space beneath a sloped parterre of grass and trees.[70] But of all these, the 1994 "Automatic Gardens" remains an intriguing representation of paths yet untraveled in Kuma's larger work: toy-like trees spinning across the sand of a dry garden landscape, raking patterns in a manner programmed to reflect ambient sound.[71] In 2004, Kuma revived the idea in his "Niwa" project, installed at the Japanese Pavilion for the Venice Biennale and then in Japan, the path of the robotic rakes traced with a calligraphic brush.

At Baisoin Temple, he lined the entry path, otherwise elegantly orthodox, with a beautiful and rare striped bamboo, elevating its effect.[72] Bamboo beds are also found at the Noh Stage; Kuma also attempted to plant it in a bath space at Ginzan Fujiya Ryokan (although the plants quickly died from exposure to sulfurous steam). Elsewhere, Kuma used one of Japan's most evocative but plainest agrarian materials – rice – to yield "a landscape with a nostalgic feeling to it" at the Takayanagi Community Center.[73]

But not all Kuma's landscapes could be called nostalgic. His garden at Murai Museum, further discussed in my next chapter, offers an unusual landscape anchored by a rusting Toyota in a weedy pond, a fringe of neglected vegetation surrounding the space. In another passage on Japanese aesthetics, academic Yuriko Saito argued,

> A garden with a wild, neglected appearance also conjures up an image of the passage of time. Instead of lamenting the fact that the object no longer exhibits the original, perfectly shaped, lustrously colored appearance, the aesthetics of imperfection elevates this fall from the graceful perfection to an even higher aesthetic plane by celebrating vicissitude and perishability.[74]

Kuma's many evocative landscapes draw deeply on the passage of time and the meaning of place.

The Murai Museum remains a rare example of nature as an ungainly presence; Kuma's inclination to pristine purity makes him, like his apparent nemesis Tadao Ando, partial to introduce nature as water. Look to the names of Kuma's projects to get a sense of its importance: Water/Glass, River/Filter, Sea/Filter, Ocean/City, Kitakami Canal Museum, and the more prosaic Seaside Subcenter of Tokyo. Yet these names do not begin to cover all Kuma's projects that rely on water for effect: his 1995 design for the Venice Biennale, for example, recreated a garden by Takamasa Yoshizaka from 40 years earlier by flooding the pavilion to the depth of 5 cm (about 2 inches). Occasionally Kuma sluices water across walls, an active presence, but he tends towards calm pools that double the presence of his buildings through

70. Published data describes the building as two stories below grade and three above, but sections show only one full story to the rear of the structure completely above the line of surrounding earth.

71. These small robots were exhibited at Takashimaya Department Store in 1994. Kuma also executed a similar project, "*Niwa* [Garden]: Where the Particle Responses" (*sic*) at the 2004 Venice Biennale.

72. This screen also serves as a remarkably rare and very traditional backdrop when viewed from the large windows of Kuma's office.

73. Kuma (2004a) p. 80.

74. Saito (1997) pp. 382–383.

reflection (perhaps the most effective way Kuma offers of burrowing into the earth). He rhapsodizes,

> The strange nature of water makes this experiment possible. Water can easily alternate between its solid, liquid and gaseous states. Water thus makes our attempts to categorize and separate the world look foolish. Water is also an infinitely sensitive receptor. It is thoroughly passive. Whereas objects are always in an active mode, water is always acted upon. Even its configuration is passively determined by its receptacle. Water is consistently passive toward every conceivable environmental factor.[75]

Kuma's careful attention to the size and effect of pools is expressed in their array: interior and exterior; long and narrow as slits or broad; shallow or of uncertain depth. One consistent gesture is the way he positions water at crucial thresholds, separating spaces from their mundane surroundings in a manner found in venerable sites like Kyoto's Gold and Silver Pavilions.[76]

Kuma also draws in other ordered forms of history and place. His 2003 Horai Bath House, a delicate open structure perched on a shelf of land, integrates and highlights an old, unusual herringbone "*kirikomihagi*" stone wall that predated the project. There is an interesting reverse used here, as he acknowledges:

> When I visited the site I found this wall was a very good one, showing very high-level craftsmanship. I decided to use that element as a part of the interior. Usually this is exterior – apart from buildings, but I decided to use that [wall] as an interior material.[77]

Many might quibble about whether there is an interior to this open-air bath, but the emphasis on the ancient wall is undeniable.

Kuma sometimes proposes his own earthen architecture; at the Nasu Historical Museum, he first hoped to build "movable earthen walls," assisted in his efforts by the renowned plasterer Akira Kusumi. They were unsuccessful, settling for the straw panels mentioned earlier. Kuma's interest, however, did not wane. He later discovered a region in Southern Japan with a surprising number of adobe structures and says he immediately called Kusumi from the site. In the resulting project, Kuma and Kusumi enclosed a large Heian-era Buddha in adobe blocks. Kuma said simply:

> The ability to make bricks from the soil in the site was very alluring. It represented the ultimate in melting into the surroundings. The material does not have to be transported any distance at all since it was already at the site.[78]

In addition to adobe and old stone, Kuma experiments with the heft of modern masonry: a screen of sliced precast concrete planks at Tokyo's Waketokuyama restaurant (a collaboration with interior designer Takashi Sugimoto, who calls his firm "Superpotato"), or customized brick, seen at his 2001 Sea/Filter, rotated on its edge to emphasize its non-bearing role. Both these systems utilize steel spines to achieve an airy appearance. Of all the materials Kuma has employed, a wall of glass and goose feathers at the Great Wall (Bamboo) House is one of the few moments where his material choice seems unconvincing. I suspect its difficulty is precisely related to the non-architectonic, non-allusive character of those feathers; Kuma's best buildings presume our awareness of traditional use, of weight. Juhani Pallasmaa eloquently argues:

> Materials and surfaces have a language of their own. Stone

75. Kuma (2000) pp. 82–83.
76. This point is made in Plutschow (2003) p. 18. Kuma echoed it in his 3 March, 2007, lecture at the Watarium Museum in Tokyo.
77. Interview, Tokyo (3 March, 2007).
78. Kuma (2007a) p. 163.

> speaks of its distant geological origins, its durability and inherent symbolism of permanence; brick makes one think of earth and fire, gravity and the ageless traditions of construction; bronze evokes ... the ancient processes of casting and the passage of time as measured in its patina. Wood speaks of its two existences and time scales; its first life as a growing tree and the second as a human artefact made by the caring hand of a carpenter or cabinet maker.[79]

Kuma's weightiest works are buried buildings, like the 1999 Kitakami Canal Museum and the oddly bunker-like 2001 Institute for Disaster Prevention. Often, his stereotomic proposals are advanced for exhibitions, with little chance of being built in their purest polemical form. The North American architect and academic Greg Lynn seems to have a finger on the reasons why, writing of Kuma's work, "... the earth is not treated as a ground but rather as a thin, flexible surface that can be modified, textured and manipulated as if it were like a cloth." Lynn continues, "In the 'Grass Net' proposal[,] the park surface of the city is equated to both (*sic*) a natural carpet of plant life, a network[-]like surface of information, and clothing."[80] While many of the projects Lynn discussed reflect the problems inherent in Kuma's early use of computers, the few built examples of Kuma's embedded architecture available suggest he has a tendency to undercut his own attempts at stereometry. Yet while he has not yet developed the same skill in these projects as in his lighter, airy work, it is clearly important to him to try.

To find a clear contrast with Kuma's earth-bound efforts, one need go no further than a cluster of structures within walking distance of his urban office. The screen wrapping the NTT Aoyama Building, only minutes from his desk, is a fiber-reinforced polymer grid floating free of the façade. The Baisoin Temple directly out his window is at its best on the southern face, a mysterious wall of paper-thin steel fins skimming the sidewalk. Less widely known is a fritted glass screen at Shibuya station, printed with digitized photographs of clouds, perhaps trendy Tokyo's version of COCON Karasuma's "Tenpyo Okumo."

While such a neat parallel as two cloud-patterned screens, one in Tokyo and the other in Kyoto, remains rare, Kuma does openly allude to place as crucial in understanding the two schools Fujimori treats as polar opposites. One approach he offers is to suggest tradition with an industrial material when working in the city, as he did in the 2002 Plastic House, later recalling, "I was pleased to hear a grand tea master mention that these FRP [fiber-reinforced plastic] square pipes were reminiscent of bamboo."[81]

In fact, while Kuma is alert to Fujimori's arguments, the younger architect is equally influenced by theories drawn directly from tea. As I briefly mentioned in the opening of this essay, Kuma wrote regarding tea master Sen no Rikyu as early as 1986, saying:

> ... Rikyu gradually shrunk the space of the tea room, ultimately arriving at a tea room of only one *tatami* mat [in size]. At a time when the splendor of Chinese imported [tea] ware was representative, Rikyu envisioned a directly opposite vector; he valued crude things, places that were narrow and cramped.[82]

Kuma observed, "Ando, in the same way, also pointed in the opposite direction from the exoticism of imported Chinese wares, exhibiting a new aesthetic of *wabi*, a new *sabi*,"[83] and finally concluded, "One point at 'Sumiyoshi Row House' represents the small, narrow space

79. Pallasmaa (2000) p. 79.

80. Lynn (1997) p. 47. Lynn is clearly influenced in his reading of Kuma by two essays: Leatherbarrow and Mostafavi (1993) pp. 115–123 and the subsequent Leatherbarrow and Mostafavi, "Opacity," (1996) pp. 49–64.

81. Kuma (2004a) p. 123.

82. Kuma (1986) p. 122. Original Japanese: …さらに利休は茶室空間のウォリュームを徐々に縮小していき、究極的には一畳の茶室にまで利達したのである。唐物に代表される華美なものに向かうベクトルが反転され、逆に粗末なもの狭苦しいものに価値が見出されるようになったのである。

that Ando indicated. That point is the interior unfinished concrete that represented his *sabi* (crude) materials. Rikyu's special quality is particularly clear ..."[84] Kuma, however, while able to offer these insights, rejected a purely raw, crude aesthetic, whether its original or the "new *wabi*" he associated with Ando.

The history of tea is varied enough for distinctly different architects to restate its aesthetics in diverse ways, and tea has thus reverberated through twentieth-century architectural practice. At Kenzo Tange's best, for example, he combined the rough and refined; although the postwar architect rejected tea as overly precious – even while writing a widely read book on the Katsura Imperial Retreat and its teahouses – the synthesis Tange fostered is found in tea. Kuma takes the position that "For [tea masters] Oribe or Rikyu, two different things meet: natural materials and industrial materials. For them the contrasting was very important. I try to do the same thing in this time..."[85] Philosopher Robert Wicks similarly stated, "... if 'imperfection' is the keynote of this aesthetics, how does one explain the meticulously raked surfaces of the dry landscape garden or the impeccably perfected movements requisite for performing the tea ceremony?"[86] Wicks goes on to assert that "By means of juxtaposing contingent, perishable [elements] (which usually have an 'imperfect' appearance) against a perfected, polished and idealized background, the contingency ... is thereby aesthetically highlighted and made more readily appreciable."[87] Thus the tearoom should not be portrayed as merely an architecture of thatched roofs, earthen walls, gnarled columns and crude pottery, but also about an elegantly lacquered lid, ornate edging on *tatami* mats or carefully defined modularity. Kuma expresses this contrast in his own work, arguing, "Usually abstraction and organic characteristics do not exist together ... That kind of coexistence of two different things together is a goal of my architecture." He continues, "Organic and abstraction are basic keywords of Japanese tradition."[88]

Teahouses often concentrate several stylized systems in a tiny space. Three different ceilings may mingle in one room no larger than 6 square meters (under 65 square feet). Surfaces are highlighted, each treated autonomously. Ando argued that in the teahouse, "The wall was made abstract until there was no sense of mass and it had been reduced to mere surface."[89] And Ken Tadashi Oshima, in his unpublished dissertation, wrote that one of the earliest architects to show an interest in the teahouse, Sutemi Horiguchi, demonstrated a strikingly similar approach to materials to Kuma's: "... covered structure allowed [Horiguchi] to freely face wall surfaces with luxurious materials such as teak, Himalayan cedar, Japanese oak, and varieties of Japanese paper ..."[90] and "... luxurious materials on the interior, such as teak floors, Japanese walnut, *paulownia*, and pear-wood for interior moldings and wall surfaces with silver leaf."[91]

While Kuma at first represented his worldly experience to Japan through postmodern architecture like the ironic Ionic M2, in the end he believes, "Each culture competes with every other and for our generation to go back to Japanese tradition is one way of competing ..."[92] As his reputation grows from a national to an international one, he feels increasing outside pressure to acknowledge Japanese tradition:

> For us, there is an expectation that [our] architectures should experiment with quintessentially Japanese design – but conditions at the present are a hopeless jumble of good and bad. Because Japanese architecture and design

83. Ibid., p. 124. Original Japanese:「安藤はそのような状況のなかにあって唐物への指向の反転し、新しわび、さびの美学を呈示して見せた。

84. Ibid., p. 125. Original Japanese: 一つには「住吉の長屋に代表される彼[安藤]の狭小空間指向。そして一つは内装打放しに代表される彼のさびた(粗末な)材料に対する指向によってである。これの特性は利休においては極めて明瞭であり…

85. Interview, Tokyo (3 March, 2007).

86. Wicks (2005) pp. 88–89.

87. Ibid., p. 89.

88. http://www.royalacademy.org.uk/architecture/interviews/kengo-kumas-craft,213,AR.html (accessed 20 February, 2007).

89. Walker (2002) p. 3. Original is in Ando (1984) p. 84.

90. Oshima (2003) p. 183.

91. Ibid. p. 198 f.

92. http://www.royalacademy.org.uk/architecture/interviews/kengo-kumas-craft,213,AR.html (accessed 9 February, 2007).

> are presently getting a lot of attention on the world stage, even when working abroad Japanese people are expected to offer up things that present beauty and an authentic feeling of Japanese harmony. You cannot merely imitate Japanese tradition simplistically, but instead I think we must create a cutting-edge Modernism that has a contemporary, new form of Japanese harmony.[93]

This "return to Japan" recalls similar shifts in Japanese architecture and literature during the early twentieth century. Architectural critic Ryuichi Hamaguchi wrote in 1956 of "... representative architects of the modern sukiya, such as Isoya Yoshida and Sutemi Horiguchi. Both underwent the [*sic*] baptism of Western architecture as young men. This led to travel abroad [in the 1920s], which in turn led to their return to things Japanese ..."[94] Writers of the 1920s also emerged by achieving a modern cast to their prose, using direct, declarative statements and emphasizing individuality, then excitingly unusual in Japanese. Yet to readers outside Japan at the time, such modernism was weak and derivative. Jun'ichiro Tanizaki, author of *In Praise of Shadows*, responded by bringing his writing and referents home, turning from the West towards Japan, and even shifting to Japanese dress; many others of his generation did so as well. Critic Kojin Karatani wrote of this "Western Paradox," "What in Japan looked avant-gardist and anti-traditionalist was actually seen in the West as simple reproductions. A regression to the 'traditional school' was actually perceived as an avant-gardist move – *a problem that continues to be felt to this very day.*"[95]

On the international stage, Japanese architects like Kuma now exploit their origins – not only in their buildings, but also in their rhetorical referents and, again, even in their dress. Unlike the early twentieth century, though, these gestures are not nationalistic or xenophobic. Kuma and his cohort weave Japanese culture into an architecture aware of and open to its encounter with the West, resulting in what author Luigi Alini neatly called "a *progressive* 'return' to tradition."[96] There are multiple constituencies demanding this echo of the past in present works: not only an enthusiastic international press, but also clients at home alienated from internationalism who support neo-regionalist efforts.

Ultimately, Kuma's architecture is both international and local; it straddles Fujimori's rustic Red and Westernized White, drawing on the best of both. His urbane architecture in particular exploits industrial production: sparkling ceramic, crisp aluminum or milky fiber-reinforced polymers. But his buildings, tucked away in far-flung, tiny towns or housing ancient artifacts – the ones that most interest me here – lean towards Fujimori's Red School, abstracting elements like *shoji* screens, *koshi* lattice doors, raised floors, and long eaves; using bamboo, adobe, thatch, straw, and paper. Because Kuma so clearly chooses at each juncture to recall tradition or emphasize the *au courant*, he also underscores how meaning – how location, cultural context or the use of a building – can be reflected in materials.

Understanding how Kuma embraces abstract and organic, rough and refined, renders his architecture legible. The stone grid swathing Lotus House or the odd use of Oya stone at his 2006 Chokkura Plaza are examples that make greater sense when seen as reflections of a community of cultures: stereometry struggling with story, both ultimately resolved in Semperian screens. Kuma has carved out a rich territory for his avid exploration.

93. Housekeeper (April, 2007) p. 90.
Original Japanese:
皆日本に対する期待があるし、和のデザインを試みる建築も多い。しかし、現状は玉石混淆です。世界中が日本の建築やデザインに注目している時代だからこそ、海外でも日本人が美しい感じる本物の和を見せていかなければならない。単に伝統を模倣するだけではなく、モダニズムの切れ味をもった現代の新しい和を作っていきたいと思っています。

94. Hamaguchi (1956) p. 59. Yoshida gets little coverage in this book because of his limited influence today. However, anyone closely studying the role tradition played in mid-century Modernism would benefit from a close look at his architecture.

95. Karatani (2001) p. 45. My emphasis. See also Karatani (1994), especially p. 34, where Karatani writes, "... in the literature of the 1930s, traditionalists formed the dominant wave ... [Giving names in Japanese order:] Tanizaki Jun'ichiro, Kawabata Yasunari, Mishima Yukio, and others albeit now renowned as traditionalists in the West, were originally Westernized modernists. At certain points in their careers, they all turned from Westernization to traditionalism, not for reasons of nostalgia, but because they thought it appeared more avant-garde."

96. Alini (2005) p. 8. My emphasis.

Murai Museum

Kengo Kuma

4

... this aspiration toward a "time" that transcends everyday lived time is the most salient characteristic of Kuma's recent works.—*Youichi Iijima*[1]

As I write in 2008, Kengo Kuma has completed four art museums: the 2000 Hiroshige Ando Museum, the 2004 Masanari Murai Museum of Art, the 2005 Nagasaki Museum of Art, done in partnership with a large corporate firm, Nihon Sekkei, the Suntory Museum of Art, opened in 2007 in Tokyo's trend-setting Midtown complex. A fifth, an expansion of the Nezu Museum, is under construction. For any architect, designing so many significant museums in a short time is noteworthy, but in addition, Kuma's approach is far from cookie-cutter, with distinctly different intentions for each museum.

Kuma's earliest art museum, the Hiroshige Ando Museum (also called the Nakagawa-machi Batoh Hiroshige Museum of Art, acknowledging its location), holds an important collection by one of Japan's leading *ukiyoe* artists. Hiroshige (sometimes called Hiroshige Utagawa, using his mentor's family name, which he adopted) lived until 1858, dying just before Japan's Edo era came to a close. The artist often worked in series, and his most famous sets of woodblock prints comprised scenic views: along the highway linking Tokyo and Kyoto, for example, or of the eastern capital itself. A major earthquake in Kobe in 1995 damaged an old storehouse; an unknown cache of hand-drawn work by Hiroshige was discovered within. The owners donated the unusual collection to the relatively out-of-the-way town of Batoh because of their ancestral ties to the area.

Art historians agree that Hiroshige's finest work portrayed water in all its forms: snow, rain, mist. Kuma's own love of water is apparently coincidental, but the architect responded strongly to Hiroshige's work; the resulting museum is one of his most important early buildings. As I noted in the last chapter, Kuma invariably indicates in lectures how Hiroshige's art – especially his woodcut "People on a Bridge Surprised by Rain" – inspired this museum. The architect follows the artist's lead, using layered, linear screens to create an overlapping spatial depth: curtains of aluminum rods slide behind louvered wooden screens, floating paper panels protected within, bamboo growing beyond. Kuma enveloped the museum in cedar slats, treated by an infrared technology that assures fire-resistance and the stability of their straight lines. The building's form and materials recall long, low wooden buildings of Hiroshige's era, rendered in layers of lines.

The museum especially focuses on the careful exhibition and storage of its collection; galleries are sympathetically scaled to the art. These spaces, the core of the building, are dark, with skillfully deployed spots pinpointing each work. Exhibition cases are understated, large panes of glass with a minimum of joints and hardware. Kuma's architecture illustrates his assertion that "Time stops while we engage in the act of looking at or capturing an image or an object with a camera or video camera. Time is made discontinuous and does not flow ..." [2] Storage areas here, rarely published, are also loving; paper

4.1 The gallery of Kuma's 2004 Murai Museum of Art, with Masanari Murai's artwork on display.

1. Iijima (1997) p. 94. Original Japanese:
...そうした日常的な、あるいは生きられた時間を超えてゆく時間への希求を、私は最近の隈の最大の特質と考える。
2. Ibid., pp. 8–9. Original Japanese:
客体を、単なる視覚の対象物と考えれば, 見られた時、あるいは写真、映像におさめた時に時間は停止する。時間は不連続で、時間は流れてはゆかない。

4.2

artworks cradled in soft cedar cabinets free of nails or other potentially damaging hardware. When I visited these rooms with two museum professionals, one of nearly a dozen museums our group saw in the span of two weeks in 2006, a curator swooned at the storerooms, claiming them the best we had found in all of Japan.

The museum thus begins with a world-class collection and wisely works from its suggestions. Kuma's building is no wallflower, but at its nucleus, it draws its inspiration from the woodcuts within, focused on the experience of appreciating the art. The architectural pyrotechnics this building is known for are beyond the galleries – bringing visitors to the site. Its interior becomes increasingly muted, detailed in progressively smaller gestures that shift the scale as visitors approach the art, in response to the relatively tiny size of most Hiroshige works. (The standard size for his woodcuts, *ooban*, is about 15 x 10 inches – 38 x 25.5 cm. – and larger *kakemono* were twice the size, 30 x 10 inches or 76 x 25.5 cm. His hand-drawn work is similar in scale.) In an astute essay on postwar museums, Charles Saumarez Smith links institutions like the Hiroshige to Louis Kahn's renowned Kimbell Museum. Smith contends Kahn privileged personal experience by using enclosed, room-like galleries, balancing exhibition areas with a building that "was expected to hold [its] own alongside *and independent of* the experience of the works of art."[3] As if describing Kuma's museum, Smith continued:

> There was a drive towards a relationship of planned and carefully controlled reciprocity between the museum as a place to visit and the museum as a ... collection of works of art. The garden ... and the café were as important to visit as individual galleries.[4]

The serene, respectful way Kuma's galleries enrich the experience of the artwork is rare in Japanese museum design today. Not surprisingly, other well-regarded private collections of Japan's cultural heritage have responded by commissioning Kuma.

The 2007 Suntory and the Nezu Institute of Fine Arts (open in 2009), emulate this museum. In fact, the Suntory has many similarities: layered screens of wood-finished louvers, glowing paper panels, and dimly lit galleries drawing the viewer into intimate enjoyment of each piece. At the Suntory, however, these materials exist in spaces scaled for crowds, as much as 10 meters high. Kuma admits, "I do not think that there is another sizable public space like this with a large surface of nothing but Japanese paper. Just using the paper is interesting."[5] In a published discussion of this building by Yukio Futagawa and Ryoji Suzuki, they relied on the spatial character and scale of the museum to make a distinction between a more nostalgic "*wafu*" Japanese style and this "new space."[6]

A public role is also emphatically expressed at the Nagasaki Museum of Art, a civic institution concerned with symbolizing the city's ambitions, designed in collaboration with the corporate architects Nihon Sekkei. Kuma produced a monumental space, grand galleries within linked through glass to broad plazas beyond the walls of the museum. While the Hiroshige Museum offers contemplative appreciation of each piece, the Nagasaki Museum entices and then entertains. Accenting this intent, exuberant electronic screens (often associated with commercial environments in Japan) abut the entrance. At Nagasaki, success is not measured in aesthetic experience, but in visitor statistics. This is not intended negatively; Smith, too, in discussing such structures, inquired "... does [the museum]

***4.2** The Hiroshige Ando Museum, completed in 2000, is a long, low building wrapped in wood.*

3. Smith (1995) p. 248. My emphasis.
4. Ibid.
5. Kuma (2006) p. 73. Original Japanese: 巨大な空間の中に、これだけの大きな面で和紙を用いた公共建築はないと思います。この和紙が持つ可能性も興味深いもので、時間が経るてば経つほどその色合いに落ち着きが増し，雰囲気に融け込む風合いになっていきます。
6. Suzuki and Yoshio (2007) pp. 58–65, especially p. 64.

4.3

4.4

4.5

4.3 *The galleries of the Hiroshige Ando Museum.*

4.4 *The largely unseen storage areas of the museum, also wrapped entirely in wood - joined without nails, as a precaution for careful preservation of the artwork.*

4.5 *Public areas of the museum are defined by layers of wood slats, slender aluminum pipe and handmade paper lit from behind and below.*

4.6

4.7

4.8

4.6–9 The 2005 Nagasaki Museum of Art, designed in collaboration with Nihon Sekkei, employs many of Kuma's architectural gestures seen elsewhere, but with a very different effect.

4.9

have a larger responsibility in the provision of public space and public experience and, indeed, public interaction at a time when so much of life and leisure has retreated into the home?"[7]

Materials play a role in defining the differences in these museums. The Hiroshige Museum is intimately scaled; local, knotty woods and handmade *washi* paper refer to the cultural ties and historical nature of the collection. At Nagasaki, Kuma wrapped the exterior in slices of imported granite; the permanent galleries inside are finished in exotic wood veneers. These materials are not modest; they proclaim the economic power of the institution.

These two museums demonstrate Kuma's careful consideration of institutional roles in a community. The Masanari Murai Museum could not offer a more different set of expectations from these others: built for a private collection bequeathed by a respected abstract artist, located in leafy suburban Tokyo. Completed in 2004, the Murai Museum remains doggedly private. On a quiet residential street, it is perhaps best called a home holding a gallery within; Itsuko Murai, the artist's widow, lives in a tiny apartment on the second floor.[8] In the first few years the museum existed, it was difficult even to find, lacking a website and offering only a minimal presence in guidebooks. Visitors were allowed only on Sundays (and, since the beginning of 2008, Fridays as well); callers come only after reserving appointments through the mail. The artist's widow prepares cake and coffee, encouraging each person to linger after viewing the artworks, to look over catalogs and chat.[9]

Kuma and Mrs. Murai, his client, conceived of this building as more than simply an opportunity to exhibit. One week after graduating from a respectable Tokyo art school in 1928, Masanari (who sometimes signed his work with a Francophile "Maçanari") boarded a ship to Paris. It was an accepted path for ambitious Japanese painters; art historian Thomas Havens writes, "Between the world wars, more than five hundred persons identified as Japanese artists lived in Paris at any given time."[10] Masanari quickly adopted bold, Jean Arp-like abstraction – but when he came home in 1932, his skillful compositions of primary colors and simple shapes were out of step with the tenor of the times. Although always understood as a progenitor of the new international art, Masanari faced a nation at best suspicious of his aesthetic approach. During World War II, local military authorities harassed Masanari (and many like him); the school where he taught, his *alma mater*, was closed. Artists willing to paint propaganda were, in the end, the only ones with access to paint and canvas. Many well-known, respected artists, including Gen'ichiro Inokuma and Tsuguharu Foujita (an odd man who also painted under the names "Tsuguji" and "Leonard") capitulated to these demands.[11] Masanari did not.

At war's end, the art world slighted Masanari (already 40) in favor of younger, more adventurous artists. It was in a particularly tumultuous period in Japan's art history; writing on the radical shifts of the era, Havens acknowledges Masanari as simply, "... a pioneering oil painter and mentor to young abstractionists after the war."[12] Masanari remained respected, but never received the recognition he might have in other circumstances. Nonetheless, he remained prolific throughout, leaving a collection of noteworthy canvasses and an arresting group of primitive sculptures, never exhibited in his lifetime.

Understanding this remarkable history, Kuma and Mrs. Murai intended not only exhibition, but also education. Whereas the architect embraced a public role for his museum in Nagasaki, here Kuma

7. Smith (1995) p. 255.
8. 伊津子.
9. Masanari Murai signed his paintings with his given name.
10. Havens (2006) p. 45. Birnbaum (2006) covers the same period.
11. See Munroe, Alexandria. "*Circle:*Modernism and Tradition," in Munroe (1994) pp. 125–137.
12. Havens (2006) p. 23.

4.10 The shaggy entrance to the Murai Museum of Art.

4.11 In the forecourt, Masanari Murai's ancient automobile stands as if sculpture.

4.12 An airy steel stair defines the back wall of the garden; another is used similarly within.

4.10

4.11

4.12

4.13

4.13–15 *The rough boards on the exterior were collected from Murai's studio before its demolition.*

challenged the allure of such entertaining institutions, instead invoking active involvement, encouraging an awareness of Masanari's struggle to create his powerful pieces. For Kuma and his client, it was as important to underscore the trajectory of Masanari's career, to bring to life its pathos.

Dead years before Kuma's commission, Masanari left behind strange, oddly appealing structures which confronted the architect on his first visit to the site: a dilapidated home and studio from 1938 and another building from the postwar period, chock full of anything imaginable. In his old age, Masanari annexed ad-hoc accretions to these modest wooden shacks, fashioning a labyrinthine collage that may perhaps have been his largest sculptural work. In a catalogue published in 1987, Masataka Ogawa, an acquaintance who had not seen the artist in 20 years, vividly recalls the studio complex:

> As I began to head towards the foyer I remembered, the person showing me around said "That way's no good." A motley assortment of stuff was piled up as far as the entry, and I was told we could not to get in from there. Yet when we went around to the rear entrance, the same was true. On top of an aged car stored there, bundles and boxes of old magazines were stacked up, junk was jumbled together in heavy piles, all of it a mountain of *rubbish*. In the garden stood a little shed and I could see, through the glass, stacks came up to the window in the same way. Finally, standing in front of a glass door facing the garden – there was a paper sign: "Please ring the bell. The door will open." And from there, we went into a room ...
>
> But inside, conditions were the same.[13]

4.14

4.15

13. Ogawa (1987) pp. 4–5. Original Japanese: 見慣れた玄関の方に足を運ぼうとしたらそちらは駄目です。と、案内者は言う。玄関にまで雑多な荷物がつまっていて、そこからは入れないそうだ。だが、裏口に回っても同じこと。放置されたオールド・カーの上には、古雑誌の束や空箱のなかに詰まった廃品などが堆く積み重られていた、まさにごみの山だ。庭に建てられた小舎のなかも、がラス越しに見ると、それと少しも変わりない。やっと庭側のガラス戸の前に立つと、『ベルを押して下さい。戸をあけますと貼り紙してある。
そこから部屋へーー。
しかし、室内も同様だった。

4.16 A part of Murai's original studio remains at the heart of Kuma's building.

4.17 The light line between interior and exterior.

4.16

4.17

Writing for the British newspaper, the *Daily Telegraph*, Yuki Sumner claimed:

> Technically speaking, the old house was not exactly a ruin. [Masanari] Murai lived, worked and taught there until his death at the age of 93. Over its 60-year lifespan, however, it did become somewhat dilapidated as the painter continually extended it on a whim. A maze evolved, with corridors that led nowhere and rooms that could be reached only by climbing over the windows from another room.[14]

Most Japanese architects would not think twice about tearing down such shacks. Tokyo houses, even those in good condition, rarely survive thirty years; when property encumbered with older houses is sold, sellers pay removal costs. But Kuma and his architect wife Satoko Shinohara were somehow taken by the muddle of Masanari's studio. Naomi Pollock, who writes often on Japanese architecture, quotes Kuma: "I thought the house was chaotic, but I like that kind of chaos."[15] Though conservancy remains rare in Japan, Kuma asked the photographer Ryuji Miyamoto, known for his sensitive images of ruins and dilapidation, to document the studio.[16]

British architectural historian Adrian Forty argued that, "The creation of buildings for commemoration is one of the oldest purposes of architecture,"[17] but this has not been true in Japan: earlier capitals were abandoned on the death of the Emperor; fires that swept the city were called the "Flowers of Edo." In nineteenth-century Japan, examples of collective commemoration were introduced from the West, just as universities, railroad stations and – yes – museums were. Japan incorporated nineteenth- and twentieth-century war memorials into religious sites, including the highly problematic internment of souls at Yasukuni Shrine. After World War II, several secular memorials to civilians were also constructed, although in ways that sometimes revealed the discomfort these caused even within Japan. A memorial hall commemorating those who died in the atomic bombing of Nagasaki, for example, was not completed until nearly sixty years afterwards; a memorial to student soldiers who died in the same war, designed by Kenzo Tange, was so little known that art historian Jackie Kestenbaum and I brought it to the attention of Japan's leading scholars in 1998, leading Terunobu Fujimori to return it to public attention in a monograph published shortly thereafter.

14. Sumner(2006). Available at: http://www.telegraph.co.uk/property/main.jhtml?xml=/property/2006/10/10/ptricks10.xml (accessed 27 March, 2007).

15. Pollock (2006) p.140.

16. Mrs. Murai originally asked Kuma to produce a full set of measured drawings and a model of the studio for display in the new museum, but the two ultimately agreed this was too expensive. Officials at the nearby Setagaya Museum suggested Miyamoto as an alternative, and Kuma, an acquaintance, asked the photographer to take on this unusual commission.

17. Forty (2004) p. 206.

4 . 18

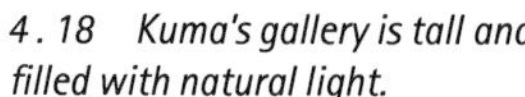

4 . 18 Kuma's gallery is tall and filled with natural light.

4 . 19–21 The original studio; the door shown in the image on the left is seen behind Kuma's steel stair in Fig . 4 . 16 and below.

4 . 19

4 . 20

4 . 21

MAÇANARI

4.22 In a piece of Masanari Murai's studio, his collection of artifacts and artworks remains.

4.23, 24 Views of the studio, showing his powerful artworks in place.

4.25 A plan of the museum shows the original studio, darkened, at the heart of the museum.

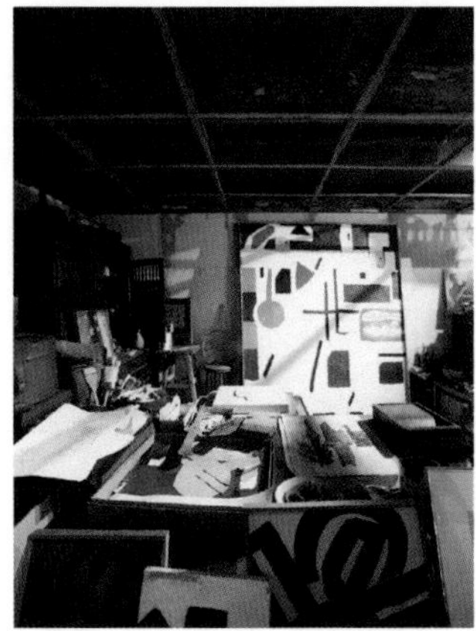

4.23

4.24

Salvaging the entire structure Murai had left behind proved impractical; Kuma realized the 1938 studio accommodated only individual movement and could not be safely adapted to public use. The architect struggled with the existing interior – he saw it as transformed, first space, then solid:

> It had an indescribable vigor. It was not just a wooden house. Nothing had been thrown away, the whole house was more than merely used for storage – it felt as if it had become one big trashcan. There was almost no space left in the rooms: magazines, drawings, anything and everything piled up within. What was once void had become a solid. The atelier existed in a sliver of space remaining. (Laughs.) Anyway, I was impressed with the remarkable house ... Usually, I think it should be possible to separate what is architecture, furniture, or trash. It was impossible to find any division; that was a real shock.[18]

Ultimately, Kuma saved a portion of the postwar studio; the remnant was carefully wrapped in durable sheets of blue plastic while construction swirled around it, finally engulfing it. The studio is now an object on exhibit, a dense, dark core nestled within a clean, contemporary box.

Kuma claims:

> I preserved, exactly in its original form, the small room that Mr. Murai used ... The atelier looks like one of the objects displayed inside the large box ... The opening thus created [where the existing studio meets the galleries] is both a discontinuity in physical space and a discontinuity in time. Mr. Murai's works are displayed in this anomalous space that acts as a threshold between the old time and the new time.[19]

At the inner recesses of the museum (what Kuma's mentor Fumihiko Maki describes as the *oku*) sits the studio: rough walls, seemingly torn; worn white paint contrasting with raw wood, the original finish like a tapestry laid against the smooth white plasterboard of Kuma's interior. Exposed underlayers offer ghostly reminders of absent areas. One of Masanari's unknown sculptures, an oversized cast aluminum figure of a man (a 1991 self-portrait), stands sentry for the studio; a door to the left is clearly blocked by the airy steel stairs, perhaps recalling how Masanari blocked openings in the original studio.

Columbia University Dean of Architecture Mark Wigley has much to say that indirectly offers insight into Kuma and his work; Wigley wrote of such places that:

> Buildings witness something that has been lost, maintaining the memory of ... a ghostly spirit that ... animates the solid object. They keep alive the sense of an earlier time. Architecture, seemingly the least mobile of the arts, has a special relationship to the idea of making time stand still.

Wigley continues, "The monument is therefore not so much an object as a space, a protected zone, a preserve for time. It evokes memory by holding a previous time against the flow of the present."[20]

The Murai Museum is not only a commemoration of Masanari's life and work, but also a collaboration between Kuma and the deceased artist. Masanari left a raw, primitive artistry the elegant architect is unable to achieve alone. Kuma conceded:

> Murai painted abstractly, but when you saw his house it was less easy to classify as either abstraction or as an ex-

18. Kuma (2003) p. 120. Original Japanese:
さっそく、東京・等々力の旧村井邸に行ってみました。そこがなんとも凄い迫力だったんです。
単なる古い木造家屋というのではない。物が捨てられなくて、家全体が、倉庫というよりは、ゴミ箱になっている感じ。スペースの残っている部屋がほんとんど無い。雑誌や、描いた絵、何もかもドンドン、積んでしまって、ヴォイドだったところも、ソリッドになっているんです。かろうじて残ったヴォイドをアトリエにしていた(笑)。とにかく、スッゴイ家に感激した…普通は、建築、家具、ゴミくらいは分かれていると思うんけど、その境が無い。それがすごくショックで…
19. Kuma (2004b) p. 72.
20. Wigley (2000) p. 36.

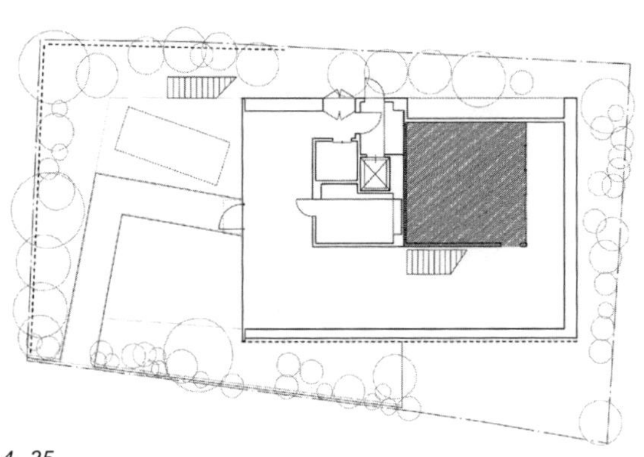

4.25

4.26 A tiny balcony above.

4.27 A balustrade, gnawed by a beloved dog, was reused in casework Kuma designed.

4.26

4.27

> pression of materiality. I think his house existed where abstraction and materiality meet. It was an expression of materiality, but it was the most extreme form of materiality.[21]

Kuma, an architect known for his materiality, employed cool abstraction in response.

Within the studio, Kuma re-placed the jumble of materials Masanari left behind, assemblages of odds and ends, a kaleidoscopic chaos. Cans of dirty paintbrushes and unfinished canvas sit as if the artist had just stepped aside; Masanari proudly proclaimed that he never cleaned his brushes. Posters and large photos of the artist contend with televisions and tools, from an unused saw to a display of old spoons. Rough chests and crates are topped with bamboo baskets, boxes of paper scrap, old light bulbs, briefcases and a man's felt hat. Paper and bamboo toys hang from the ceiling. An overwhelming assemblage, it is jumbled together with precious art. Elsewhere in the museum are apple crates Masanari assembled as shelves, an oddly asymmetrical old door, a bronze bell, and the stair banister of the earlier studio, gnawed into a sensuously slender-waisted shape by a long-dead dog. Kuma placed Masanari's rusty 1960s Toyota Crown, the very car Masataka Ogawa found many years before buried in bundles of newspaper, in the garden forecourt: a valued sculpture, its voluptuous rear fins a clear contrast to the clean lines of Kuma's muted, neutral architecture.

The success of this museum results from how Kuma created a low-key background for Masanari's robust remnants. The interior, perhaps merely because of its modest budget, intelligently deploys simple, industrial materials with minimal fuss. Finishes are straightforward: a good-quality concrete slab in one area, the former studio's old wood

21. Kuma (2003) p. 121. Original Japanese: 村井さんは抽象画家だけど、家を見て、抽象、具象という分類がかすんでかんじられた…村井さんの家は、具象と抽象の彼岸に会ったんじゃないかと思う。具象と言えば、具象の極地。

4.28

4.29

flooring in another, white painted plasterboard walls and screens of expanded metal. At the entry, Kuma concentrates the infrastructure: an exposed wide-flange beam and a rolling shutter offer the only articulation; a set of ducts, lacking even air grilles, snake above the entrance, effectively lowering the ceiling and increasing intimacy.

It is easy to miss the care taken to achieve artlessness, the way surfaces smoothly meet or the nearly complete lack of window frames – effects easy to draw but unusually hard to build. Internally, Kuma allows little leeway; his only attention-getting effort is in the thinness of his stairs and screens. He mutes his pyrotechnics – a contrast to the hyper-aestheticization of the Hiroshige Museum. When the Murai Museum was completed, Kuma reflected:

> When you looked at Murai's house, it was a unification of architecture, furniture, and trash. It was effectively detail-free, an architecture developed without regard for detail, where detail had no meaning. None of the details particularly seemed to matter ... It was all one thing, without any unnecessary effort, just relaxed conditions.[22]

On the exterior, Kuma allowed himself some leeway. The approach to the museum rises between two weedy pools bounded in thin, rusty Cor-ten sheet. Water meets the glass wall of the museum almost perfectly, with only a narrow line of trim separating the two reflective planes. A ragged fringe of trees wraps the space, showing no evidence of the conventional care often given to tiny plots in Japan. Years before Kuma designed this landscape, he acknowledged:

> ... the gardener is held captive inside the garden and is unable to stop the flow of time. There can be no temporal "point" where the goal is reached and completion is achieved. There is no completion for a garden. Time continues to flow forever.[23]

Even the slender canopy over the entrance is effective; for an instant Kuma upstages Masanari's remnants, but in a small gesture, lost as one passes within the building. The false note for this museum is its exterior screen, which Kuma once suggested is no more than a modest fence. The louver-like layer, made from wood scraps that clad Masanari's studios, is not rough enough to reveal the primitive strength within. I am perhaps unfair to compare. Masanari worked with a carpenter clearly unconcerned with any of the niceties of the craft as it is practiced in Japan (even Mrs. Murai describes the man as strange); the exterior siding saved from the original building is of oddly varying thickness.[24] Kuma, usually well served by the precision of the Japanese construction industry, could hardly achieve such brutish results. The only real value of this exterior screen is that it reduces expectations of what lies within.

Some day, this museum will be annexed to a larger and well-regarded public institution nearby, the Setagaya Museum of Art. Setagaya is already a generous and sympathetic supporter, curating exhibitions and sending over volunteers to staff the Murai Museum. Exhibitions ably reflect Mrs. Murai's initial goals: the entrance area quickly establishing Masanari's skills with one or two bold canvases, followed by artifacts from Masanari's early years, delicate watercolors of exotic scenery or photographs of the dapper Masanari abroad. Large, accomplished canvases fill the rest of the gallery.

The remains of Masanari's studio offer a fascinating juxtaposition to the well-lit minimalism of the gallery, strong spots throwing deep, dramatic shadows into the space. The shift in scale, material and light

22. Ibid. Original Japanese:
村井さんの家を見て、建築と家具とゴミが一体化している状態はまさにディテール・レスな状態だと思いました。建築のディテールを問うことに意味は無いし、どのディテールも突出していない気持…それが、村井さんの自宅には無い。全部一様に無駄な力が抜けて、リラックスしている状態。

23. Kuma (1997) p. 9.

4.30

4.28, 29 An artwork by Murai, never exhibited in his lifetime.

4.30 The original studio's wooden floorboards, reused on the balcony.

4.31

4.31 A foyer area at the entrance is made more intimate by adding ductwork that drops the ceiling height.

4.32 Looking from gallery to garden.

indicates Kuma's temporal discontinuity. While one can imagine this disarray remains untouched since Masanari's death, it is clean and constantly fine-tuned by Mrs. Murai. Lately, the widow seems to be reenacting her late husband's hoarding, drawing solid out of void, the studio and its environs increasingly filling with unfinished canvases, boxes of kitchen tools, old clothes and magazines. Even so, the studio will never hold the shock for us it did for Masanari's contemporaries. Clifford E. Clark dissected the difficulties of using material culture as a lens on unwritten histories: "... as objects age, their meanings change ... one generation's castaways sometimes become the next generation's treasures."[25] This is certainly true in the studio; the cheap, disposable toys, bowls and baskets are now exhibited in many other museums as valued folk art of an earlier era.

On the second floor, the exhibition tends towards Masanari's later years. Visitors then return to the low lobby tables that once furnished Masanari's studio, where fat catalogues from his shows, augmented by cake and conversation with Mrs. Murai, complete the education offered. The tale of Masanari's life as related by his widow is entwined with – and perhaps even overshadows – his art; the museum is not a dry, scholarly archive. No attempt is made to communicate the collections that hold Masanari's works; the Setagaya Museum archives will ultimately play that role. Here, the architecture empowers a personal account of the artist, embodied not only by his output but also through the unusual environment he created.

Kuma once claimed, "I want to recover the Japanese tradition of weaker buildings."[26] He was confident he could be muted at the Murai Museum and still speak volumes. His best work draws on the substance of each architectural event to evoke meaning, using the physical and cultural context of each project as a departure point. Often, Kuma does so by highlighting these elements within a contrasting composition of rough and smooth, old and new. Oddly, while the Murai Museum expresses these dichotomies with remarkable skill, it is – and probably will remain – unique within the architect's *œuvre*, because of the genuinely astonishing vigor of Masanari's robust remnant. Kuma's architecture is, in response, unusually reticent.

4.32

24. *Shitsunai* (May, 2005) pp. [57]–61, siding thickness discussed on p. 61.

25. Clark (1991) p. 75.

26. Interview with Jeremy Melvin, "Kengo Kuma's Craft." Available at: http://www.royalacademy.org.uk/architecture/interviews/kengo-kumas-craft,213,AR.html (accessed 28 March, 2007).

4.33

4.33 *The street elevation.*

4.34 *The rough, ad hoc construction of Murai's studio is a foil for Kuma's careful control.*

While the decision to build a small, independent museum was one Mrs. Murai and her husband agreed to during his lifetime, she argues it was she who first envisioned an architecture embracing the environment Masanari left behind.[27] She chose Kuma after reading his book *Han Obujekuto* [Anti-Object], which eloquently outlines his approach: he speaks of his struggles to satisfy the needs of clients with no money, his attempts to unify a love for the history of places with contemporary expectations and demands, his passion for materials and materiality, and his efforts to achieve modest, understated effects. All these spoke directly to Mrs. Murai. She may in turn have strengthened Kuma's awareness of memory and the passage of time; notably, his *Makeru Kenchiku* [Defeated Architecture] was published the very week of Masanari's one-hundredth birthday, a week before the museum opened.[28]

In his earlier architecture, Kuma alluded to a common past through paper screens and local woods, but the Murai Museum of Art demonstrates a crucial shift. The communal yielded to the idiosyncratic; even Masanari's car, positioned as it is in a pool of water, is less likely to be seen as a shared historical referent than as an oddly individual relic. The artist's life presented many challenges: his tale was one of initial hope, wartime persecution, and an odd hoarding in his later years. Kuma could hardly presume to present this life as one that museum visitors might find familiar. Masanari's early move to Paris will seem exotic even to most Japanese today, the impact of World War II on citizens is rarely acknowledged openly, and Japanese society as a whole tends towards neatness, quickly eradicating the rubbish of daily life. The dilemma presented by this challenge caused Kuma to consider material and its meaning at a more personal level than he had, enriching and enhancing his subsequent structures. The Murai Museum offered an unusual occasion, a point when a client opened new territories for the architect.

In the essay I mentioned earlier, Adrian Forty argued that commemorative structures hold "The expectation that works of architecture can prolong collective social memory of persons or events beyond the mental recollections of individuals who knew or witnessed them at first hand ..."[29] The Murai Museum is poised to accept the inevitable shift from the personal commemoration offered by Mrs. Murai with cake and coffee, to reinforcing broader recognition of the artist and his worth.

Since completing this museum, Kuma has instigated other opportunities to draw on the personal memories of clients, especially in the quasi-domestic environment of the Ginzan Fujiya *Ryokan*. He seems poised to layer these symbolically important elements, the personal and the collective. Pieces expressing meaning for his clients commingle with those the architect adds as a narrative of his own development. However, for the moment, such gestures lack the power and poignancy of this first foray into the personal, in part, simply because the memories evoked are openly nostalgic in tone and far too easy to apprehend. The role memory will play in future works, the opportunities Kuma may have to again incorporate such resonant allusions, both remain unknown, a pregnant potential.

27. Such private museums are far from rare in Japan; they allow owners to maintain valuable collections and simultaneously avoid excessive taxes. According to a recent article, the Japanese Ministry of Education, Culture, Sports, Science and Technology estimated there were 56,614 museums in the country in 2005.

28. Kuma (2004c).

29. Forty (2004) p. 206.

4.34

Outlandish Amateur, Polished Professional

Terunobu Fujimori and Kengo Kuma

5

5.2

Fujimori and Kuma appear poles apart, though in reality they frame the opposite ends of the range of Fujimori's Red School. Other architects are also straying into regionalism - not out of inclination, but because conditions call for it. Comparing and contrasting the ideas embedded in Kuma's and Fujimori's output unfolds the latitude of this alternative "Red School" approach to architecture.

Both Fujimori and Kuma unearth innovation from the rich territory of history and tradition. A popular and dauntingly prolific architectural historian (author of a mind-boggling sixty books), Fujimori's enthusiasm for the past is understandable. Kuma is also passionately interested in history, reflected in his work both as a practicing architect and an occasional author; he has penned a handful of books offering thoughtful observation on architectural events spanning centuries. Both men consciously avoid established approaches to tradition in their authorship; in their architecture, both avoid simply following the established practice of overlaying Modernism with the sixteenth-century *shoin* style. Perhaps their architectural approaches are the result of their inclination to reflect, to research, and to rethink, also expressed in their writing.

Yet Fujimori and Kuma do not perceive the same past. Fujimori's rare acceptance of Shinto represents living, spiritual ties, an open

5.1 Terunobu Fujimori's bristling wall at his 2000 Camellia Castle is made up of slate interspersed with grass.

5.2 Kengo Kuma's woven oya stone at his 2006 Chokkura Plaza.

5.3 The interior of Fujimori's 2003 Kuan, a teahouse hidden behind a Kyoto temple.

embrace of his rural origin. But he is no rube; Hiroyuki Suzuki suggests far more when he calls this University of Tokyo professor a "noble savage." Fujimori, a Meiji scholar, embraces the innocence of earlier eras. His past remains present, echoing artist Taro Okamoto's assertion that "Tradition should breathe in our lives and in our work. ... tradition exists not so much in the past as in the present ..."[1]

Fujimori makes explicit and recognizable references to history, Japanese or international; however, he is not concerned with accuracy. As historian Stephen Vlastos asserted:

> ...tradition is not the sum of actual past practices that have perdured into the present; rather, tradition is a modern trope, a ... representation of socially desirable (or sometimes undesirable) institutions and ideas thought to have been handed down from generation to generation.[2]

Fujimori adapts the past with enthusiastic pragmatism and a perhaps somewhat perverse intuition. In his book *The Fujimori Way of Using Natural Materials*, he aggressively repudiates any Romanticism:

> I'm telling you, with Romanticism, people are always saying how great it was in the old days. We had great materials, great craftsmen, and had a lot of time. And yet! If you ask me, it is just like riding a speeding bullet train while saying, "The old steam engine trains were grand."[3]

Interestingly, things that appear old in Fujimori's architecture often have shallower roots; most Japanese might mistake his *namako*-like diagonals cladding the Camellia Chateau in blades of grass as adapting something ancient, but the fat plaster it alludes to was actually invented at the point when Japan was avidly modernizing in the Meiji era.

5.3

1. Okamoto,. "What is Tradition?" in Munroe (1994) p. 381.
2. Vlastos, Tradition: Past/Present Culture and Modern Japanese History," in Vlastos (1998) p. 3.
3. Fujimori *et al.* (2005) p. 197.
Original Japanese:
ロマン主義の中には、昔がいいっていうのがあるんですよ。昔は材料はいいし職人がいいし時間だってあって。でもね。僕に言わせると、新幹線に乗りながら「昔の蒸気機関車が良かったな」って言ってるのとおなじようなものだと。

5.4

To Kuma, however, the past is no longer alive; it is a rich, inspiring archive. Scholar Stefan Tanaka says modernization in the Meiji era shifted

> ... [Japan's] relation with the past: the integration of inherited ideas and practices as a part of life ... replaced by the separation of pasts as something to be admired – as tradition, authenticity, natural, etc. – ... it disappears from life but is perhaps preserved as objects.[4]

Kuma reflects modern thought: tradition is based on our abstract understanding of shared social views. Kuma's relationship to history is idealistic; his effort to add new concepts to an established canon is progressive, building on and within already established architectural practices. For Kuma, tradition is timeless; his history offers fluidly interchangeable but unchanged moments. This is why the younger architect could nimbly ditch Western postmodernism for Taut and tea, why Kuma is untroubled when he apes the structural systems of temples in a modern town hall built of unwanted wood.

Their shared interest in tea, yielding very different approaches, underscores how each embraces tradition. Fujimori acknowledges the lasting influence of the *sukiya* style, arguing that even today,

> In Japan, *sukiya* offers a model. It's clearly a style, but one practiced and practiced for a long time without winding to a conclusion. Its vitality has been enhanced for 400 years without cooling. If you were to point to the same period in Europe, you would be talking about Neo Baroque Style ... [yet] *sukiya* endures.[5]

But both intellectually and formally, Fujimori ignores the established face of tradition, instead returning to the dawning days of tea and

5.5

5.4, 5 Kuma's inflatable teahouse at the Museum of Applied Arts in Frankfurt, installed in 2008.

4. Tanaka (2004) p. 21.
5. Fujimori (2006d) p. 21. Original Japanese: 日本には数寄屋という先例がある。スタイルとしては完成しているのに、やってもやっても行きついて終わるということがなかった。生れてから４００年も飽きずに続いている。ヨーロッパでいうならネオ・バロックと同時代のスタイルだ。漸近線的完成過程の中にいると、数寄屋４００年状態だろう。

5.6 Fujimori's rough façade, at Soda Pop Spa.

5.6

to tea master Sen no Rikyu. Rikyu's is *wabi* tea, tea in its most rustic form. Rikyu's tea is an event. Fujimori, too, is a ritualist, not an aesthete; his is tea "short-lived like a morning glory."[6] And so Fujimori inclines to modest materials; the conventions imbued in today's teahouses are too luxurious and meticulous for him. His works are so simple Fujimori can, and does, build many himself.

Kuma's is an erudite appreciation. He explores established aesthetic theories; he is inspired by close study of structure and screen, opaque and translucent, exotic import set against the crude or plain. Kuma draws on an informed connoisseurship of the aesthetics of tea; his expertise is encouraged by aficionados who ask him to accommodate their ancient and valuable teahouses.[7] Early on, Kuma rejected Rikyu's *wabi* tea and Ando's insightful adaptations of *wabi* to today. Kuma loves the luxury of beautiful stone and rare or expensive woods, and only uses the restraint so evident in tea to prevent this luxury from becoming excessive.

But architects have an annoying habit of constantly evolving. Even as I wrote this text, Fujimori's tiny structures seemed to grow more ornamental, with mother-of-pearl embedded in plaster and entrances framed in gold leaf appliqué. Kuma, meanwhile, is increasingly interested in temporary architectures as event, a moment of communication.

The difference in the two architects is also evident in Kuma's openness to employing the words *"wabi"* and *"sabi"* where Fujimori will not; Kuma accepts oft-employed abstractions of the past. In his book *Makeru Kenchiku* (Defeated Architecture), Kuma recalled the controversy surrounding his installation at the 1995 Venice Biennale. The theme was "Identity and Alterity" (the second word blending "alterna-

6. Plutschow (2003) p. 139.

7. Lotus House and the house in Kyoto, called "Yien East," are both part of building complexes with ancient teahouses, designed for an avid tea practitioner. The Nezu Museum and Suntory Museums also incorporate valued teahouses. Kuma, as I note in my earlier chapter, also designed a number of temporary teahouses as installations in cultural settings, both at home and (more recently) abroad.

5.7 *Kuma's always-clean ceramic stripes, at the 2007 Suntory Museum.*

tive" and "identity"). Japanese art critic Junji Ito proposed as pavilion theme *"suki"* [elegant pursuits], linked linguistically to the tea style *sukiya*. Kuma's account of the fracas that followed could also describe his own experiences elsewhere:

> [Kunio] Motoe criticized the *"Suki"* argument in the newspaper, saying Ito blithely emphasized things that were only Japanese, with no thought of art concerned with the essentials of universality ... Shuuji Takashina came to Ito's defense, quoting Tenshin Okakura, "Travel abroad in *kimono* if you think your English is good enough, but never wear Japanese clothes and speak in broken English." Ito, Takashina suggested, was pursuing a course akin to this. ... Motoe's faction, the "universal side", criticized the concept of *"Suki"* as simplistic Orientalism ... But for the *"Suki"* side, *the concept could also overcome Orientalism to expose a deeper truth at its core.* Ours was not an effort to ingratiate by accommodating the expectations of the West ... but to expose critical thinking vis-à-vis the West.[8]

Kuma is remarkably unafraid of romantic notions of Japanese tradition; he assumes they indicate deeper meaning worthy of mining.

Both men, it should be said, appreciate not only Japan's uniqueness, but also its universalities. Arata Isozaki once wrote, "For Japanese Modernists – and I include myself – it is impossible not to begin with Western concepts."[9] But while both Fujimori and Kuma understand architecture is international, introduced from beyond the nation's shores more than a century ago, the West remaining a strong source of influence, both unabashedly acknowledge early Modernist antecedents. They again do so differently: Fujimori admires Le Corbusier;

5.7

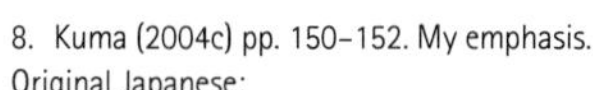

8. Kuma (2004c) pp. 150–152. My emphasis. Original Japanese:
日本館のコミッショナーの選定に際し、はじめてコンペ制度が導入され、高階秀爾を審査委員長とするコンペで選ばれたのは美術評論家の伊東順二による「数寄–複方言への試み」という企画であった。ビエンナーレの全体テーマとして揚げられたのは「自己性と他者性」。...コンペ方式も話題を集めたが、より話題となったのは、国立美術館の本江邦夫の批判に端を発した普遍論争である。本江は伊東の「数寄」案は、いたずらに日本的なものを強調するだけで、美術に不可欠な普遍性に対する思考が欠如している、と新聞紙上で批判した。...それに対して、高階秀爾は伊東弁護の論を寄せた。高階は「英語が自由に話せるなら、和服を着て洋行しろ」という岡倉天心の言葉を引き、伊東の案は「和服」を通して普遍的な場とコミュニケーションを図ろうとするものであるとしたのである。...簡単にいえば、本江たち「普遍派」サイドは、数寄」のコンセプトは単なるオリエンタリズムにすぎないと批判しているわけである。...一方、「数寄」サイドは「数寄」のコンセプトの中にオリエンタリズムを超えた真の他者性の表現を見つけ出し、そこに西欧への迎合ではなく西欧への批判を見出そうとするのである。
As an interesting aside, several years after Kuma wrote this text, Ito became the Director of the Kuma-designed Nagasaki Museum of Art.

9. Isozaki (2006) p. 65.

5.8 Wood joinery at Fujimori's 1997 Nira House.

5.8

Kuma studies the works and writings of the German school.

One notable indication of the international character of Japanese architecture is the relatively high reliance on *katakana* language, words borrowed from the West. Any journal article in the field is peppered with technical terminology borrowed from English and other European languages – *concrete, glass, steel, Vierendeel truss, earth anchor, engineered wood* – and borrowed words from the arts and humanities: *amenity, design, concept, sequence, approach, symmetry, balance, level.* I became aware of this first when listening to lectures in Japanese on Kyoto gardens and suddenly noticing the loss of this borrowed language, the point reinforced when reading Japanese-language texts on religion, both fields more explicitly indigenous and far less international in their word use. Time, the temporal reach of these disciplines, is reflected in the words chosen.

Time plays another role as well. For Fujimori, time uncoils in the act of climbing ladders and swaying on the slender legs of *Takasugian*, the "Too Tall Teahouse." Time is visceral, a four-dimensional aspect of architecture. Kuma adapted videos to his lectures early in order to underscore the rhythm calibrated in his louvers and lines. He pulls the body from light to darkness, occasionally matching falling light to increasingly intimate scale to slow one's steps. Procession and movement, the experience of unfolding a building by walking through it (unable to understand it merely through careful study of plan and geometry), is also seen in the buildings by other architects I discuss in the pages ahead.

Fujimori and Kuma are also attracted to natural materials, and this underscores another way their architectures embrace time. Change is evident in how each occasionally engages the seasons with shag-

5.9 Steel splines in the structure of Kuma's 1996 River/Filter.

5.9

gy building skins of plants that bloom and die. Parts rot and decay. Fujimori experiences the wood he uses as, first, living trees; he cuts them, incorporates them to emphasize their natural forms: barked edges, fragile branches projecting outward, cracks opening in drying planks – all suggest evolving life. He also accepts that materials deteriorate and crumble. In a 2005 book, Fujimori acknowledges:

> How artificial and natural materials relate, make no mistake, that has been a fundamental theme in my work. "Artificial" and "natural" are polar opposites when it comes to maintenance.
>
> Artificial – by which I mean "architecture" – through various tricks, you try to proceed without doing any maintenance. Twentieth-century architecture, particularly Japan's post-war buildings, demand that they be maintenance-free. Concrete is representative, walls and bridges said to last an eternity [literally, "ten thousand years"]. Our thinking has arrived at a point when we expect them to last forever without maintenance. That lie has been out in the open for only the last 20 years, but that is the intention when using technologies like steel, concrete, glass, sealant – even while it is evident that these are not really maintenance-free.
>
> But natural materials weather easily, slowly deteriorate. It is okay that this is their destiny.[10]

For Fujimori, life is engaged; for Kuma, is it represented, nature illustrated not through decomposition, but through intellectual appreciation of origins. Although he has expressed an openness to aging, Kuma tightly conscribes conditions, endeavors to overcome unpredictability. His wood at the 1996 River/Filter was allowed to crack

10. Fujimori *et al*. (2005) p. 197.
Original Japanese:
人工と自然の関係をどうするか、というのが私の仕事の基本的テーマに違いないが、"人工"と"自然"はメンテナンスについては正反対の性格を持つ。
人工, つまり建築は、もともとできるだけメンテナンスをしなくてすむように工夫されてきた。とりわけ20世紀建築、その中でも戦後の日本は"メンテナンスフリー"を謳い文句に揚げてきた。その代表が鉄筋コンクリートで、万年塀とか万年橋の呼び名があったように、永遠にメンテナンスフリーと思われてきた。このウソが暴かれるのはここ20年ほどのことで、より進んだ技術のはずの鉄もコンクリートもガラスもコーキングも、決してメンテナンスフリーなんかじゃないことが明らかになっている。
一方、自然の素材は、もともと風化しやすく、次第に劣化するのが宿命といていい。

5.10 *Fujimori is inclined to embed, as seen here at Soda Pop Spa.*

and cup, but today he relies more often on veneers affixed to plywood or aluminum, the stable industrial materials beneath maintaining form and shape. At the Hiroshige Ando Museum, the architecture exploited a unique infrared technology that stabilized and fire-protects the wooden slats. Kuma blends "low tech natural materials, high tech function," again straddling the line between Fujimori's Red and White.[11] When decrepitude intrudes, as with the inevitable aging of bamboo, Kuma plans for replacement and architectural rejuvenation.

Inevitably, natural materials are often local. Why import woods when so many are available close to home? Fujimori chops down timber minutes from his childhood home, slices slabs at the village sawmill before going to check on mom. But his preference is for plebian woods. Kuma, too, uses familiar timber and locally quarried stone, but he seems to particularly prefer Japanese woods with rich historical connotations, like *paulownia* and *hinoki*. Kuma wants people to recognize a fine-grained, costly wood, to understand it was once limited to important architecture by sumptuary laws, but he also likes exotic, imported woods when he wants to render a surface unusual and unfamiliar.

Both confess to a love for craft, possible because of the slippery way the word is used today. In an unusually precise investigation, Paul Greenhalgh pointed to three ways that the word is used:

> ... craft as we now understand it was largely an invention of the nineteenth and twentieth centuries, and ... this invention comprised three distinct elements. The *politics of work* gave it most of its intellectual structure and all of its ideological power, the *vernacular* gave it its ethnic credibility and its enduring tie to rural and traditional practices

5.10

11. Kuma (2006) p. 72. Original Japanese: ローテクな自然素材でハイテクな機能.

5.11 Aluminum rods are lightly and loosely suspended in the entrance area of Kuma's 2003 One Omotesando.

5.11

> and the decorative arts were the age-old genres which have been collected as "the arts not fine".[12]

Fujimori and Kuma advertise the individual contributions of others; they heed this "politics of work." They collaborate when they fabricate. They search for adept artisans. But Greenhalgh's remaining definitions differ, each illustrated by these designers. Greenhalgh stated that:

> The vernacular refers to the cultural produce of a community... It is as close to nature as a culture can get; the unselfconscious and collective products of a social group, unpolluted by outside influence. It carries the mystique of being the authentic voice of society ... pre-industrial, rural communities.[13]

Fujimori's craft. Greenhalgh continued, "[craft's] attractiveness ... lay in the fact that it stood outside such notions as professionalism, specialization, authorship or academism," again befitting Fujimori, avid amateur. Another author argues, "all craft represents a counter-culture."[14] But these ways of thinking about craft are inappropriate for Kuma, who instead aims for a refinement assessed in production costs and rare materials, areas Greenhalgh assigned to decorative arts.[15]

Fujimori and Kuma are enthusiastic innovators. Fujimori transformed his construction team, introducing amateurs and artists – but because he is untrained as an architect, he inclines towards existing answers in construction and detail.[16] Materials meet based on empiricism and observation. One odd mismatch in his effort to engage others is that the professionals and builders who participate in his work are often surprisingly conservative in their contributions. Kuma, by contrast, relies on close and ongoing collaborations with

12. Greenhalgh (1997) p. 111. This summation is effective, but the full discussion of these points is better seen in another chapter by Greenhalgh in the same book: "The History of Craft," Dormer (1997) pp. 20–52.
13. Ibid., p. 31.
14. Rees, "Patterns of Making: Thinking and Making in Industrial Design," pp. 116–136 in Dormer (1997).
15. Greenhalgh, in Dormer (1997) p. 30.
16. See Fujimori (2006d) p. 16.

5.12 Kuma speaking with the esteemed tea carpenter Yoshiaki Nakamura and Nakamura's son, Kohseki.

5.12

accomplished craftsmen. He challenges them to generate multiple mock-ups suggesting new methods in old materials. He is not only directly designing, but establishing allies in his efforts.

These two approaches to craft result in differing materiality. Fujimori is excessive and inefficient, attested to in fat columns, thick timber planks, and lumpy plaster. As a result, Fujimori's buildings are volumetric. Kuma wants weight, intrigued by the earth, burrowing into or slicing open ground.[17] But he reduces materials to their minimum: paper-thin veneer, unseen structure. In the end, Kuma's architecture is frequently frontal. These two unintentionally illustrate the alternative approaches David Leatherbarrow and Mohsen Mostafavi propose in an essay entitled "Opacity":

> ... the negative consequences of modern building practices [offer] sufficient grounds for proposing a return to thick-wall construction whether in fact or in appearance. This would be accomplished by a return to pre-industrial methods of construction or by the development of the clearest possible distinction between the inner, insignificant and industrialized parts of a building and its outer, figurative and "designed" parts.[18]

Lastly, Fujimori audaciously ignores many expectations applied to architects. He is unaware of economics, unconcerned with the short-term implications of inefficient human labor spent on his structures or the long-term costs of perishability. Fujimori at his most quintessential also shows an offhand disregard for the fundamentals of professionalism; he ignores conventions of life safety in his tiny teahouses. The simple basics of egress – two exits, predictably smooth transitions, large openings, easy-to-use handrails – are anathema to

17. Both architects struggle with stereometry. While reflecting an awareness of weight, neither succeed. Perhaps in Japan, where Shinto traditions are sometimes said to enjoin cutting the earth (and rituals of expiation are still held today), grounded architectures might not come naturally. Yet there are clear historical precedents for weighty works, especially the graceful curve of castle walls and early, Jomon-era pit buildings.
18. Leatherbarrow and Mostafavi (1996) p. 49.

the effect Fujimori intends in making us aware of movement. Instead, he offers tiny, crawl-though apertures and wobbly, handmade ladders. His smallest structures often lack lighting, heat or other mechanical means of creating daily comfort. He is little interested. Fujimori's architecture is an art; this incompatibility with the norms of the profession is inherent in the most radical architects he calls Reds.

Kuma oversees a large office; his practice ranges from ephemeral, experimental structures to major institutions serving tens of thousands of people annually. The tiny teahouses he sometimes designs are innovative and often very expensive, not unlike Fujimori's – but they are anomalies. Economics is at the heart of keeping the office underway. Kuma is concerned for his clients, concerned about comfort. Visiting a teahouse he recently brought to Kyoto, I found workers meticulously installing an invisible array of electric lines, plumbing, and heat – updated amenities. His architecture, excepting the most artful, accommodates anyone, blind or sighted, in wheelchairs or freely mobile, even in the most disastrous events. Kuma's office is embedded in the profession.

Thus, while Fujimori can rely on artists and willing amateurs to achieve his architectural effect, Kuma cannot. Concerned for costs and construction schedules, Kuma collaborates with established craftsmen who know and understand the field of construction. Fujimori works one piece at a time, each personal; even his openness to humor is a reflection of his amateur outlook, free to risk causing misunderstanding or offense through seemingly small jokes. Kuma's clients, governments and institutions responsible for cultural heritage, insist his work be far more circumspect.

This inclination to the personal, handmade and homely, is not something that can be separated from the deepest shades of Fujimori's Red School, at its heart more than merely a cruder, weedier body of work. It is easy to dismiss the most oddball architects as ignoring many of the practical demands placed on architecture today – but Fujimori's conception of a Red School of radicals emerges from the fact that they revive in architecture things that were lost as practice became professional. Victoria Meyers eloquently argued in an essay in the *Journal of Architectural Education*, "If architecture is an analogue for human memory, we might well wonder what contemporary minimalist space refers to human memory today. As a reflection of contemporary life, perhaps it communicates that we are losing access to memory ..."[19] Through an openness to history and place, to ritual and humor, Fujimori's Red School offers an architecture that, in its opposition, may perhaps reinvigorate Japanese practice today. Kuma and his work illustrate adaptations. Other architects, offering alternative approaches, are introduced in the pages ahead.

19. Meyers (1999) p. 92.

Radical Reds

Looking Back at Japan's Radical Reds

Team Zoo, Osamu Ishiyama, Kazuhiro Ishii, Itsuko Hasegawa, Hiroshi Naito

6

ARCHITECTURE, AMAZEMENT, AMBIGUITY, AMBIVALENCE, AMITABHA
BLOOD spouting – BANG!!
Manifestation of CRACK – that is architecture
DIGNITY DIVERSITY
EARTH covered with numerous cracks, EMBARRASSMENT
FEMININE and masculine
GRACEFUL GRAVITY
HEART HEAT HUMOR HEAVEN HELL
INTELLIGENCE IMAGINATION IMITATION
JOY JAIL JUMP
KALEIDOSCOPE
LIGHT and shadow organize architecture
MOUNTAIN MIMICRY
form should not seek after NOVELTY
ORDER – we are searching for.
PRAY PLAY
QUADRILLION
RED REPETITION RAINBOW
SKY SEA SCIENCE
TIME and TIDE wait for no man.
UNIVERSE is packed in architecture
VAST VERNACULAR VOID VIRTUE VIOLENCE
WIND
XEROGRAPHY XYLOGRAPH XEROX
YOGA YES
ZODIAC ZIGZAG ZOETROPE ZOMBIE

–ZOO[1]

6.1 Team Zoo's 1981 Nago City Hall, decorated with a pride of oddball lion-like shishi.

Team Zoo

When I first visited Jinchokan Moriya Museum, Fujimori stood under a blooming crepe myrtle and recounted his interest in Le Corbusier's disciple Takamasa Yoshizaka and a group of Yoshizaka's disciples, a band of collaborating offices all named after animals. In 2007, Fujimori again reflected on the group:

> ... the fact is that if Tomita and the others kept doing what they did at Nago City Hall after that, I probably would not have done anything. If she and the others had fully carried out [what began at] Nago City Hall, well, there would have been no necessity for me to do any architectural design.[2]

In 1971, Waseda graduates Koichi Otake and Hiroyasu Higuchi ventured to Okinawa at Yoshizaka's recommendation, joined by Reiko Tomita, who came to Yoshizaka after studying under Kenzo Tange at the University of Tokyo. At the time, Okinawa was impoverished, viewed in Japan as a foreign territory; it was under U.S. occupation until 1972.

Yoshizaka punningly collapsed the words for walking (*aruku*) and "architect," calling himself an "*arukitekuto*."[3] One manifesto-like missive from Atelier *Zo*, founded by the three younger architects, announced, "We walk around the village, survey the landscape, observe how people are living and investigate the local history. In this way we eventually uncover clues or keys for expressing the locality in our designs."[4] Culture is not in the elite arts for Team Zoo; it is in an extremely local version of Joe-Six-Pack society, unearthed in the banal moments of everyday existence. Yet, in truth, these architects have always been at their best when far from home – in slightly exotic

1. Atelier *Zo* (1985) p. 7. Emphasis added to underscore alphabetic structure; to my knowledge, no Japanese version of this list exists. An early and slightly different form of this manifesto is found in Frampton (1978) p. 97 – which raises the interesting point that Frampton never addressed whether this collective might better fit the outlines of his theories of Critical Regionalism.

2. Interview, Tokyo (4 June, 2007). Original Japanese: ちょっと残念だけど、ね、確か、ね、もし，名護市庁舎、あの用のこと、ね、ずうっとう富田さん達がやっていたら、僕やること無かったかも知れないね．名護市一杯あればね、僕、建築設計する必要がなかった。。。

3. Kuba (2007) p. 16.

4. Available at: http://www.zoz.co.jp/ (accessed 6 July, 2008).

6.2

6.2 *The "green" roof of city hall, planted with grass.*

6.3 *Corridors are designed to catch breezes.*

6.3

locales like Okinawa or Taiwan, where they are perhaps more fully inspired to investigate everything, no matter how mundane.

For more than a decade in Okinawa, these young designers produced modest master plans and simple architectural schemes for community groups and children, lightheartedly dubbing themselves Atelier *Zo* (Elephant). Kazuhiro Ishii, an architect and author, offered a sweeping appraisal of the group, asserting *Zo* favored,

> ...the masses, rather than capitalists; medium to triflingly tiny manufacturers instead of large industry; Asia over Western Europe. I do not know, but perhaps by chance they reflect the future, close to the day of a fight against the "White Australia Policy," racial problems in South Asia, the difficulty of rescuing refugees. They are Asiacentric.[5]

Joined by Kinya Maruyama's Atelier *Mobile* (Running Bird), they launched the larger entity called Team Zoo, bursting on the professional scene by winning a 1979 competition for new city offices in Nago, a town of 46,000 midway along Okinawa's western shore, a town Atelier *Zo* knew well from earlier projects. The group had, in fact, done the master planning for Nago City Hall and the area – but had to fight for the commission in the first open competition held in Japan in ten years. Still, in the end, Team Zoo was selected from 300 entries.[6] The sympathetic jury included Fumihiko Maki and Kiyoshi Seike, an architect who penned an enduring book on Japan's traditional timber joinery and, in his own residential work, combined *tatami* with steel shipping containers.

Artist Keiji Usami declared of the alliance of animal-named ateliers, "Their work is a mixture of the achievements of Modernism and the things it cast aside in the process of pursuing abstraction and universalism ..."[7] Team Zoo itself asserted, "Modern architectural spaces have abandoned decoration, allegory and individuality,"[8] and repositioned Le Corbusier (who was, after all, their mentor's mentor) by quoting him as saying: "Make houses of wood and stone and with grass roofs. This is architecture ... I am glad to say 'This is beautiful.' Here is where art comes in."[9]

Critic Hiroshi Watanabe proposed that, "What the team members seem to abhor most of all is consistency, at least consistency of any stylistic form. Their works are exuberant, sometimes to the point of being boisterous and unconventional, sometimes to the point of being grotesque."[10] Team Zoo's ateliers – at least a dozen separate studios, practicing as planners, architects and interior designers – are surprisingly varied. Some, like Maruyama's Atelier *Mobile*, today tend to express ornament over established vernacular, or topographical undulations inspired by the earth. Others, like Tsutomo Shigemura and Keiko Arimura's Kobe-based Atelier *Iruka* (Dolphin), are almost academic in their use of the vernacular, incorporating white plaster walls and gunmetal grey glazed roof tiles. Deliberately alluding to Christian Norberg-Schultz, Shigemura wrote, "... we wanted to continue the tradition of nameable objects, materials, and craftsmen's techniques, which have a deep meaning ..."[11]

The proposal for Nago City Hall was an antithesis to other architecture of the time. Most of Japan was enamored with technology, but Yoshizaka's disciples proferred a primitive, passively cooled structure that was far from institutional: wind corridors channeled sea breezes through open offices; grass topped the building. There were pocket-like *tatami* platforms seeded throughout the interior to encourage lazy intervals like a game of *go*. A lattice of concrete block tangled

5. Ishii (1982) p. 215. Original Japanese: それは資本家より一般大衆であり、大企業よりは中小零細企業であり、そして西欧人より亜細亜人である。ひょっとすると将来彼らが白豪主義や、南アの人種問題、難民救済問題などと闘う日も近いのかも知れない。亜細亜主義者なのだ。.
6. Hara (1982) p. 5.
7. Usami (1985) p. 95.
8. Toh (1978) p. 53.
9. Atelier Zo (1993) p. 139. No citation of the original source is included.
10. Watanabe and Emanuel (1994), s.v. "Team Zoo" p. 946.
11. Shigemura (1991) p. 51.

6.4

6.5

6.4-6 *Each of the lions were made individually.*

with blazing pink bougainvillea-shaded breezeways and broad patios – and while concrete block might seem unremarkable, its implications are underscored in a 1982 description of Team Zoo's work, a Japanese journal explicitly noting block as "a material introduced by the American military ..."[12] Nago City Hall was far away from the gung-ho, go-go attitude driving much of Japan, Team Zoo's structure underscoring Okinawa as a still-languid tropical outpost only recently occupied by a foreign force, and its architects as equally unusual.

Patrice Goulet once wrote that Team Zoo's "... buildings can appear so normal to some, so traditional even, ... so vulgar to others."[13] There were odd ornamental accretions along the building's formal face: 56 pairs of guardian *shiisa*, a talismanic creature combining aspects of lions and dogs.[14] Made by numerous craftsmen, the collection was ostentatiously diverse, many twosomes engagingly inept. Team Zoo professed a desire to concentrate on community structures, but founder Hiroyasu Higuchi complained, "... these large [government] authorities give us a hard time ..."[15] Understandable, perhaps, that these stodgy bureaucrats were not wholly sympathetic; Goulet reflected:

> The way in which they work, the notions they rely on, the objectives they pursue, the buildings that they build are always different from the majority of architects' work in Japan and elsewhere.
>
> Their taste for life, their absolute lack of respect for rules, the pleasure they take ... their affection for craftsmen, their enthusiasm for teamwork, ... their respect for tradition, ... their humor and gaiety all serve to reinforce their eccentricity.[16]

Led by Higuchi and Tomita, Atelier *Zo* is invariably the heart of the collective called Team Zoo. The Atelier *Zo* website lists seven central principles: expressing place, understanding building use, diversity, sensory and emotional experience, enhancing and enjoying nature, "*aimaimoko*" (something unlimited and ambiguous), and, finally, that building should be "exertive," of which they say,

> We favor: a bunch of people rather than machines; human wisdom rather than knowledge; continuity rather than speed; passion and zeal rather than reason; excessiveness rather than adequacy; extranorm [*sic*] rather than the norm; endless questions rather than a conclusion.[17]

Many may think Team Zoo is disinclined to theory, ignoring intellectual threads in the loose weave of its work. They quote foreign philosophy, cite science, and, in one of their most successful projects, the 1986 Yoga Promenade in Tokyo's Setagaya Ward, employ pavers produced by the photographer-turned-tile-craftsman Shuuji Yamada, stamped with French verse and Japanese *haiku*. Characteristically, the bookish rhymes are undercut by the ridiculous moment when an unexpected explosion of water knocks over a squealing child in nearby pools. That, in a nutshell, is Team Zoo.

Writing on a "toilet park" by the group – for a lavish Japanese architecture journal, no less – Richard Weston declared, "'The beautiful arts', the American critic and planning theorist Paul Goodman has written, 'are made of cheap stuff, of mud and speech, humming and drumming, daylight and rock, available to anybody'."[18] Mud, it seems, is especially important to these architects, Higuchi arguing: "Earth is our most common and familiar resource."[19] Rammed earth, sprouting soil, plaster in every imaginable color and texture, softly rounded stones of red brick, gaudy tile mosaics and those almost-ubiquitous

6.6

12. Team Zoo and Atelier Mobile (1982) p. 10.
13. Goulet (1991) p. 22.
14. These are called both "shisa" and "shiisa" when discussed in English. The second is a more accurate rending of native pronunciation.
15. Higuchi and Miyake (1993) p. 73.
16. Goulet (1991) p. 24.
17. Available at:: http://www.zoz.co.jp/ (accessed 6 July, 2008. An earlier version of these can also be found in Kenchiku Bunka 建築文化 [Architecture Culture] vol. 48, no. 564 "Aimaimoko" あいまいもく [Ambiguity] (October 1993) pp. 24–37.
18. Weston (1993) p. 189.
19. Higuchi and Kusumi (1993) p. 94.

6.7

6.8

6.9

6.10

6.7–10 Handmade kawara tile pavers sport poetry and slip-resistant textures; inside a fountain there are bits of brick, tumbled to resemble river rock, all at the 1986 Yoga Promenade.

6.11 *The path of Yoga Promenade.*

roof tiles, some shaped like demons – even concrete, pocked with expressive rock; all are found in Team Zoo architecture, finishes worked by the architects' own hands, their own ungainly effort. Higuchi recalled, "There is an old man in Mawaki who helped us; he has a tunnel-shaped kiln. He doesn't attend to the firing process meticulously ... So his products are not standardized; the color and strength vary ..."[20] And that suits them fine. Maruyama argued, "Perfect things sometimes seem unapproachable. There's warmth and beauty in foolish or broken things."[21]

In 1993, two years after Akasegawa nicknamed Fujimori "Neolithic Daddy," the esteemed critic Riichi Miyake said of Atelier *Zo*:

> Their sensitivity reminds us of "Jomon" people in [the] Japanese prehistorical period, who spent their life ... hunting and fishing, beyond the limits of the hierarchy ... Jomon people can move wherever they want, and create certain dynamism full fo [*sic*] aggressiveness and mobility in spite of low productivity.
>
> Atelier Zo alludes to the image of [an] already-lost-homeland.[22]

Team Zoo's intentions, far more than its odd names and varied architectural output, were important as Fujimori framed the outlines of the Red School. Their plebian playfulness and their lavish love of mundane materials like mud were clearly carried over. Fujimori also learned from these ateliers that small buildings based on big ideas had an outsized influence on others. The group was the most ostentatiously open to incomplete architecture, the most exuberant, the best known abroad for their unusual attitude. But there were others as well, eccentric designers who influenced the framing of Fujimori's philosophies. I introduce a few of them in this chapter.

6.11

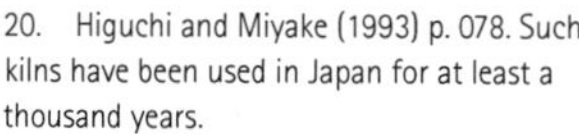

20. Higuchi and Miyake (1993) p. 078. Such kilns have been used in Japan for at least a thousand years.

21. Kuba (2007) p. 16.

22. Miyake (1993) p. 127. The Japanese text is a somewhat lengthier explication; see pp. 126–127 of the same volume.

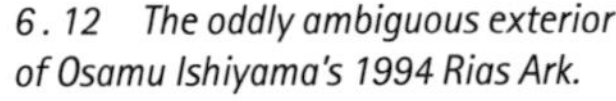
6.12 The oddly ambiguous exterior of Osamu Ishiyama's 1994 Rias Ark.

6.12

Osamu Ishiyama

Tradition is something that rises in the consciousness only when it is about to be forgotten.—Isamu Kurita[23]

When Toyo Ito acknowledged a reinvigorated Red School while sitting on the sod roof of Fujimori's house, the three others in the group were radical Reds: Fujimori himself, Waseda Professor Osamu Ishiyama, and Kazuhiro Ishii.[24] Ishiyama and Ishii are on every loose listing that Fujimori offers of this school. Disparate as these other three designers are, Ito, Ishii and Ishiyama also worked together once, on the 1991 "Visions of Japan" exhibition organized by Arata Isozaki at the Victoria and Albert Museum in London. Ito's liquid-crystal-lined psychedelic space entitled "Dreams of Japan" is by far best known now, but Osamu Ishiyama and Kazuhiro Ishii also arranged interiors. Ishii's included a pair of elaborate pillar-and-bracket pieces, one weirdly assembling and disassembling itself, and a Japanese hearse, capped, as they conventionally are, with an intricately carved timber top; he crashed the hearse into a wall to complete the installation. In this setting, Ishiyama was almost understated, his interior organized around a comic replica of a well-known Tokyo temple gate, its allegorical guardian a "beckoning kitty" abutted by brightly lit vending machines, Godzilla rising above the happy chaos, his cry heard throughout the galleries.

Ishiyama is a tough critic of convention, once complaining, "Today's architectural style has become boring. Smooth, sparkling ... high tech skyscrapers, things calculated to the millimeter, architecture that looks cheap. That is what is being built now, all you see is dull stuff."[25] For both Fujimori and Ishiyama, their architecture is instead oddly angular. Ishiyama's "Open Tech" is a sort of Whole Earth hippie-ish Hi-Tech: canting wood columns or open-web steel trusses almost invariably expressed, interiors chock full of improvised industrial artifacts, exteriors capped with gyrating gizmos, a sense of ongoing stabs at construction, capricious stops and starts. Ishiyama is ostentatiously in love with Akihabara, an area in Tokyo that attracts old audio geeks and kids scavenging parts for cobbling computers; these days Akihabara's obsessive *otaku* reenact anime, hooking up with cos-play cuties suited up as come-to-life cartoon characters. Ishiyama argues impish employ of sophisticated technologies is a typically Asian appropriation – and who can counter this, with robot puppies recently the rage? The Waseda professor is less interested in the eventual elegance of the objects he engenders than in the fun of fabrication: in a 2008 book, he included his House for a Pioneer – still unfinished after nearly thirty years, and, according to Ishiyama, now happily veering away from his original design.[26] His kit-of-parts approach emerged in the era shortly after Archigram, but is more unpretentious – and more comprehensive, including ancient craft along with corrugated steel and computer-driven customization.

Far earlier than Fujimori, Ishiyama also argued "... anyone can build houses."[27] He acknowledged, "I was born in 1944, and in my youth there were still self-built remnants left in towns and villages like ancient ruins ... my trips to self-built works are a kind of sentimental nostalgia."[28] He authors popular books and magazine articles promoting visits to oddball firetraps improvised by amateurs.

In spite of his position as a professor in the architecture department of one of the nation's leading private universities, Waseda

23. Kurita (1983) p. 132.

24. Interestingly, today Ito suggests that his own position is increasingly equivocal; he recently wrote of this day, 'At that time, I was said to be 'White School'..." [Original Japanese: 当時, 白派と言われていた私。。。]. My emphasis. See Ito (2007) p. 55.

25. Ishiyama (1986) p. 23. Original Japanese: 今風な建築のスタイルはつまらないものになった。ツルツル、ピカピカな、つまりハイテクな超高層ビルや、きちんと隅々まで計算しつくされ、デザインされたビルディンが俗っぽいものとして眼に映りはじめている。それが今風にたてられていればいるほどに、つまらないものに見えてしまう。

26. Ishiyama (2008a), pp. 50–55.

27. Knabe and Noennig (1999) p. 133.

28. Ishiyama (2008a), p. 105. Original Japanese:
一九四四年生まれの私の少年期、町や村にはまだセルフビルドの残滓(さんじ)
が遺跡のように残っていた。... それではセルフビルドへの旅はセチメンタルな郷愁なのだろうか。

6.13

6.14

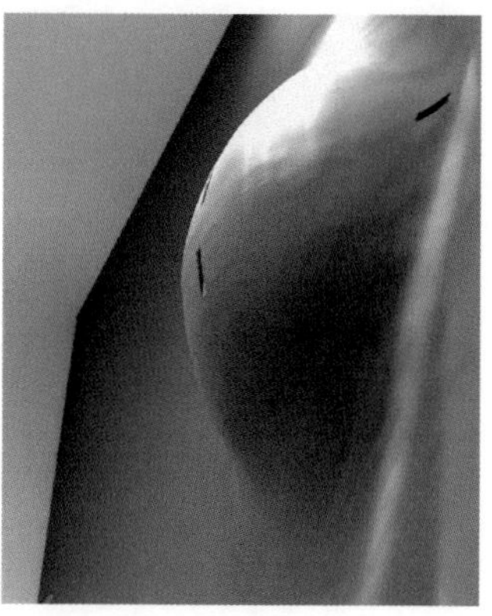

6.15

6.13, 14 In a community known for its fishing, Ishiyama suggested new ages of exploration in his odd embellishments on the roof.

6.15 A bulge, inspired by shipbuilding.

6.16 Ishiyama's 1984 Izu Chohachi Museum was ultimately a critical influence on Fujimori.

University, Ishiyama predicts the eventual obsolescence of the profession and its pomposity. He is okay with unimposing projects: when once asked to make a museum, he started by simply placing cartoonish coin collection boxes along a pier in the small town, an effort to engage. Ishiyama avidly invents ephemera – cardboard emergency toilets, flashy parade floats, inflatables, events. It is hard to say what you might call his signature style when he is often unconcerned with building anything – and when he does, Ishiyama, like his predecessor at Waseda, Takamasa Yoshizaka, adapts to the immediate environment he finds, with uneven and unexpected architectural outcomes.

Ishiyama's early masterpiece, the 1975 Fantasy Villa (Gen-An), is an odd construction of corrugated culvert and colored glass; German critic Manfried Spiedel asserted it is one of a set of "sheet-metal huts [which] approximated a wabi-aesthetic."[29] Even so, I saw rust, but no relation to Fujimori's Red; the forms did not seem to fit. Even more contradictory was Rias Ark, wrapped in duraluminum panels pinned by titanium rivets from a jet-fighter production plant, two pink sci-fi spaceships perched upon its roof; shipbuilders produced a sensual, pregnant bulge on the surface of the building, its only role as a memorable ornamental fragment.

Ishiyama proffers fictions: tales of Dracula, death and sailing ships.[30] He designed a residence around a raccoon, and a structure said to be swallowing a boulder. Something, a sense of private mysteries as acceptable to evoke, is evident in both Fujimori's and Ishiyama's architecture. Ishiyama's "Works for Minorities" seem unusually solicitous for Japan; one allowed anyone in a wheelchair to float in the forest.

Ishiyama's are experiential environments; his 2001 Helen Keller Tower, a library for the blind, is dark inside, where footsteps crunch across a bed of gravel; its exterior is dressed in bells and singing strings. He described it, ironically entitled "Tower of Silence," as:

> Thousands of different sounds ... perfo[r]med depending on the vagaries of the breeze. The fine wires attached to the corners ... resonate with a consummate music and the edges of the aluminum panels on the surface will produce fine sounds. Both snow and ice will adhere to the tower and sometimes, clothed in ice, it will undoubtedly play a rousing symphony in the blizzard.
>
> On rainy days, both inside and out, the tower will perform an amazing watery quartet. The guttering on the inside and outside of the tower is designed in a complex configuration so that people can enjoy the sound of the water as it flows down in small waterfalls.[31]

It was not the form of Ishiyama's architecture that most influenced Fujimori, but, again, Ishiyama's ideas. Ishiyama even earlier evoked the unpretentious places of the early tea masters; he assumed that a raw energy lent built works authenticity; he argued that the walls between architects and everyone else were better razed. Yet in Ishiyama's architecture there is one clear influence on Fujimori, a collection of structures in the town of Matsuzaki, dating from a decade or so starting in the early 1980s.[32] Ishiyama said of the site:

> This town is the "Commonwealth of Craft," you might call it a secret place. It is not well known that they are beginning to build a wonderful garden ... When you go off to the

29. Spiedel (1991) p. 30.

30. Parts of this section were first presented in a paper I gave, "The Influential Outsider: Two Examples from Japan," Association of Architectural Historians, London (April, 2003).

31. Ishiyama, Osamu. Translated by Bruce Holcombe. "Tower of Silence" described on his website as "published in cooperation with the Japan Finland Design Association," April, 2001. Available at: http://ishiyama.arch.waseda.ac.jp/www/en/tokachi.html (accessed 13 February, 2008).

32. Ishiyama's daughter marvels that even today, "... it's been about 30 years ... but people from the town still come to [him] to design something really small." E-mail from Tomomi Ishiyama, received 12 July, 2008.

6.17

6.18

6.17–21 The Chohachi Museum was designed to incorporate craft, while the 1997 Annex, also by Ishiyama, is made of curtain wall and concrete.

6.19

6.20

6.21

6.22 *A 1984 clock tower in Matsuzaki, also by Ishiyama.*

6.22

> commonwealth, you have to complete formalities.
>
> ... I am not talking about a passport or a visa. To go to this commonwealth, you must prepare your heart. Adults or children, uncles and aunts, in the deepest corner of each heart they have a feeling ...[33]

Ishiyama designed a number of small but significant structures for the town, starting with a museum celebrating the skills of an Edo-era plasterer called Chohachi, and quickly following with:

> Three bridges cross the Nakagawa River, the large Tokiwa Bridge, Hamacho Bridge, and the Shinshima Bridge, respectively [representing] the present, the past, and the future. At the foot of the Tokiwa Bridge is built a clock tower. Its style is contrived from various symbols of the town of Matsuzaki. It also strikes the hour of 25 ... that is, it tells a time that does not exist. Then the clock "bongs" 13 times ...[34]

In his Matsuzaki buildings and the books he has written about them, Ishiyama was open to a kind of rejigged reminiscence, recently insisting, "Everyone has nostalgia. It is something very important you cannot dismiss ... I think it is necessary to explore the structure of nostalgia more thoroughly."[35] In each project in the town, Ishiyama strained to prop up Matsuzaki's uniqueness as a place, goaded by a politician (once a member of the avant-garde art troupe called Gutai) who wanted this architecture to be at once richly local and yet so up-to-date and global it might be exhibited in New York's Museum of Modern Art.[36]

Undoubtedly, Ishiyama's initial effort in Matsuzaki, the museum for Chohachi, set the tone for subsequent structures. Two of the nations' finest plaster craftsmen completed the curving walls flanking its front entrance, a form they demanded for its difficulty. Hiroshi Watanabe wrote:

> As with other traditional crafts, plastering is dying out in Japan. The Chohachi Museum has been likened by town residents to a giant white bird, and that seems apt, for this structure is a swan song for a building art. Yet the museum and other projects being carried out in the town are by no means elegiac. Instead, they have the innocence and high spiritedness we associate with an earlier era.[37]

Ishiyama himself argues:

> Because they came from throughout Japan, men of the wet trades, plasterers who used the palms of their hands to lay plaster on these walls, the white of the walls has a strange charm is exquisite. Dry goods from a factory have a whiteness of a different complexity. It is the flow of time, a oneness with nature. That wall will age over the years like human skin. It will absorb hardship, stains will rise to the surface, wrinkles spread, the months and years accumulating. But it will also sparkle wonderfully. After finishing the museum, ... I started to help with the townscape. My friendships increased, acquaintances became dense.[38]

Ishiyama connects with craftsmen, encrusting the Chohachi Museum in riotous reliefs, in the end even accepting the result is often kitsch. Ishiyama is William Morris' enduring acolyte, not Fujimori, the former concluding a recent essay on the Englishman, "The fact that we must learn from William Morris is, at this moment, huge."[39] Unlike Fujimori's abiding artist allies in ROJO and the *Jomon* Company, Ishiyama seems to be always searching for new alliances with artisans

33. Ishiyama (1986) p. 10. Original Japanese: …この町が職人たちの共和国、つまり言ってしまえば秘密の花園でもあり、彼らが不思議な空中庭園をつくりはじめていることはあんまり知られていない。この共和国にでかけるのにはそれなりの手続きが必要だからだ。手続きと言っても、パスポートやビザがいるわけではない。この共和国に行くのにはある種の感覚を用意しなくてはならないのだ。…大人でも、子どもでも、おじいさん、おばあさんでも、みんなが胸の奥深くに持っている感覚だ。

34. Ishiyama (1987) pp. 106–107. Original Japanese: 那賀川に架かる三つの橋、ときわ大橋、浜丁橋、新島橋は、それぞれに現在[written above in *futagana* as "いま"]、過去[written above in *futagana* as "むかし"]、未来[written above in *futagana* as "これから"]を見立てている。ときわ大橋のたもとには、時計塔が建てられる。この時計塔のスタイルが、松崎町につくられつつあるさまざまな仕掛けを象徴している。この時計塔は、２５時を打つことがある。２５時、つまりありえない時間を刻むのだ。時間が１３のボンを打つ時それぞれの橋から河面を見おろせば、そこには不思議な町の不思議な光景が写し出されていると言う。

35. Ishiyama, Osamu by Mie Moriyasu (2008b) p. 160.

36. Ishiyama (1999) p. 151.

37. Watanabe (1991) p. 27.

38. Ishiyama (1987) p. 107. Original Japanese: 日本中から集まってくれた水の職人でもある左官職たちが手のひらで塗り込めてくれた壁だから、この壁の白さは精妙なものだ。工場でつくられてくる乾式な部品としての白さとは違う複雑さをもっている。それは時の流れとともに歴然とする。この壁は人間の皮膚のように歳を取ってゆく。辛酸をなめ、しみを浮き出させ、しわを刻みながら、年月を積み重ねる。しかも細妙に輝く。美術館完成後、町づくりのお手伝いをするようになった。知り合いの数も増え，付き合いも濃いものになっていった。

39. Ishiyama (1999) p. 37. Original Japanese: ウィリアム・モリスから学ばねばならぬことは今だからこそ大きい。

6.23, 24 The two major volumes of Kazuhiro Ishii's 1992 Seiwa Puppet Museum, unusual shapes rendered in familiar vernacular materials.

or investigating emerging areas of industry.

Fujimori spoke at a symposium celebrating the Chohachi Museum's completion, sharing the stage with two almost-silent plasterers. He compared Ishiyama's architecture there to Sutemi Horiguchi's exquisite, early structure called Shienso (which has also influenced others discussed in this book).[40] Fujimori, active at the time only as an architectural historian, acknowledged:

> The truth is that until now – in our world [of architecture] – there has not been much careful thought given to the work of plasterers. No thought was given to it. It's a particularly distant world; somehow a plasterer comes and does his thing, goes away without us paying it much attention. Compare that to carpentry, discussed until you are sick of it ...[41]

One of the closed-mouthed craftsmen sharing the stage simply stated in response, "If there were no plasterers, it would not be possible to make a traditional plaster wall."[42]

Ishiyama was not just looking to the past in plaster; his avid interest in Akihabara was also entwined in Matsuzaki's museum.
He argued:

> Raw industrial materials, rough natural resources. That is now the struggle on the stage of this small town. Steel and soil. Aluminum and timber. The white of plaster and the white of paint. They meet in the scenery of the town, they melt together, each one starting its own song.[43]

And yet, unlike his other architecture, here the past and place are allowed to have the upper hand.

Of all the architects I discuss, only Ishiyama boldly has taken on town planning, *machizukuri*, the romantic regionalism far more pervasive than Fujimori's Red. Hiroshi Watanabe once wisely wrote:

> Like a person, a town must construct an identity or risk having it constructed by others. Over the last twenty years, municipalities all over Japan have felt the need to create ... distinctive images for themselves ... when traditions are in short supply, enterprising towns ... have been known to invent them.[44]

Ishiyama openly acknowledged that here history was flaunted like a brand, used to tempt tourists to the town – yet he designed each element so that it would also charm a child. His position was exceedingly unpopular in the architectural press, but in the town of Matsuzaki and among his artisan allies, there was deep appreciation for his architecture – and for his effort to acknowledge that where they lived was also loved, the tales of their tiny town no less important to the elite architecture professor.

Fujimori discovered the charm in an architecture of open naïveté. His child-like sketches, long-legged teahouses and goofy façade faces all, in the end, owe much to Ishiyama.

40. Parts of this symposium are excerpted in Ishiyama (1986) pp. 39–63.

41. Ibid., p. 52.

42. Ibid. Original Japanese: 「左官がいなければ, 日本の伝統建築の壁はできないはずですが....

43. Ibid., p. 182. Original Japanese: 工業化された素材と自然の素材。これがいま、小さな町を舞台にしてせめぎ合っている。鉄と土。アルミと木。漆喰の白とペンキの色。それが町の風景の中でぶつかりあったり、融けあったりでさまざまに唄いはじめている。

44. Watanabe (1991) p. 22.

6.23

6.24

Kazuhiro Ishii

> *... tradition is not the past, but is a creative, active, protean and formative principle of the present.*—John Clammer[45]

In the late 1990s, Osamu Ishiyama opined, "The nearest architect to me is ... Ishii ... All the others are rather strange to me."[46] Kazuhiro Ishii often toiled for tiny towns in far-flung corners of Japan, also often facing approbation from architectural elites for his efforts. His best-known work remains a small performance site for the 400-year-old practice of puppet theater called *bunraku*, located in a village in southern Japan, built under a rural outreach program spearheaded by Arata Isozaki and then-governor Morihiro Hosokawa (who later commissioned a teahouse by Fujimori, One Night Stand). Architect and critic Thomas Daniell wrote: "... Ishii's Seiwa Bunraku Puppet Theatre (completed in 1992, as part of the Kumamoto Artpolis program ...) was the first wooden public building in Kumamoto Prefecture since the war, and at the time an almost illegal act. ... construction was begun without seeking the necessary permission from the national building authorities in Tokyo."[47] Ishii believed the building was key to changing codes: after 2000, individual prefectures were allowed to set their own local building laws, and wooden architecture was on the rise. Ishii asserted, "I use the old vocabulary to keep the old towns alive."[48]

At Seiwa, Ishii employed plaster finishes and traditional *kawara* roof tiles over a structure he described as "based on the temples and shrines of Nara ... learned from the techniques established by the Buddhist monk Chogen ..."[49] – but in spite of its ancient inspiration, the result is not one but two innovative organizations of overlapping beams; one round, the other square, both ponderous and precarious.[50] Ishii argued, "*Bunraku* stages tragedies [dealing with feudalism, money and love], so a light ceiling structure would be unsuitable. Rather, the ceiling should be heavy."[51] The structure was particularly striking because its innovation emerged from an untutored approach. As Ishii related:

> Once in a while someone asks me, "Did you learn about wood construction in school?" The fact is, lately schools teach professional topics like steel or concrete construction, but almost never teach how to build in wood. At most, they teach various wood joints, that's all.
>
> And when I answer that way, people ask me to tell them where I learned to build in wood. And I say: "Truthfully? *Waribashi,* cheap chopsticks."[52]

Ishii later jocularly referred to himself as "*Waribashi* Chogen," claiming links to both those cheap chopsticks and the twelfth-century monk credited with introducing transformative construction techniques at Todai-ji Temple.[53] Obviously, Ishii's early education encompassed basic structural concepts, but he put it to innovative use, applied to an ancient material. Almost instantly, these buildings received international acclaim.

Ishii recalled,

> On the day of the topping off ceremony [for the Seiwa Puppet Theater], about half the village leaders wrote their names on the back of the ridge beam ... First the mayor and then all of us climbed up into the heights of the structure. The mayor said, "I'd like to offer a message ..." and stopped,

45. Clammer (1995) p. 122.
46. Knabe and Noennig (1999) p. 128.
47. Daniell (2000) p. 58-63. It is likely that these advances will be rolled back in light of more recent construction scandals. Ishii also relates this story in his book Kenchiku no Chikyuugaku 建築の地球学 a.k.a. The Geocosmology of Architecture (1997) on page 290.
48. Buck (1997a) p. 18.
49. Ishii (1994b) p. 45.
50. Gutdeutsch (1996) p. 83. Ishii elsewhere also credits that the temple and shrine carpenter Akio Takigawa 滝川昭雄, who built the bracketed column for the "Visions of Japan" exhibition, with advice on the Seiwa Puppet Theater.
51. Ishii (1997) p. 288. Original Japanese: 「文楽では悲劇を演じるので軽い感じのものは似合わない。
52. Ibid., p. 290. Original Japanese: 木造は学校で学んだのか、ということを時々聞かれる。ところが、最近の学校では鉄骨造、コンクリート造は専門的に教えるが、木造はほとんど教えない。木の継ぎ手のいろいろを、教養的に教えてくれるのが関の山だ。
それならばいったい私はどこで木造を学んだのだろうと教える。それは実は割り箸なのだ。
53. Ibid., p. 291.

6.26

6.25 This rounded shape is rare in Japan and more likely an allusion to Chinese temples, although Ishii never clearly made this connection.

6.26 Each volume is independently expressed, giving the complex the character of a village.

6.27 Chuta Ito's 1935 Yushima Seido, in an unusual Confucian style.

6.27

> and a great number of the village people collected below, so I figured he would speak to them. But the fact is that his message was directed at "the gods of the mountains." And then I thought, "Well, after all, of course." ... In the mayor's speech, he asked the mountain gods to preserve the life forces of the architecture for three millennium.[54]

In the early years after its construction, the theater drew 10,000 people a month to Seiwa, which had a population of only 4,000. Performances, earlier offered twice monthly, were for a while held 30 times each month.[55] Again and again in Japan, clients are tempted to turn these architectural successes into commercial opportunities. Ryoji Suzuki's remarkable religious buildings at Kotohira Shrine, which I discuss later in this book, were followed by a commission for a posh marble-clad café and restaurant placed lower on the slope, pompously offered as an outpost of Tokyo's upscale Ginza shopping streets. At Seiwa, Ishii was commissioned to follow his theater with a building to sell local produce. Its brief and budget were far less grand than that of the original structures. Ishii, though, responded by reaching farther for his inspiration:

> It is called the Seiwa Municipal Products Center. An image of China and an image of Japan are most strongly established, of course, in the square form of the traditional hall. It is true there are differences in things like the depth of the eaves, but basically, this is Chinese ... You see the *Bunraku* Theater and the Products Center placed in a line and you think "This is Asia." Other countries wrap China like a ring, in a form that reflects cultural links. The features of Asia become [this] scenery through straightforward modernization, the form modern, non-Western, with new possibilities. I think this is a situation of global modernism.
>
> History is entering a new era, the new Asia gropes towards cooperation. Suddenly, I understood who I was designing my architecture for. Who would see it? Who would listen? It was Asians, the Chinese. In Japan, I am not much understood, but here China would naturally understand. It lived with Asia recorded in its DNA.[56]

Maybe Ishii was overly ambitious; I have no evidence he struck a chord elsewhere in Asia with this architecture. Nonetheless, it is worth emphasizing how rare his perspective was in the early 1990s; in a 1988 study of Japanese high school students, for example, nearly 60 percent declared that their nation was not a part of Asia.[57]

Ishii once acknowledged, "I have been skeptical of Modern Architecture" – in spite of an education that included study at Yale University under Charles Moore, James Stirling and Vincent Scully.[58] After publishing a book in 1977 on his experiences abroad and then translating Denise Scott Brown and Robert Venturi's *Learning from Las Vegas*, Ishii published two volumes in 1985 that marked his turning inward towards Japan: *Thoughts on Sukiya* and *Reclaiming Japanese Architecture: After America*.[59] Ishii claimed that, "... [Bruno] Taut's *Diary of Japan* played a major role in conceiving the traditions of our architectural form. Published in 1939, to me it is a very valuable text, which I read after Professor [Fumihiko] Maki recommended it."[60]

Ishii recommended visiting eight buildings in his book *Reclaiming Japanese Architecture*, as excerpted on his office website – all, he eventually revealed, designed by the nineteenth-century architectural historian Chuta Ito.[61] Ishii underscored another point as well:

54. Ishii (1992) p. 183. Original Japanese:
上棟式の日、棟木の裏に村長の半分ほどが名前を書き込み、展示室棟上部、通称バットの斗きょう＊が組み上がり、甲斐敏(name of mayor)村長はじめ私たちは上に乗った。村長が「口上を申し上げます」と切り出したとき、てっきり足元に集まっている大勢の村人に口上を申し上げるのかと私は思った。ところが村長が口上を言われたのは「山の神様」にあててだったのである。そのとき私はああそうだったのかと思った。関係者一同のこの頑張りは、それぞれに目的のあってのことであろうが、それらが総合化されえたのは「山の神」の存在への近世的想いだったのだ。清和の近世はこうして近代と調停を果たした。村長の口上にあったこの建築の三千年の生命を山の神に伏して願うものである。

55. See Ishii (1997) p. 291.

56. Ibid. pp. 344–345. Original Japanese:
清和村立清和物産館」と呼ばれている。中国のイメージが日本のイメージとして最も定着しているのは、もちろん四角い「堂」である。庇の深さなどの差こそあれ、基本は中国のものである…文楽館と物産館が並んでいるところを見ていると、これはアジアだと思う。中国の周囲を環状にめぐる諸国のカルチュラル・リンクの姿である。アジアの風物が、そのまま近代化されていく風景、こうした非欧米型の近代化が新しく可能になった。世界的な近代化の状況であると思う。
歴史は新しいアジアの連携を模索する時代に入ってきている。そして、自分が設計した建築を誰に見てもらいたかったのか、誰に私の建築の話を聞いてもらいたかったのか、急にわかってきた。それは、アジア人であり中国人なのである。日本ではなかなかわかってもらえないことが、ここ中国では自然にわかってもらえるのだ。DNA的記憶にアジアは生きている。

57. Iwabuchi (2002) p. 212. The original survey was credited to Murai, Yoshinori with Kazuo Kido and Takashi Koshida, *Ajia to Watashitachi* (1988).

58. Ishii (1989) p. 12.

59. Ishii (1985a). Ishii also lists a third text on his office website, which he calls Nihon Kenchiku no Saisei 2: Ishii Kazuhiro 日本築の再生2: 石井和紘 [Rebirth of Japanese Architecture 2].

60. Ishii (1994a) pp. 189–90. Original Japanese:
私たちの伝統像の創出に大きな役割を果たしているものに、たとえば「日本—タウトの日記」... がある。1939年に出版されたこの重要な書物を私は、槇先生のお勧めによって読んだ。

61. Taken from his office website, http://www.ishiiarc.com/book/saisei.html (accessed 1 January, 2008).

6.28, 29   The complex construction within Seiwa Puppet Museum owes nothing to the past.

6.28

6.29

the buildings he listed remain popular ones, sites integrated into the country's cultural life, like Meiji Shrine in Tokyo where millions worship on the first days of the year. Chuta Ito, too, argued Japanese architecture should be seen as fundamentally of Asia. Ishii's efforts, though, like Ito's, isolated them from being appreciated, offered at a time Japan seemed unable to understand.

Ishii accepts history as a jumble of archetypes stored in architecture's attic, especially drawing on two important threads at the heart of Japanese architectural tradition, saying, "*Sukiya* is a world of the individual, but Nara's temples and shrines are things of society."[62] In his contribution to the 1991 exhibition "Visions of Japan" at the Victoria and Albert Museum, Ishii rebuilt both the Chogen-inspired column I described earlier in this chapter – and a tea space that opened and closed like a flower, a physical expression of folding paper models used in earlier eras in Japan. A distinction, however, is easy to observe in Ishii's work: *sukiya*, which he once called "a treasure trove for architects," remains in the private realm, with the exception of this exhibition.[63]

Kengo Kuma wrote of Ishii, "He is an incomparable presence … He has history on his back. He groans under the yoke of [the] history of architecture on his shoulders and continues designing. His works are connected with history strongly, deeply, and sometimes poignantly."[64] Early in his own career, Kuma shared many interests with Ishii, like a love of *sukiya* and a formal approach allied with post-modern pastiche. Ishii's architecture also, like Kuma's later works, received awards for its material sensibility, albeit more minor ones: a tile prize in 1987 for "Gyro Roof" (sometimes called "Spinning House"), built for the owner of a roof tile company; an award for wood at the Seiwa Puppet Museum. Wood has also been an invariable element in Ishii's architecture; he even introduced rough logs wrapping streetlamps in the lively Akasaka entertainment district of Tokyo where he had his office.[65]

However, while Kuma offers a clean, simple approach, Ishii is the opposite. The older architect wrote in 1989, "… I cast aside all pretense of perfect beauty …"[66] The straightforward way Ishii blended past and present in his puppet theater is more often elusive. Instead, his work is awkwardly collaged, past struggling against the present, yielding an overall effect at best uneasy. Ishii acknowledged "… the usual criticisms: Too choppy and too hard to get a visual grasp of; too lacking any integrating elements."[67] He claimed an "obsession with the individual parts of a building …"[68]

Ishii's referents are dizzying, ranging from samurai helmets to pro wrestlers. In a sprawling residential complex called Sukiya Village, Ishii quoted not just China and Chogen, but reconstructed Bruno Taut's Glass Pavilion cheek-and-jowl with an adaptation of Sutemi Horiguchi's masterpiece from 1926, Shienso. For several years, he offered his thoughts on architectural tradition in an ongoing series published in the widely read journal *Shinkenchiku*, covering technique, history, the environment, "self-sufficiency," wood construction, and, in a culminating essay, "An Architecture of the Earth Sciences."[69] In the end, Ishii's architecture suggests an indiscriminate love of place and past, a love of lumber as an expression of innovation and older times, an almost oversized obsession with craft. But it is a dizzyingly kaleidoscopic – like Ishiyama's, an individualistic, eccentric exploration.

62. Ishii (1992) p. 183. Original Japanese: 数寄屋は個人の世界である。しかし，奈良の社寺は公共のものである。

63. Ishii (1989a) p. 13.

64. Kuma (1989b) p. 19.

65. Although street names are rare in Tokyo, this one is named. It might be translated as "Single Tree Road" [一ツ木通り], acknowledging those unusual light poles.

66. Ishii (1989a) p. 11.

67. Ibid., p. 12.

68. Ibid., p. 14.

69. The series ran as: "Jiko Henkaku Jidai no Kenchiku (1) Toshi' 自己変革時代の建築(1)-都市 [An Era of My Change (1), Cities] (March, 1994); "Jiko Henkaku Jidai no Kenchiku (2) Gijutsu" 自己変革時代の建築(2)-技術 [An Era of My Change (2), Technology] (May, 1994); "Jiko Henkaku Jidai no Kenchiku (3) Rekishi" 自己変革時代の建築(3)-歴史 [An Era of My Change (3), History] (August, 1994); "Jiko Henkaku Jidai no Kenchiku (4) Kankyo" 自己変革時代の建築(4)-環境 [An Era of My Change (4), Environment] (November, 1994); "Jiko Henkaku Jidai no Kenchiku (V) Jichi" 自己変革時代の建築v一自治 [An Era of My Change (5), Autonomy] (April, 1995); "Jiko Henkaku Jidai no Kenchiku (6) Mokuzou" 自己変革時代の建築(6)-木造 [An Era of My Change (6), Wood Construction] (January, 1996); "Kenchiku no Chikyuu Gaku" 建築の地球学 [Architecture's Earth Studies] (July, 1996).

6.30, 31 An aluminum tree in Itsuko Hasegawa's 1990 Shonandai Culture Center.

6.30

Itsuko Hasegawa

> *Architecture is a vessel to hold people's rich and ambiguous sentimentality, changing seasons, climate and the mysteries of the universe. That is what I … call a poetic machine.*
> –Itsuko Hasegawa[70]

Itsuko Hasegawa, only a few years older than Ishii and Ishiyama, was privileged to work closely with two of Japan's architectural giants, men who struggled with connecting the past and present: Kiyonori Kikutake and Kazuo Shinohara. (In some ways, her experience is similar to Tomita's.) Hasegawa entered Kikutake's office in 1964, when it was one of the most exciting places to be. The older architect is best known today as one of the original Metabolists, a group that exploded upon international discourse with a brazen pamphlet circulated at the 1960 World Design Congress; Kikutake proposed changeable cities floating on the sea. It is less well understood abroad that Kikutake was the most experienced of the Metabolists; the idea of adaptable architecture came from his postwar professional practice, reusing old timber in new housing for war widows and children. Hasegawa recalled, "During the 1960s, … I was interested in Kikutake's attempt to integrate notions of the traditional Japanese lifestyle with developments of Western technology …"[71] She stayed with the office for five years, then in 1969 entered Kazuo Shinohara's lab at the Tokyo Institute of Technology. After two years, she became Shinohara's assistant, an honor and responsibility far greater than the expression suggests in English – the experience almost inevitably leads to a career as an academic.

Shinohara himself once reflected that, "In the 1950s, … my strong affection for traditional architecture led me to pursue a career in architecture …" His earliest buildings were powerful explorations of vernacular forms, like the elegant "House in White" from 1966 – a simple Japanese tile roof over a square plan, wide *shoji* screens reflecting the same unusual proportions as the plan, a *daikokubashira*-like column standing in the open interior space between living and dining areas.[72] Another he built while Hasegawa was in his lab, the 1974 Tanikawa House, was one of the crowning achievements of his career, defined by an internal sloping floor of pounded earth, populated by braced timber columns posed like living trees. In an interview in 2007, Hasegawa recalled how, before joining the Shinohara lab, she took a trip through rural Japan, looking especially closely at villages and vernacular architecture – only to learn upon arriving at the university that Shinohara's work was entering a new phase less focused on tradition. Even so, Hasegawa stayed for seven years, until she left to establish her own practice in 1979.

Hasegawa's initial designs of allusive residential environs were widely admired. She quickly progressed to more ambitious works and in 1986 won a competition for a large children's museum and culture center in a bedroom community of Tokyo, besting 214 other entries. The jury, which included Fumihiko Maki, Arata Isozaki, and Kiyoshi Seike, said of her proposal:

> The original peoples of this area, who settled Shonandai in the Jomon era, surely had direct experience with "a line of mountains and mountains overlaying rich fields, and occasionally you see the broad waters of the sea or an endless sky" … as imagined by Hasegawa. We chose this entry

70. Toy (1993) p. 10.
71. Hasegawa, Itsuko *et al.* (2000) p. 98.
72. This house has recently been moved and reconstructed. See Shinkenchiku 新建築 [New Architecture] (June, 2008) pp. 111–124.

6.31

6.32

6.32 The plaza at Shonandai argues for an awareness of nature and a lost way of living.

6.33 Aluminum trees along a kawara tile river.

6.34 Grape arbors entwined in steel cable and stained glass.

> because we expect that this place might offer a viscerally emotional experience to contemporary residents.[73]

Hasegawa brought the history and landscape of Shonandai to life because, as she prepared for the competition, she researched the ancient sagas of the site and visited it – obvious actions in many countries, perhaps, but unlikely to have been common among her competitors.

Finalists included Hajime Yatsuka, Kunio Hayakawa, and other now established and respected architects. (Toyo Ito, who also worked in Kikutake's office, entered a scheme that made it into the final 38, but no further.) The three premiated entries were by Hasegawa, Shin Takamatsu, and Sei Takeyama, who called his firm Amorphe. Looking at these proposals today is a shock: Takeyama offered a pompous PoMo neo-Grec structure that seems implausible anywhere but in a Leon Krier sketch (and especially absurd in Asia), while Takamatsu's was a collage of parts reminiscent of Isozaki's now generally derided Tsukuba Center. Both are surprisingly dated, while Hasegawa's proposal seems, if anything, even more suitable today than it did then.

Hasegawa's rhetoric, too, was prophetic, yet little listened to. She seemed completely unconcerned with or unaware of the controversies that would emerge. She asserted:

> For our postwar society, the most often used word is "modernization." People also scream about our "regional era," but this merely indicates a plan to modernize and unify a bunch of urbanized "mini Tokyos" with Tokyo at their heart. Modernization is a Western principle that comes with our destruction, that yields loss. Today's international economic society welcomes the eras of technology or of this so-called

6.34

73. Kenchiku Bunka (1986) p. 55. Original Japanese: 縄文の湘南台に澄んだ原湘南人もきっとこうした「…山々が重ねった豊かな野、時には広大な海にも、無限に続く空にも…(設計案旨原文のまま)」を体験したと想像される。現湘南人が、その追体験を行なえる場となる可能性を期待してえらんだ。N.B. There is a rather nice pun in the original, where the words for "original peoples" and "contemporary residents" are homonyms – suggesting that this text was perhaps written by Isozaki.

6.35–41 Children play in the waters of Hasegawa's rippling artificial river.

6.35

6.36

6.37

6.38

6.39

6.40

6.41

> "New Middle Class" – but now we can correct course. The wisdom to divert modernity's centralization is in complexity and diversity, in division and dispersal, starting naturally by making the act of freeing ourselves from urbanization and centralized authority. I am thinking of a new regionalism, a reverse course from what we have so far followed.[74]

Hasegawa instead offered,

> ... the kind of cosmos or religion of shrines with forests or mountains, the liquidity and diversity of a place where animals and plants flourish together, people and nature exist in harmony, a place of mystery and symbolism, a town made up of labyrinth and neighborhood quarters ... rather than saying I'll make architecture, this is a work of making topography. A plateau, a river, a bridge, a *torii* gate, a pyramid, a sea of trees, luxuriant forests ...

She continued with the evocative phrase the jurors quoted, "a line of mountains and mountains overlaying rich fields, and occasionally you see the broad waters of the sea or an endless sky."[75]

Hasegawa's proposal evoked a bed-time tale: a large silvery globe rose over a roofscape of concrete, aluminum and glass reminiscent of a small village, at its heart an open space cut by a meandering brook in *kawara* tile. As Hajime Yatsuka claimed at the time:

> Hasegawa's winning proposal is sharply different from the commonly held, monumental image of public cultural facilities; it is like a fairy-tale village on the moon out of a children's book. Now people are waiting for its completion to see whether it will reveal any new architectural horizon, or succumb to the danger of becoming another "Disneyland."[76]

Some, however, did not wait. While the Japanese architectural community is often incestuously clubby, this courtesy was not extended to Hasegawa; in a discussion of the projects published with the announcement of Hasegawa's landmark success (she was the first woman to win such a competition, and also unusually young, though already in her forties), critic Makoto Ueda derided her solution, "as naïve as a child's drawing."[77] Koji Taki, a philosopher and esteemed architectural critic who lived in the Shonandai area, was brutal in his many essays and interviews, referring to the project in one short piece alone as kitsch, gaudy, pop, idiosyncratic, and eccentric.[78]

The completed building presented plenty of playful touches: blue and green marbles above perforated aluminum ceiling panels, seashells embedded in concrete walls and floors, an old-fashioned fillip of a cloud carved in plaster, and animal tracks embossed in tile pavers. Kazuhiro Ishii was one of the few Japanese to respond positively in print to the enormous effort involved in rendering this 10,530 square meter (113,344 square foot) structure as a richly evocative architectural expression. His opening line in a short essay written on Shonandai was, "Aaah, I felt this architecture is the first realization of the methods of our generation."[79] The critical community abroad, too, found Hasegawa's achievement at Shonandai invigorating. Udo Kultermann called it "... one of the most significant works of contemporary architecture in Japan."[80] Peter Cook, while tending to undermine Hasegawa's accomplishment by referring to her by only her first name, encouraged his countrymen to save up simply so they could come to Japan and see Shonandai, praising it as "a sheer delight" and "... the most engaging building of the last five years."[81]

Kultermann wrote:

74. Ibid., p. 56.
75. Ibid.
76. Yatsuka (1988) p. 10.
77. Hara and Ueda (1986) p. 73.
78. Taki, Koji. "A Dialogue-Based Programme," in Toy (1993) p. 13. Elsewhere, Taki called the ideas behind the project "particularly boring" [非常につまらない]. See Taki (1991) pp. 140–152.
79. Ishii (1989b) p. 35. Hasegawa was born in 1941; Ishii and Ishiyama were born in 1944 and Fujimori in 1946.
80. Kultermann (1998). Unpaginated text accessed on-line via Wilson Web.
81. Cook (1990) pp. 30 and 35.

6.42 Cloud-like patterns on Hasegawa's concrete.

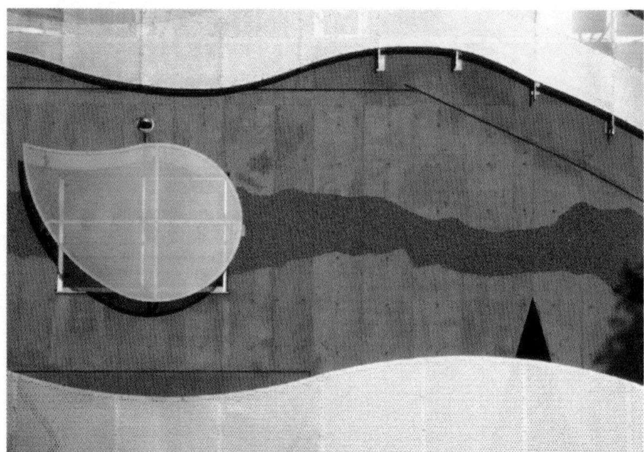

6.42

> From her earliest realizations of architectural works it is evident that one of Hasegawa's major goals was the continuation of the tradition created by Kazuo Shinohara in the sense of bringing together the old Japanese heritage of construction with contemporary technological reality ... While a technologically dominated reality is articulated, the inner solution and meaningful shape in the final result transcends these elements and integrates them into the spirit of the Japanese tradition.
>
> The early buildings of Hasegawa clearly represent her aspiration to follow the model of Shinohara, to unite old Japanese construction methods with contemporary technology.[82]

It was precisely this blending of old Japan and new that was the point of contention differentiating the two critical communities. While the Japanese architectural world was unable to assess an embrace of the past as anything but retrogressive nostalgia, architects elsewhere in the world saw that Hasegawa was not simply looking backwards, but instead endeavoring to integrate Japan's past with its forward-thinking present.

It is difficult to see how this point might have been missed even in Japan, frankly – why there was such a willingness to see the project as overly sentimental. Hasegawa did, it is true, work with the plasterer Akira Kusumi, and with Shuuji Yamada, the tile craftsman.[83] But their traditional materials were mixed with airy perforated aluminum trees and sailing ships, ochre-colored concrete walls holding aloft the enormous silver globe. Hasegawa, like Ishii and Ishiyama, proposed a blending of established and innovative, explicitly arguing nearly twenty years ago for a construction of "two types of technical skills, digital skills and anti-digital ..."[84] In Japan, most saw only that there was an element of imagination in the "anti-digital" elements Hasegawa incorporated – and felt architecture too serious to be thus emasculated.

In addition to the approbation Hasegawa faced for her formal approach, she took on other important struggles at Shonandai. Her initial residential work prepared her to embrace a collaborative process involving users early on, while most architects and bureaucrats of the time saw the public sector at an elite remove from daily life. Mitsugu Okagawa wrote only a few years later:

> Itsuko Hasegawa's victory in the Shonandai Culture Center design competition in 1986 was a watershed event for the new era of public architecture in Japan. Not only had a small architectural studio led by a woman won a large public design competition, but Hasegawa and her design team had proposed a totally new approach in the history of Japanese public architecture in terms of concept, design and construction process, as well as in facility management.

Continuing,

> ... public architecture has represented images of the government authorities more than anything else. The quality of architectural design has been judged on how well the message of the government was embodied in the buildings ... In this [postwar] period, public architecture was seen as an appropriate vehicle for the expression of modernistic forms. However, this kind of public architecture projected a somewhat aloof and isolated image to society in general. Modern Japanese public architecture ... lacked popular appeal.[85]

82. Kultermann (1998) n.p.

83. For more on this point, see my earlier book, *Japanese Architecture as a Collaborative Process* (2001) pp. 102-104.

84. Hasegawa, Itsuko by Koji Taki, (January, 1991) p. 141. The term "digital" is used in the original in *katakana* English, notable at this early date. Original Japanese: そうしてここでの技術は、デジタルなものと反デジタルのものが配置される事になったのです。

85. Okagawa (1995) p. 24.

6.43, 44 Winsome house-like shapes at Shonandai were intended to link Hasegawa's work with buildings around it, but today the surroundings lack the residential character she embraced.

6.43

6.44

Hasegawa challenged this head-on, engaging throughout design development in workshops involving anyone, from tykes to the elderly. She recalled, "Local officials ... were embarrassed and frustrated dealing with an architect like me. ... Some older officials treated me as if I were a radical social activist. They would not cooperate ..."[86]

Officials were also offended by her gender. At a time when fine-tuning design decision-making was done on site, she recalls:

> One thing that really surprised me at Shonandai ... The local bureaucrat supervising the project felt that, like the sumo wrestling ring, women should not be allowed to enter a construction site. He sent me a letter asking me not to come! What a surprise ... I knew that if I could not go, I could not complete the project...[87]

Eventually, Hasegawa was able to get on site. But while the Shonandai Culture Center was a major effort that established her internationally and shifted the scale and nature of her office's subsequent work, critical resistance at home made it a poignantly mixed success, poisoned by her pain. In the architecture that followed, Hasegawa pared down her aspirations. She continued to rely on workshops with the public to refine building programs and explore new ways of managing facilities – though even as late as her Niigata Performing Arts Center, completed in 1998, officials opposed the undertaking. But she also determined that for the project following Shonandai, the 1994 Sumida Culture Factory, she would present a light, modern aesthetic more palatable to her colleagues in Japan. Her ensuing architecture never afterwards expressed so strongly her love of the land, and it is only recently that she has again begun to incorporate older forms of architectural craft into her efforts.

86. Hasegawa, Itsuko in Taki (1997) p. 16.

87. Interview, Tokyo (7 December, 2007). Original Japanese: 湘南台の時びっくりしたんだけど、ね。市役所の担当者が相撲の土俵みたいにね現場はね女性は入っていけませんから、「来ないでください手紙が来たから. 驚きでしたよ. 菊竹さんにこんなこと有って, 槇さんにも相談したんですよ。「どうしてやったら良いんですか、私が現場に行かないとできない。。。

6.45 *A door at Hiroshi Naito's 1992 Sea Folk Museum, painted by the artist Ken'ichi Matsuda.*

I returned to Shonandai while I was putting the finishing touches to this book. All too often, Japan's public buildings age appallingly. Only a few years after completion, important architecture is often found empty, abandoned and unloved. But on a sultry summer Saturday, Shonandai, although showing rust here and there, mostly sparkled. A veil of ivy now clung to the ochre concrete (just as it often covers ancient wooden houses in Japan). Clusters of children played in the waters of the winding brook, some shaded by dangling grapevines that the architect selected almost two decades earlier. Inside, the building overflowed with families. Hasegawa listened to children in her workshops once; inside and out, as a result, Shonandai and its exhibits were remarkably unchanged, shrieking kids slipping down the same slides, seriously investigating the same aluminum forest, seated on the same small chairs. Children are perhaps more unchanging than we might think – instead of evidence of a digital generation, these were happily engaged in older forms of play. But nearby, newer municipal construction suggested the city's bureaucrats had somehow missed the lesson: a plaza linking two transportation lines was a dull space lined in granite – and it was empty and unused.

Shonandai Culture Center was completed in March 1990; it was in February of the following year that Fujimori would finish his first work, the Jinchokan Historical Museum. It is fair to say that the approbation Hasegawa faced cleared away competition; only someone like Fujimori, already successful in other avenues of architecture and unconcerned with approbation, might take up the task of blending past and present in the years immediately afterwards. One younger architect, however, was well on his way to completing a remarkable work that remains the crowning effort of his career.

Hiroshi Naito

> *Materials, whether they be stone or whatever, are garrulous, aren't they? Natural materials are garrulous.*—Hiroshi Naito[88]

Born in 1950, Hiroshi Naito is closer to Kengo Kuma in age than to these others, years younger than Fujimori. Yet at its best, Naito's architecture fits quite comfortably within the work of the more radical Reds. Naito shares many experiences with that earlier generation. He was educated at Waseda, studying under Takamasa Yoshizaka, like Ishiyama and two of the founders of Team Zoo. Like Itsuko Hasegawa, Naito worked for Kiyonori Kikutake. Naito's first published project was a Tokyo art gallery intended for the blind, and he initially embraced an architecture that emphasized experience over simple aesthetics. Yet at the same time, Naito's approach was from the start a more intellectual one than the others in this chapter exhibit.

Even in his student days, Naito was attracted to a theme that remains central in his work: time. His thesis project was a cemetery – a challenge, he noted, until Yoshizaka advised his young pupil, "You have to think about death ..."[89] Naito explained:

> In architecture, I suppose we have two main types: one is where time passes slowly – cemeteries, museums, and spiritual places. One of my works, the Sea Folk Museum, belongs in this category, since time seems to flow very slowly there ... When I designed this museum, I had to think about very long time-spans, up to two hundred years. But in contrast, when I design a commercial building, I need to retain a sense of the rapid changes that will happen ... The

88. Kuma with Hiroshi Naito (2004) p. 64.
89. Knabe and Noennig (1999) p. 100. The interview with Naito was on 15 August, 1997.

6.46

6.46 Each of the museum's buildings was an oversized expression of local forms and materials set into an up-to-date landscape.

6.47

> mistake of our architecture today is that we are confusing these two.[90]

Oddly enough, at the time Naito said this, he had actually completed several other museums. But he rightly singled out the Sea Folk Museum as unusually successful at slowing time, a complex of low structures located in a whaling town that seems almost at the end of the world, easy to imagine the institution enduring a hundred years or more.

His client insisted on this latter point. The museum earlier inhabited a 1972 building designed by the award-winning architect Hiroshi Hara; in 1985, only 13 years after its completion, the client commissioned Naito's new buildings. Naito often argued that Hara's lightweight aluminum structures quickly corroded in Tobu's salty sea air – but in truth, the earlier institution's obsolescence was perhaps as much a result of Japan's changing economy; the Seibu-Saison group (department store, real estate, and rail enterprises), extremely active in Japan's overheated "Bubble" economy, aggressively adapted art and architecture as a way of branding. In the 1980s, Saison proposed the tiny town of Tobu become the site of an artists' colony, and Naito, through some luck, was selected as the architect. The scheme incorporated the Sea Folk Museum, along with spaces for sculpture and the arts. While most of the proposed master plan was never built, the small museum, without support from Saison, soldiered on.

Naito asserted that in reaction to the rapid obsolescence of Hara's earlier architecture and the modest means of the museum, his material and formal choices for the new structures were guided by pragmatism:

> It is low-cost architecture. By using the old traditional

90. Ibid.

6.48

6.47, 48 An unloved, local stone was used to draw together buildings and landscape.

TOKAI

materials we could reduce the costs of construction ... If new materials had been cheaper, we would have used those. ... if we want to make a building that will last for a hundred years, we have to look at buildings that were built a hundred years ago ...[91]

He began with careful consideration of the roof, which ultimately determined the overall form of the buildings making up the complex: after deciding that only *kawara* tile would resist salt air, he set the span and slope.

Naito once suggested, "Architecture should be like people, who age naturally even as they try to resist time."[92] But in fact he does not embrace aging and decay: he painted cedar boards with a coat of tar to protect them, and happily incorporated longer-lasting materials like concrete and steel. Naito, when turning to traditional materials, is unlike the others in this book, far more likely to emphasize those that endure, like stone, not fragile *washi* paper or soft *paulownia*. He did not begin with a romantic view of architecture, arguing that as a student, "... I took no delight in these nostalgic, traditional materials or methods ..."[93] He was aware that economics make craft often impractical. In a long passage written while completing Sea Folk Museum, Naito lamented that traditional plasterers were abandoning their trade, turning in their tools for low-skill vocations relying on pneumatic hoses. He concluded, "... we are witnessing the end of the crafts spirit and technologies that have lasted since the Edo era."[94] He never attempted to ignore or overcome this tendency; his wooden glulam structures were updated industrial elements in a country where woodcraft is still often an obsession.

Yet the Sea Folk Museum, he acknowledged, was "... reminiscent

6.50

6.49, 50 The gallery interiors, glulam ribs reminiscent of whales' bellies and ship's hulls.

91. Ibid., pp. 105–106.
92. Hagenburg (2004) p. 134. Hagenburg quotes this statement from elsewhere, without citation, in an interview with Naito.
93. Knabe and Noennig (1999) p. 106.
94. Naito (1993a) p. 158.

6.51 The dark finishes of the warehouse-like museum structures resemble older techniques painted with tar or whale oil.

6.51

of old fishermen's huts, the walls of which were soaked in whale oil. Indeed, the whole complex evoked memories of traditional villages."[95] Naito insisted:

> When I show people around this museum, ... many things float up in their minds.
>
> It's like being in the belly of a whale, reminds you of the ribs of a ship's hull. The exterior of the collections building resembles a Japanese *kura* storehouse, the exhibition wings are similar to large sheds – a variety of impressions. You cannot say that any of these is a mistake. When we were making the study models, when we saw the building as it was emerging in reality, every one of them flitted through our minds. It's interesting that so many resemblances appear in the result. But those things that come to mind, we did not build to create those resemblances.[96]

The architect argued he simply accepted allusions as an outcome incidental to his efforts. In fact, he worried,

> ... this is a fishing village in the Ise Shima region, and from a long time ago it has been an environment of roofs and stone walls, so the client asked that, as we designed, we keep this in mind.
>
> From the beginning, this was a difficult way of thinking [for me]. However, while anyone looking can nostalgically embrace the shape of the land, you do not know what to do with that shape, what is ahead. The thought existed that nothing but Disneyland [would result from] transforming that shape.[97]

Starting with Sea Folk, the esteemed Japanese-American photographer Yasuhiro Ishimoto, who once collaborated with Kenzo Tange in 1960 on the book *Katsura: Tradition and Creation in Japanese Architecture*, has regularly documented Naito's work. In fact, Naito felt that his efforts were so unlikely to be appreciated that he feared Japanese magazines would not bother to send photographers, and this was the reason he asked Ishimoto to photograph this sprawling complex – underscoring how out-of-step this building was with the interests of the critical community.

The museum, like all the most successful buildings in this book, is

95. Gutdeutsch (1996) p. 87.

96. Naito (1992) p. 198. Original Japanese:
この博物館に人を案内すると、それぞれいるいるなことを思い浮かべるようだ。
鯨のお腹の中みたいだとか、船の龍骨のようだとか、収蔵庫の外観は蔵みたいだとか、展示棟は大きな納屋のようだとか、さまざまな印象をもつようだ。どの印象も間違ってはいない。スタディ模型ができたときや実際に立ち上がっていく建築を見て、そのどれもが頭の中によぎったことがあるからだ。結果として現れたこうした数似性は面白い。しかし、そういうものを思い浮かべて、それに似せてつくったわけではない。

97. Ibid.

another kind of lens, magnifying and enhancing our understanding of its cultural context at scales both large and small. The landscape, for example, was unusually eloquent, terraces carved from stone and soil. Naito explained,

> The large stone walls and plinths are built with local stone by a mason from the area, a famous craftsman from the Daiozaki area. The black stone that we used heavily along the approach and the pond area is usually thrown away in this area, considered waste; its unit price was cheap, so we built the landscape up with this stone at its center.[98]

The overall organization was so successfully nestled into the land that at first glance it appeared no more than a casual collection of working warehouses – though up close, the care and discipline of each placement was apparent; Naito noted, "We settled on the architecture suggesting at a single glance that it was a vernacular grouping."[99] The brooding black walls of exhibition areas and the crisp contrast of white storage structures are as elegant as Ishimoto's monochrome photographs.

The architect also wielded texture as his tool: pounded earthen floors in the collections, the doors standing sentry with finishes as invigorating as abstract artworks. He wrote:

> The entrance doors play an important role in the overall design of the museum. The architecture is jammed with ideas, the natural environment and cost concerns in a terrible rivalry ... The doors are large ones, a square 3 meters on each side, made of wood to reduce the overall weight, but faced in lead for fire resistance.
>
> For their finish, since the collections buildings are white on their exterior, I selected black, and the exhibitions buildings are black, so I chose red. The collections buildings suggest the image of night, the soul of the fishing folk sealed within, and the exhibition structures are bursting with life, the recollections of lifestyles in the bright light of day, and I thought the doors could express this. From the beginning, I thought the collections and exhibition buildings could express the opposition of life and death.
>
> I asked Ken'ichi Matsuda to finish the doors. A year passed with a variety of studies done on the collections and exhibition [buildings] before starting production; in the end, there was a hard struggle at the construction site before completion.[100]

At the edge of the eave, roof tiles end with a small symbol. Most might innocently overlook it. But these marks were inspired by talismans that women diving for pearls in the area once wore.[101] Those who understand these gestures are again reminded that these buildings exist to hold a whole heritage of practices; they draw the eye and the intellect. Naito once pointed out, "... Modern architecture was about eliminating the particularity of place ... It's my desire to reconnect all these things that were dismantled and scattered."[102]

I once accused Jun Aoki of thinking too much on the Aomori Museum, which I introduce at the end of this book (Chapter 9); Aoki remained conflicted to the end as to the outlines of the story he wanted his building to tell. At Sea Folk Museum, by contrast, Naito was able to benefit from ample time, deepening and enriching the story of the building and its place in layers and increasingly intricate details. Naito designed the complex over thirteen years, in three

98. Naito (1993b) p. 35. Original Japanese:
大きな石垣は、この近くの石職人で有名な大王崎の職人に近場の地石で作ってもらった。アプローチ周辺や池に大量に使われている黒い石は、この辺りでは通常捨ててしまう屑石で、単価が安いのでこれを中心に環境を組み上げた。.

99. Ibid., p. 34. Original Japanese:
一見バナキュラーな建築群にまとまりを持たせている.

100. Ibid. Original Japanese:
扉は、博物館の計画全体のなかで重要な役割を演じている。建築自体は、コストや自然条件との厳しい相克のなかで、ある意味では理詰めで作り上げられる。システムとしての建築に、揺らぎを与える要素が当初から必要ではないかと考えていた。扉は大きいもので3m四方の大きさがあり、総重量の関係で木製で制作し、防火性能を持たせるためにその上に鉛を張りつけた.
扉の仕上げは, 収蔵庫の場合は白の外壁に対して黒、展示棟の場合は黒の外壁に対して赤と決めた. 収蔵庫は、漁民の魂を封印するような夜のイメージ、展示棟は生き生きとした生活を想起させる昼のイメージが、扉で表現できないものかと考えた。当初から、収蔵庫と展示棟は、死と生の対比的な表現の中に在るべきではないかと考えていた。
扉の仕上げは松田研一氏にお願いした. 収蔵庫、展示棟、それぞれ制作前に一年ほどの膨大なスタディを経て、最終的には現場での悪戦苦闘の末、出来上がった。
Matsuda was also related to Naito by marriage; in a 2008 interview, Naito said he appealed to the artist to consider this as an opportunity to exhibit. Matsuda probably agreed because of the early involvement of the Saison group and a board of directors for the artists' colony that included many of Japan's leading artists. As a result, Matsuda worked on this effort relatively inexpensively – but other than doors for a home Naito has in Kamakura, the artist has not been involved in subsequent architectural efforts.

101. While these eave-edge tiles are unusual, in general, the roof tiles are absolutely standard, allowing for easy maintenance.

102. Naito (2002) p. 118.

phases stretching from 1985 through 1998 (with the crucial effort concentrated between 1985 and 1993), the institution growing as artifacts in the collection more than tripled in number during design and construction.[103]

Naito once asserted, "... I would like my architecture to live in its place, as an organism does, putting down roots, and sharing in the communities' history ..."[104] Yet he worried, "... most Japanese towns are not built upon a foundation of history. One cannot turn to history's presence in a townscape ..."[105] continuing, "Earthquakes, which occur anywhere in Japan, have also kept us removed from a sense of history's continued accumulation."[106]

To draw on the nature of each place and to become a part of the rich history of each region is not easy to achieve, although in Naito's case, a series of fitting projects followed the Sea Folk Museum, especially an institution on the rocky Ibaraki shore memorializing Tenshin Okakura, author of *The Book of Tea*. Naito's other oft-awarded architecture, the Makino Museum, was a tribute to an important botanist woven into the topography of its site, reflecting the architect's later thoughts on "sheltering earth."

But Naito says he began to see architecture differently in the years following these early works. He, more than most, is deeply aware of the economic impact of recent years. Tiny towns and rural regions, he argued in a 2008 interview, do not need an architectural embellishment, a mere object. Naito has turned to longer efforts, to larger-scale public works. You will find the Makino and Okakura Museums in the heart of new parks. Naito's 2005 Arts Center is part of an ambitious plan to entirely remake the town of Masuda, in an out-of-the-way corner of Shimane Prefecture. Naito is probably one of the few designers in recent years who includes a dam control center in his portfolio. He seems, of late, particularly interested in designing rail stations, which are a good fit for the architect's engineering interests.

In an odd shift, Naito's architecture went from something inspired by the arts, detailed with care and close attention, to often offering the most detailed element in larger schemes. Now in the Civil Engineering Department at the University of Tokyo, public works are of far greater interest to the architect. The result is not felicitous from an architectural perspective; Naito seems simply to recycle successes in subsequent structures. His Fuji Rinkai Seminar House is at the foot of Mt. Fuji – stone plinths, which evoke the rocky shoreline at his Sea Folk Museum, seem abstracted and out of place at the seminar house, the long lines of the blackened wood walls as unusual in the area as an aluminum cube. Naito also transplanted brown-glazed tile roofs tried first in Shimane to a similar structure in Medellin, Columbia. The Sea Folk Museum exaggerated and drew attention to the unique practices of its place, but these subsequent structures seem not so knowing.

Once in a while, Naito is drawn to more intriguing opportunities, and the occasionally artful commercial commission demonstrates he might again produce an architecture as inspiring as the Sea Folk Museum. But the niche that Naito enjoyed early on, a heady blend of public good and artistic ambition, was a product of the aggressive economic approach taken by the Seibu-Saison Group in the late 1980s, and Naito seems less confident when called upon to make a choice between two.

103. The collections buildings were designed and constructed between 1985 and 1989, the exhibition buildings from 1988 to 1992, and places for study were completed in 1998. The first two phases, which took over seven years, are the most powerful.

104. Naito and Magnago Lampugnani (1996) p. 92.

105. Ibid.

106. Ibid., pp. 92–93.

6.52

6.52 *Stacked kawara tiles at Waro Kishi's 2003 interior in Kyoto, a showroom for Zen Buddhist religious articles.*

6.53 *A view of a sales counter in the same space.*

And Others

Ishii and Ishiyama offer untamed architectural appetites that inverted the conventional hierarchy of the profession – their love of technology old or new is seen in over-complex detail, often at the expense of overall form and organization. In the twentieth century, as the profession of architecture evolved in Japan, there was still a place for these kinds of practices, for buildings that took years to design, for oddball eccentrics.

Perhaps it is inevitable that the architects who are most radical, most illustrate Fujimori's Red School tenets, are less well known – and, as Riichi Miyake indicated many years ago, less productive. They rely on handicrafts now hard to find. They study places and histories with close care, consult with shrine carpenters more knowledgeable about the curve of roofs or craftsmen well schooled in a mundane art like mud and plaster.

In an interview with Waro Kishi, architectural historian Ken Tadashi Oshima pointed out, "... Sutemi Horiguchi went to Europe in pursuit of Western models and then returned [to Japan] to study traditional tea architecture." Kishi, who studied architectural history before establishing his Kyoto office, responded:

> That was also true of Isoya Yoshida. He went to Europe and then, on returning to Japan, adopted a more traditional viewpoint. That's been the pattern of Japanese architects who revert to a traditional point of view ... I've long wondered if there wasn't some other path. That's why I've deliberately distanced myself from Japanese architecture ...[107]

Kishi claimed, "I've tried to imagine myself as a foreigner living in

6.53

107. Waro Kishi, interview by Ken Tadashi Oshima. Kishi (2000) p. 73.

6.54

6.55

6.54, 55 Another area of the show-room is more traditional in character, with a low table on chestnut planks showing skillful working with an adze.

6.56 Kishi's 1997 Yamaguchi Memorial Hall in the town of Ube is more typical of his work.

Kyoto ..."[108] He only reluctantly incorporates elements of tradition, and when willing to do so, engages the past in a way that is established, not exploratory.

Naito and Kishi were born in the same year, as if marking a moment when time began to shift significantly in Japan; the other architects I discuss in this chapter are older. Fujimori holds in his heart an animism nearly unheard of in contemporary Japan, nurtured in a once-isolated village. Hasegawa's childhood home had a *douma* floor; today young Japanese architects are likely more familiar with carpet than pounded earth, or even *tatami*. In internationalizing, architecture in Japan is safer, sleeker – but less aware of the particularities of place.

6.56

In 2006, Kengo Kuma admitted:

> Time and again I have had the feeling that perhaps it is only because Fujimori-San did the 1991 Jinchokan Moriya Historical Museum and thus broke free ... that I have been able to do my work of the last ten years or so. For me as well, the role [Fujimori] established really served as a kind of protection.
>
> To me, architects of the Red School like Ishii and Ishiyama, who emerged before the protection Fujimori offered were really taking on a difficult way of thinking. On the other hand, architects who came after Fujimori created his protection have been freed ...[109]

Riding a taxi through Tokyo recently, Kuma told me of another wonderful work coming his way, for a new *kabuki* theater. It was not yet confirmed that he would get the job – and yet, we both agreed, who else might? Oddly, even while Kuma's efforts to engage past and place have struck a chord with Japanese clients, few others, even from his own office, are willing or able to follow in his footsteps.

Perhaps in the increasingly rigid outlines of professional practice in Japan today, it is no longer as possible to be regionalist or Red – in spite of the obvious opportunities offered. But in the following section, I discuss three projects where clients and context argued for just such an approach – from architects most would not think of as inclined in this way. I call these architects "Reluctant Reds."

108. Ibid.

109. Ito et al. (2006) p. 93. Original Japanese: そこで改めて感じたのは、藤森さんが『神長官守矢史料館』(九一年)によって『篠原大号令』を破ってくれたから、ここの一〇年間のぼくの仕事がやれたのかもしれないこと。ぼくにとっても、ある種の楯のような役割を果たしてくれたのです。. その楯ができる前に出っていった石井さん、石山さんたち『赤派』は、結構, 大変な思いをしていたと思う。一方で、藤森さんの楯ができた後に建築家になった人たちは、抽象化という 呪縛から自由なことができるようになってきた。

Reluctant Reds

旭社
高木清司

Remaking the Landscape of Kotohira Shrine

Ryoji Suzuki

7

Konpira, situated in the island of Shikoku, is a shrine for which sailors and travellers have a peculiar devotion.

When I first visited it some seventeen years ago, it was in Buddhist hands. On going there again last November, I found it in Shinto, but ... not more changed than was the exquisite view ... that greets the traveller from the summit of the hill, up where the temple buildings extend.
—*Basil Hall Chamberlain, 1893*[1]

The path upwards through the grounds of Kotohira Shrine (still often colloquially called by the friendlier nickname Konpira-san or "Mr. Konpira") is notorious for its imposition on visitants – 785 steps, say most sources, but the official guidebook argues there are 786 steps upward to the Main Shrine, but also one downward step at the point where shops yield to sacred. The number "786" can be linked phonetically to *nayamu* – the Japanese word for "suffering" – so convention is to subtract that one downward step, leaving 785.[2]

The long, winding route up the steep mountain leads into a dark, leafy forest near the top, then out onto a bright plateau 251 meters (nearly 825 feet) above sea level, with a magnificent view of the town at the mountain's base and the Inland Sea beyond.[3] Fewer and fewer climb these steps each year. Unlike the far better known poles of Ise or Izumo, Kotohira is rarely studied by architectural academics and seldom recommended to foreign tourists. Not so long ago, however, it was "... one of the most popular destinations of the nineteenth century, compared by writers of the time even to the shrine of Amaterasu at Ise."[4]

Kotohira's treads mark a varying rhythm. Broad expanses of flat granite worn smooth by innumerable visitors' steps bracket gentle clusters of only a few risers, establishing peaceful interludes along the path. Other stretches are alarmingly steep or cling to the edge of slopes, overlooking a landscape that falls away abruptly. In a reminiscence, the renowned architectural scholar Teiji Ito recalls that he first wrote of this route in 1960.[5] Ito produced a pamphlet, which he remembers entitling *The Linkage of Japanese Space*, and shared it with a coterie of internationally respected architects attending the Tokyo 1960 World Design Conference.[6] He had already written a number of books, including a comprehensive series on the architecture of Japan's countryside, produced with the now highly influential photographer and publisher Yukio Futagawa, but in this recent essay Ito credits the unfolding turns of his long and successful career to this pamphlet.

The scholar recalled that he did not expect to reach the Main

7.1 The 1837 Dawn Pavilion at Kotohira Shrine in Shikoku is one of the few buildings remaining that reflects the site's earlier ties to Buddhism.

1. Chamberlain (1893) pp. 365–366.
2. *Kotohiraguu Ofisharu Gaidobukku* 金刀比羅宮オフィシャルガイドブック [Kotohira Shrine Official Guidebook] (2004) p. 12.
3. Ibid., p. 31.
4. Thal (2005) p. 3.
5. My description of Ito's encounter with Konpira is based on Ito, Teiji. "*Honden he Michibiku Takumi na Fuukei*" 本殿へ導くたくみな風景 [Ingenious Scenery Guides to the Main Shrine] *Shikoku Shinbun* 四国新聞 [Shikoku Newspaper] (21 September, 2003). Available at: http://www.shikoku-np.co.jp/feature/kotohira/25/index.htm (accessed June 12, 2007).
6. Ito gives the title as *Nihon no Kuukan no Renzoku* 日本の空間の連続 [The Continuity of Japanese Space] in his 2003 essay, although I can find no evidence of this title in even the most comprehensive bibliographies and collections. As an aside, the Metabolists also offered an acclaimed tract at this meeting.

7.2

7.2 *A belfry built in 1710 is in the Kamakura hakamagoshi style, also Buddhist; it sits just outside the entrance to the shrine.*

7.3 *One of many Shinto torii that mark the rising path to the shrine.*

7.4 *The landscape along the path.*

7.5 *A plan of the path to Kotohira Shrine, from its Nio gate just above the steps shown at the bottom of the page, to the inner precincts of the shrine at the top of the page.*

7.3

Shrine, disabled as he was – Ito had only one functioning lung. However, commerce offered enticement; two nimble men could take him up in a simple carrier. He paid, riding through a clutter of shops and occasional stone *torii*, only to discover that the porters would merely drop him halfway, 365 steps upward, but not within the shrine. (Today, porters carry the physically handicapped to the top, but this remains rare. Even tiny children are expected to climb.)

Ito felt unable to turn away at this point, where town gives way to shrine. It is a particularly intriguing interval with its odd combination of entrance markers. The narrow stone landing overlooks a squat belfry built in 1710 in the Kamakura *hakamagoshi* style (referring to its skirt-like lower floor) where a bell still peals each morning and evening. A large, dignified gate built in 1649 marks the threshold to the shrine, visitants passing between the two elaborately carved wooden demon-like guardians. Both structures are oddly indicative of Kotohira's history; they are normally found at Buddhist temples, not Shinto shrines like Kotohira – far more suitable to the threshold of a shrine is a simple *torii*, like the one that sits just within the gate. This simple post-and-lintel frame marks the procession to all Shinto shrines, following a 1907 order by the Emperor Meiji.[7]

Until the middle of the nineteenth century, shrines and temples often coexisted, and Japanese Esoteric Buddhism (found on mountain sites such as this) agreeably blended the traditions of many gods. Historian Sarah Thal traced the history of Kotohira in her 2005 book *Rearranging the Landscape of the Gods: The Politics of a Pilgrimage Site in Japan, 1573–1912*.[8] She argued the power of this place transcends any faith: "Mountains in Japan have long been associated with sacred powers, whether as abodes of the dead, sites of medita-

7.4

7. Fridell, Wilbur M., *Japanese Shrine Mergers, 1906–1912: State Shinto Moves to the Grassroots* (1973) writes that an Imperial order in 1907 required shrines to distinguish their presence by a *torii*, an outer worship hall and a main sanctuary. Konpira, whose Main Shrine was rebuilt shortly before this order, lacks an outer worship hall.

8. Thal (2005). While I have relied on many other sources on Kotohira as well, Thal's book was a particularly important resource for the historical discussions found in this chapter.

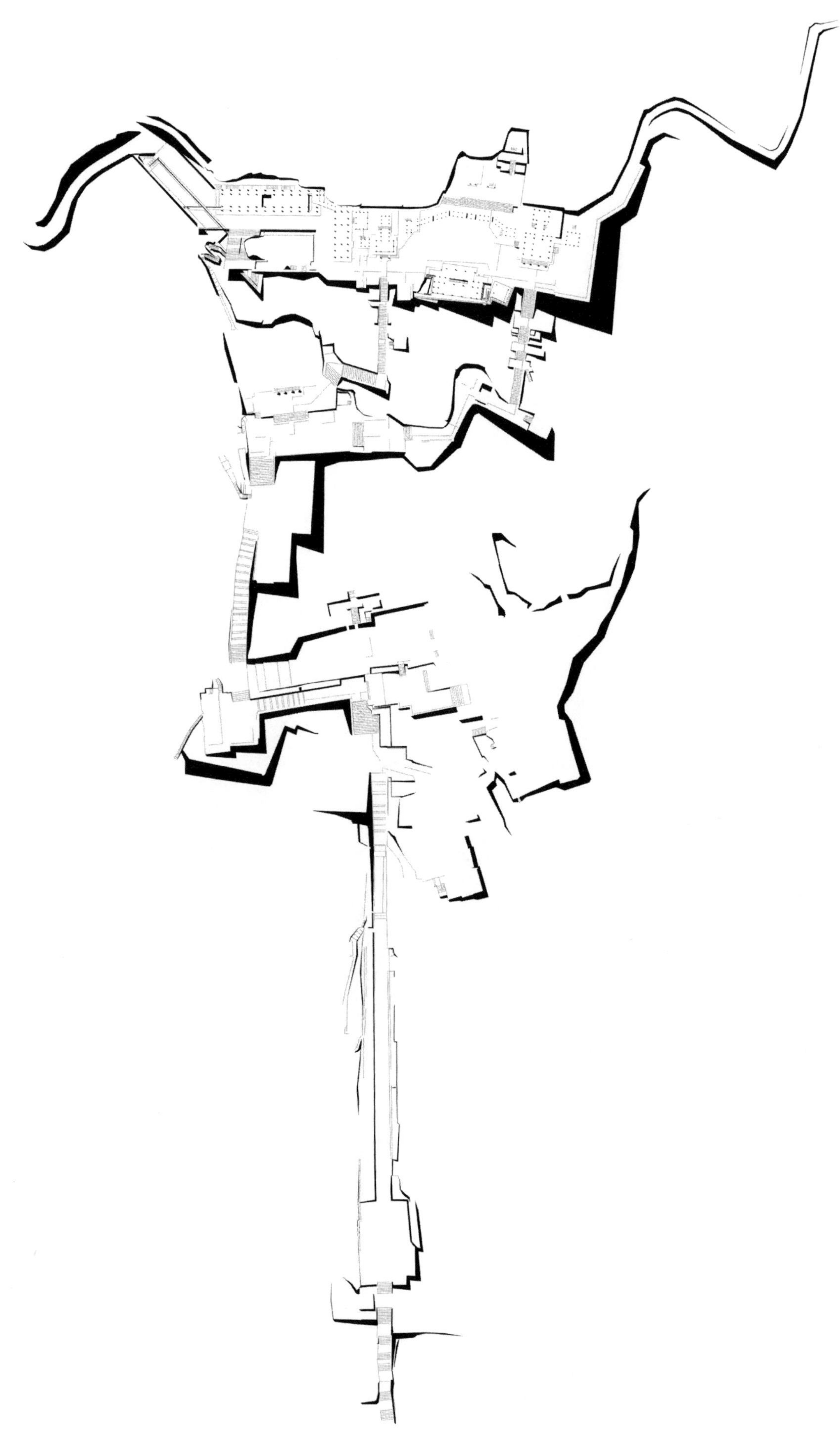

7.5

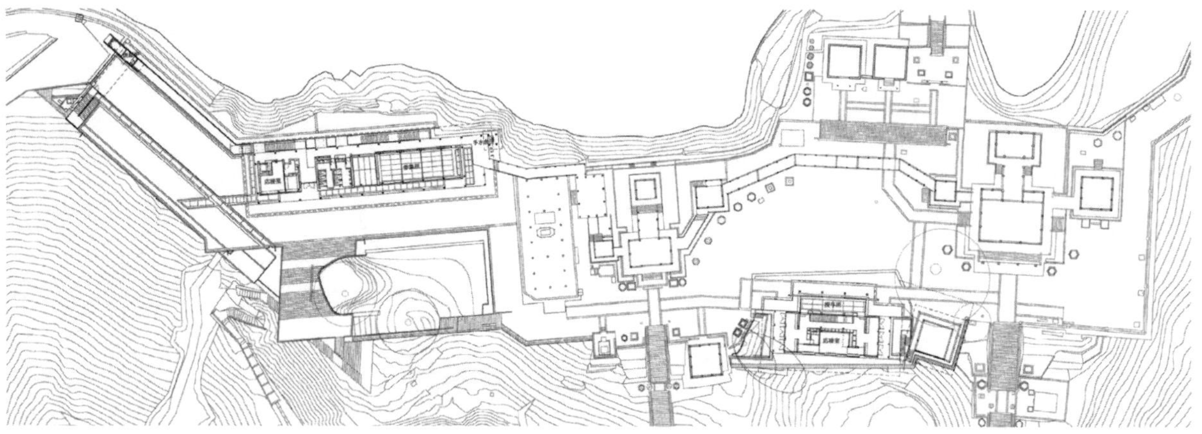

7.6

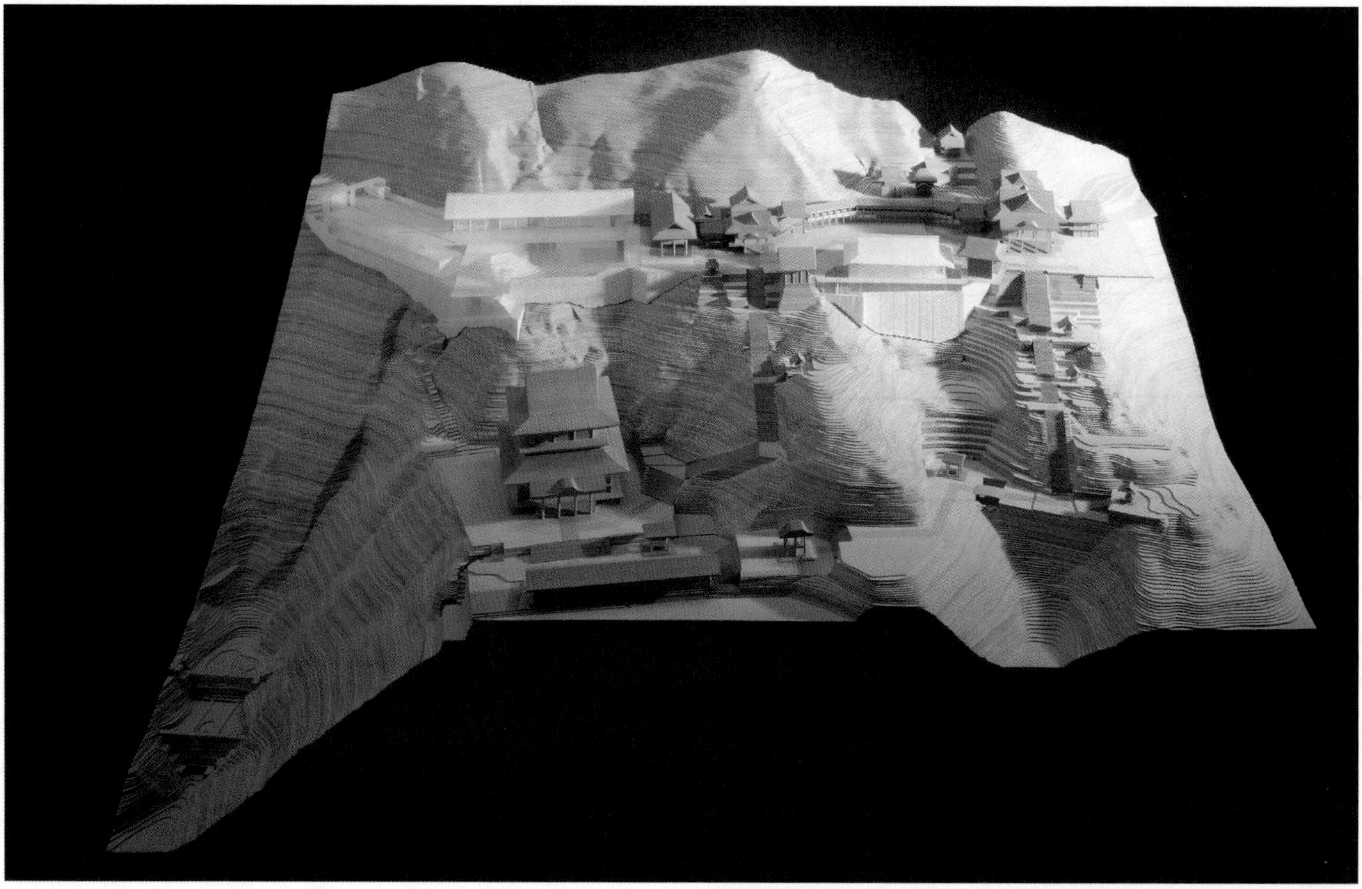

7.7

7.6, 7 The inner precincts of the shrine include new buildings designed by Ryoji Suzuki: the conferment building sits between the two sets of stairs and the Saikan to the far left in the plan . Both are shown in white in the model.

7.8 The Nio gate at the entrance to Kotohira, the legs of a Shinto torii visible beneath its curtains.

7.9 The Nio gate, built in 1649, is the other remaining structure that reflects Kotohira's past as a place of more than one religion.

7.8

7.10

7.11

7.10 A large propeller is a symbol of Kotohira's ties to the shipping industry.

7.11 The Main Shrine, built in the miyadera-zukuri style, in 1878.

tion, sources of life-giving water, or homes of powerful gods and spirits."[9] Shinto gods (*kami*) coexisted comfortably here with not only with esoteric Buddhism, but also with nativist water sprites (*kappa*) and troublesome goblins (*tengu*). For over a millennium, Thal writes, people were untroubled by Kotohira's diversity of divinities. But even though this rich fusion once existed, I know few other sites where a Buddhist gate is closely followed by a Shinto *torii*.

Just beyond this point, a straight path nearly 150 meters long beckons – deceptively easy and cool, shaded under a canopy of cherry trees, suggesting the road ahead will be an effortless one. In truth, of course, 421 steps remain. Ito climbed, stopping frequently along the way, always drawn deeper towards the upper reaches of the shrine; anyone visiting the shrine feels the same upward pull today. A demanding stretch follows, and then widens into Kotohira's "Cultural Zone," a quiet plateau where visitors discover other oddities: a cartoonish statue of a dog (because a worshipper was once said to be too busy to come himself, and sent his dog as proxy instead) and a gigantic, gleaming propeller, acknowledging that this mountain shrine protects seafarers. While resting in the Culture Zone, visitors explore two museums: a dignified building from the Meiji era holding many Buddhist artifacts (materials desacralized as the site shifted from Buddhist to Shinto, from the popularly named Konpira-san to Kotohira) or another more recent structure dedicated to Yuichi Takahashi, one of Japan's earliest artists to work in oils, painting from daily life: shells, flowers, a plasterer at work, a fishing boat on the sea.[10]

Rising, a turn marks a small rest house where one can stop for a cup of tea, opened in late 2007.[11] The building is nearly invisible beneath a broad platform overlooking the rolling landscape, simply an overlook along the path. Those that go below find a weaker version of two modern buildings up ahead – but while the shrine was generous when funds were needed for its religious structures above, this building reflects its commercial character in less committed construction.

With this turn, Kotohira's path at its most intimidating unfolds, framed on each side by stone monoliths, the monumental volume of the 18 meter (nearly 60 feet) tall Dawn Pavilion looming far above. Climbing towards it, visitors leave the Culture Zone and enter the sacred site above. Like the belfry and the guardian gate found at the threshold to the shrine, the 1837 Dawn Pavilion is an oddity to architects and religious adherents, also clearly Buddhist. While the Main Shrine to be found further up the path is delicate, airy and open, capped with a *hinoki* cypress bark roof of graceful curves, the Dawn Pavilion is powerful, monumental and dark. It is in the classic shape of a temple, with thick columns supporting an extensive system of projecting brackets under a heavy verdigris double roof. The undersides of the eaves are carved into a rare and remarkable riot of rolling waves, articulating the ferocity of the sea.

More of the shrine's buildings were once – like the Dawn Pavilion, the gate and belfry – Buddhist in their iconography. In 1868, the newly formed Meiji government reshaped Japan, demanding people align themselves with their local Shinto shrines. Ise, the pinnacle of this new, codified religion, was also cleansed of Buddhist structures, said to have numbered 300, both large and small.[12] Professor Fumio Tamamuro pointed out that, "Because a plethora of Buddhist monuments and buildings lined the approach to the Grand Shrines [at Ise], a new road was constructed ..."[13] He estimates "... of the approximately 200,000 Edo-period temples, about 74,600 survived ... In other

9. Ibid., p. 46.

10. Takahashi lived and painted at Kotohira for one year, in 1880. Interestingly, in an unpublished 2004 Ph.D. dissertation, Akiko Takenaka-O'Brien notes that Takahashi had earlier proposed a Western-style museum at Yasukuni Shrine in Tokyo around 1871. Takenaka-O'Brien states there were no exhibition venues large enough for Western paintings until the 1881 completion of Josiah Conder's Imperial Museum in Ueno Park in Tokyo. According to her, Giovanni Vincenzo Cappelletti, the designer of a museum of war-related artifacts at Yasukuni Shrine completed in 1882, was a close friend of Takahashi's; the painter donated a large painting to Yasukuni to be displayed in the Cappelletti structure. See Takenaka-O'Brien (2004) pp. 119–120.

11. The "*chajo*" [茶所] has many of the same gestures as Suzuki's work I discuss in this chapter. Unfortunately, the budget was far more limited here and compromises are evident. For example, Suzuki's structures above rely on slim steel, but this building is rendered in cheaper concrete. Notably, Suzuki has no intention to include this lower edifice among his most successful projects, which he always entitles an "Experiment in Materials."

12. Hardacre (1986) p. 32.

13. Tamamuro (1997) p. 503.

7 . 12

7 . 12 Another view of the Main Shrine, with its flowing hinoki cypress bark roof.

7.13 The shinsenden, adjacent to the Main Shrine, also under a cedar bark roof.

7.13

words, two out of every three temples that existed during the Edo period were burned to the ground as a result of the suppression of Buddhism."[14] Some religious communities bravely retained their Buddhist traditions, but most (like Kotohira) recognized that the shifting tenor of the times demanded they remake themselves – as Shinto shrines. Two years after the Meiji government demanded a newly purified Shinto, Kotohira's pagoda, symbolizing the enshrinement of Buddha's remains, was torn down.[15]

To strengthen the Shinto character of the site, not only buildings were destroyed; Buddhas were burned and sutras and other valued artifacts sold cheaply to whomever would buy them. By 1874, the authorities at Kotohira had destroyed "almost every lantern and signpost that sported a goblin *tengu*'s fan or contained Buddhist language."[16] Allan Grapard, a University of California professor who has written often and passionately on the traumatic sundering of Shinto and Buddhism, noted, "... innumerable statues, paintings, scriptures, ritual implements, and buildings were destroyed, sold, stolen, burnt, or covered with excrement."[17] Stunned by this nationwide purge, Tenshin Okakura, Ernest Fellanosa, and others argued for the aesthetic importance of Buddhist artifacts. As a result, the Horyuji Temple in Nara, for example, sold significant parts of its collection to the State, objects now maintained in an exquisite museum designed by Yoshio Taniguchi – sited not in Nara, but in a park in the nation's capital, with other art and history collections.[18]

The desire to salvage once hallowed artifacts was also the impetus for the 1904 museum found in Kotohira's lower "Culture Zone." Many of the works on display are Buddhist, while others depict nativist spirits; my favorite on a recent trip was a tableau of *kappa* water sprites playfully farting water at each other. Sarah Thal, the English-speaking expert on Kotohira, relates that the distinction between sacred and secular was sometimes lost on adherents in the Meiji era, who worshiped Buddhas in the museum by praying towards its blank exterior walls. She argues that repositioning the religious artifacts as art was an innovative solution, one that made Kotohira "the first shrine in the country to display Buddhist statues, scrolls and other artifacts permanently in its own museum."[19] The result was to redefine Kotohira as a Shinto shrine, but also as a conservator of a rich cultural legacy – the inheritor of both sacred and secular, a position the shrine aggressively embraces today.

While the Dawn Pavilion remained apparently too beautiful to destroy, the abbot understandably rebuilt Kotohira's Main Shrine in 1878, making it more in keeping with Shinto aesthetics. Thal argues "... the buildings of the main hall were indeed 300 years old and in need of repair, [but] the rationale was certainly also to rid the architecture of its Buddhist motifs and decorations."[20] Ambiguously, its style is not based on common archetypes sporting easily recognized diagonal finials (*chigi*) projecting from the roof. Instead, the Main Shrine follows the *miyadera-zukuri* style, a name combining the characters for shrine (*miya*) and temple (*tera/dera*).[21]

The sweeping *hinoki* bark roofs of the Main Shrine require regular replacing, done on a cycle of 33 years. In 2004, when the shrine was last re-roofed, the priests at Kotohira also initiated a dramatic reorganization, "... the large-scale 'New Konpira-San' plan."[22] Mindful of the need to maintain the history of the site, but equally aware of how Kotohira has in recent years embraced the challenges of modernization, the priests chose an architect who could do both: Tokyo-based

14. Ibid., p. 504.
15. Thal (2005) p. 143.
16. Ibid., p. 180.
17. Grapard (1984) p. 245.
18. The way that noteworthy Buddhist artifacts were redefined as art is beyond the scope of this chapter, though clearly related to the theme of this book. Tanaka focuses in particular on the fate of Horyuji, noting that its "... artifacts, now constituted as art, were emptied of previous meanings and became important historical data..." (2004, p. 170), resulting in "... the transformation of the Horyuji into a ghost town: it is shorn of its spirits and powers, and now symbolizes a dead, but valued complex of buildings" (ibid., p. 177). A somewhat different position, offered in greater detail, can be seen at McDermott, Hiroko T. "The Horyuji Treasures and Early Meiji Cultural Policy," (2006) pp. 339–374. It is notable that the style Taniguchi chose for his exquisite museum refers to the abstraction of tradition as it developed in the middle of the twentieth century (relying in part on imperial *shoin* precedents), not to the style of Horyuji itself. In other words, Taniguchi's style indicates the building's state ties, not the collection's earlier religious ones.
19. Thal (2005) p. 33.
20. Ibid., pp. 155–156.
21. Another name for this style is *gongenzukuri*. Although one of the styles conventionally used for shrines, it is, relatively speaking, an outlier. As the scholar Mary Neighbor Parent wrote when explaining her focus only on the Buddhist roof, "... for the most part, shrine buildings were limited to three styles up to the fifteenth century; the *shinmei*, *nagare*, and *kasuga* styles" (1983, p. 9). These three, far more recognizable styles, relied on *chigi*, the diagonal finials perched above the gable, and/or cigar-shaped billets (*katsu'ogi*) running along the ridge line.
22. "*Dai'ichiwa: Yutaka na Bunka kono Chi kara*" 第一話。豊かな文化この地から [First in a series: From a Place Rich in Culture] *Shikoku Shinbun* 四国新聞 [Shikoku Newspaper] 6 April, 2003. Available at: http://www.shikoku-np.co.jp/feature/kotohira/1/index.htm (accessed 12 June, 2007). Original Japanese:

二〇〇四年九月の「平成の大遷座祭」へ向けて、大規模な「ニューこんぴらさん」計画が進行中だ。旭社から本宮までを信仰の中心となる「神殿ゾーン」、それより下の宝物館や書院、現在の社務所周辺を「文化ゾーン」として再編整備する計画。二十一世紀の庶民信仰と文化の核となる基盤が、徐々にではあるが私たちの前に姿を見せ始めている。

一九七一(昭和四十六)年以来、三十三年ぶりとなる遷座祭。本来は風雪に耐えた本宮の屋根の葺(ふ)き替えを中心とする"若返り"工事が主だった。今回はそれに加えて、現在の社務所とご神札授与所を統合して本宮周辺に新築するほか、神楽殿や絵馬殿も移転。大規模な"リニューアル"工事になっている。

7.14

7.14 Another view of the entrance to the shrine, the Nio gate.

Ryoji Suzuki, who also later guided the little tea structure passed on the upward path. Suzuki's charge was far from easy; he repositioned a small wooden stage hundreds of years old and inserted two large, entirely new buildings into the most sacred heart of the shrine: a 528-square-meter (5,683-square-foot) building directly facing the Main Shrine, where amulets are sold, the "conferment building," and a more imposing 1,727-sq m (18,590-sq ft) structure further south, enclosing ritual spaces and offices. The ancient stage, the *Shinrakuden*, was actually relocated twice, ultimately to be placed on a dramatic steel-plate cantilever that juts out 8 meters (over 26 feet) over the forest below, just where the path upward reaches the Main Shrine.[23]

In order to accomplish this complex reorganization, the edges of the site were redefined, enclosed within an imposing retaining wall, of which Suzuki wrote:

> For the very deep base of the *Juyosho* [conferment] building, ... we hardened the foundation, built a base of local *Aoki* stone. We picked *Aoki* stone not only because it is a local and extremely beautiful granite, but also because the [museum] building at Kotohira and many other structures at the shrine also employed this stone, making it a material intimately associated with the site. Thirty-two centimeters each in section, the longest are stone columns of 3 meters in length; in total there are nearly 1000 of these below the two buildings, and the total width of the retaining wall is 150 meters. The tallest area is in front of the [conferment building], built up of four vertical tiers, where the retaining wall is more than ten meters tall – of course the tallest in Japan, and possibly unprecedented in the world ... In order to viscerally scrutinize the size, we built [full-scale] mock-ups and repeatedly tested the strength of the attachment hardware ...[24]

All this was done without intruding on non-stop worship at the shrine. Furthermore, as Suzuki wrote, "Untamed nature and tradition were observing us from the very beginning."[25] Because of the amalgamation of Shinto and nature, every effort was made to preserve and even enfold the huge trees interspersed throughout the narrow site. Kotohira is richly endowed with colossal trees: according to arboreal specialist Motoi Toyota:

> ... a 1991 survey done by the then Environmental Agency (now the Environmental Ministry) in the area of the shrine, [showed] there were 33 trees with a trunk circumference of greater than 3 meters [nearly 10 feet] – and in the near future, the number was expected to substantially increase.[26]

In the new southern courtyard he created, Suzuki surrounded a large camphor tree with a curving wall of steel, and he lovingly carved a balcony-like walkway around another tree on the downhill side of the conferment building. It is perhaps a testament to the very tight conditions where these structures were built that – in spite of significant effort by the contractor – in the end the latter tree succumbed. Tellingly, the architect and contractor did not leave this loss evident, altering the walkway to erase the evidence of the missing tree.

Although the scale and complexity involved in weaving these two structures into the core of the shrine were unprecedented in Suzuki's career (much of his work remains modestly residential), the shrine chose him with confidence. For one thing, there was the simple – but in Japan, not unimportant – fact that Suzuki had second-hand but

23. In fact, the cantilever is more dramatic than it appears, because Japanese structural codes would not let the engineer, Masato Araya, tie into the visible retaining wall; the actual cantilever extends 9.5 meters, or about 31 feet. In addition, a tree to the inboard side of the cantilever caused Araya no end of difficulty as he worked to protect its roots. It remains healthy, suggesting he was successful.

24. Kotohira Shrine Office (2005) p. 12.
Original Japanese:
。。。深礎工法によって固められた基礎のうえに地元産の青木石によって建ち上げられています。青木石が選ばれたのは、それが地元産の優れた御影石であるばかりではなく、宝物館など金刀比羅宮の随所で使われてきた親しみのある素材であるからです。三二センチ角の断面を持つ最長で三メートルの大きな石柱をひとつの単位とし、これを総数で約一千本ほど役入して、授与所側と斎館側とを合わせると、全長一五〇メートルにも擁壁を構築します。授与所前に当たるもっとも高い部分では、四段ほど垂直に積み上げることによって擁壁の高さは十数メートルにもおよび、日本ではもちろん、世界でもほとんど前例のない、完全に垂直の擁壁を形成しております。実際のスケールによるモックアップを造って検討を加え、また、取付金物の強度試験も何度も繰り返し....
The stone used for this base is the same stone used for the monoliths that line the path to the shrine.

25. Suzuki, Ryoji (2006) p. xvi.
Original Japanese:
野生と伝統が最初から持ちかまえていた。

26. Toyota, Motoi 豊田基 (2004) Available at: http://www.shikoku-np.co.jp/feature/kotohira/53/index.htm *(accessed on June 11, 2007)*.
Original Japanese:
環境庁(現環境省)の巨樹に関する調査(一九九一年)によると、お宮の社叢には幹周り三メートル以上の巨樹が三十三本も集中してあり、近い将来、この数はさらに増えていく可能性が高い。白峰神社周辺の大谷地区には、特にクスノキの巨木が多い。

7.15 Ryoji Suzuki's Saikan reads initially as a one-story structure.

7.16 Suzuki's conferment building, closer to the Main Shrine, is also under a flowing bark roof.

7.17 Seen from below, the conferment building is revealed as larger and more monumental.

7.18 The interior of the conferment building.

7.19 An exterior detail of stone and rusted steel.

7.15

7.16

7.17

7.18

7.19

7.20

7.21

strong personal ties to shrine authorities, through an old and intimate friend, Kyoji Takubo, who has collaborated with Suzuki once before. Takubo, instrumental in the effort to reorganize and reinvigorate the shrine is, in turn, a childhood friend of Kotohira's head priest, Yasutsugu Kotouka.

Suzuki was also able to offer one extremely appropriate precedent: his 1993 Kou'unji Temple in a suburb of Tokyo.[27] There the architect faced an unusual site, a bowl-like declivity into which he inserted his temple. Suzuki capped painted steel H-shaped columns on the exterior with a familiar hipped tile roof recalling the Nara era (710-794). Between the temple and its surrounding landscape, Suzuki employed a rich layering of stairs, catwalks and overlooks that turn the steep topography from an oddity to an advantage. In seeing this building, apparently, the shrine officials became convinced that Suzuki was understandably the best architect for their site as well.

Suzuki displays a life-long fascination with stairs in his work, perhaps partially inspired by Fumihiko Maki, who has also used stairs as an expressive device; Suzuki worked within the Maki office for two years in the 1970s, while remaining in the employ of contractor Takenaka. The younger architect can offer many examples of exuberant stairs, the best known his 1987 Azabu Edge Building in Roppongi, crested with a flight that seems almost an urban microcosm of Kotohira's intimidating slope. A roof of imposing stairs was also key at his 1990 Folly for the Osaka Flower Exposition; it was here that Suzuki also first explored the powerful effect of tall slabs of rusted Cor-ten steel – a material also exploited at Kotohira. More recently, Suzuki's 1998 Ashikita Youth Center in Kumamoto internalized stairways in a fashion that had earlier been expressed only in his residential structures, establishing the experience of moving through interior spaces as mysterious and enigmatic.

At Kotohira, Suzuki draws on all these devices, and yet is almost restrained in his use of stairs, making them subservient to the overall volume of the buildings he has created. They are nonetheless an important part of the way he links his structures to Kotohira's context. He argued:

> Each set of steps are resolutions of careful investigation concerning each slope of the hill, the inclinations and declinations, making the most of each winding corner, of each straight path ... Just as if watching a film, composed of numerous sequences of stairs.[28]

His published sketchbooks on the development of the shrine propose "... to make a hole in the stairs, to scrape off the stairs, to twist the exterior through the stairs, to stab into the interior, to turn the exterior inside-out ..."[29]

The most notable exterior stair is found in the new southern courtyard, in front of the larger office structure further from the Main Shrine, the one called the *Saikan*. Suzuki engages the slope falling away in front of the building with a wide, cascading granite stair (the same local stone used for the retaining walls). The broad steps seemingly end in a cantilever jutting over the landscape below – but the landing at the bottom is actually a turning point, and another tiny stair continues towards the Dawn Pavilion.

Within the *Saikan*, a space not open to the public, Suzuki uses stairs to accommodate the unseen complexities of the interior. Opposite the entrance, two apparently redundant flights hang in the open air under the large roof, only differing in the material of their

7.22

7.23

27. The name is sometimes written in English-language texts as Kohunji.

28. Suzuki, Ryoji (2006) p. xvi.

29. Ibid., p. 371. Original Japanese: 階段に穴を開けること、階段に削り取ること、外部を捻って、内部に突き刺すのと、外部を裏返すこと....

7.20 The Saikan also reveals itself to be larger on approach.

7.21 Broad steps from the Saikan follow the slope downwards towards the Dawn Pavilion.

7.22 The interior of the Saikan combines river rock and cypress with rusted steel structural slabs.

7.23 Suzuki's stepped pavilion for the 1990 Flower Exposition in Osaka was also an exploration in rusted slabs of steel.

7.24

7.25

7.26

7.24 Suzuki's 1987 Azabu Edge in Tokyo demonstrates his long interest in steps and stairs.

7.25–28 The 1993 Kou'unji Temple in a suburb of Tokyo, where Suzuki earlier explored bringing together modern steel structure with the materials and textures that easily express a religious role.

7.27

7.28

treads. These connect the upper level, a relatively modest 623-square-meter (about 6,700 square feet) footprint, with the remaining 1,104 square meters (nearly 11,885 square feet) concealed below. One stair is finished in gleaming golden Japanese cypress (*hinoki*) and the other is stone. But these flights are not redundant; the stone treads are for those wearing street shoes – for outside visitors, deliverymen, and others moving from the entrance to the private offices below. The wooden treads of the second stair accommodate the daily life of those working within the shrine, wearing on their feet only mitten-like white *tabi* socks when in its sacred spaces, and stocking-footed visitants receiving rituals.

It is worth a brief digression to point out the thoughtful articulation of these stairs, which, like those climbing to Kotohira itself, offer an uneven rhythm. The landings are longer than might be expected, and interrupt the flights not at the midpoint, but higher. The balustrades – detailed in a simple way that the architect has relied on for at least two decades – and the thick structural steel flat bars that interrupt to carry the stairs are articulated in two separate rhythms, reminiscent of Suzuki's passion for jazz.

The architect naturally extends the ritualistic character of his stairs to the floors as well, distinctly isolating raised wood plank planes from the darker granite of pavers where shoes are allowed. The gleaming wooden aisles that outline the box-like village of enclosed interior rooms are spatially compressed, but natural light falls through slits cut into the steel deck above and through the loose enclosure on each long face of the building. (Along each edge, Suzuki's signature gap, or *vide*, allows butterflies to float through freely, and birds dart across or make their nests within.[30]) The path to the inner offices of the head priest sits immediately beneath a glass-block line in the ceiling; light illuminates this narrowing artery as it extends from an open, undefined area towards the most intimate spaces of the structure. Throughout the *Saikan*, in fact, procession is marked by light: light from the open sky; white, artificial light tucked into the underside of the immaculate boxes housing internal spaces; light doubled through its reflection on stainless steel edging and baseboards. Suzuki says, "It is a small thing, but the light is all placed at the floor level, so in the evening the floor is lit, creating a feeling that [each volume] is floating."[31] Floating within a space embedded in the ground.

The modest conferment building closer to the Main Shrine also hides two stairs: for each, a thin, folded steel plate hovers inches above the lower floor, ostentatiously avoiding the final riser that would connect the two levels. The structures of these buildings employ three major elements: steel decks, H-shaped columns visible on the exterior of each building, and internal steel monoliths the engineer, Masato Araya of Oak Engineering, calls "*walumns*," combining the words for wall and column.[32] The floor decks symbolically act as barriers separating pure from profane, *kekkai*; commonly fences, but Kotohira's topography justified horizontal planes playing this role: "an absolute horizontal surface that isolates above the ground and underground."[33] Suzuki pointed out, "The Vierendeel structure's form above and the H-shaped steel below do not penetrate this steel floor, which is expressed as a *kekkai* barrier. I did not permit the elements above and below to be mixed."[34] Elsewhere, he has written:

> Everything was welded together, supported by welding each piece to the structure above. ... there is a steel

30. A revealing set of notes from a 1999 lecture lists five "intervals" that repeatedly inform his work: gaps (using also the French word "*vide*"), stairs, hollows (*creux*) and columns, clearings (*clairiere*), and "frame/screen/opening." See http://www.ryoji.co.jp/atelier/01menu.html (accessed 23 August, 2007).

31. Futagawa and Takamatsu (2004) p. 42. Original Japanese:
小さなことだけど、照明は全て足元に入れていて、夜は床が光ることで、浮いてような感じになる。

32. 壁柱.

33. Suzuk (2007) p. 74.

34. Futagawa and Takamatsu (2004) p. 42. Original Japanese:
上のウィーレンディールのラーメンを形成しているH型鋼は、結界としての鉄床を貫いていない。上と下が混じってしまうことを禁じています。

7.29 Within the Saikan, slabs of steel as much as 2.4 meters wide and six meters tall mark the inflection in the plan.

7.30 The plan of the lower floor of the Saikan reveals the structure's spatial complexity.

7.31 The slab between the Saikan's lower and upper floors is sliced through, bringing sunlight below.

7.29

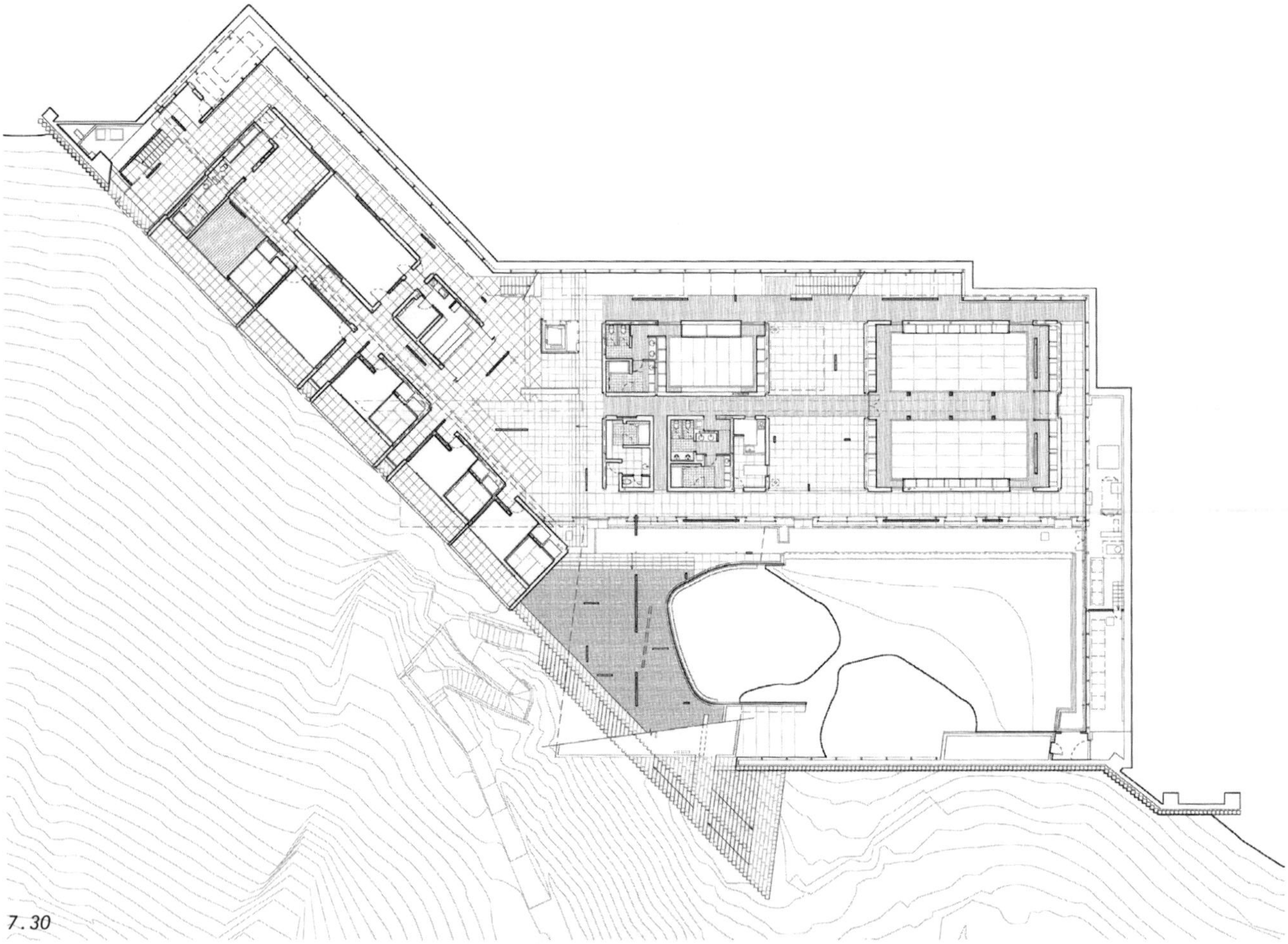

7.30

7.31

7.32 A stair at the conferment building stops just shy of touching the floor below.

7.33 One of two long stairs in the Saikan.

7.34 Light falling on steel and cedar.

7.35 An open space in the Saikan, where structural engineer Masato Araya's skillful handling of the steel structure makes it almost disappear.

7.36 Along the corridor of the Saikan's lower level, breaks between offices frame earth and sky beyond.

7.32

7.33

7.34

7.35

7.36

7.37 The path from the Saikan to the Dawn Pavilion below.

7.38, 39 The stairs of the Saikan also hover above the floor, not touching, the two territories separated by a slice of space.

7.40 Offices within the lower level of the Saikan expressed as perfect and pristine.

7.37

> plate stair that comes downward from the greenery. I wanted to suspend the stairs without any joints, so that the lowest step is actually floating 3 centimeters [above the floor].[35]

Suzuki's emphatic handling of this plane echoes Kuma's observations on the importance of raised floors in Japanese architecture, but Suzuki also offers more modern referents, entirely suitable to this seafarers' shrine (which enthusiastically supported the navy during many recent wars), calling it "A flat, artificial ground made of steel, positioned at the same level as the 'shrine zone,' and reminiscent of an aircraft carrier deck, separating aboveground from underground ..."[36] Elsewhere, Suzuki proposed that:

> ... the steel floor has a floating sense, an image like a boat. A boat, or perhaps one might suggest an island – a feeling that a separate world was constructed. The construction of this artificial plinth was done with the same technologies as boat building.[37]

The remarkably adroit spatial effect of the thin internal *walumns*, at turns disappearing and dominating, is surprisingly overlooked in discussions of these interiors. When architect and engineer first discussed structure, they decided a simple grid would lack needed artistry; instead they chose Mondrian as a model, breaking the plan into a looser grid and randomly rotating *walumns* in both directions. The open space of the lower floor in the conferment building blends with the leafy landscape outside a 23½-meter [77-foot] long expanse of mullion-free glass. At this opening, Araya's structure is nearly invisible, the *walumns* no more than a hand-span deep (12 centimeters, or about 5¾ inches) and only half a meter (19 inches) wide. By setting these structural elements perpendicular to the window, Araya renders them nearly inconspicuous.[38]

The structure is even more arresting in the larger spaces of the *Saikan*; in addition to rotating the direction of the *walumns*, Araya also allowed for variation in the width of each support. A walkway on the lower level is symmetrically flanked by pure white boxes enclosing inner space; columns are held back from the edges, drawing attention first to the boxes themselves, but also accenting the space of the walkway within. The formal foyer between is flanked by two areas similar in form and finish, but distinctive simply by the way the architect and engineer deployed the structure in each. In the open area towards the front, a cluster of three thin, nearly invisible vertical members establishes spatial continuity with the exterior – Araya says that Suzuki wanted to avoid any structure at all, and points out how two of these columns are parallel to the direction of sight when looking outside, thus rendering them close to invisible. In the area on the other side of the bisecting aisle, under a large opening in the floor above, only one wide *walumn* is present, a seemingly ancient monolith, recalling the standing stones that line the path through Kotohira. Yet this is far from the largest and most remarkable of these *walumns*; at the juncture where the *Saikan* inflects in plan, an open space is dominated by three 6-meter (over 19½ feet) tall slabs, the broadest 2.4 meters (nearly 8 feet) wide, exhibited like artworks. Charcoal-like strokes cross their surfaces, reminiscent of rough sketches on a Rothko, the result of accident. The steel was wrapped in wrinkled plastic when brought to the site; trapped moisture drew these lines. Suzuki, the son of an abstract painter, saw their beauty and accepted it. (But while the effect at Kotohira was not deliberate, such paint-

35. Ibid. Original Japanese:
...全溶接に拘ったのは目地を完全に無くしたかったから.目地は工業化の刻印でコンクリートですら打ち継ぎに目地が現れますからね。完全な目地無しが可能なのは唯一、全溶接の鉄だけです.
全溶接ということもあって、そこからいろんな物を溶接で吊っているんです。例えば、鉄板から緑に向かって下に降りていく大階段。これも吊られていて、一番下の段で三センチくらい浮いている。

36. Suzuki (2004) p. 64.

37. Futagawa and Shin (2004) p. 42.
Original Japanese:
実際にはあの鉄床は浮遊感のある船のようなイメージもあるのです。船って島に例えられたりもするように、もうひとつの別の世界を構築している感じがあるでしょう。この人工地盤の構造も造船技術と同じやり方でつくられている。

38. The greater work of the structure occurs against the foundation to the west, in a long shear wall.

7.38

7.39

7.41

7.42

7.43

7.44

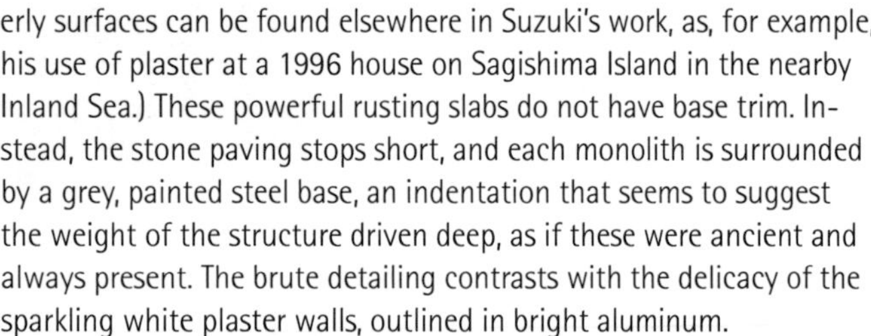

erly surfaces can be found elsewhere in Suzuki's work, as, for example, his use of plaster at a 1996 house on Sagishima Island in the nearby Inland Sea.) These powerful rusting slabs do not have base trim. Instead, the stone paving stops short, and each monolith is surrounded by a grey, painted steel base, an indentation that seems to suggest the weight of the structure driven deep, as if these were ancient and always present. The brute detailing contrasts with the delicacy of the sparkling white plaster walls, outlined in bright aluminum.

The rusted steel used throughout the structure yields a variety of textures. The raw, rough surfaces of Araya's *walumns* are repeated in rusting steel cobblestones the artist Takubo placed in the courtyard of the *Saikan*. But in areas where steel might come in contact with the hand, it is sealed and has a leathery finish. More intriguing is a flaking steel drip edge running the length of the roofline above the private offices in the *Saikan*. Suzuki stated, "The surface of steel was left to rust in order to respect the material's properties, as it would record the passage of time."[39] Tomoaki Tanaka once remarked on "... Suzuki's pursuit of 'material memory'..." continuing, "Materials necessarily take on a temporal dimension, the moment they are freighted with the concept of memory."[40]

39. Suzuki (2004) p. 64.

7.45

7.41 A guardhouse, seldom seen, is a cubic contemporary structure made entirely of welded steel.

7.42 Under the eaves of the Saikan, its modern architectural gestures are less obvious.

7.43 Part of the steel plinth separating the two levels of the Saikan.

7.44 Another view of the Saikan's two levels.

7.45, 46 Beneath a stair, steel cobblestones by the artist Kyoji Takubo.

7.47

7.47 The 1934 Kudan Kaikan, originally "Soldiers' Hall," an example of the Imperial Roof Style, its tiled roof peeping above a modern concrete and brick base.

7.48, 49 Hiroshi ("Jin") Watanabe's 1937 competition design for what was then the Imperial Household Museum (now the Tokyo National Museum) is a particularly accomplished expression of the Imperial Roof Style.

7.48

In a public discussion in March, 2007, architect Souhei Imamura challenged Suzuki:

> In both the 1991 Seijo Kou'unji Temple ... and in the 2004 Kotohira Shrine Project, you adopted a classical Japanese roof. In these two, a temple and a shrine, was this a constraint you were given? Or is it something you dared to do? After all, these days the opportunity to design a roof is almost nonexistent.[41] Normally, the roof is flat; there is no awareness of the roof ... after your talk today, I have come to think ... that you don't like flat roofs and have approached the problem of the roof from that way of thinking.[42]

Suzuki began his response by discussing some of his buildings topped by stairs:

> Thinking about the roof, and stairs above a roof, in the end, ... I have a bad feeling about [capping a building with] a horizontal line. I don't mean a slope is automatically better ... But for me, perhaps these stairs emerge as another line of inclination.[43]

But he then went further, articulating his use of the roof as based in a lost heritage:

> ... in truth, I think a roof that is essentially flat, that has no presence, is undesirable. Until [the end of] Japan's Edo Era, architecture – as a rule – had a roof. That roof was a part of the character of the building, but today we rarely have the chance to build such a roof, and making one has become unfashionable.[44]

One of the more serious American academic researchers on Japanese architecture, the late Mary Neighbor Parent, spent years of her life closely focused on this subject. In the opening sentence to her book, *The Roof in Japanese Buddhist Architecture*, Parent notes, "The roof is perhaps the most attractive, compelling part of Japanese architecture; it holds an undeniable fascination, especially among non-Japanese, for its graceful proportions set off by sophisticated and intricate support systems."[45] Today, when few architects make a serious study of the roof and few people take the time for either historical studies or religious pursuits, the appeal Parent ascribes to non-Japanese, writing in the 1970s, can probably be extended to urbane Japanese as well. As long ago as 1983, Isamu Kurita observed, "The fact that Japanese are seeing charm and depth in their own tradition reveals how alien it has indeed become."[46]

At the March 2007 discussion where Imamura challenged Suzuki, the older architect also acknowledged:

> When we began working on Kotohira, this became very clear to me: the roof and the landscape are connected. Modern architecture has a simplicity, like the launch of a white ship; we have arrived at a point where it is sharply divided from the landscape. This includes Le Corbusier, [or] contemporary architecture's "white cubes;" the feeling is that ... the roof is no longer necessary. In the case of Kotohira, the slope of the mountain, the inclined forest thicket, the cliffs – in the midst of all this to suddenly and abruptly introduce a long rectangular box is completely incompatible. The older remains are all around, wonderful Edo Era architecture which all have roofs, an architecture that is connected to and enfolded in the landscape. These roofs exist

40. Tanaka (2003) p. 155.

41. 今村創平。The word both Imamura and Suzuki are using for roof is 屋根 [*yane*], which implies a sloped roof; a different word is used for flat roofs when speaking Japanese.

42. Discussion on 11 March, 2007 at Aoyama Book Center in the HMV Store, Shibuya, Tokyo. Transcript available at: http://mdr.sub.jp/tenplusone/0705_suzuki_yatuka/suzuki_yatuka04.html (accessed 12 June, 2007).

43. Ibid. Original Japanese:
屋根と屋上につく階段のことを考えますと、やはり水平線に対しての居心地の悪さという理由がありますね。だからといって水平でなく斜めであればいいというものでもないわけです。僕の場合は、もうひとつの傾斜する地盤として、階段が出てきているのかもしれません。

44. Ibid.
屋上をまっ平らにすることの根拠のなさが、気持ち悪いと思っています。日本の江戸時代までの建物には必ず屋根があるわけです。その屋根というものは一体なんなのか、と考えながら、しかし今のわれわれがそういう屋根を作ることの根拠もないわけで、くすぶっている状態がありました。

45. Parent (1983) p. 1 of Foreword.

46. Kurita (1983) p. 131.

7.49

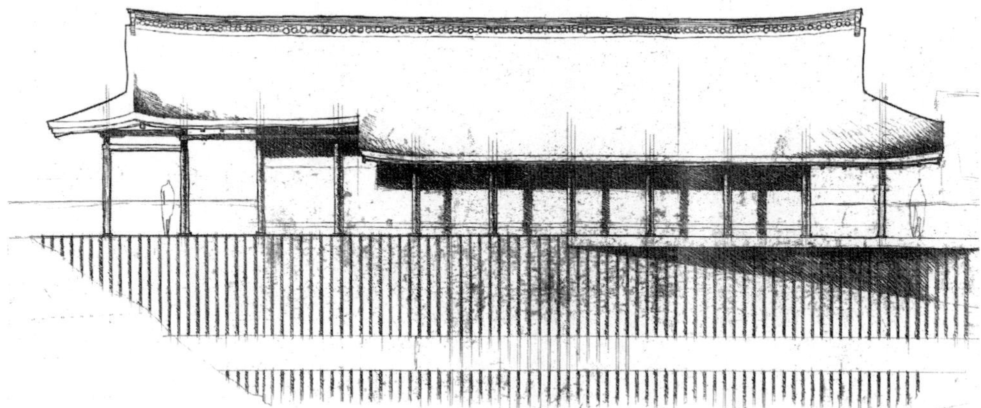

7.50

7.50 *Ryoji Suzuki's early sketch for the conferment building demonstrates the degree to which the final design was influenced by collaboration with a shrine carpenter.*

> in a very powerful setting. So, from the beginning, I felt I wanted to do a proper roof. Not a roof that was a modern roof with a simplified gable, but a roof that was a classical form, within Japanese history – that is what interested me. You normally cannot do something, so you think you do not want to do it.[47]

In the West, a heavy roof has a pacific character, often used to reflect that a building is residential or rural; the way Suzuki and Imamura speak, arguing this choice is daring, something that cannot be done, must seem decidedly odd. A brief interlude in twentieth-century Japanese architecture has freighted the roof with weighty associations. As the nation lurched from advocacy of all things Western towards constructing a nationalist identity, it arrived at a point where key institutions were capped in large, tiled roofs, in the style known as *Teikan Yoshiki*, or the "Imperial Crown Style." For a short period, the critic Noboru Kawagoe wrote, "... advertisements for public architecture requested that *all* structures be of 'a Japanese style founded in Oriental taste.' Many ferro-concrete buildings covered with heavy tiled roofs were designed and constructed ..."[48] David Stewart, in his book *The Making of a Modern Japanese Architecture: 1868 to the Present*, baldly argues that such an approach became "the recognized emblem of Japanese nationalism, and, later, expansionism."[49] Although both Stewart and Jonathan Reynolds, offering a more detailed discussion on the origins of the style,[50] demonstrate that well-meaning Westerners were the first to propose capping modern structures with a roof reminiscent of tradition, the long history of the Japanese roof became tainted by the insistence on such an approach by mid-century fascists.

Suzuki's stance was not taken naïvely; writing of his Kou'unji Temple, Suzuki acknowledged that religious buildings in Japan involve "... some degree of political conflict between 'modern' and 'traditional' principles."[51] And earlier, writing on other matters, he reflected that:

> [W]hat is needed now is none other than a 'political science' of architecture. It hardly needs pointing out that this will not be a Fascist kind of political science, which could seek to impose a single value on the whole and control it, but rather a kind of 'public' or 'democratic' political science in which a plurality of values can coexist, free to spark off tensions from each other.[52]

At the moment, most Japanese architects are far more willing to rely on abstractions of traditional architecture than to employ historical conventions in a straightforward way. (This probably also accounts for architects' inclination to adopt the freer *sukiya* style over more ordered historical prototypes.) Japanese architects have little opportunity to develop a deep understanding of the nation's rich and demanding architectural history, whether through education, commissions or even observation.[53] Traditional buildings like temples and shrines have an uneasy relationship with the practice of architecture; the profession was brought to Japan in the mid-nineteenth century, primarily in the service of Western building styles and typologies. Constructing classical religious structures remained in the firm control of carpentry guilds, and is so even today. Gregory Clancey, writing on the historical role of carpenters (using the Japanese word, *daiku*) argued that the reasons went beyond prosaic ones:

> Possessing ... knowledge was as essential to the identity of the *daiku* [carpenter] as possessing woodworking tools,

47. Discussion on 11 March, 2007, at Aoyama Book Center in the HMV Store, Shibuya, Tokyo. Transcript accessed at: http://mdr.sub.jp/tenplusone/0705_suzuki_yatuka/suzuki_yatuka04.html (accessed 12 June, 2007).
Original Japanese:
金刀比羅をやってみてはっきりとわかったことは、屋根はランドスケープに属してる、ということでした。近代的な建築は、あたかも白い船が出航してくるように単体で、ランドスケープから切り離されてでてきているわけです。コルビュジエも含め、現在建っているホワイト・キューブも、まさにそういう感じで、その場合には屋根というものは必要ないわけです。金刀比羅の場合は、山の斜面や森の鬱蒼とした傾斜や断崖のなかで、いきなり長方形の箱を持ってきたら強烈な違和感が出てくる。また周りに古い遺構があり、江戸時代の良い建物のいくつかが屋根を持っていて、ランドスケープの繋がりの中に建築を巻き込んでいく、とても強い装置として、屋根が存在していた。そこで、最初から屋根をちゃんとやりたいと思いました。そして、近代建築にはまる正三角形切り妻のような屋根ではなくて、日本の歴史に入りこんだ古典としての屋根造形の方が面白いだろうと思いました。普段やらないので、やりたくなった。

48. Kawagoe (1968) p. 19. My emphasis.

49. Stewart (1987) p. 107.

50. Reynolds (1996a) pp. 38–47. Cherie Wendelken offers a more open-minded discussion of this style. See Wendelken (2000) pp. 819–828 available at: http://muse.jhu.edu/journals/positions/v008/8.3wendelken.html

51. Suzuki (1992) p. 73.

52. Suzuki (1987) p. 36.

53. Many years ago, one of my American graduate students, Sarah Lavery, came to Japan on a National Science Foundation Fellowship and asked Tokyo's best-known architects when they had last visited a temple or shrine. Most, unlike Suzuki, were simply unable to remember recent occasions other than shrine visits at New Year, when the pressing crowds and temporary protective apparatus hardly encourage thoughtful study.

7.51

7.52

> books, patrons and so forth ... It also acted out *daiku* closeness to Shinto and its priesthood, a religion deeply entwined with forests and trees. To this day, Shinto shrines are nearly always wooden and *daiku*-built ...[54]

Except for carpenter-architects who specialize in such structures, the opportunity Suzuki has experienced, to design two religious complexes, is one few are likely to enjoy today.

When discussing his 1993 Kou'unji Temple, Suzuki pointed out, "It is not an easy task to follow all the strict rules and orders of complexity, which have been traditionally applied for [*sic*] classical temples in Japan. So I had to 'study' hard, right from the beginning."[55] The architect also acknowledged others' contributions to his effort at Kotohira:

> I aimed for the characteristic curve found in roofs ... I did a lot of research, asked many questions of a history professor and of the shrine carpenter. The way we initially laid out the drawings of the roof and its reality today are completely different. Other than the roof I had a pretty clear grasp of proportions, but the roof was a different matter.[56]

He especially credits a carpenter, Nobuyuki Yamamoto of Fujita Shaji:[57]

> ... I did not make choices [about the buildings] alone, but was able to ask specialists about many points. Truthfully, the Master Carpenter was a sagacious fellow who saved me. This project was actually a first experience for him, too, but he treated it all as an adventure. He responded with great flexibility. Thanks to him, this audacious outcome came together. Neither had ever done something like this before, but we were thinking we might be able to accomplish something we had never done, or maybe not ...[58]

Having decided to use a traditional roof, Suzuki faced confounding choices: "Should I do a Tenpyou [era] roof, a Kamakura [era] roof? (Laughs.) And I thought ... if I did both, one could be delicate and the other powerful."[59] Although he does not draw a parallel between the Dawn Pavilion and the Main Shrine, one monumental and the other delicately curving, it is hard not to assume that this was part of what drove Suzuki to accept the challenge of producing not merely one convincing roof form, but two distinctly different ones. Today, the Main Hall faces the floating Kamakura-style roof over Suzuki's nearby conferment hall, and the heavy, tiled Tenpyou-style roof of the *Saikan* seems linked to the monumentality of the Dawn Pavilion immediately below. Suzuki explained the implications of these two choices, saying:

> ... the *Saikan* was tile from the beginning. Immediately adjacent is the existing roof sheltering votive tablets [the *Ema* Hall] and it was also tile. So the new *Saikan* building (the "*Ryokutaiden*") is a tile roof, too. And it naturally developed that there were two roofs, with extremely different characters. The conferment building is held lower than the Main Shrine, but with the delicate sense of its *hinoki* bark roof. The other, the *Saikan* building, is deeper within the precincts, 48 meters [157 feet] long; a large, extensive roof finished in both convex and concave tiles. I thought of these two buildings as contrasting. The conferment building was from the beginning [in the style of] the Kamakura era [1185–1332], and the *Saikan* has the feel of the *Tenpyou* Period of the Nara era [c. 710–794].

54. Clancey (2006) p. 29.

55. http://www.ryoji.co.jp/atelier/01/B0/B0-12.html (accessed 14 June, 2007).

56. Discussion on 11 March, 2007 at Aoyama Book Center in the HMV Store, Shibuya, Tokyo. Transcript available at: http://mdr.sub.jp/tenplusone/0705_suzuki_yatuka/suzuki_yatuka04.html (accessed 12 June, 2007).
Original Japanese:
独特のそりのある、...を狙っています。これについては、歴史の先生や宮大工に聞いて、随分研究しました。図面に落としても、屋根だけは、図面と実際の印象が全然違うのです。屋根以外は全部プロポーションが分かるのですが。屋根だけは別ものでした。

57. 藤田社寺の 山本信幸。

58. Futagawa and Shin (2004) p. 44.
Original Japanese:
もちろんぼくだけでは決めれなくて，色々な方面の専門家に考えてもらいながらです。棟梁が実に聡明な方で救われました。彼にとっても初めての体験で、色々と冒険だったようです。とても柔軟に対応してくれ、おかげで大胆になれた。お互いにやったことはないけれど、かつてないところまでいけるかもしれない、あるいはははずしちゃうかもしれない。。。

59. Ibid. The Tenpyo era was between 729 and 748 and is part of the Nara period (c. 710–794).
Original Japanese:
ようし天平をやろう、鎌倉もやろう、というような(笑)。どうせやるのなら、この際、繊細と豪放の両方ともやってしまおう、と思いました。

60. Futagawa and Shin (2004) p. 43.
Original Japanese:
一方、斎館は元々瓦だったし、また隣り合っている既存の絵馬殿も瓦なので、新しい斎館棟(緑黛殿)も本瓦葺きです。そうすることで、二つのタイプの極端に性格の異なる伽藍が出てきたと言える．一つは、本宮より低く抑えた繊細な感じの檜皮葺きの授与所棟。そして敷地奥にある、長さ四八メートルと伸び伸びした大きな本瓦葺きの斎館棟。その二つの建物を対照的に考えていったわけです。イメージとしては、授与所は鎌倉初期で、斎館は奈良天平という感覚。(P)授与所では、とにかく桧皮をいかに綺麗(きれい)に見せるかということを研究しましたよ．

7.53

7.54

7.55

7.56

7.57

> In order to display the beauty of the *hinoki* bark roof on the conferment building, I did my research.[60]

Suzuki elsewhere elaborated:

> For the conferment hall facing the Main Shrine I chose a *hinoki* [Japanese cypress] bark roof. Every 33 years at Kotohira, because of the *hinoki* bark [finish], they hold a rite of renewal, they remove and reroof with *hinoki* bark. *Hinoki* bark is today a very expensive finish, yet I felt that it was the only choice. If you use *hinoki* bark, there are no joints in the roof finish. With tile or a metal panel roof, joints are inevitable, but *hinoki* bark has no joints if the roof is made of a certain thickness. I aimed for the characteristic curve found in roofs from the early part of the Kamakura Era [1185–1332].[61]

Mary Parent argued of Japan's architectural history that, "The only historical genre of building that reveals real continuity of development is temple architecture, the mainstream of Japanese architecture until the early fifteenth century. Extant examples from the earliest period, encompassing the Nara ... are few ..."[62] Later in the same text, she wrote, "In the ancient period, exactitude in aligning rafters was not demanded, but from the end of the Kamakura period, workmanship became conspicuously precise ..."[63] continuing, "By about 1430 ... no conspicuous changes [to the roof] are apparent."[64] In other words, by picking the bold power of the Nara era and the graceful curves of the Kamakura period, Suzuki also used two roofs that refer to the beginning and end points of the development of roof form in Japanese architecture.

The larger tile roof capping the *Saikan* is assiduously correct and

61. Discussion on 11 March, 2007 at Aoyama Book Center in the HMV Store, Shibuya, Tokyo. Transcript available at: http://mdr.sub.jp/tenplusone/0705_suzuki_yatuka/suzuki_yatuka04.html (accessed 12 June, 2007).
Original Japanese:
本堂の向かいに建っているお礼所は檜皮葺にしました。金刀比羅では、33年がかりで檜皮をためて、遷座祭ごとに屋根を葺き替えます。この檜皮は現在ではとても高価な材料です。それが使えるということで、檜皮葺しかないと思いました。檜皮を使えば、目地なしの屋根ができるわけです。瓦とか金属パネルというのは必ず目地が出てしまいますが、檜皮だったら目地なしで、ある厚みで屋根を作れる。独特のそりのある、鎌倉の初期の屋根を狙っています。

62. Parent (1983) p. 24.
63. Ibid., p. 181.
64. Ibid., p. 182.

7.51 Shrine carpenter Nobuyuki Yamamoto and an assistant.

7.52 Two development models of the conferment building roof, a full-scale drawing of the gable behind.

7.53 A wooden bearing block sits on a steel wide flange.

7.54 Suzuki and Yamamoto lay out the curve of the conferment building's gable full scale, using wood and paper cut-outs.

7.55 Grids are used to transfer the curve from full-scale templates.

7.56 The conferment building's two structural systems meet, welded steel supporting intricate wooden joinery.

7.57 The roof of the Saikan, simpler structural systems.

7.58

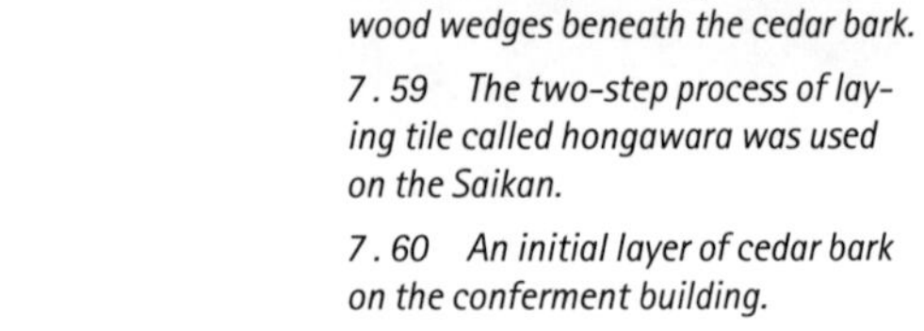

7.58 The springy curve of the conferment building's cantilever is further accomplished by layers of wood wedges beneath the cedar bark.

7.59 The two-step process of laying tile called hongawara was used on the Saikan.

7.60 An initial layer of cedar bark on the conferment building.

yet it relies on unusual prototypes. The model for this building is a no-longer extant eighth-century structure, the Choushuudou at Nara's Toshodaiji temple.[65] Suzuki's first sketches were inspired by the current Choushuudou, a result of permissive twentieth-century repairs, an elaborate *kiritsuma* roof combining a gable end with a skirt-like section turned up in an exaggerated curve. He simplified the *Saikan* to its present form: two diagonal braces atop a rainbow beam, purlins sitting directly on top of pillars, resulting in a modern directness. Parent also indicates, "Nara ... period buildings are characterized by low eaves ..."[66] and this lower eave line lends a sense of intimacy to what is an imposing structure. When visitors first view the *Saikan*, the roof seems to lightly hover, its brackets concealed in the dark shadow of the eaves.

Any roof form depends to a large degree on the structure beneath. The structure of the *Saikan* is exposed. By contrast, the conferment hall draws from the thirteenth-century Kamakura period when false ceilings commonly concealed the complex structure needed to achieve flowing shapes. The fluid form of this roof justified the use of expensive *hinoki* bark as a finish, a pliant material. The hidden framework (allowably unruly because it is concealed) and lightweight roof finish also allow for unusually long cantilevers, another feature of the era – one that Suzuki exuberantly flaunts at Kotohira.

Parent suggests the polar opposites seen here: "The roof in Japanese architecture has both charm and grandeur. Its form is animated by flowing curves and by deeply overhanging eaves lightly curved at the corners and, by its form as a whole, which is like *a huge cover over all*."[67] Notably, these two roof styles are not commonly associated with shrines – but when shrines were mingled with temples, they

7.59

sometimes adapted such a form. Parent explained:

> ... in order to compete with the imposing structures erected within the precincts of Buddhist temples, Shinto shrine architecture did emulate them to a certain degree ... Japanese history has witnessed the ... amalgamation of the two religions, so that Buddhist structures are sometimes found within shrine precincts or vice versa.[68]

Considering Kotohira's history, then, adapting Buddhist architectural forms for these two new Shinto structures was not entirely odd or unprecedented. Nonetheless, it is clear that the client knowingly per-

7.60

65. 唐招提寺.
66. Parent (1983) p. 27.
67. Ibid., p. 8.
68. Ibid., p. 9.

7.61

7.62

mitted Suzuki to encompass these allusions, and also that these roof styles were far from inevitable: there is no eighth-century Nara-era precedent within the shrine precincts and the only Kamakura-era structure I am aware of is the bell tower outside the entrance to the shrine. By using these styles, Suzuki recalls the long-destroyed structures of Kotohira's Buddhist past.

In both of Suzuki's Kotohira buildings – one roof simple and massive, the other fluid and gracefully dainty – the roof is the most imposing feature of the building. Parent speculates:

> One reason for the often disproportionate size of the roof to the body of the building is that perhaps such a combination developed consciously from the necessity of using humble materials which could be offset by an imposing roof. Also, the psychological preference for a simple intimate interior had to be counterbalanced by an impressive exterior. This could be resolved by the huge roof.[69]

Suzuki offers a strong architectural presence on the exterior; since most visitors to Kotohira will never enter these two new buildings, this gesture is a generous one. Nonetheless, there is much to be appreciated inside, where the spaces are surprisingly intimate, in sharp contrast to the character of each roof. The welded steel structure yields an unexpectedly airy space. Suzuki explained:

> With a roof like this, if you were to build the whole structure entirely following the era, today it would be kitsch and out of place. I had to sever it somewhere. So the columns became steel. A roof from time immemorial, juxtaposed with steel, a material of today.[70]

While the roofscape and its wooden structure closely follow the conventions of tradition, inside these buildings are audaciously contemporary – subtly marked on the exterior by the H-shaped steel colonnade, but only fully appreciated within. Ironically for the pilgrims who pass unknowingly by these structures, their most modern elements are hidden, accommodating monks robed in archaic apparel.

Earlier I argued that there is more than one way to view history; Fujimori sees a continuum, while Kuma draws on a past that is made up of fixed moments. It would be easy to argue that Suzuki, authoritatively employing two distinct styles from the periods that bracket the historical development of temple roofs, sees history as Kuma does. But this overlooks the way Suzuki integrates his buildings into the site. The treads that rise through the shrine date from many moments in its development. While some stones are hundreds of years old, Suzuki's stairs are a continuation of this path, using the same materials found throughout the shrine. He did not treat the priests and their work as ancient, but instead offered contemporary interiors of white plaster with marble chips, aluminum, and dramatic, rusting steel. At Kotohira, Suzuki offers both views of history: a sense of time as something known and fixed, something which can be quoted, and a sense of time unrolling like a scroll, unfolding like a film.

7.63

7.64

69. Ibid., p. 207.

70. Discussion on 11 March, 2007, at Aoyama Book Center in the HMV Store, Shibuya, Tokyo. Transcript available at: http://mdr.sub.jp/tenplusone/0705_suzuki_yatuka/suzuki_yatuka04.html (accessed 12 June, 2007). このように屋根は、当時のやり方を踏襲しつつ作っていったわけですが、でも建築全体をそうしてしまうと、今度はキッチュになって、浮いてしまうわけです。どこかで切断しないといけない。だから柱は鉄でいきたいと思いました。鉄という現代的な材料とぶつかるように、古来の屋根がある。

7.61 The conferment building's buoyant curves are only possible with its lighter hinoki bark roof finish.

7.62 The cleaner and more modern look of the Saikan is an expression of its simple structure, but it is the older of the two roof forms Suzuki drew on, dating to the eighth century.

7.63, 64 The most modern parts of this architecture are inhabited by priests, and only rarely seen by the public.

Ancient Izumo and Oku

Fumihiko Maki

8

Ise and Izumo, be it remarked, are the Mecca and Medina of the Shinto cult.
—*Basil Hall Chamberlain*[1]

In the Spring of 2000, preparations for a festival at Izumo Grand Shrine, the oldest shrine in Japan, accidentally unearthed a pillar estimated to be nearly 800 years old. It was an immense three meters (nearly ten feet) in diameter, composed of a trio of fat cedar logs banded together with steel, buried at the point where today worshippers enter the innermost precincts of the Grand Shrine. Shortly afterwards, two similarly bundled shafts were found nearby. For years, scholars have debated the existence of a vermillion lacquered shrine said to be an improbable 48 meters tall (157 feet), known only through a single drawing from the Heian period (794–1185).[2] The placement and arrangement of these wooden fragments demonstrated conclusively the towering shrine truly existed. The unprepossessing timber lumps were displayed shortly after, in the early days of May in the same year; over 2500 people lined up before the exhibition opened, and in a few days nearly twenty thousand people viewed the artifacts.[3]

The earlier structure on this site, called the Great Shrine of Kitsuki, was reached by a ceremonial stair that must have been terrifying to climb.[4] The thick timber columns supporting the shrine were driven directly into dirt, vulnerable to decay; the name "Kitsuki" refers to this practice. Of today's shrine, Arata Isozaki writes that Japan's earliest architectural historians "... believed the style of Izumo *Taisha* [Grand Shrine] in Shimane Prefecture – *taishi zukuri* or *sumiyoshi-zukuri* – to be the more original of the two [shrines of Ise and Izumo] in terms of Japan's Shinto typologies."[5] Unlike its politically more central cousin Ise, Izumo is no longer rebuilt on a regular schedule (if indeed it ever was – this point, too, is being debated); the practice has certainly not occurred since the late eighteenth century. Many historians say the shrine's unusual size assured that regular reconstruction was economically oppressive. While now only half the height of the old Kitsuki Shrine, Izumo Grand Shrine is the tallest in Japan at 24 meters (just short of 79 feet). Its unusually monumental scale is reinforced throughout the grounds, in features like the huge rope hanging from its eaves, the nation's largest *shimenawa*, 8 meters – about 26 feet – in length and weighing about 1.6 tons.

Pritzker-Prize-winning architect Fumihiko Maki proposed an uncommonly solemn and monumental museum to house the artifacts found at Izumo, a distinct contrast to the delicacy customary in his work. Maki was particularly suited to the demands of this project. Over the course of a long and productive career, Maki has thought a great deal about the demands of modern public buildings, especially museums. He has also reflected deeply on how architects today address traditions – especially the history of places – in their work. An apt title Alex Krieger used for a brief discussion on Maki's work offers an insightful analysis of his strengths in an epigrammatic eleven words: "To Remain Modern, to Return to Sources, and to Employ Time."[6] Maki differs from the other architects I have so far discussed; he sees the past as Kuma does, unchangeable and timeless moments, albeit al-

8.1 Fumihiko Maki's 2006 Shimane Museum of Ancient Izumo employs materials and colors unusual for the architect.

1. Chamberlain (1893) p. 366.
2. This structure's height – and other features like the length of its stair – continue to be debated; height estimates are based on an ancient children's textbook that described it in relation to other known structures.
3. The timing of the display helped a great deal; it was during the Golden Week holiday. An article in the *Shimane Nichinichi News* on 8 May, 2000, reported that between 10:00 a.m. and 4:00 p.m. on the first day, 9,500 people attended; on the second, when the exhibition ran from 9:30 a.m. to 4 p.m., 9,300 people attended, for a total of 18,800 viewers. In an earlier piece I wrote on this museum, the attendance numbers I relied on were casual reports estimating closer to ten thousand attendees. See Buntrock (2006b) p. 44-49. Importantly, it was also announced that this was going to be the only opportunity to see all three bundles together. For more on this find, see Imafuji, Akira 今藤啓 and *Kenchiku Toshi* [建築都市] Workshop, ed. *Taisha Kenchiku Jisho* 大社建築事始 [The Beginning of Taisha Architecture] (2002), especially two chapters: Fujisawa, Akira 藤澤彰. "*Kodai Kenchiku Sukeiru*" 古代建築スケール [The Scale of Ancient Architecture] pp. 9-47 and Matsuo, Mitsuaki 松尾充晶. "*Chichuu Kenchiku no Suke-ru*" 地中建築のスケール [The Scale of Architecture Embedded in the Earth] pp. 49-73. Terunobu Fujimori and Toyo Ito also have essays in this book.
4. For more on the current state of archaeological theories related to these findings, see Matsuo (2004). Available at: http://www2.pref.shimane.jp/kodai/about-kodai/matsuo.htm (accessed 1 May, 2005).
5. Isozaki (2006) p. 119.
6. Krieger, Alex. "To Remain Modern, to Return to Sources, and to Employ Time" (1993). Krieger's title is itself a quote of Ricoeur's "... how to become modern and return to sources."

8.2

8.3

8.2, 3 The Grand Shrine of Izumo is one of Japan's most venerated Shinto sites.

8.4 A small shrine within Maki's chic shopping complex, Hillside Terrace in Tokyo.

tered as our understanding grows. But in the end, Maki uses history to highlight and underscore the modernity of his work, assertively juxtaposing the two knowingly and deliberately. Maki explained this reading of history as it related to an observation deck he designed, overlooking the roof of Izumo Grand Shrine, "After coming in contact with the ancient collections within the museum, from the observation deck you can feel the overlap of the past and today, created in the 'real time' of this place. The architecture and its environment display multiple histories in a meaningful dialogue."[7]

Internationally, Fumihiko Maki is best known for his evolving design of a complex of buildings at Hillside Terrace, constructed between 1969 and 1992.[8] Developed in six stages, the grouping demonstrates Maki's growing skill in manipulating public and private space and his increasingly elegant detailing. Although often overlooked, Hillside Terrace also offers a noteworthy elucidation of Maki's handling of nature and cultural history, in a precedent directly linked to the Shimane Museum of Ancient Izumo.

When Hillside Terrace first broke ground, the surrounding district was leafy and suburban, but close enough to Shibuya – a major transportation node – to anticipate change. Maki incorporated the precincts of a Taisho-era villa bordering his site on the south, a lushly overgrown zone destined to become distinctive. The first two phases of his design mediate deliberately between a retail façade pressed hard against the street and Maki's framed views of the compound's treetops. In Phase Three, Maki awkwardly faced a new challenge: a small shrine atop a *kofun* (a burial mound, perhaps never used, of unknown age, but believed to date as far back as the seventh century). Maki left the mound untouched, respectfully squeezing new retail activity against the edges of the site. Economically, this is the weakest retail zone of the complex, notable only because neither the architect nor the developer has made any effort to fine-tune the territory in later phases of construction.

While his design in Phase Three might be less successful commercially than the other phases of Hillside Terrace, it yielded one of Maki's most influential essays, first published in English in the journal that also debuted Phase Three to an international audience: "Japanese City Spaces and the Concept of *Oku*." Maki argued in this essay:

> For Japanese, the land is a living entity. At the foundation of this idea there is a feeling of deep respect for the land based upon its reverence – a feeling deeply rooted in folk beliefs ... the Japanese do have a strong aversion towards removing existing wells or *tumuli*.[9]

His explanation of the embedded and innermost space called *oku* does more than merely justify the presence of a burial mound in a chic shopping complex. Maki's work since has been almost always organized with an awareness of the importance of the *oku* within; silent open spaces, sometimes lush and green, expanding and somehow empty at a point when most Western architects would choose to highlight the heart as overfull and active.

The essay established Maki as an insightful interpreter; his effort reflects what Kuma suggested when he wrote of overcoming "... Orientalism to expose a deeper truth at its core."[10] Maki was not interested in encouraging a romanticized view of Japan, but his international experiences also made him fully aware that he saw the world differently because of who he was and where he has lived. Early in his career he worked and taught in the United States for a number

8.4

7. Maki, Fumihiko interview. Maki (2007) p. 102.
8. The nearby Hillside West, a detached annex to the original complex, was completed in 1998.
9. Maki (1975) p. 62.
10. Kuma (2004c) p 152. Original Japanese: 数寄のコンセプトの中にオリエンタリズムを超えた真の他者性の表現を見つけ出し...

8.5

8.6

8.7

8.5 A large study model of a crucial space at the Shimane Museum of Ancient Izumo, used by the Maki office in design development.

8.6 Maki's sketch of the museum shows the relationship between his museum, the Izumo Grand Shrine, and the landscape.

8.7 Maki's competition drawing of the view from his museum, the sacred landscape of the Kitayama range dominating Izumo Shrine's magnificent roof.

8.8

8.9

of years, and also traveled widely. Unlike Isozaki, the more international Maki does not profess that today's Japanese have merely become Western. In 1979, Maki wrote of his time abroad, "... I went to America, but the real meaning of my stay ... [was] in having been able to take a good look at postwar Japan from a distance."[11]

Maki's theoretical and international outlook extends beyond his own work. Ryoji Suzuki and Kengo Kuma each recall their time in Maki's office as pivotal; Suzuki says that the two years he spent in the office were something like being in an intellectually intense research lab. According to both, Maki frequently engaged staff in complex and challenging discussions about the places where he traveled and the changes Japan faced. These experiences freed each of the younger architects to shape their own approaches to theory and to time, taking on influences from both at home and abroad.

In his reflections on what he saw, Maki contrasted Japanese and Western spatial hierarchy. In the essay on *oku*, he argued indigenous Japanese beliefs embraced a multiplicity of weighted moments in the landscape – in contrast, he wrote, monotheistic religions value a single, visually celebrated center. Maki outlined how distant mountains and unseen shrines stood as spiritual *foci* in Japan. He argued:

> By discovering the significance of woods and land in light of Japan's ethnological history, we can further extend our awareness of the pervasiveness of the idea of inner space. Many of the mountains revered as divine are covered with beautiful wood or rise in smoothly rounded curves.[12]

Perhaps it is fair to say that Maki hungered for just such a site as Izumo. In conversations thirty years after the essay, Maki echoed his earlier arguments as he pointed out how the museum site addressed two culturally important precincts: Izumo Shrine and the virginal forests shrouding the Kitayama mountains looming over the museum.[13] Of these, he mused:

> ... perhaps the scenery of the Kitayama mountain chain has not changed since ancient times, and to the left somewhat beyond [our building] is the Grand Shrine of Izumo. When building a new structure in such a place – where nature reaches out, where there is a sense of continued existence from the past, in a particularly serene setting amongst the mountains – I wanted to establish a form that would not damage the setting, to meet the serenity of the context, you might say to make a fusion of the two. How to establish this dialogue was the primary theme from the beginning.
>
> Before [the Shimane competition], I went to Venice and walked through the Piazza San Marco. Just a bit distant from [the piazza] is a small museum of works by Leonardo da Vinci and I went there. I saw within a sketch he had done of the Piazza San Marco, and it seemed exactly the same as the scene that I had just enjoyed. It left a very strong impression on me. Today in Japan, it is almost impossible to experience the sensation of scenes that are the same as four or five hundred years ago. But the garden-like space at Shimane [Museum] offered just such a possibility.[14]

Botond Bognar argues "... Maki's designs do not respond only to the physical attributes of the natural or urban environment, but also to an imaginary or, as he calls it, 'primary landscape' that exists in the collective memory..."[15] Writing the essay on *oku* in the 1970s, a time

11. Maki and Hara (1979) p. 4. The Japanese text gives a somewhat lengthier explication; see p. 142 of the same volume.

12. Maki (2000a) p. 25.

13. *Kitayama* means "North Mountain," a name clearly defining the mountains in terms of their relation to Izumo Shrine.

14. Maki interview (2007) p. 102.
Original Japanese:
島根 が建つ敷地を見ると、おそらく古代から、背後の北山山系はあまり変わらなくて、左後方には出雲大社があるわけです。その場所に新たに建築をつくる時に、自然な流れで、昔から存続している非常に特徴ある穏やかな山並みを、あまり損なわない形にしたいと言える、穏やかな背景に対して、融合とは言わないですが、建築がどのように対話するかが、初めから第一テーマだったわけです。

以前、ヴェネツィアの行った時に、サンマルコ広場から歩いて、少し離れたところにあるダ・ヴィンチの美術館に行ったのです. そこにあった彼が描いたサンマルコ広場の絵を見て、今自分が見てきた広場とダ・ヴィンチが見たものと同じであったという、強い印象を受けました。今、日本の中で、四、五世紀前の風景を実感として体験できるということはほとんどない。しかし、『島根』の田園の中では、それが可能なわけです。

8.10

8.11

8.12

when the profession in Japan tended to eschew tradition in favor of technology, Maki addressed the role cultural memory plays in perceptions of a place. While others attended to vernacular structures, Maki was more interested in the vernacular landscape; the forms he adopts and adapts are often attempts to recreate that landscape. He has always been moved by mountains, and often incorporates pyramids as artificial mountains in his work. Not surprisingly, when looking at the dual poles of the Grand Shrine and the even more venerable mountains, Maki focused on the mountains in particular:

> This site is large, around 6 hectares, immediately adjacent on the east to the ceremonial approach leading to Izumo Grand Shrine. The scenery of the shrine is one with the line of the *Kita* [North] Mountains, this environment endowed through *shakkei*, or borrowed landscape. The landscape and the architecture become a lucid whole.[16]

Younger staff, when discussing the museum, its relationship to Izumo Shrine and its surroundings or the landscape designed by Toru Mitani often use religious terms – but Maki always returned to the fact that he offered a public building in these precincts.

Maki is one of the most international of architects; Fujimori once called him quintessentially White School. His office was established in 1965, and more than 40 years have passed, with the Museum of Ancient Izumo completed at the end of 2005 and opened to the public in 2007.[17] Maki's earliest work, the 1960 Steinberg Hall for Washington University, was one of the first permanent works of architecture constructed in the United States designed by a Japanese architect, completed only a few years after a 1955 motel designed by Junzo Yoshimura.[18] Active throughout the world, the Maki office currently has commissions from both the United Nations and the Aga Khan. He has designed a Christian church and is working on a small synagogue, less interested in religion for its specific ties than in its cultural resonance in the lives of individuals and places.

In his essays, Maki frequently observes how differences between Japan and the West can be understood through traditional spatial concepts that still overlay and inform the daily lives of citizens in Japan's most global city, Tokyo. Maki's efforts to draw appreciative awareness of Japan's traditions and how they remain reflected in the landscape are complex; he is deeply aware that during his lifetime reinterpretations of the indigenous religion of Japan, Shinto, promoted nationalist political goals. Maki simply ignores this era. Indeed, like others from his generation, he parses Shinto closely, making a distinction between the formal religious order and an animist faith of tiny shrines diffused throughout the country – simultaneously validating Japan's oldest religious beliefs for their cultural importance, while rejecting the political cult that emerged in the Meiji era. One scholar, focusing on the elimination of small shrines that occurred as Shinto was consolidated, offered the following distinction:

> The rich diversity of the Japanese Shinto tradition has tended to focus at two principal levels, the national and the local. The broadest national level of prewar Shinto was what we in retrospect call State Shinto (*kokka Shinto*). Although the heart of State Shinto was the modern shrine system (Shrine Shinto), State Shinto extended beyond the modern shrine system (Shrine Shinto) ...
>
> At the local level, Shinto has been deeply rooted in the lives of the people through many folk practices centering in

8.8 Maki on site.

8.9 The lightness of the museum's more secular spaces are achieved through genuinely skillful handling of the steel structure.

8.10 Concrete formed in cedar recalls the use of similar boards in wooden shrines.

8.11 Large hardware needed to carry the museum's steel slabs.

8.12 Conservation work underway within the museum during its construction.

15. Bognar. Original in "Toward Another [New Age] Modernism: Three Recent Large-Scale Works by Fumihiko Maki," *Space Design (SD)* no. 340 "Fumihiko Maki, 1987–1992" (January, 1993) p. 44.

16. Kondo (2007) p. 99. Original Japanese: 本敷地は、約六ヘクタールの広さを有し、出雲大社の参道東側に隣接し、北山山系が出雲大社と共有の借景となっている恵まれた環境である。そのためランドスケープと建築が一体になった明快かつおおらかな環境の創出を目指した。

17. Customarily in Japan, museums allow time for the building to off-gas and for staff to become accustomed to them before opening to the public.

18. Yoshimura's structure at the Museum of Modern Art was rebuilt in Philadelphia, but it was originally expected to be temporary. Other Japanese architects, of course, immigrated to the U.S. and took up practice; Maki's experience simply reflects the emergence of a new model of global practice.

8 . 13

8 . 14

8 . 15

8 . 13–15 The museum is composed of a central volume under a dark steel roof, bracketed on either side by contemporary volumes clad in elongated expanses of curtain wall.

8 . 16 A dark slate wall facing the street.

8.17

8.18

> home and community. A central feature has been the worship of the local tutelary *kami*, or divine spirit, which protects each hamlet, village, or neighborhood.[19]

The mid-twentieth-century repression and political exploitation associated with Shinto make casually conflating shrine and State taboo today. Reflecting that stance, Maki studiously avoids the word "Shinto," associating it with the more recent religion. He instead draws upon agrarian origins, looks to the veneration of land and nature. In an interview, he clarified, "I am not interested in recent history of Shintoism at all. I am more interested in basic human nature and the idea of god ..."[20] He addresses the forms of these older landscapes: spatial compression, weight and shadow, horizontality and veiled depth.

But the Museum of Ancient Izumo is a publicly funded structure sited on the grounds of one of Japan's most important shrines. The separation of state and religion established by the U.S. Occupation Forces in the years after the end of World War II and generally maintained since offer awkward refuge here; the museum inevitably contradicts efforts to maintain a separation of sacred and secular. In response, Maki's museum and its landscape instead oscillate between its embrace of nature as an extension of the surrounding sacred landscape, deliberately shadowed by the symbolic presence of Shinto, and treatments that are studiously secular – hierarchical, light, and transparent, reflecting the public nature of the museum. Maki's design alternatively accepts and denies each influence, tradition and today, providing a tension that runs through the Museum of Ancient Izumo and enriches it. As one moves deeper inside, his references to the past fall away; what remains within is a decidedly modern space.

In the West, defining a museum as a non-secular cathedral is hardly a new idea, and it is easy to argue that the erosion of religious culture in late-twentieth-century Japan inevitably led to similar conditions. Critic Charles Jencks proposed that we are "... about to enter a post-Christian [post-religious] age where culture is taking the role of religion ..."[21] He outlined roles the museum usurped from religious sanctuaries, but warned,

> ... artists, curators, and architects are not happy with the comparison. They do not themselves use the religious metaphor, yet at the same time they seem unwilling to deny the spiritual and expressive ... they seem reluctant to either give up the religious role or take responsibility for it.[22]

Looking closer at the experience at Izumo, it is clear Maki embraced paradigmatic aspects of traditional sacred places in spite of his discomfort. In a deeply insightful book that elaborates on the sacred roles of architecture, *The Hermeneutics of Sacred Architecture*, Lindsay Jones offers up a comprehensive theoretical examination of sacred architecture's power. These points are summarized in the Foreword to the book:

> [Sacred architecture] ... *orients* participants: 1) to the universe itself by presenting a microcosmic replica; 2) to rules, precedents, standards, and convention displayed in sacred architecture; 3) to stars and heavenly bodies with which sacred architecture is aligned ... sacred architecture *commemorates*: 4) the deities and ultimate realities housed or recalled in sacred architecture; 5) the mythical and miraculous episodes of sacred history; 6) the social order of authority and economic arrangement legitimated (or some-

19. Fridell (1973) pp. vii–viii. Fridell goes on to note that in the late nineteenth and early twentieth centuries State Shinto was often positioned politically as a *non-religious* approach to encouraging patriotism:

It was from about 1897 that the principal Shinto publications began to press the interpretation that the shrines were 'non-religious'. This view emphasized the ethico-political rather than the religious dimensions of the multi-faceted Shinto tradition. It was difficult, of course, to deny that religious elements such as prayers, fasting, purification rituals, etc. did actually play an important part in State Shinto. Yet the government and shrine leaders did their best to play these down. They held that the shrines taught no religious doctrines, and that shrine ceremonials (saishi) were non-religious in nature.

(ibid., p. 5)

20. Interview (Tokyo) 13 June, 2005. Maki spoke clearly on the subject::

In my essay I have never discussed "Shinto" ... I simply said that the Japanese religion is a combination of animism and shamanism. That is all I said. I have never said "Shinto." I mean we revere nature. In shamanism, god is not just one but ubiquitous, which was the case for why we have a small shrine in a garden or even the rooftop of modern buildings, which is a situation we quite often see. But I have never discussed this animism and shamanism with the word "Shinto".

Maki went on to say, "Whatever I have said is very similar to what Shinto teaches. But I have never dug into Shinto religion or history, except of course I just see a certain phenomena as interesting and I analyze and understand. But never around Shintoism. Shinto has tangentially come into my organization under certain circumstances."

21. Jencks (2000) p. 44.

22. Ibid.

8 . 17, 18 *The procession to the main entrance is flanked with katsura trees, symbolically linking the secular building to Shinto shrines.*

8 . 19 *One's first view of the museum, seen from the street above, the Kitayama range as a backdrop.*

8 . 20 *Toru Mitani's landscape offers both up-to-date abstraction and suggestive symbolism.*

8 . 19

times challenged) in the politics that swill around sacred architecture; 7) the ancestors and the deceased brought to mind in the ritual commemorations held within sacred architecture... sacred architecture *contextualizes* the presentation of: 8) theater enacted against the backdrop of sacred architecture; 9) contemplation, especially where sacred architecture becomes the focus for meditation or devotion; 10) offerings of appeasement, aiming to please sacred beings through the very process of construction; 11) pure sanctuary, a state free from imperfection.[23]

Taking into account that references to the universe and sky are less suitable when discussing Japanese pantheism, Maki's Museum of Ancient Izumo demonstrates a remarkable overlap with this framework for sacred spaces. In a revealing comment written in 1999 (two years before his competition-winning design for the museum), Maki stated, "Being able to confirm firsthand that architecture *can indeed communicate an unconscious group aspiration* has been the most important fruit of my work as an architect in recent years ..."[24] While Maki does not create a place for offerings of appeasement and worship, he contextualizes contemplation, explicitly expressed in terms of Izumo's sacred precincts.

Maki's expression of the Shimane Museum as both sacred and secular is played out in an alternating articulation of movement through the building. The procession begins with an unmarked threshold, avoiding a distinction between the site and the shrine. At this point, the visitor stands above the museum and sees the structure overwhelmed by and united with the mountains and forests beyond. Maki offers the building as a relatively minor feature in this divine landscape; considering its enormous size, this perspectival trick is no small thing. Immediately, the shift to a secular reading of the site is imposed; from this raised vista, the visitor steps down to the museum grounds. This is a repositioning; traditionally shrines are higher in the mountains, demanding upward movement.[25]

In a few paces, visitors step from an open space linked to the mountains to what will eventually leaf out into a quiet internal grove. A berm to the west encloses a grid of *katsura* trees sheltering the broad path leading to the museum.[26] This shift is not only spatial, but a literal right-angle turn; it again signals a return to the sacred: in conversations, Maki's staff repeatedly referred to these trees as *shinboku*, "holy trees", and landscape designer Toru Mitani engaged me in a lengthy discussion about preceding the word with an honorific, writing or saying *goshinboku*. In an interview, Mitani noted, "... the *katsura* tree is valued religiously. In Japan, the *katsura* tree is often planted at shrines."[27] Invoking an important local myth, Yoshiki Kondo, the project architect wrote:

> The trees ... lined up along the main approach are *katsura* trees, such as those where the white heron [the goddess] *Kanayako* [lit. 'child of the metal worker'] rode alighted, and she then taught the craft of making steel on that spot.[28]

Mitani also incorporates gestures in the landscape connected to another important myth, the *Kunibiki Shinwa*, the tale of the god Omitsunu pulling a clump of small islands to Japan (the *kunibiki*) to increase the size of his kingdom. Referring to this legend, Mitani carved the words "*Izumo no Kuni Fudoki*" in archaic letterforms on a broken path along the western edge of Maki's building. Many of the trees in the more secluded northern lawn are multi-trunk clusters; Mitani

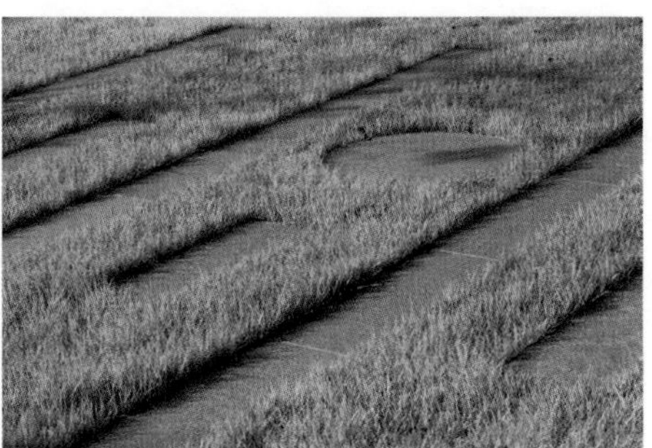

8 . 20

23. Sullivan, Lawrence E. "Foreword: Monumental Works and Eventful Occasions," in Jones (2000) p. xvi. This framework is evident in the Appendix to Volume 2, *Hermeneutical Calisthenics: A Morphology of Ritual-Architectural Priorities*, pp. 296–332.

24. Maki (2000b) p 7. Emphasis mine.

25. The gesture, however, is not untried in Maki's work. An early precedent is his generally unknown 1970 Senboku Archaeological Museum, nestled in the earth in opposition to the wide, grassy park that surrounds it. Maki may have repeated a descending path in Shimane in response to the two buildings' shared archaeological ties.

26. *Cercidiphyllum japonica*. The trees mark seasons, leafing out red in the Spring, changing to a blue-green in summer, and an apricot yellow in the autumn. They also have a slight fragrance, leading them to be called the "Cinnamon Tree." Their other English name is "Judas Tree."

27. Interview (Tokyo) 27 June, 2005.

28. Kondo (2007) p. 99. Original Japanese: 鉄本来の重厚な素材感を表現している。また、メインアプローチの並木は、金屋子神が白鷺に乗って桂の木に舞い降りて、たたら製鉄を伝授したことから桂の並木道としている。

8.21, 22 A small classroom structure on the museum's grounds is more assertively contemporary.

8.21

8.22

linked these to other legends recorded in the eighth-century *Izumo Fudoki* (Records of Izumo) which describe *Ou no mori*, a small clump of trees in the province of Ou thought to be the remnants of a walking stick planted by Omitsunu.[29] Notably, Mitani's references support the distinction Maki drew; they are not part of the formalized religion called Shinto, but its earlier animistic antecedents.

The northern lawn at the foot of the mountains is also easy to read as secular, in spite of the symbolism of the clumps of trees. A studied landscape of rough vegetation, designed by Harvard-educated Mitani, it owes much to contemporary concepts of large-scale geometric landforms, minimalism, and spatial effects of a flat *parterre*. Gunter Nitschke, discussing movement from the profane world to Ise Shrine, points to "... the interesting issue of where on the site the sacred starts and the profane ends."[30] A similar vacillation regarding sacred and secular exists in this landscape.

Many years ago, Maki argued: "A place ... is a dramatic stage on which contemporary mythic ceremonies are held. To create architecture is to build places and to give life to 'time' (i.e., past, present, and future)."[31] Elsewhere, he wondered,

> What *sort of time* are we to dramatize by means of form or material in architecture, particularly public architecture? That, I am beginning to feel, is a major issue for architecture. Architects hitherto have been concerned with expressing time only in the sense that they were anxious to employ the latest building technology. Is it time for us to broaden our horizons in this regard?[32]

Maki manipulates time through procession and through a richly symbolic language of materials. For the informed visitor to this site, its

29. 意宇の森.
30. Nitschke (1993) p. 63.
31. Maki (1986) p. 140.
32. Maki (1985) p. 19. Emphasis mine.

8.23

8.24

8.23 *The pearly glass of a long curtain wall facing the parking lot encloses offices.*

8.24 *Copper, marked with a green glass comma resembling ornaments of the Jomon era, marks the main entrance.*

8.25 *The wall wrapping the museum, cedar-board-formed concrete clad in Cor-ten steel.*

symbolism holds many references to the history of this place – but for the uninitiated, the Museum of Ancient Izumo will seem decidedly modern.

In 1985, Maki laid out a strategy for procession,

> ... public character is expressed through the use and design of territory – in the sensitivity to borders, both marked and unmarked, in the multiple lengthening of space by means of *shoji* and other screens; and in the spatial arrangements structured not by the idea of center but by the idea of depth (*oku*).[33]

Maki's essay on *oku* offers insight into the formal character of the Museum of Ancient Izumo as well; he struggled to define *oku*, but ultimately gave up on language and pointed instead to two artworks accompanying the essay: a large, empty plaza painted by De Chirico (reflecting Western space) and a woodblock, *"Atagoshitakoji"* from Hiroshige Ando's "Hundred Edo Scenes." The Japanese woodblock shows a roadway curving along the edge of a tall, nearly windowless building, a tree-shrouded slope beyond; the temple for which the print is named is nowhere to be seen. A path paralleling a mute wall, nature dominating the scene without establishing a focus – these are echoed at the Museum of Ancient Izumo, Maki's use of an unarticulated wall of corroded weathering steel running along the approach to the museum, 120 meters long and 9 meters tall (almost 394 feet long and 30 feet high).

Maki's architecture is internationally recognized for its airy elegance and refined delicacy, features that are the result not only of his well-known collaborations with Japan's very supportive construction community, but also reflect the intimate size of many of Maki's most successful projects. (The footprint of the 1985 Spiral Building, for example, is a mere 1,462 square meters or 15,736 square feet.) Maki early on defined his palette of materials as a simple one, expressing "...a faith in concrete, glass, and steel and the forms these materials take."[34] Aluminum has become another reliable favorite over the years. Until quite recently, his work maintained a muted palette in shades of brilliant white and sparkling silver, highlighting and accentuating buildings' sculptural and spatial qualities. This limited color range allowed his buildings to be read as abstractions, appreciated intellectually and formally. They suggested a sort of perfection not often associated with Japan's cities, and a certain architectural idealism that reached beyond Japan's shores. Maki became known and respected for his clean, serene modernist architecture, detailed to a level of precision measured in fractions of a millimeter.

One might have expected the Museum of Ancient Izumo to rely on the juxtaposition of Maki's characteristically delicate hand against the wild landscape and robust architecture of Izumo Shrine. Maki has also shown a tendency to break large structures down into what he called "semantical" volumes that reflect a building's inner workings; the terms "fragmented" and "fragmentary" seemed to naturally spring up when discussing his work. The enormous unrelieved volume of this museum, rendered in tall slabs of rusting steel, does not follow those conventions; its powerful effect is made more formidable by its dark, massive materials minimally detailed, terms that precisely reflect the descriptions scholars use for Izumo Shrine itself. The result is monumentality appropriate to the museum and its site.[35]

Maki's Cor-ten wall and copper doors recall ancient iron and bronze artifacts found on this site in the early stages of construction,

8.25

33. Ibid., p. 16.

34. Maki (1986) p. 7.

35. Notably, Maki also created simple, relatively unbroken forms for two earlier buildings: the Kyoto Museum of Art, standing adjacent to a large orange *torii* that leads to Chuta Ito's Heian Shrine, and the much smaller Church of Christ in Tokyo. Both are, like the Museum of Ancient Izumo, designed with a concern for the weight of history and the role of religious culture. In such structures, Maki seems to eschew the artful collaged layering he has applied elsewhere, and to reject human scale, in order to communicate dignity and gravitas.

8 . 26–29 At some points on its exterior, Maki's museum is uncharacteristically monumental - and yet also somehow mute, a result of his handling of the Cor-ten steel slabs.

8 . 27

remnants of the advances in metallurgy that began in this area of Japan.[36] Maki made that connection explicit:

> We are finding many remnants around this region ... iron, iron pieces; to some extent this Cor-ten is a modern product, but it relates to important findings and exhibits of this museum ... I'd like to share the spirit of old cultures with the new building we are making.[37]

His project architect argued that, "The Corten steel wall stands next to the main approach, recalling the *Kanayako* myth of *tatara* steel making."[38] While Fujimori, Kuma, and Suzuki employ materials with a long history in Japan – *paulownia*, paper, *hinoki* – Maki symbolically exploits a distinctly contemporary material to recall the past. (Cor-ten was first used architecturally on Eero Saarinen's John Deere Building, completed in 1963.) Maki's concrete, too, delicately formed against the raised grain of cedar boards, recalls rather than replicates the thick, horizontally laid cedar board walls of Izumo and Ise. Many years earlier, Maki wrote, "I believe it to be critical to the design process that one constantly references the material nature of one's proposals to both their historical and geographical context."[39] And elsewhere he offered:

> It is ... this persistent expression of culture ... that must form the basis of a true modern vernacular. The design and construction of individual buildings capable of speaking to both the traditional past and industrial future of Japan depends on sensitivity to historical fact. The challenge facing the architect today is to understand and contribute to this integration of intangible traditions with tangible artifacts – to link together the historical character of our

8 . 28

8 . 29

36. This is a point Maki makes in "Shimane Prefectural Museum of History and Folklore, Shimane, Japan" (2003) p. 97. Note that the title refers to an earlier name for the project. Also Interview (Tokyo) 15 January, 2004.

37. Interview (Tokyo) 15 January, 2004.

38. Kondo (2007) p. 99. Original Japanese: メインアプローチに沿って佇む外壁のコールテン鋼は島根の金屋子神話に登場する「たたら製鉄 を想起させるもの。。。

39. Maki (1988) p. 110.

8.30

8.31

8.30 *Maki's 1997 Kaze no Oka, a creamatorium, is defined by a carefully constructed procession, drawn by light.*

8.31 *A ritually important space in Kaze no Oka.*

8.32 *The entrance at Kaze no Oka.*

> culture with the development of a built ... landscape ... such a challenge involves the investigation of industrial artifacts for their more *evocative* natures, searching among them for a specific character related to regional tradition.[40]

The museum's Cor-ten façade is detailed simply, divided into stout one-and-a-half-ton panels 1.5 meters wide and 9 meters high (5 feet by 29.5 feet), about 4 centimeters (1½ inches) thick, separated by a dark reveal less than a centimeter (three-eighths of an inch) wide. This brooding volume emphasizes the museum's size, underscored by black slate marking out key areas. Even for those who have watched Maki's work closely, these finishes may still be a surprise – but they are not unprecedented. Throughout his career, Maki has periodically experimented with building in dark, heavy materials, but these projects were met with a lack of critical enthusiasm: e.g., the 1972 Osaka Prefectural Sports Center, the 1974 "glass mountain" Maki designed for Tsukuba University, and an aquarium Maki designed for the 1975 International Exposition in Okinawa. (The 1976 Austrian Embassy is another such building, but it is formally closer to Hillside Terrace in its modeling; notably, this is the site where Kengo Kuma worked for Maki so many years ago.) In the 1980s, Maki turned to the bright, sculptural structures that come to mind today. Sheathed in shimmering stainless steel, they melted away in spite of their colossal size; the first phase of Makuhari Messe, for example, was a gargantuan 130,000 square meters (1.4 million square feet), and yet feels remarkably intimate and exquisitely detailed.

In the much smaller *Kaze no Oka* Crematorium completed in 1997, Maki found critical acceptance for these saturated, earthy tones. Writing for the *Japan Times*, David Buck called the complex "a bold

40. Ibid. My emphasis.

8.32

8.33

8.34

8.35

8.33 The exterior of Kaze no Oka is an early precedent for Maki's handling of color and weight at his Museum of Ancient Izumo.

8.34 A space for memorial services at Kaze no Oka.

8.35 Mitani's landscape at Kaze no Oka employs gestures taken up again in the Museum of Ancient Izumo.

8.36 At an entrance to the Museum of Ancient Izumo.

8.37 Maki's grand stair in the glass-wrapped entrance hall of the museum.

and irrepressible hymn to the sacredness of the site."[41] *Kaze no Oka* is in a relatively remote location, but those able to visit it recognized an important approach was emerging in Maki's *œuvre* at a time when he was nearly 70 years old. The complex houses spaces for funeral and memorial services and features a crematorium that serenely accommodates ritual actions undertaken by grieving family members. Toru Mitani, landscape designer for the Museum of Ancient Izumo, also designed the landscape wrapping this crematorium; it is one of the finest contemporary landscapes in Japan, with spaces that comfort and mystify.

The Maki office's written description of *Kaze no Oka* explains these colors and their implications: "We used grey or black colors (such as concrete, slate, plaster, steel, or granite) to establish a basic palette, while brown materials, such as Cor-ten and wood, were used as highlights."[42] The essay continues, "… The architecture's earthy tactility connotes the primordial relationship among life, death, earth and sky."[43] Maki repeated this term "primordial" in our first interview regarding the Museum of Ancient Izumo. *Kaze no Oka's* material richness is very closely reflected in the more recent Museum of Ancient Izumo: elegant stone in muted colors follows the paths people take through the building; heavy, Cor-ten slabs rise from the earth; and severe black accents frame moments of transition.

Over the two-year period when the Museum of Ancient Izumo was under construction, Mr. Maki and I repeatedly discussed how history existed in his architecture. Maki resisted my initial efforts to link his work to Fujimori's Red School, unwilling to exist under another's rubric. But as I completed this text, he wrote, "The crematorium is probably the most representative project … expressing *Oku* … Furthermore it is one of a few Red buildings I have done."[44] These two points are not unrelated. At *Kaze no Oka*, Maki's careful choreography follows the processional pace of cremation, curling around a still pool of water. The ritual of loss and mourning unfolds architecturally. You enter in darkness, turning towards light only when leaving the remains of loved ones in the kiln, then wait in a quiet, serene space wrapped around a stair. Inevitably drawn upward, you stand overlooking Mitani's landscape – and if you leave the building to enter it, you will discover a deep cut in the lawn, from which the wind emerges in eerie moans, mystery evoking Maki's *Oku*. The complex is visceral and heavy, accepting its emotional and ritual roles. Maki's modernity, luminous and light, has been muted.

At *Kaze no Oka* Crematorium, the Cor-ten steel walls literally rose out of the landscape as if left over from ancient eras. This gesture is not repeated at the Museum of Ancient Izumo, but the building's overall form, recalling rippling landscape, again encourages these dark materials to be read as rooted. Maki contrasts the Cor-ten steel with a crystalline glass pavilion, delicate curtain wall meeting slabs of steel, a treatment entirely new in his work. Where visitors stand at a distance, the large gestures of steel and stone dominate; closer, the places where hand and eye engage, Maki's jeweler-like detailing sparkles in its settings. Adrian Stokes, a Modernist author and artist, once wrote:

> Dichotomy is the unavoidable means to architectural effect. It has, of course, many embodiments … heaviness and lightness, sheerness and recession or projection … lit surfaces and shadowed surfaces, a thematic contrast between two principal textures, that is to say, between rough and smooth. I take this last to symbolize all, because it best

41. Buck (1997b) p. 17.
42. Maki (2000c) p. 44.
43. Ibid. Original Japanese:
独自性をさらに強調するために、斎場、待合、火葬棟は、それぞれレンガ、コールテン鋼、コンクリートという異なる材料によってしあげられている。
44. Personal communication by e-mail from Fumihiko Maki, 24 December, 2007.

8.36

2F
3F
展望
テラス

8.38

8.39

marks the "bite" of architectural pleasure on the memory.[45] The brooding Cor-ten wall contrasts with a glass vitrine, of the same height but half its length, thrusting westward from the building as if bridging between the holdings within the museum and the Grand Shrine of Izumo itself. This glass-enclosed area houses public functions – reception desk, ticketing, sales, café, toilets – in what again appears a deliberate juxtaposition of sacred and profane. The dark, earthen tones of the rusting façade, grounded by its exaggerated horizontal sweep, emphasize historical weight. By contrast, the glass entry court is luminous and, looking from the north, appears to be floating on an adjacent reflecting pool. Its entrance is marked by a *magatama* – an enlarged, comma-shaped bead, in a shape worn during the *Jomon* period, rendered in a solid green piece of soda glass that looks like jade, one of the few gestures within the building where Maki uses form, not material, symbolically, but for the most part, this glass case is a contemporary and clearly secular space.

Standing within this area, one again confronts the Kitayama Mountains, not as an object so much as an overwhelming presence: the "*oku*" heart of Maki's design ahead but unreachable. Inevitably, visitors will be drawn up a ceremonial stair that calls to mind the elongated stair of the thirteenth-century Kitsuki Grand Shrine; the beautiful, curving roof of Izumo Shrine itself is just barely visible from the upper observation platform. Maki once wrote:

> Somehow I suspect great directors first conceive a few great scenes and then want to make a movie in order to portray these scenes ... architecture is also able to adapt the same attitude when we are designing complex buildings. In many cases, I have wanted to produce certain spaces, scenes.[46]

This scenographic link between the museum and Izumo Shrine is underscored by the fact that early in the process of making his competition-winning proposal a reality, the architect arranged for equipment to be brought to the site so that he could confirm the view.[47] Nature, though, may yet prevent this unusual prospect from being accessible; deciduous trees growing taller began to shield the shrine when I visited the construction site in the summer of 2005. The authorities of Izumo surely would not object to this intervention; the observation deck privileges the secular role of the museum, since looking downward on Japan's significant religious sites is an unusual experience.

Throughout this secular zone, modernity is emphasized. No discussion of the entry lobby would be complete without acknowledging the contributions of furniture designer Kazuko Fujie, who has been collaborating on Maki's projects for over 20 years.[48] She describes the fluidity of her work as driven by the idea of "the density of spirit" evidenced in air, water, clouds, mist, wind, and the flow of water.[49] Below the observation area, a tiny museum shop of paper-thin white painted steel and glowing glass shelves reinforces the way those elements of the building that are most luminous and diaphanous are reflections of today's secular (and, in this case, commercial) world.

In 1973, Maki wrote, "The approach and entrance to a building are of great concern to me ... I much prefer a work which quietly receives entrants."[50] Nitschke, in a slim volume that parses traditional Japanese processional patterns, notes that typically, "... we actually arrive at our destination several times; we arrive in stages."[51] Moving into and through the museum, the visitor never encounters a pronounced threshold, the processional experience instead uniting the museum's contents with its context. The spaces of this glass pavilion overlap

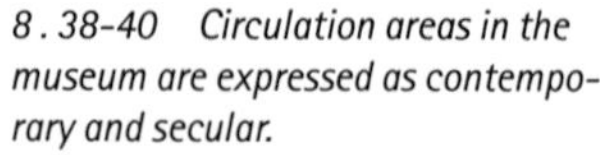

8.38-40 Circulation areas in the museum are expressed as contemporary and secular.

8.40

45. Adrian Stokes, quoted in Jones (2000) p. 68.

46. Maki, Fumihiko interview. Maki (1987) p. 70.

47. Interview (Tokyo) 15 January, 2004.

48. In another reflection of the way the Japanese architecture community remains incestuous, Fujie is the daughter of a former partner of Arata Isozaki's. Maki has long employed her furnishings as signature moments in his buildings.

49. Fujie (2007) p. 83.

50. Maki (1973) p. 19.

51. Nitschke (1993) p. 39.

8.41

8.42

8.43

8.41–44 The rusted steel slabs wrapping the museum's exterior penetrate and terminate one end of the entrance hall, their rough expression of weight magnetically drawing visitors further within.

8.44

8.45

8.46

8.45, 48 Benches designed by Kazuko Fujie for the museum's central space are lit from within, lightening their effect.

8.46, 47 The slim steel shelves of the tiny museum shop, also by Fujie, express its contemporary character.

8.47

8.48

8.49 *The second tier of the entrance hall, looking outward.*

8.49

with the exterior, but also project into a light-filled lobby on the east side of the Cor-ten wall, that separates two lobby spaces. Echoing the manner in which the west end of the pavilion looks over Izumo Shrine, the eastern end of the observation deck ends in a second-floor platform that overlooks the remains of Kitsuki Shrine. The three once-banded logs, the archaeological finds from 2000, are located in this space, housed in a delicate hexagonal display case designed by Maki's office. Siting these archaeological remains at this point, and in a case shaped like the Izumo crest, seems also to suggest the way shrines such as Izumo frame a pillar at their core.

The green stone floor in this room refers to other riches of the Shimane area's history as well: jade, a stone highly valued by Japan's *Jomon* and *Yayoi* cultures. Serene, shadowed spaces, a single exhibition area Maki designed, are deeper beyond. (Other, exhibition areas were designed under a separate contract.) Thus, interior spaces behind the Cor-ten wall offer both centrality and unseen *oku*, informed contemporaneously by Japanese and Western spatial strategies. In his essay on *oku*, Maki asked, "Does the *oku* disappear when it is exposed?"[52] He answered himself: "In many cases, the *oku* has no climax in itself as the ultimate destination begins to be unfolded. One rather seeks drama and ritual in the process of approaching it."[53] Elsewhere, he elaborated:

> Innermost space as an ultimate destination often lacks a climactic quality. Instead, it is through the process of reaching the goal that drama and ritual are sought. Horizontal depth, rather than height, is the key. The approaches to temples and shrines turn and twist ... This structuring of spatial experiences includes the dimension of time.[54]

The cavernous archival areas of the museum, holding innumerable treasures, are the inner depths that daily visitors will not reach, but will, perhaps, be a part of their awareness of the building: looking down a long corridor, one sees it ends in a mysterious, flat-black door. This hidden area is like the construction of traditional religious spaces, where the innermost areas of shrines are not entered but merely acknowledged.

Maki layers time in the procession through the museum: strongly allusive landscape looking towards the mountains and the mists of history matched by light, modern interiors reflecting a present period and framing the ancient artifacts exhibited within. He once argued, "Quite possibly – though this is mere speculation – an age in which people are optimistic and expansive produces a more 'open' architecture ... than an age when people are pessimistic and self-protective."[55] His design for Shimane Prefecture offers both a protective wrapping that looks back to earlier ages and a light, luminous interior, with the most hopeful spaces of the Museum of Ancient Izumo – those that are secular and modern – ultimately dominating the experience of the building. Maki uses the past as a platform for the present, drawing a distinction, yet enfolding both into this important work.

52. Maki (1975) p. 59.
53. Ibid.
54. Maki (2000b) p. 26.
55. Maki (1973) p. 21.

Archaeology and Architecture

Jun Aoki

9

Neon and *tatami* can co-exist, to the destruction of neither. This, damn it, is the conceptual triumph that may save the world ...—*Charles Moore*[1]

In 2000, 44-year-old Jun Aoki won first place in a national competition for the Aomori Museum of Art, besting many of Japan's leading architects, including Kisho Kurokawa and Itsuko Hasegawa. The art museum was an exciting project: the initial budget was a fairly generous 12 billion yen (about $112 million) for a 14,000 square meter (150,000 square foot) facility; three rare Chagall backdrops would be in the permanent collection.[2] Writing in a widely read architectural blog, Akira Suzuki emphasized the (at the time) unusual nature of this competition: "As an open public competition, famous and little-known architects, senior and emerging, all architects participated on an equal basis, their designs judged on skill and insight."[3]

Aoki's model for the competition suggested little in the way of above-grade structure. The jury, which included Toyo Ito and Terunobu Fujimori, selected the proposal because it responded to the site in a way both audacious and remarkably sensitive, proposing a series of earthen trenches, looping and linear, incised into the large grassy park encompassing Aomori's most important tourist attraction. These trenches deliberately echoed the adjacent archaeological dig, the Sannai Maruyama Neolithic Remains.[4] Galleries floated over the excavated areas, the mismatched upper and low regions meeting like loosely fitting dentures.

Aomori is an out-of-the way place, in Japan's rural north. The area is slow to change; some call it backwards and provincial, others extol it for maintaining strong ties to traditional ways of life. Speaking around the time of the building's opening, Aoki argued "the essence of Aomori as timelessness," continuing, "... it has a feeling that time has stopped, there is no future."[5] Millennia ago, this area was one of the largest and most important *Jomon* [Neolithic] settlements in Japan – but it is also a very new site, discovered only in 1992. Aoki is quite clear that the two places are linked, writing:

> The memory of the Jomon era is the spiritual heritage of Aomori, and its symbol is the Sannai Maruyama Jomon relics [*sic*]. When visiting the relics, we are overwhelmed to see trenches dug out of the soil. It is this geometrical view of earth which is characteristic of the site through its "unearthing". To form this kind of space into the exhibition space without changing its nature is the fundamental strategy behind the building of the [art] museum.[6]

The archaeological site is pocked with narrow vertical trenches carved into raw, red soil. These trenches seem only loosely linked. The logic of their order is hidden; the field still almost untouched. Aoki proposed embodying archaeology in his art museum, loosely grouping large volumes (ultimately orthogonal, losing any lyrical looping). He wrote:

> ... in this art museum we extend the character of the archaeological dig and its relics. I felt this logic transcends any arbitrary stance I might take ... In the Sannai Maruyama

9.1 Jun Aoki's 2006 Aomori Musuem of Art, wrapped in a skin of white brick.

1 Moore (1978) p. 6. The title alludes to a 1905 book by architect Ralph Adams Cram, of which Moore tellingly wrote in the same essay that it "... told me a lot about Ralph Adams Cram but not much about my Japan" (ibid., p. 5). Moore also notes in this essay that he made time during a whirlwind visit to Japan to see a gymnasium by his former student Kazuhiro Ishii, an early work by Tadao Ando, and climbed to Kompira, using a colloquial name for Kotohira Shrine. This essay can also be found at: http://www.coldbacon.com/art/moore-japanesearchitecture.html (accessed 31 December, 2007).

2 The budget was considerably reduced in the end, the final 21,133-sq m (227,474-sq ft) building costing just over 10 billion yen (roughly $114.5 million at average currency exchange over the construction period).

3 http://www.telescoweb.com/node/79 (accessed 3 October, 2007). Original Japanese: 公開建築設計競技とは、有名無名、老いも若きも、すべての建築家が同じ条件で腕を奮い、デザインと技と知恵を競うイベント。

4 Also referred to in English as the Maruyama Sannai site, as will be seen in quoted publications.

5 Aoki, Jun interview with Makoto Watanabe 渡辺真理 and Yoko Kinoshita 木下庸子. "*Aoki Jun Intabyuu: Aomori Rashii Bijutukan he no Kaitou*" 青木淳インタビュー：青森らしい美術館への回答 [An Interview with Jun Aoki: Replies for an Art Museum Like Aomori] アーハウス [Ahaus], no. 3 (March, 2006) p. 18 (first quote) and 20 (second). Original Japanese: 青森らしいを『無時間性』で表現」and「未来とかがない時間が止まっちゃった感覚・無時間性・タイムレス ...

6 http://tenplusone.inax.co.jp/aomori/text.html (accessed 19 July, 2005). Translation by Naoko Shinogi.

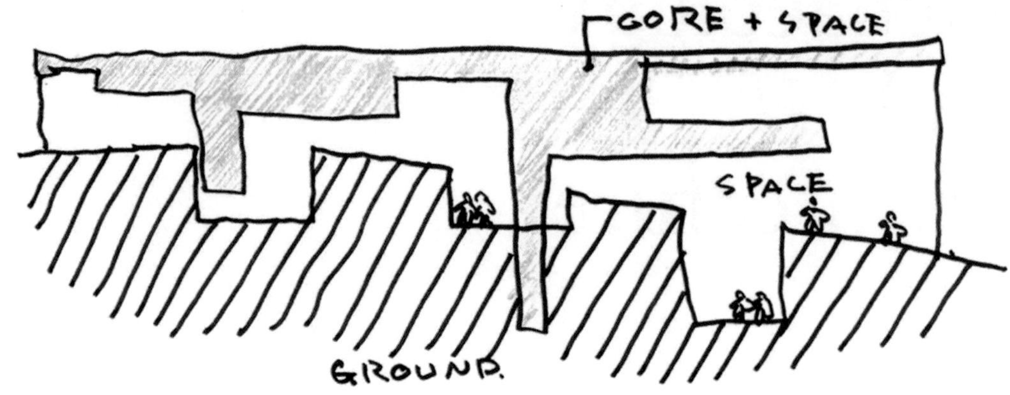

9.2

9.3

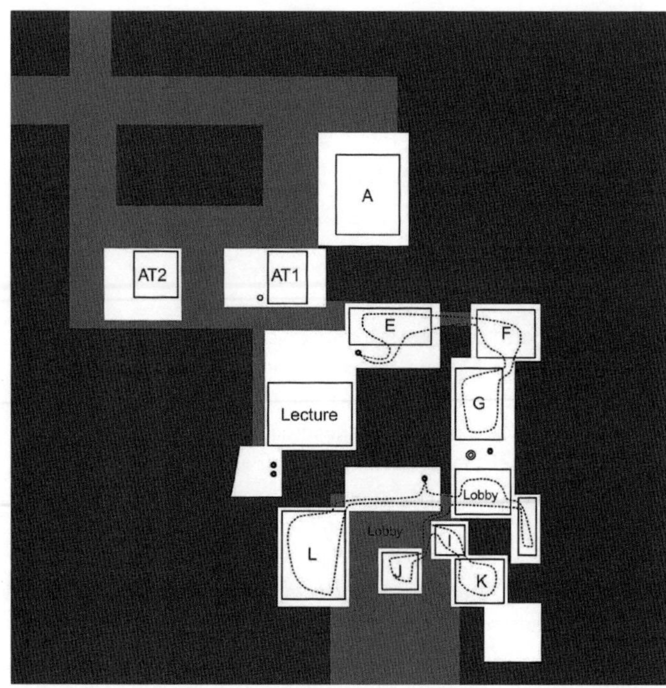

9.4

9.2 Aoki's early sketch shows how the two parts of the museum, carved trenches and suspended spaces, come together.

9.3, 4 Diagrams of the lower levels, B2 to the left and B1 to the right.

9.5 An axonometric isolates the two parts of the museum.

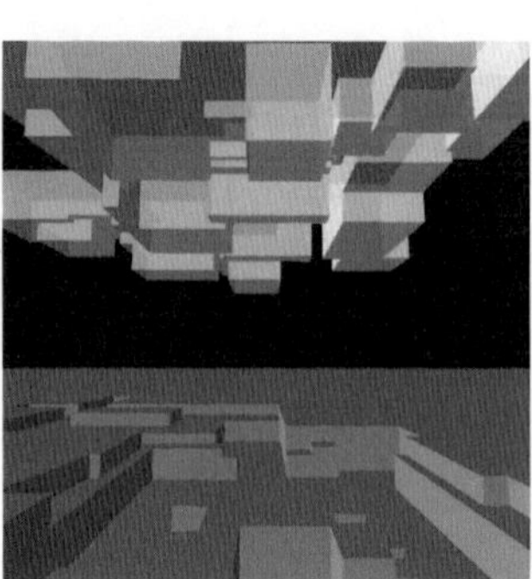

9.5

9.6

9.7

9.6 Arrows point towards exits, marked on the tamped earthen floors.

9.7 A slice of space cuts through the central gallery exhibiting three important Chagalls.

> Archaeological Site the space has a charm derived from the survey methods in the trenches The soil is cut in a grid, horizontally and vertically.[7]

The Aomori Museum of Art offers a very different view of time than other buildings in this book. While other architects instill meaning in their work, Aoki asserts that he wants to transcend telling tales. The Aomori galleries demand curators and artists engage more aggressively with his building – that they, not the architect, bring to the site meaningful ways of understanding and appreciating it. He emphasized: "... the nature of the work is dependent on how it is positioned in the art museum, and particularly on the galleries in which it is displayed."[8] Aoki's museum is intended to be constantly changing. He avoids any obvious, over-riding order; he offers visitors a path that is not about procession, only discovery – exploration instead of organization. The interior experience at the Aomori Museum of Art begins from seven disparate entrances (six on the ground level and one at the lowest exhibition level, facing the Sannai Maruyama site). Aoki's interlaced galleries offer movement in multiple directions, constantly confronting with choice: straight ahead, slipping diagonally, turning right or left, rising or descending – the two floors of gallery space connect via four sets of open stairs and two independent elevator cores.[9] There is no single path.

As one moves through the galleries, the choice of how to proceed is rarely clear, never predetermined. The museum staff, however, struggle with this concept and frequently attempt to impose order. Usually, museum visitors in Japan are directed along a single path by small signs describing a set route. Aoki acknowledged this norm:

> From the entrance to the exit [of most museums], along a line with no deviation as if drawn with a single pencil, large numbers of people smoothly flow in a single direction, a controlled fashion. ... [the path] is quite likely to be a tube-like space of a consistent width, all the way to the end. The convention ... is generally that space is organized around a single line of movement, as if drawn with one stroke.[10]

Josep Maria Montaner, in the book *Museums for the 21st Century*, writes of the "self-involved museum" which is "... full of multiple visions, with double spaces and alternate routes through the use of different stairways, elevators ... with an extremely intense materiality in its details and textures."[11] Aoki's museum fits this model; while public, it is unconcerned with public experience. Each visit is a private interlude unearthing new interpretations of the site. Tellingly, when Aoki presented the museum experience to the clients, his animation of the galleries moved through them from the point of view of a somewhat off-balance and errant child.[12]

While other architects might combine a loose path with a clear circulation spine, Aoki offered only equivocal organization. Of an earlier project, Aoki wrote:

> I believe that architecture and cities today draw too clear a distinction between "what is being linked" and "what is linking." Architecturally speaking, rooms and hallways, or purposeful space and linear space ... grossly impoverishes both architecture and cities.[13]

Rejecting the rational, he argued that in this museum, "the chain of our perceptions moment-by-moment from this or that surface do not add up into a consistent overall picture of the architecture with clarity, but rather is experienced as a near-chaotic assemblage of mo-

7 Aoki (2004) p. 112. Original Japanese:
ぼくはここでつくられる美術館にその遺跡が持っている発掘現場としての質を延長させることを提案した。それがその場所を美術館としてつくっていく論理として、ぼくの恣意を超えて、多くの人が納得できる論理だと考えたからである。そこで美術館をつくるとき、ぼくはそこで開館後になにかをつくっていく人の行為を、空間によって先取しないために、あるいはそれを基本的には想定しないところで設計を進めていくことができるために、発掘現場としての質を持ちだしたのである。
三内丸山縄文遺跡のなかで、空間としてもっとも魅力的なのは、トレンチと呼ばれる発掘方法で調査された場所だった。土が縦横にグリッド状に切られている。その側断面には地層となって各年代の遺構が現れている。そういう土でできた上向きに凸凹な地形をまず築く。そのトレンチ空間が美術館として定義される。そして、その上から下向き凸凹の構造体を被せる。構造体のなかには、ホワイトキューブの展示室が含まれている。上向きに凸凹な地形と下向きに凸凹な構造体との間に隙間の空間が生まれる。そこの「土の展示室」とする。土と言っても、具体的には、床をタタキ、壁を版築とした人工的な空間である。

8 Ibid. Original Japanese:
美術館の展示室は、どんな場合でも、それ自体、ひとつの世界を持っている。それはまず、外の日常的な世界とは別の世界である。そして、そういう展示室で展示するということは、それをもうひとつ別の空間にすることだ。。。そうであるから、作品のあり方は、それが置かれる美術館、特に展示室に依存する。

9 In addition to the open stairways, the lowest gallery floor is also served by five sets of fire stairs and three staff elevators accessible only to those with right of entry to secure areas of the building. It is both annoying and amusing to try to work out the linking stairs and elevators using either published drawings or when visiting the museum. I found circulation oddly elided in drawings and diagrams, reminding me of the tale of Kent Kleinmann and Leslie Van Duser being surprised to discover an uncharted room when documenting an oft-published building by Adolf Loos.

10 Aoki (2004) p. 125. Original Japanese:
... 入口から出口まで、交差のない一筆描きの動線で構成し、群衆をスムースのワンウェイの流れに制御する。...幅の一定なチューブ状の空間で押し切ることだって可能だ。いずれにしても、博覧会施設は総じて、一筆描きの動線を空間構成の骨格として持つ。

11 Montaner (2003) p. 93.

12 Hosaka, Kenjiro "The Aporia of Creating an Art Museum," private, in-house translation by Hiroshi Watanabe, received from the Aoki office.

13 "Mamihara Bridge," (Spring, 1994) private, in-house translation received from the Aoki office.

9.8

9.9

9.8–10 The whitewashed brick volume of the museum hovers over earthen trenches to the rear, intended for sculpture and workshops.

9.10

9.11

9.12

9.13

9.11–13 On the museum's exterior, Aoki alludes to Northern European Modernism and to nineteenth-century structures still seen in Aomori and the area.

9.14 *The nearly cubic central space, featuring three large Chagall backdrops.*

mentary epiphanies. There is no conclusive hierarchy relating one image to the next. Instead, our jumbled perceptions keep wavering back and forth aimlessly between scattered images."[14] Aoki perhaps needed to expunge any ordered circulation because Japanese museum visitors are so accustomed to structured sequences they would not otherwise avail themselves of the exploratory aspects of this museum. Still, I confess to reservations. Sometimes a clear and obvious order is wanted, especially in emergencies; in the panicky moments following a fire or earthquake this building would not be easy to exit.[15]

From 1983 to 1990, Aoki worked for Arata Isozaki, Japan's most intellectual architect. In an influential book entitled *Postmodernism in Japan* (published at the time Aoki was working in the office), Isozaki described his own desire to enrich the 1983 Tsukuba Center Building by re-introducing aspects lost in Modern structures: labyrinth, complexity, ambiguity, and symbolism.[16] Aoki, influenced by Isozaki's obsessions of that era, takes these further. He celebrates the labyrinthine, quoted in an article on the museum saying, "In a space like a maze, don't you have the sense of lightly drifting?"[17] Justification for his effort lies elsewhere on the same page. In a photograph, Aoki is seated in the central space of the completed museum. Two backdrops by Chagall are immediately behind him; the one over his left shoulder portrays St. Petersburg floating in space.[18] In a 1962 discussion of the painter's theatrical *tableaux*, critic L.L. Zimmerman argued these reflect Chagall's "varied concepts of reality".[19] Representing ecstasy over the rational, Zimmerman describes the works as "... puzzling to many, and dismissed as undecipherable by some."[20] The critic almost anticipates Aoki's museum when he writes, "In [Chagall's] subjective world, physical elements disjoint themselves, recombine ... or float unfettered ..."[21] Considering these Chagalls are the most important pieces in the museum collection, it is perhaps appropriate that Aoki attempted to create just such an experience within.

The semantics of Aoki's two layers – suspended, additive "white" areas proffered as modern, and the exhumed earthen spaces rooted in history and vernacular tradition – are thus drawn from two initial influences on the art museum. The Chagall backdrops, 15 meters wide and 9 meters high (just short of 50 x 30 feet), demanded overscaled, contemporary spaces. The trenches recall the place where the museum stands, both the rural landscape of Aomori and the nearby archaeological trenches. The museum's permanent collection is also split between soil and smooth, with works reflecting both the rural privations Aomori knows too well and Japan's emerging affluence and internationalism. Ichiro Kojima's photographs from the late 1950s and early 1960s depict farmers working with wooden-wheeled, horse-drawn wagons. Scrap-wood sculptures by Yoshishige Saito, stark black, are three-dimensional calligraphic strokes. Tiny sketches by anthropologist and Waseda University professor Wajiro Kon meticulously detail the shacks thrown up in Tokyo immediately after the 1923 earthquake. And Shiko Munakata, self-taught, produced bright woodcuts, inspired by Amori's Nebuta festival and its colorful paper floats. Yet the collection also includes Matisse lithographs, pop art by Tetsumi Kudo, and postwar cartoons by Toru (Tohl) Narita, the creator of Ultraman. Even so, Aoki, reflecting the pretensions of a Tokyoite, worried that, "Building yet more-of-the-same white cubes ... few artists would see any special reason to go all the way there [to Aomori] to exhibit ... there was a real need to create a unique space such as could exist only in Aomori."[22] Writing for a publication put out in

14 Aoki (2006a) p. 15.

15 As if to reassure, the museum offers a video guide to the museum on-line, albeit one which elides some of the most confusing moments in moving through the building. See http://www.aomori-museum.jp/ja/guide/tour/ (accessed 11 October, 2007).

16 Isozaki (1989) p. 50.

17 Aoki (2006b) p. 019.

18 Zimmerman (1962) pp. 204–205. Portrayed as the hero, Aleko (for whom these pieces are named), is an aristocrat who joins a gypsy camp out of love, in the process shunning civic culture.

19 Ibid., p. 203.

20 Ibid., p. 204.

21 Ibid.

22 Aoki (2006a) p. 016.

9 . 15

9 . 16

9 . 17

9 . 15 Gallery spaces shift from light to dark, as if slicing off each space to highlight its independence.

9 . 16 Scrap-wood sculptures by Yoshishige Saito, one of Aomori's most important twentieth-century artists, are featured in a permanent gallery installation.

9 . 17 Photography in a large gallery designed for flexibility.

9.18

9.19

9.20

anticipation of the museum's opening, Aoki claimed, "Earth will render the space particularly strong and individualistic. Our proposal to apply this individuality was not born from it. It was Aomori, this particular place in Aomori, that brought forth this kind of space."[23]

Diagramming the building, the pull of these two influences is clearly articulated as "white" vs. "earth."[24] White galleries are timeless and autonomous, enclosed spaces where the edges of walls and floors dissolve into an even glow. Earthen galleries offer richly textured surfaces highlighted by light and shadow; these walls and floors will change and grow more figured as they are patched and altered. Aoki's artificial trenches exist in their purest state outside, in open-air courtyards to the west of the building. In line with his initial proposal, apparently excavated earth surfaces meet additive painted planes in loose overlaps, enclosing these galleries as interstitial events, neither wholly of the soil, nor the smooth.

Aoki's original competition models very clearly describe the potential power of an excavated space. The sides of the proposed trench-like galleries canted 60 degrees, jutting rods projecting outward, dangling artworks in the air – mounds of earth, ambiguous assertions in internal spaces. The proposed floor buckled, flat and ramped areas adjacent, underscoring the subtractive way the spaces were first conceptualized (rather than the additive way the galleries were ultimately constructed). Shallow differences in height established areas that appear simultaneously as floor and inviting seat, a peculiar proposal in a public building in Japan, where people are unlikely to remove shoes or to sit on a floor where others walk shod. In the completed museum all this is lost: floors are relatively flat, dangerous differences in height deleted; no inviting seating plinths remain; walls are gently battered, not assertively banked, less allusive of mounds, losing any illusion of a captured exterior.

Aoki hoped to construct these walls of rammed earth. For economic reasons, he abandoned the idea early on; rammed earth is very labor-intensive, unrealistic in public works. Vertical surfaces are instead constructed of clay and cement mixed in a stiff, zero-slump composition, shot through a hose and smoothed as it sets, a process David Easton, the Napa Valley-based originator, calls *pise*.[25] The approach was tweaked for Japan by plasterer Akira Kusumi working with ceramics manufacturer Inax, resulting, for example, in more hand-trowelling and even some cob-construction-like surfaces, built up in lumps. Yet in spite of the fact that this finish is rooted in a process developed in California, the design team wanted the soil to be understood as of Aomori and Japan, vernacular, reinforcing this through word choice. Aoki and his team call these walls "*hanchiku*" – a long-standing method of constructing the thick, battered, rammed earth walls enclosing gardens and temples. Japanese architects have choices when describing innovations, enlarging the use of a familiar domestic term or adopting a borrowed foreign expression. Aoki usually speaks an international architectural *patois* – at Aomori, for example, he relies on the word "trench" when discussing the earthen areas of the building, and calls a horizontal structural member a "beam," rather than writing the Japanese character for beams, *hari*.[26] His choice of the Japanese term, recalling handmade *hanchiku* in his industrial process, is deliberate.

There are other ambiguities evident in this construction. The design team matched the color of walls on the Sannai Maruyama site – but, notably, not the red earth of the trenches; they matched the artificial,

23 Aoki (2001) p. 3. Original Japanese: 土は空間に非常に強い個性を与えます。しかし，その個性は，そこで行われることの想定からうまれたものではありません。青森の，この場所だからこそ、生まれてくる空間なのです。

24 See, for example, "*Aomori Kenritsu Bijutukan*" (Data) *Shinkenchiku* 新建築 [New Architecture], vol. 81, no. 9 (September 2006) p. 226.

25 Easton himself is playing with words. *Pise* is a loose adaptation of the French term for rammed earth, *pise de terre*; Easton's appropriation of the term for his approach can also confuse one's understanding of the material and its construction. In the English translation of a small booklet the Aomori Museum of Art published on its facilities, the English text does rely on this word, *pise de terre*, while the Japanese text uses *hanchiku*.

26 Aoki (2006d) p. 7. Similarly, in a subsequent essa, Aoki uses the words "exterior" and "interior," rather than the native Japanese alternatives. See "*Aomori Bijutuka*," p. 10.

9.18 In an entrance corridor, the structure is exposed.

9.19, 20 Visitors are drawn by stairs to discover new spaces.

9.21

9.22

chocolate-colored explanatory walls used in exhibits elsewhere on the site. Aoki confessed that he wanted to resist employing a color too obviously alluding to actual soil conditions in the area.[27] As a result, the hue is itself a simulation of a simulation, an intellectual conceit that adds looping layers to one's reading of the building. The color is also appealing; these sepia walls richly complement art. Reds and yellows in paintings seem more vivid; the fine-grained delicacy of photographs is underscored against the rough texture of the earthen finish.

Dark surfaces also demanded the design team take a different approach to lighting these spaces. As Hideyuki Nakayama wrote of the museum, "... matte brown pounded *tataki* floors and molded dirt *hanchiku* walls readily absorb light and reflect virtually none ... most of the building is made of earth and white paint, materials at either extreme of the luminosity scale ..."[28] An even glow (the effect found in the white galleries) is not possible in a room with dark, rough surfaces. Instead, Aoki accepts shadow; paintings are framed and highlighted by dark shadow separating the painted surface from the soil wall. Because the soil is not reflective, light also drops off at the high ceilings of these galleries. The upper reaches of these rooms are obscured.

Oddly articulated edges and gaps between galleries also increase a sense of mystery. Gaps have become almost a signature device in Aoki's work, here underscoring the slippage where white plasterboard and rough earth meet, perhaps deliberately drawing on an insight artist Brian O'Doherty offered on "white cube" environments:

> The 19th century looked at a subject – not at its edges. Various fields were studied within their declared limits. Studying not the field but its limits, and defining these limits for the purpose of extending them, is a 20th-century habit ...[29]

Soil-infused materials are inherently unclean. Phoebe Crisman, an architecture professor at the University of Virginia, recently wrote, "When we do encounter dirt or decay in a museum ... human beings' futile battle with time and material change becomes poignantly evident."[30] Aoki's proposal to juxtapose expensive and valued artworks against dirt emphasizes their fragility and the potential for destruction in all artworks – as well as the potential disintegration of the soil surfaces themselves. Not surprisingly, in the early stages of design Aoki faced strong resistance from national and local bureaucrats towards his use of earth, yet he had no choice but to fight for an idea so much at the heart of his initial, competition-winning proposal. So the construction team needed to understand outcomes, to assure the client that their use of clay, while based on empirical tests, was sufficiently rigorous to inspire confidence. There have been great advances in soil-based construction in the last 10 years, but earth in its natural state remains a poor choice for a seismically active zone. Paul Oliver, the leading historian of vernacular architectures and their lineage, makes the point that, "Though the technology of earth construction may be simple, the technology for testing it is complicated and expensive."[31] The walls' safety was studied in a variety of exposure and stress tests. Assessments extended to multiple gas chromography tests in order to find a suitable soil on the site.[32] Aoki's effort to reassure Aomori officials is underscored by an extensive appendix to the elegant monograph published on the building, a 28-page bilingual section presented on toothy, ochre-colored paper that contrasts with the glossy white pages otherwise used throughout the book.[33]

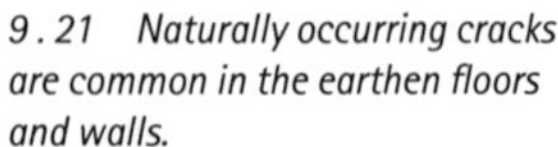

9.21 Naturally occurring cracks are common in the earthen floors and walls.

9.22 Applying the hanchiku walls with a hose.

27 Aoki's position is contradictory; the team went to a great trouble to use soil from the site, testing dozens of samples.

28 Nakayama (2006) English, p. 44. Japanese, p. 34.

29 O'Doherty (1976) pp. 26–27. This text can also be accessed without pagination on-line at: http://www.societyofcontrol.com/whitecube/insidewc.htm.

30 Crisman (2007) p. 413.

31 Oliver (1983) p. 32.

32 "Appendix: Soil Report," in Aoki *et al.* (2006) p. 16. These tests assured that the organic content of the final mix was less than 1%.

33 Ibid. See especially section 3, pp. 8–21 only. Notably, the English text is abbreviated, since the editors were reluctant to take on the costs of translating technical materials from Japanese.

9.23

9.23 The hanchiku walls were sprayed over dense rebar.

9.24 Brick exterior walls are detailed as if to deny they are made up of smaller units, no joints evident on the large expanses.

9.25 The dark chocolate of the hanchiku walls contrasts with areas where the mix of earth and mortar has not yet been applied.

9.24

9.25

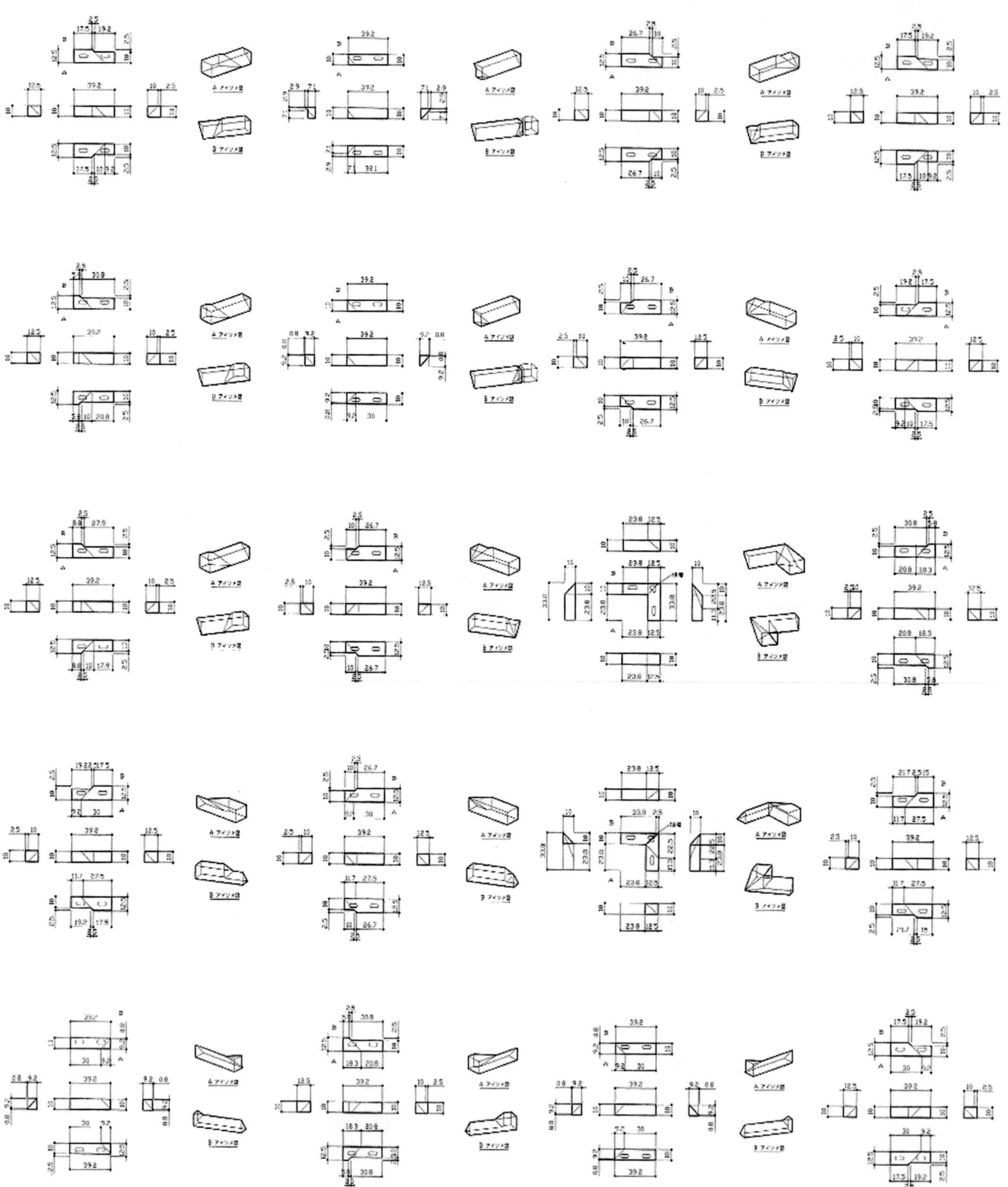

9.26

9.27

9.28

9.29

Through tests described in this section, Aoki and the development team suggested they could confidently predict how these soil surfaces would age and change.

Yet while the broad nature of outcomes was predictable – the team, for example, knew these finishes would crack – the way cracks would emerge, their length and patterns, were unforeseeable. Riverine fissures fall at consistent distances in the interior, suggesting they are shrinkage cracks, a natural result of the curing process.[34] This expression of change – some predictable because of artists' acts upon the surfaces and elsewhere unguided and natural outcomes – adds interest to the earthen surfaces. Aoki and the construction team understood they could avoid cracking by introducing control joints, but for the interior, they chose not to do so.[35] Architects avoid unpredictable cracks by cutting regular kerfs, "control joints," to collect stresses – and just such cuts are present outside on the museum's *hanchiku* walls.

For the floors, Aoki again uses a traditional word, *tataki*, compacted with mechanical tampers, only the shallow gaps and narrow notches inaccessible to machinery done by hand. Minor variations in pressure in any location still give the finish a pleasant unevenness and an irregular density. These finishes are the most crazed and cracked. Before the museum opened there were already patches in place, due to the normal wear and tear of any construction site. These repairs prevented the museum staff from treating the walls and floors as precious. Yet even with the inevitable patching and cracking, it is unclear whether the surfaces, in spite of their sensuality, can ever achieve the vitality Aoki intended. In a published interview with Aoki, Ryue Nishizawa, a partner in the firm SANAA (also recently integrating similar cracking in concrete slabs in New York and Aomori), called Aoki's walls "too pretty," arguing they lack the force of the Sannai Maruyama trenches.[36]

The surfaces will, nonetheless, continue to change, the natural result of an ongoing slate of exhibitions, becoming a palimpsest of the life of the wall and the life of the gallery. Aoki located most of the earth-based finishes in the lower, temporary galleries, assuring that they will be altered more quickly than if used only for the permanent collection above. He also contends that these rougher walls have greater compatibility with contemporary art (more likely to be exhibited in these spaces than the permanent galleries), arguing that earthen surfaces are suitable to artwork that is messy, incorporating fire or other dirty materials.[37] Troublingly, in the Aomori Museum of Art, exhibition spaces are not isolated from each other; all share the same mechanical systems and are spatially linked, with no intervening walls. Conservative curators would be unlikely to exhibit art that might threaten the life of the relatively fragile Chagall backdrops, tempura painted on cotton canvas – but in line with Aoki's expectations, the Aomori museum included a fire-breathing robot by Kenji Yanobe ("Giant Torayan") in its second exhibition, "Art and Object: the Affinity of Jomon and Contemporary."

While trench-like spaces in the Aomori Museum of Art are the strongest, with a robust, sensual presence, Aoki also serves up a number of more conventional galleries, where hanging and rehanging artworks is easily erased by non-professionals using spackle and paint. In writing about these areas, Aoki argued he accommodated contemporary expectations for an art museum with what he calls "White Cube" galleries. The largest of these, Aleko Hall, housing the huge Chagalls,

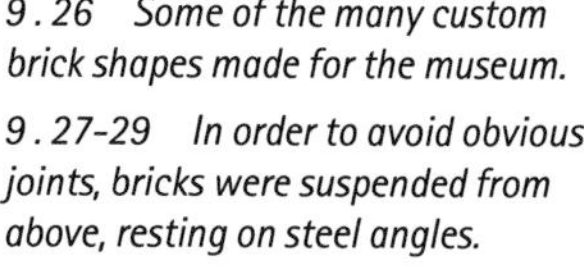

9.26 Some of the many custom brick shapes made for the museum.

9.27–29 In order to avoid obvious joints, bricks were suspended from above, resting on steel angles.

34 The mixture also contains cement.

35 Even for the exterior walls, control joints were never inevitable; at one point during construction Aoki assured me he had decided not to cut any such joints into the walls – but in the end the construction team was concerned that cracking would lead to dramatic failures. Over time, water seeping into exterior concrete, freezing and expanding, can stress it; frozen water or rusting steel rebar (which also expands), can push chucks of cementious material out of a wall, a process called spalling. Notably, exterior walls and pavements at the Aomori Museum of Art are also reinforced with more expensive stainless steel rebar, so there was some effort to avoid spalling (due to rust) early in the construction process.

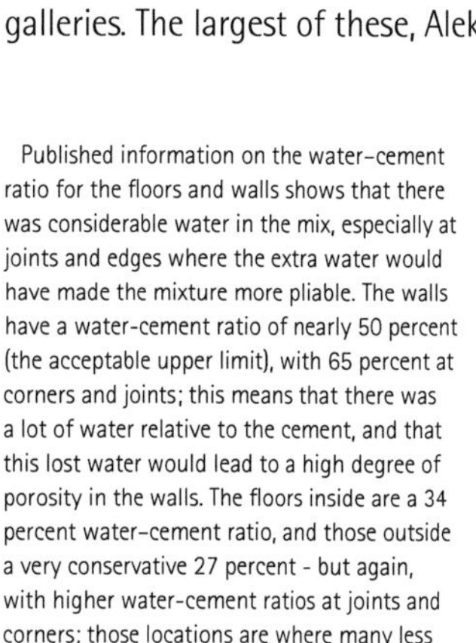

Published information on the water-cement ratio for the floors and walls shows that there was considerable water in the mix, especially at joints and edges where the extra water would have made the mixture more pliable. The walls have a water-cement ratio of nearly 50 percent (the acceptable upper limit), with 65 percent at corners and joints; this means that there was a lot of water relative to the cement, and that this lost water would lead to a high degree of porosity in the walls. The floors inside are a 34 percent water-cement ratio, and those outside a very conservative 27 percent - but again, with higher water-cement ratios at joints and corners; those locations are where many less evenly spaced cracks have appeared.

36 Aoki, Jun with Ryue Nishizawa (2006) p. 68.

37 In the 1960s, many contemporary artworks were banned from group exhibitions because they incorporated materials like rotting food; Aoki may be reacting to this era as much as the reality today.

9.30

9.31

9.30 *A modern space, the café.*

9.31 *The rougher earthen walls are in sync with works of art from Aomori's recent past, such as this photograph by Ichiro Kojima.*

9.32 *One wall of the museum is closer to lumpy cob construction.*

is in fact nearly cubic: heart-breakingly close to square in plan and marginally shallower than it is broad.[38] The term "White Cube" has been widely used in Japan of late, and acknowledges a pivotal 1970s text by Brian O'Doherty.[39] O'Doherty, an artist, described such spaces in an insightful but abrogating way:

> ... The ideal gallery subtracts from the artwork all cues that interfere with the fact that it is "art." The work is isolated from everything that would detract ... This gives the space a presence possessed by other spaces where conventions are preserved through the repetition of a closed system of values.[40]

He continues,

> ... Unshadowed, white, clean, artificial, the space is devoted to the technology of esthetics. Works of art are mounted, hung, scattered for study. Their ungrubby surfaces are untouched by time and its vicissitudes. Art exists in a kind of eternity of display, and though there is lots of "period" (late modern), there is no time. This eternity gives the gallery a limbolike [*sic*] status ...[41]

In Aoki's "white" galleries, walls are stripped of any relief or interruption; no base trim or picture rail, no windows – the room enclosure seems to disappear. Floors are finished in a glossy white epoxy. In the strongest galleries, lighting (from the ceiling, but reflected by the glossy floors to create a bright, shadow-free space) is pure, clean, strong and uniform, creating a sense that the artworks are simply floating. Aoki and his staff designed much of the lighting in the office, consulting closely with the mechanical engineers P. T. Morimura and three independent lighting firms. The result varies widely; the whitest spaces lit to 4200 Kelvins, while other areas incorporate yellowy, 3500 Kelvin lighting.

White spaces enclosed in brick are treated with special care; Aoki clearly reflected the conflict between Japan and Western interpretations when detailing the masonry walls, the design team pulled by the ambiguity of these materials as both modern and traditional. Aoki insisted on hand-laid brick to achieve a rougher surface, yet simultaneously devised a complicated approach that undermined any reading of the brick as weighted. The expanse underscores the resulting artificiality of the finish; white-painted masonry extends without joints or visual interruption 79 meters (259 feet) on the longest façade, expansion joints carefully camouflaged.[42]

Gregory Clancey, writing on material choices following the 1923 earthquake that leveled Tokyo, goes so far as to state that afterwards, "Brick and stone were virtually banned ..."[43] Because it is difficult – indeed, impossible – to design traditional, bearing brick walls to survive repeated strong earthquakes, unitary masonry materials such as brick and block are little used in Japan today. However, as Clancey also points out, for many years before giving up the material, "the standard brick wall was subjected to an orgy of reinvention."[44] The atypical way that Aoki employs brick at Aomori, then, may not seem so odd at home, where many other architects (Kazuyo Sejima and Kengo Kuma included) have also rethought the modest brick.

A book on the Aomori Museum of Art illustrates 25 specially produced, non-standard brick shapes – clearly defying the conventional logic of masonry construction.[45] Unusual shapes are particularly noticeable at the intersection of soffits and ceilings, where the brick underside runs perpendicular to the bond of the wall above, with no

38 Aleko Hall is 21.7 x 21.65 meters (roughly 71 x 71 feet) in plan and 19.5 meters (just short of 64 feet) in height.

39 O'Doherty (1976) p. 24.

40 Ibid.

41 Ibid., p. 25.

42 Aoki (2006c) p. 92.

43 Clancey (2006) p. 222.

44 Ibid., pp. 180–181. It is worth pointing out, though, that while there are some technical benefits to Aoki's novel system (reduced cracking in the mortar joints), it does not reduce labor, and most likely considerably increased labor costs.

45 Aoki *et al.* (2006a) p. 203. These unusual shapes were used to create the sharp edges at openings, suggest that corners were the result of two mitered bricks meeting, and to accommodate the steel lintels supporting the brick. In addition, there are three brick thicknesses: 50, 75 and 150 mm.

9.32

9 . 33

9 . 34

9 . 35

9 . 36

9 . 37

9 . 33, 34 The brick is rendered as almost weightless, with narrow slits of space and oddly abutting edges.

9 . 35, 37 The two territories of the museum are clearly and cleanly articulated in their contrasting finishes and colors.

9 . 36 A hovering wall, the gap a subtle structural trick.

9.38 *A visitors' area at a lower entrance to the museum which Aoki thought particularly important because of its proximity to the Sannai Maruyama site.*

9.39 *Jomon era pottery is mingled with contemporary art in an early exhibition, reflecting the architect's own ideas.*

9.38

sense of thickness in evidence. Aoki points out:

> ... the bricks have been cut at 45-degree angles and merely tacked up in place, more an image of brick-patterned wall paper [*sic*] than real laid brick ... the actual lintel cannot be seen, only rows of brick. Likewise, the underside of the eaves [soffits] are covered with brick. Impossible by means of stone masonry, thin-split bricks are set into glass-fiber reinforced concrete (GRC) to form lintel and ceiling panels that are then cemented into place ...[46]

At window openings, the oddness of the system is even more pronounced; brick corners end in a knife-edge, visually emphasized by slipping the opaque wall forward across the glass like a curtain. From inside, supporting galvanized steel hangers and the unpainted edges of the brick curtain wall are visible. One of Aoki's staff most closely involved in the museum, Toru Murayama, explained the intentions of this odd detail: "... at the inside of openings in the brick wall, [bricks] are cut at 45-degrees and through this device a heavy, thick impression of the wall is converted to a light, thin impression."[47]

In Japanese clothing design, a popular conceit is to turn seams outward so fraying edges are exposed; Aoki has taken a similar approach architecturally, revealing the inner workings of wall cavities and structure at windows and air vents. Structure and building skin are thus presented as independent systems (an homage to Scott Brown and Venturi's "decorated shed"). Aoki argued for the intellectual pleasure this layered construction was to offer, saying, for example, "... we always imagine the backsides [*sic*] we cannot actually see. The backsides [*sic*] being the real state of things, we are forever trying to picture the substance of things from their surfaces."[48] The architect relied on an industrial system developed in Napa Valley to update vernacular *hanchiku*, while in his white areas, he ironically employs complex brick construction as the exterior finish, relying on the flexibility of Japan's fabricators to remake a material more often found abroad.

The clean lines of this white-painted brick exterior also link this building in Northern Japan to many in Northern Europe. But while Westerners date architectural modernism from the early twentieth-century shift to glass and steel, for Japanese architects, the shift was earlier, heralded by brick banks, railroad stations and warehouses that were a feature of mid-nineteenth-century industrialization. Such buildings were once widely distributed across Japan, but few remain today. Yet northern Japan's relatively dolorous economies offered little incentive to tear older structures down; relatively speaking, there are proportionately more structures from the Meiji era in this area than affluent urban centers such as Tokyo. The nineteenth-century references implied by Aoki's brick walls are underscored in his incongruous application of arched openings and heavy steel doors that slide on exposed rails, similar to doors widely used in old warehouses in Hokkaido, north of Aomori. Aoki struggled to find a way to explain these gestures, and often called them droll; they are offered with amusement, the arches and heavy doors contrasting with the wallpaper-like superficiality of the walls. The brick also encourages other allusions to Japan's modern architecture; the project architect linked them to the work of Kunio Maekawa, a mid-twentieth-century architect hailing from nearby Hirosaki, known for his brick and brick-like tile finishes.[49] These loosely overlapping references are deliberate, establishing what Fredric Jameson calls "... the complacent eclecticism

46 Ibid. p. 014.

47 Aoki (2006c) p. 92. Original Japanese: 皿に煉瓦の小口は内側に４５カットされており，そのことが重く厚い印象を軽く薄い印象に変換している．軒天やアーチ上部の煉瓦は，それぞれGRCに25mmにスライスした煉瓦を打ち込んだもの。。。 N.B.: These angles actually seem to vary in the building; in some sections, the cut angle is closer to 60 degrees.

48 Aoki *et al.* (2006a) p. 015.

49 http://www.tezzo.net/aomori/museum3.html, 22 April, 2004 entry (accessed 21 July, 2005).

9.39

9.40

9.41

9.40 The lush colors of each piece of art seem to be accented by the dark backdrop of earthen walls.

9.41 Three sculptural figures exploiting the possibilities Aoki offered in his earthen surfaces.

9.42

9.43

of postmodern architecture, which randomly and without principle but with gusto cannibalizes all the architectural styles of the past and combines them in overstimulating ensembles."[50]

Aoki is influenced here by Isozaki. In 1989, Isozaki argued: "Anything occurring in the history of architecture – even the history of the world – is open to quotation. But the important point to notice is that, once quoted, things lose their original meaning and generate new meanings ..."[51] This is the approach Aoki adopts, simultaneously offering up gestures that recall local history, while equivocally rejecting that they imply deeper intentions, or indeed, that they should be taken seriously. Isozaki allowed "... the details to speak clearly but to generate new meaning by drowning each other out" achieving "... a style, in which continuity is lacking and confusion is allowed to persist ..."[52] Aoki also offers a set of carefully articulated and unrelated events, without concern for any ordered understanding or appreciation, a loose montage of floating fragments. Aoki's architecture seems to be deliberately going by a postmodern playbook, as described by Fredric Jameson in his 1991 *Postmodernism, or, The Cultural Logic of Late Capitalism*:

> ... all these features – the strange new feeling of an absence of inside and outside, the bewilderment and loss of spatial orientation ... the messiness of an environment in which things and people no longer find their place – offer useful symptomatic approaches to the nature of postmodern hyperspace ...[53]

The lack of hierarchy or intention renders these gestures ultimately empty and superficial – and yet also emphasizes how deep the expectation of acknowledging history is for architects today. On the one hand, Aoki had little choice but to represent Aomori's unique history, and yet he found himself able to do so only ironically.

In peeling away these layers at his large openings, Aoki also reveals an oddly syncopated structure, undermining any sense of technological artistry. (He calls it a "lump of structure".[54]) At exterior openings or inside along the ramp connecting the café and shop to the rest of the building, the clumsy steel trusses are deliberate; oddly, the engineer, Yoshiharu Kanebako, is far better known in Japan for elegantly concealing his work. According to Aoki, the structural engineer resisted the architect's affectation of randomly exposing structure, designing trusses so that their members would not fall oddly across window openings. In order to achieve his goals, Aoki simply waited until the structural design was complete, the engineer designing the trusses to best accommodate loads. The architect then relocated openings in his later documents to create awkward frames for the gawky trusses – much to the discomfort of the engineer, who frets that people might see this structure and think him inept.[55] But columns are so neatly concealed the effect underscores the oddity of seeing these trusses; in places, brick walls literally stop inches from the floor with no apparent support. One wide face of Aleko Hall hovers a hand-span above the floor; in another gallery, drape-like brick is emphasized by an unsupported corner thrusting into an adjacent space. These gaps vary in effectiveness; those a mere 150 mm (6 inches) are often too subtle to be easily appreciated (a problem made worse by the tendency of museum staff to locate signage at the unsupported corner of Gallery G), but elsewhere a brick wall stops 400 mm (nearly 16 inches) above ground, deep enough to resonate as odd.

But the ability to understand Kanebako's skill or recognize the so-

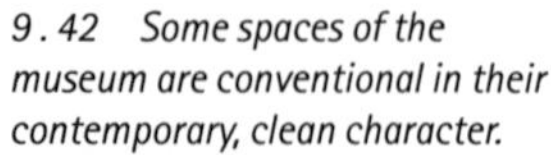

9.42 Some spaces of the museum are conventional in their contemporary, clean character.

9.43 One of the permanent galleries, housing work by woodcut artist Shiko Munakata.

50 Jameson (1991) pp. 18–19.

51 Ibid., p. 59.

52 Ibid., p. 57.

53 Ibid., pp. 117–118.

54 Aoki (2006d) p. 7. Original Japanese: 物理的には, 構造体の塊。。。

55 Aoki's trick is one possible because of the more flexible approach to documents in Japan. For more on this point, readers can turn to my first book, *Japanese Architecture as a Collaborative Process* (Buntrock, 2001).

9.44

9.45

phistication in Aoki's masonry walls is arcane, requiring an up-to-date knowledge of art discourse, of architecture and of construction to appreciate. Problematically, for people who do not comprehend the cunning construction, there is little satisfying material use or detailing in one's initial experience of the Aomori Museum of Art.[56] Visitors are well into the building before the texture and detailing of earthen walls and floors offer such a broad appeal, where the sensual colors and nubby surfaces require no specialist knowledge for their appreciation.

As a result, a sense of inscrutable, unknowable influence, of a little-understood order, is inherent in Aoki's art museum. The architect often describes the galleries through analogies: an abandoned urban lot (a *harappa*) or a deserted elementary school temporarily employed for an art installation, suggesting a poignant awareness of lingering, but lost, pasts:

> ... the walls of the classroom, ambiguous reactions to children's spirit and hopes ... to enter a [Japanese] school "without removing your shoes" affected even our hearts in its assertive character, a space transformed into its polar opposite ...
>
> Why was the [former] ... elementary school an exceptional site for an art museum? ... The abandoned ... elementary school, just like a vacant field, is a place with a sense of people [having once been active there] – a place that reflected a set of rules now cut off, the basis for those rules lost.[57]

Although Aomori's museum was a new structure, Aoki embraced this concept of reuse, citing not only abandoned urban lots and reclaimed schools, but also old warehouses exhibiting art. Aoki, echoing his mentor Isozaki, refers to ruins, but contends:

> While I was making this building [the Aomori Museum of Art], I kept telling myself it was a ruin. Only now have I come to understand what I really meant by that. A ruin does not simply refer to a material object that has decayed and broken down, leaving only partially sound remains. A ruin is something once thought out according to a coherent logic ... whose originating bases have since been lost ...[58]

Returning to the book *Museums for the 21st Century*, Josep Maria Montaner writes of these places as "anti-museums." Montaner argues "The results ... are always labyrinthine and never completely finished ..."[59] While Montaner may question such outcomes, the characteristics he identifies were ones Aoki desired.

Notably, Aoki's Aomori time is not simply a portrayal of time free of the past, but equally free of the future. In writing of the experience he intended at Aomori, Aoki offered, "We must transcend planning concepts. In order to do that, we must value only the present moment."[60] Aoki offers up an unrooted, aimless past of freely floating symbols and references, matched by a suspended timelessness in his almost invisible white galleries. Writing of the museum, Aoki argues "... superfluidity makes the architecture, in my view, a present-moment conflux of flow lines."[61] Juhani Pallasmaa once spoke of architectural experiences as "*verb* forms rather than ... nouns."[62] At the Aomori Museum of Art, Aoki expresses an architecture of nouns and verbs, but avoids applying any grammar, insisting that communication is the result of the interpretations of each individual.

56 Although you can reach the earthen trenches to the west of the building without entering it, most movement through the museum does not start from these trenches.

57 Aoki (2004) p. 13. Original Japanese: 教室の境を曖昧にし、子供たちのいろいろな精神的欲求に対応して、あらかじめいろいろな場所を用意してあげようとしてつくられた、押しつけがましく、人の心にまで土足であがり込むような小学校のつくり方とは対極にある空間である。...牛込原町小学校がどうして「美術館」として優れていたのか。...廃校となった牛込原町小学校は、原っぱと同じく、人間の感覚とは一度は切れた決定ルールによって生成し、しかしその決定ルールが根拠を失った空間だったのである。

58 Sawaragi, in Aoki *et al.* (2006a) p. 31.

59 Montaner (2003) p. 122.

60 Aoki (2004) p. 193.

61 Aoki *et al.* (2006a) p. 17.

62 MacKeith (2005) p. 60.

9.44, 45 Aoki's exterior may offer allusions that are inaccessible to most museum visitors.

Reluctant Reds

Fumihiko Maki, Ryoji Suzuki, Jun Aoki

10

Be careful not to digest time poorly.
—Takamasa Yoshizaka[1]

By focusing on three isolated works by Fumihiko Maki, Ryoji Suzuki and Jun Aoki, I could create the wrong impression of their overall output; the buildings I write of here are anomalies, outliers in these architects' *œuvre*. Maki and Suzuki have strayed into such territory on occasion over their long careers, but most of their work is more clearly Modern. Aoki, younger, is better known for sparkling Louis Vuitton boutiques wrapped in layers of graphic film, glass tubes, fine steel meshes and aluminum filigree. While he, like Kuma, is interested in isolating finishes for effect, the Aomori Museum of Art is unique within his architecture because of its overt effort to acknowledge a primitive past.

Still, as Vincent Canizaro asserts in an excellent anthology, "Regionalism is voluntary; ... it is a choice made by a practitioner ..."[2] Or is it?

The oddness of these projects within each architect's portfolio underscores an important point: they are, at best, reluctant Reds. While Kuma argues that his architecture was made possible by Fujimori's pioneering, the architects I discussed in this section are not inclined to the rough and rustic. They do not Orientalize in rhetoric and attire. They are unsympathetic to incorporating the aesthetics of tea. Instead, they adopted regionalism in response to the challenge of a specific project, the demands of clients unwilling to be entirely international. Their equivocation is evident in the architecture I present, each offering elements of both tradition and today. Suzuki closely follows the orders and proportions of ancient architectures on his exteriors, but within he offers an airy space, articulated by an unusual and elegant steel structure. Maki also highlights the modern at the heart of his building – but while Suzuki's contemporary spaces are almost a secret within the structure, for Maki, the modern exists as an outcome and an end result, the past a setting for the present. Aoki, by contrast, expresses no such hierarchy, instead establishing a postmodern pastiche open to individual interpretation, blending what he brings to the site with what he observed in its environs.

The most experienced of these, Maki is inclined to the idea that "... the present is the very flower of modernism."[3] His is an architecture of our global era. The scale of his work is large, sized for the busloads of tourists brought to the site each day and to the symbolic role of the museum in the region. Nonetheless, the power of place drove his design: the looming Kitayama range resonated with Maki's intellectual appreciation of *oku*. He argued, "The interest of the Japanese in the subtlest contours of the land is grounded in a strong, perhaps abnormal, attachment ... attachment to the land remains very much alive, even within completely modern socio-economic institutions."[4] Maki is fully engaged with a meaningful vernacular landscape and it was in the landscape designed by his protégé, Toru Mitani, and in his own mountain-like museum that Maki most strongly acknowledged the

10.1 The ticket counter by Kazuko Fujie, in the entrance hall of Fumihiko Maki's Shimane Museum of Ancient Izumo.

1. Yoshizaka and Atelier U. (1998) p. 379. Original Japanese: 人間は時間の消化不良を常に注意しなければならない。
2. Canizaro (2007) p. 10.
3. Maki (1993) p. 6. Maki is paraphrasing Octavio Paz.
4. Maki (2005) p. 15.

past invested in this place. Outside, the two designers acknowledged the *kunibiki* myth, carved in a path slashing through the site; few will miss the green *magatama* marker at the door – but mostly Maki inclined to rusting Cor-ten finish instead of form to make his point. Early on, he asserted, "... it is possible for us to express time by means of materials ..."[5] Maki's expressions of past and place in the landscape of the Museum of Ancient Izumo increasingly give way to a lighter, modern architecture, one that relies on glass cases from Germany and glowing custom furniture for effect.

The architect underscored his preference for ancient Shinto over its more recent reshaping in the way he confronted the Kitayama mountains, while only offering a nod from a discrete observation deck toward the structures of the Grand Shrine. The platform is nonetheless a crucial moment in this museum, where Maki looks outward on the past.

Aoki was also inspired at Aomori – in a very challenging competition - to take on the presence of the past found in a place. But for Aoki the raw primitiveness of Aomori apparently held no innate appeal; he ultimately turned to art as a more important way to understand his use of earth. Aoki was untroubled by his limited knowledge of the roots of rural Aomori, sampling like a hip-hop hotshot. He might appear to share Maki's preference for abstraction and intellectual appeal, but while the form of Aoki's museum is scaled similarly to Maki's, his volumes also cleanly cubic and with no sense of provenance in modeling, Aoki's materials and finishes offer a crucial difference. Alan Colquhoun, writing in a different context, aptly summarized this yawning gap:

> ... many interesting contemporary designs refer to local materials, typologies, and morphologies. But in doing so their architects are not trying to express the essence of particular regions, but are using local features as motifs in a compositional process in order to produce original, unique, and context-relevant architectural ideas.[6]

Aoki underscored the conceit of his earthen walls as an artistic gesture, the reproduction of a replica; he cloned the colors of explanatory exhibitions inside a museum on the Sannai Maruyama site, not the surrounding soils bared in trenches. He pursued a path the noted writer on postmodernism, Frederic Jameson, called "a simulated relationship to the past rather than a commemorative one."[7]

Aoki's earthen surfaces are, however, open to age, are in fact intended to insistently express the life of floors and walls as art exhibitions unfold over time. Aoki embraced cracking and crumbling, assured that it would occur in ways beyond his - or the curators' - control. He alone amongst these architects not only accepted that time would have a hand in his building, but went further, attempting to unleash time within his work.

But museums are by definition modern buildings, though many must also grapple with the past. Inevitably, other functions more firmly necessitate architects take on tradition - temples and shrines, *noh* or *kabuki* theaters, teahouses and *kaiseki* restaurants, leisure sites such as *ryokan* and *onsen* hot springs resorts. These insist upon convention, although a few unusual examples of any can be found. Contemporary churches in the West are far from rare, so this distinction may seem odd to outsiders - but the segregation of native and modern that began in the Meiji era still holds sway in Japan today. Buildings rooted in the country's culture are expected to embrace

5. Maki, in Munroe (1985) p. 18.
6. Colquhoun (2007) p. 10.
7. Jameson (1991) p. 390.

10.2 At Jun Aoki's Aomori Museum of Art, brick ends in a knife edge.

10.3 Glass skylights and slits in the steel slab of Ryoji Suzuki's Saikan at Kotohira Shrine undermine its otherwise traditional exterior, drawing attention to the steel columns adjacent.

traditional aesthetics; in some cases, to do otherwise is to undermine the accepted choreography of their use, as Fujimori did in his *tatami*-free teahouses.

Suzuki had little leeway in the narrow confines of an ancient shrine. He acknowledged, "With the existence of an intact, overwhelming nature and the amazing tradition which traces back some 500 years, it was required that facilities ... be added anew ... keeping mountain and trees intact in order to respect the landscape that has been cherished by worshippers for a long time."[8] He once told me with amusement that another architect initially considered for Kotohira proposed a two-story building looming over the Main Shrine in order to allow people to admire its elegantly curving roof - and was sternly reminded of the history and hierarchy of the site. Suzuki took this history, this hierarchy, to heart. Maki's directorial gesture, the quiet contemplation of overlooking an ancient shrine, achieved what Suzuki's rival could not at Kotohira.

These three architects ally themselves most closely to Fujimori's construct of a Red regionalism in the intimacy of their architecture, the way these buildings unfold, reveal themselves through movement or procession, link to the landscape of place. Suzuki's stone steps continue the path winding through Kotohira shrine, subtly echoing the odd rhythms of the site. His shadowy spaces and narrow internal stairs slow time. Movement through Maki's building underscores equivocation, shifting awareness the way one might see in a stroll garden, visitors alternately looking outwards to the past and inward to the present. Aoki cuts trenches into the soil of his site as if establishing an over-scaled extension of the archaeological dig next door, the two territories linked, the boundaries blurred. But he in fact offers a more provocative idea than a simple unfurling of past to present, his architecture disinclined to direct, lacking any clear hierarchy or processional path. Aoki hopes each visitor will discover the architecture at Aomori anew, a device Tadao Ando also deploys so skillfully in his smaller structures. Aoki's architecture owes something to the quantum science of Schrodinger's cat, undermining any sense of a centered or certain world.

In comparing Fujimori and Kuma, I explained how each employs a different understanding of time. For Fujimori, the past and the present are a seamless whole, while Kuma is aware of the Meiji era as a moment of separation, the beginning of the modern era. In Kuma's construction, we cannot return to earlier eras, only view them from our own, draw on the past as a rich archive. Suzuki, I would argue, ambiguously straddles these two positions; he offers an architecture rooted in an overlapping sense of both pre-modern and modern perceptions of time. The architect recreated forms from earlier eras, but he also relied on our recognition of Kotohira's economic impracticality, our understanding of rare materials and skills underscoring that these buildings are not comfortably of our time. As one author insightfully observed, "The chance for things to age and to become ruin has diminished in the age of turbo capitalism ..."[9]

Suzuki accepted unpopular precedents, rebuilding in the disciplined style of the Tenpyou and Kamakura eras; he researched buildings no longer extant, available only in publications, and visited structures that required travel to Nara and Kyoto, where Tokyo-based architects rarely have reason to roam. In the end, as he acknowledged, these uneconomic efforts at study were insufficient; the most traditional areas of his architecture owe a great deal to a carpenter. Only Suzuki,

8. Suzuki (2004) p. 64.
9. Huyssen (2006) p. 10.

of these three, was able to fully embrace craft – and even then his reliance on the shrine carpenter, Nobuyuki Yamamoto, was at some level simply pragmatic. In spite of his respect for the carpenter's contributions, it took the architect some effort to find Yamamoto's name for me – or even the name of the company, Fujita Shaji, one of a limited coterie that engages in such work. Suzuki is not fetishizing craft, though he respects its results and appreciated his unusual opportunity.

At Kotohira, Suzuki erected an architecture that exists in the cycle of time, articulated in its *hinoki* bark. The roof of the conferment building will be replaced in 33 years, along with the roof of the Main Shrine it faces - and 33 years after that, and again and again, until an easily anticipated time when these curving canopies are simply seen as one. Suzuki understands it is unlikely these roofs will be compromised by the economic inclinations of an unthinking client; this allowed him to embrace decay and ongoing, expensive maintenance.

Aoki, on the other hand, could only abstract the archaeological trenches of the adjacent Sannai Maruyama site for his public client, sanitized clay shot through a hose. The effort involved in actually mounding earth was economically impractical. Maki and Aoki relied on construction contemporary in character, expressed as much in Maki's fair-faced concrete and Aoki's singular brick as in their regionally resonant use of steel and soil. The way these architects employed vulnerable materials is, oddly, also evidence of their resistance to Fujimori's Red.

Aoki and Maki acknowledged the distant past without attempting reconstruction, both relying only on primitive references. The age of the adjacent, ancient landscape is emphasized in Maki's architecture, drawn in distinction to his soaring public spaces framed in glass, while Aoki's efforts to acknowledge the *Jomon* in his earthen walls owe something to mid-century artistic debates, making these soil surfaces simultaneously modern.

Each of these three has employed an understanding of time that accepted both past and present, but each architect ultimately embodied a differing arc of time: Suzuki accepted the past, Maki's modernism prioritized the present, and an uncontrollable future is evident in Aoki's architecture. In the end, the examples offered in this section reflect how these three designers took a selective stance, in some ways remaining comfortably within international modernism, yet also adapting aspects of rusticity and regionalism. It is they and their architecture that establishes a bridge between the professionalism demanded of public work and the unconventional character of Fujimori's Reds. Those I have introduced in these chapters till a fertile ground cleared by others, architects who often operate outside the norms of the profession, the architects who initially inspired Fujimori and his understanding of the Red School – the radical and unrepentant Reds.

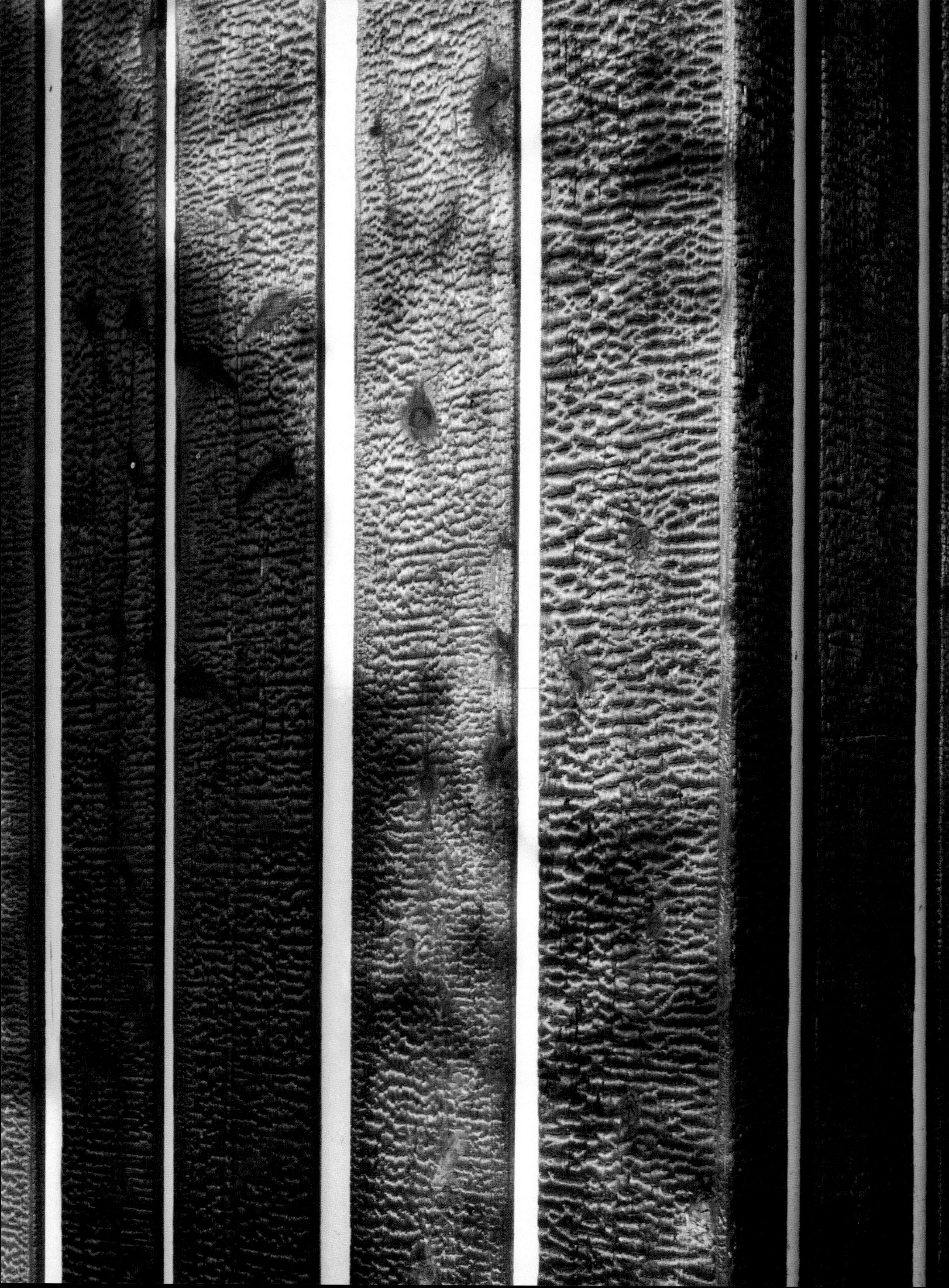

Conclusion

The Red School: From Deepest Red to Palest Shades of Pink

... standing stones require the presence of fallen stones.—*Juzou Ueda*[1]

The attributes of the Red School can be listed in a rolling roster: raw and robust, raffish and ragtag, rambunctious and reckless, rough and rudimentary, refreshing and resplendent, risky and risqué, recalling Rikyu, regionally responsive. The Red School rots and inclines to ruin; it is made of rust, rammed earth, red brick, random rock rubble or recycled rubbish. It is about being rooted and having a roof. It is a rich rhapsody. It is, in the end, rare.

And that should come as no surprise; it is exceedingly hard to be in the band of really Red architects, immerse in the stories of place or project, drawing deeply from the well of meaning or a moment in time. Instead of walking away while others build, Red architects remain, bringing their own awkward efforts to construction. To be a radically Red architect is to exert not merely intellectual effort in one's work, but sweat.

Wood will decay, paper tatter and fray - even stone, over time, is smoothed and softened. Yet an assuredly avant-garde architect best known for curving concrete and slim steel structural sandwiches, Toyo Ito, acknowledged that when he built a house in 1983 with a pounded earthen floor, "... I was shocked to discover that the muddy-smelling dirt ... was far more compelling and powerful than my own contemporary design."[2] Perhaps history and tradition are worn thinner in time, yet their essential power remains, a winnowing all we are witnessing. Perhaps this temporal moment is not so unlike the middle of the nineteenth century, when carpenters' works were assessed as temporary by Western professionals washing up on Japan's shores, and yet they endured. The alien architects' brand-new buildings of hard materials and foreign technologies are almost entirely gone now, while the temples and shrines they derided still stand at the center of many cities.

But I worry that this book will outlast more than one building of which I write.

Mark Wigley once remarked that architects can be defined and divided by their response to the idea that "Bodies last longer than the buildings they occupy."[3] Red architects, even while accepting ruin, idealize age. White architects, even while arguing the superiority of steel, idealize ephemerality. The distinction is in the way architects see and slow time, in its expression and embrace.

Age is illustrated most often in the fabric and finishes of construction. Tea master Rikyu's abiding influence means that for some even today "rather nondescript, mundane materials such as paper, wood and straw receive as much attention and celebration as, or sometimes more appreciation than, luxurious materials such as gold, opulent fabric, or precious stones," as Yuriko Saito asserted, continuing, "There are no lowly objects or materials."[4] But at the moment, not many practicing architects, professionals serving public demand, appreciate mundane materials - only, it would appear, Kengo Kuma. Just as Fujimori found few artisans enthusiastic about the idea of rethinking their trade and exploring its edges, architects and clients today are increasingly likely to limit their efforts to known systems - stable,

11. 1 Terunobu Fujimori's 2007 Yakisugi ("Charred Cedar") House.

1. Iwaki, Ken'ichi. (2001) "The Logic of Visual Perception: Ueda Juzou," [N.B., title employs Japanese name order] in Marra, ed., p. 309.
2. Ito, Toyo with Koji Taki (1994) pp. 21-22.
3. Wigley (2000) p. 31. Wigley is clearly echoing the oft-repeated Futurist argument that "Our houses will last less time than we do, and every generation will have to make its own."
4. Saito (1999) p. 262.

steady, and thus successes. Clients, in spite of their desire to reflect history in the places most meaningful to them, are also understandably fearful of an approach some argue is at its best open to ruin or risk.

In my opening chapters, I asked of Fujimori's fragile follies, "Is it architecture?" Increasingly, others answer it is not. Architecture is often assessed by a few points culled from those criteria centuries older: commodity, firmness - and, somehow in our present age, only dwindling demand for delight. Architecture is too often little more than a consumer good, characterized by a more contemporary definition of "commodity" in our dictionaries. Meaning is in short supply, replaced by simple branding.

There are certainly important technological issues facing our field: energy or engineering for earthquakes. These must be considered; increasing complexities are one of the reasons that clients are conservative today, uncomfortable with their inability to assess. Architects do not always inspire confidence, either. Japan's leading practitioners too often design structures that quickly and unintentionally corrode, buildings easily outlasted by bodies. Such structures represent not the propensity for ruin in the Red School, but the ephemerality of the White, dainty materials and details done without worry for durability. At least a designer like Ishiyama or Fujimori anticipates ongoing, modest maintenance. It might be wiser to admit at times, as they have, that buildings need constant care, to accept the idea that sometimes we should design so simply that anyone can build. But we demand more certainty and longevity of our buildings.

Clients have good reason to grasp for solutions that give them greater confidence, even misguided or not wholly valid ones. In the final months of 2005 it came to light that an architect/engineer named Hidetsugu Aneha took advantage of recent revisions to pre-construction plan checks to design dozens of concrete structures with inadequate reinforcing steel, placing savings in pennies before people – and other egregious examples have since emerged. The condominiums those optimistic owners bought no longer exist, but their mortgages will last many decades more with no relief. Books outlasting buildings, bodies outlasting buildings - we can understand the advantage at some intellectual level. Debt outlasting design? No obvious appeal, even intellectually; far less easy to argue for. But Aneha engaged in *roughshod* work, not Red's rough, his cutting corners an inevitable outcome of constructing commodities, not architecture.

Fumihiko Maki - hardly, in the end, one of the Radical Reds! - agonized over

> Today's endless process of scrap-and-build cities, the treatment of real estate as an investment trust, and the emergence of a world in which developers and corporate management play the central role, the continued practice of competitive bidding for architectural services, and the trivialization and dissipation of the architectural profession ...[5]

It is far too easy to argue that opportunities like Maki's museum, or Suzuki's buildings at Kotohira, are no longer the mainstay of the profession in Japan, if indeed they were ever more than an intellectual touchpoint. Contractors and commercial offices design an increasing proportion of those structures that were once expected to have greater meaning.

Twenty years ago, at the cusp of Japan's Bubble era, Itsuko Hasegawa envisioned the "mini-Tokyos" in Japan's future, superfi-

5. Maki (2005-2006) p. 327.

ciality spreading into smaller cities. This is globalization's hierarchy, each community aping larger urban areas, yielding a situation where, "Expressed simply, Tokyo fashions appear in the provinces with no time lag as Tokyo-origin brand shops dominate the scene, while the individual character of the regions[,] on the other hand[,] has become diluted ..."[6] as Riichi Miyake recently argued.

Maybe architecture belongs only in urbane environs or as odd outposts beyond major metropolises. Maybe it should only culminate in conservative construction by comfortable and comforting corporations. In this case, the fact that Japanese architects are almost entirely in Tokyo, are disinclined to root themselves in regions, is entirely understandable. But it is in just such a citified setting that the contemporary commodification of construction is at its most extreme. As Maiken Umbach and Bernd Huppauf argued: "Globalization is ... predicated on a fiction: the *fiction* of placelessness ... centers of power like New York, Tokyo, and London create a special order around them - they structure the system of globalization geographically. Globalization ... establishes hierarchies ..."[7] The reflection of an agglomeration of economic activity is seen in short-lived structures that have no intention of becoming important icons, no intention of encouraging an appetite for expensive and ongoing maintenance. If a building is to be allowed to be obsolete, it is an advantage that it will, over time, become uninteresting, unloved, and unwanted.

But we have arrived at a point when Itsuko Hasegawa is unlikely to engage in competitions for public projects; she laments that clients now count the number of licensed architects her office can offer up - and the small firm is unable to compete with larger commercial companies. Surely the bureaucrats are more comfortable with these corporations, but the public who once had a voice in Hasegawa's work is not well served, the resulting buildings less likely to be loved.

Those that aspire to the utmost in technological sophistication inherently accept rapidly becoming obsolete and out of date. Ito poignantly penned the tale of his own family's inability to conserve one key concrete house offered up early in his career; in 1997, Sejima won an Architectural Institute of Japan award for the Multi-Media Workshop in Gifu, a construction site I discussed in my first book - and only ten years later it was shuttered. This intense innovation is a lingering echo of the economic exuberance of the late 1980s and early 1990s. When Japan dominated the international economy, both urban and rural clients demanded buildings underscoring the nation's position as a global leader, optimistically and enthusiastically celebrating progress in architecture's effervescence.

What are the alternatives? Wendell Berry, an acute observer of cultural change, acknowledged, "... a 'regionalism' based on pride, which behaves like nationalism. And there is a 'regionalism' based upon condescension, which specializes in the quaint and the eccentric and the picturesque, and which behaves in general like an exploitive industry."[8] One cannot blame architects for their wary unwillingness to engage these ideas in light of the options he offers, but as I argued in this book, there are perhaps other ways to build, to acknowledge diversity and differences. A long-time editor of the UK's *Architectural Review*, Catherine Slessor, envisioned an architecture where

> Regionalism addresses the particularities of place and culture. It mines everyday life and perception for intentions about a truly progressive future. It aims to sustain a close and continuous relationship between architecture and the

6. Miyake (Spring 2007) pp. 08-09.
7. Umbach and Huppauf (2005) p. 12. My emphasis.
8. Berry, (2007), p. 37.

local community it serves. Crucially, it learns from experience. It tinkers, crafts, accepts, rejects, adjusts, reacts. It is immediately rooted in the tangible realities of its situation: the history, geography, human values, economy, traditions, technology and cultural life of a place.[9]

In arguing that anyone can build, oddball architecture professors and their allies are arguing for broader engagement, one possible by architects anywhere. Radical Reds appeal to the public, their popularity seen in the wide dissemination of photographs of Fujimori's funny follies - yet Red designers are aging.

In my first book, I concentrated on a group I called "lead architects," borrowing a concept from Eric von Hippel.[10] The economist studies how a "lead user" will define new technical territory for a larger group; I saw Toyo Ito, Fumihiko Maki, and others playing this role for the profession, each exploring how to achieve new structural and performance innovations. It might be argued that the unusual group I call Radical Reds also attempted to be leaders - not technical leaders, clearly, but willing, even in spite of the uneconomical nature of their work, to advance new ideas about how to draw the past into the present, challenging the accepted ideas about what our profession should be. Paul Valéry is credited with the aphorism, "... the true tradition in great things is not to do again what other people have done, but to rediscover the spirit that created great things ..." The Radical Reds play just such a role; they offer, as I noted in my introduction, not a nostalgia reaching to restore the past, but one open to reforming it, one that reflects upon what should not be lost.

But Fujimori, Ishiyama, and the other Reds are approaching the ends of their careers. Their adult lives started in the 1960s, a time of change throughout the world. Younger architects, raised in quieter and more comfortable times, are understandably less inclined to go as far. *Tatami* is often more foreign to them than titanium. Isozaki once asserted, "... despite being Japanese ourselves, today we see Japan with the eyes of a foreigner, precisely like those of Lafacadio Hearn or Bruno Taut ... [due to] the process of modernization, we see Japan from a viewpoint similar to Westerners." [11] Isamu Kurita effectively parsed the problem to get at its roots: "... the very international-ness of the life-style makes the traditional arts appear quite alien and exotic. We look at our tradition the way a foreigner does ..." [12] Not all Japanese live an international life, but its urbanites, including its urbane architects, assuredly do.

Perhaps the need for people who challenge the profession will wax and wane. Maybe one should look not only to see who is pushing the envelope, but how the edges of that envelope alter, at times enlarging, at times quite small. Maybe it is enough that at the right moments architects like Maki, Suzuki and Aoki are able to embrace deeper meaning in their work, and at other times the most successful of them turn out triumphant towers.

Professionals who present both past and present, who place the Red within a modern (or even post-modern) frame, the Reluctant Reds and architects operating in the palest shades of pink, are the ones most able to endure today. I do not mean their architectures necessarily endure. I mean that as architects, they do. And in the end they plant a larger imprint on our places.

And yet, Alan Colquhoun correctly queried, "If buildings are to retain their quality of uniqueness as symbols, how can they also be the end products of an industrial system whose purpose is to find

9. Slessor (2000) p. 16.
10. See my *Japanese Architecture as a Collaborative Process* (2001).
11. Isozaki (1996) p. 8.
12. Original in Kurita (1983) p. 131

global solutions?"[13] I confess, I miss the magic when confronted with a surfeit of overly professional projects; I am at least sometimes inclined to architectures incorporating amusement and delight. But I am Berkeley-based. It would be easy to argue that I am simply one of the weirdos of Wurster Hall, expressing the eccentric appetites of an academic. I know a robustly Red architecture is a luxury few enjoy today, accessible only to some, the built equivalent of artisanal breads or riding bikes to work. I know it is an architecture few can afford, especially in an eroding economy like Japan's. I know there are many ways to be an architect, many methods of remembering. But architecture would be diminished if only articulated in weightless Whites and perfumed pinks, lacking the passions of Fujimori and his radical fringe, the heart of the Red School in Japan.

13. Colquhoun (1985) p. 29.

Bibliography

Akasegawa, Genpei (1990) *Sen no Rikyu: Mugen no Zen'ei* 千利休：無言の前衛 [Sen no Rikyu: Vanguard of Silence], Tokyo: Iwanami Shinsho.

Akasegawa, Genpei (1991) "*Otousan wa Joumon Datta: Doukou no Shi*" お父さんは縄文だった：同好の士 *[Neolithic Daddy: Men of Similar Tastes] Kikan Me* 季刊め [Me Quarterly], (November), pp. 7-8.

Akita, Kimiko (2005) "Interactions in the Onna-yu: The Women's Section of a Bathhouse in Japan," unpublished Ph.D. dissertation, Ohio University.

Alini, Luigi (2005) *Kengo Kuma: Works and Projects*, Milan: Electa Architecture.

Anderson, Stanford (1982) "Types and Conventions in Time: Toward a History for the Duration and Change of Artifacts," *Perspecta*, vol. 18, pp. 108-117.

Ando, Tadao (1984) *Buildings, Projects, Writings*, New York: Rizzoli.

Aoki, Jun (2001) "*Tsuchi no Tenjishitu*" 土の展示室 *[Earthen Exhibition Space] A-ism*, vol. 4 (June), p. 3.

Aoki, Jun (2004) *Harappa to Yuuenchi: Kenchiku ni Totte sono Ba no Shitsu to ha Nani ka* 原っぱと遊園地：建築にとってその場の質とは何か [The Empty Field and the Amusement Park: What Is the Architectural Duality of Each Place?], Tokyo: Ookokusha.

Aoki, Jun (2006a) trans. Alfred Birnbaum, Jun with Noi Sawaragi and Hideyuki Nakayama, *Jun Aoki: Complete Works 2: Aomori Museum of Art*, Tokyo: INAX Publications.

Aoki, Jun (2006b) "*Meiro mitai de Fuwa tto fuyuu Suru Kanji Deshou,*" 迷路みたいで フワっと浮遊する感じでしょう？ a.k.a. "Modern Rendezvous for Art and Architecture," *Title* (November) pp. 14-19.

Aoki, Jun (2006c) "*Aomorikenritsu Bijutsukan*" 青森県立美術館 *[Aomori Prefectural Museum of Art] section entitled "Gaiheki"* 外壁 [Exterior Wall], *Shinkenchiku* 新建築 [New Architecture], vol. 81, no. 9 (September) pp. 76-93.

Aoki, Jun (2006d) "*Kaikoubu no Diteiru*" 開口部のディテール *[Details for Openings], Kobetsukai to Shite no Diteiru* 個別としてのディテール [Details Derived from Individualized Solutions], Tokyo: Shokokusha.

Aoki, Jun with Ryue Nishizawa (2006) "*Zushiki to Ru-Ru: Aomori Bijutukan wo Megutte*" 図式とルール：青森美術館をめぐって *[Methods and Rules: Enfolding the Aomori Museum of Art], Shinkenchiku* 新建築 [New Architecture], vol. 81, no. 9 (September), pp. 66-69.

"*Aomori Kenritsu Bijutukan" (2006) (Data) Shinkenchiku* 新建築 [New Architecture], vol. 81, no. 9 (September) p. 226.

Arashiyama, Kozaburo 嵐山光三郎,(2006) "*Konsento Nuita ka! Shuukan Asahi Rensai Essei 432*" コンセント抜いたか！ 週刊朝日連載エッセー ４３２ *[It's Unplugged?! Weekly Asahi Essay 432], Shuukan Asahi* 週刊朝日 [Weekly Asahi], available at http://www.lamune-onsen.co.jp/yuumeijin.html (accessed September 6, 2007).

Atelier Zo (1985) *"Zou no Uchuu – Sukeiru wo Meguru Juugo no Tabi"* 象の宇宙 – スケールをめぐる15の旅 a.k.a. "The Universe According to Zo: Fifteen Levels of Scale," *Space Design (SD)*, no. 254, "Atelier Zo" (November), pp. 5-36.

Kindling, speared on steel, in the clerestory of the tearoom in Akasegawa Genpei's home, the 1997 Nira House.

Atelier *Zo* (1993) *"Tochi to Tsukuru 12 no Houhou"* 土地をつくる12の方法 a.k.a. "Making Landforms: 12 Givens," *Kenchiku Bunka* 建築文化 *[Architecture Culture], vol. 48, no. 564 "Aimaimoko"* あいまいもく [Ambiguity], (October), pp. 69-140.

Baljon, Cornelis J. (1997) "Interpreting Ruskin: The Argument of the Seven Lamps of Architecture and the Stones of Venice," *The Journal of Aesthetics and Art Criticism*, vol. 55, no. 4 (Autumn), pp. 401–414.

Bergdoll, Barry (1997) "John Keenen and Terence Riley, Tectonic Collage," *Perspecta*, vol. 28, "Architects. Process. Inspiration," pp. 148-159.

Birnbaum, Phyllis (2006) *Glory in Line: A Life of Foujita*, New York: Faber and Faber.

Bognar, Botond (1993) "Toward Another [New Age] Modernism: Three Recent Large-Scale Works by Fumihiko Maki," *Space Design (SD)*, no. 340 "Fumihiko Maki, 1987–1992" (January) pp. 42-44.

Boym, Svetlana (2001) *The Future of Nostalgia*, New York: Basic Books.

Buck, David (1997a) "Rotation in Harmony with Nature," *Japan Times*, 28 June, p. 18.

Buck, David (1997b) "Ground Graffiti: A Modernist Listening to the Earth," *Japan Times*, 22 November, p. 17.

Buntrock, Dana (2001) *Japanese Architecture as a Collaborative Process*, London: Spon Press.

Buntrock, Dana (2006a) *"Chiisa na Kenchiku wo Ookiku suru koto"* 小さな建築を大きくすること *[Making Small Buildings Large] 10+1*, no. 44 (October), pp. 142–145.

Buntrock, Dana (2006b) "Shimane Museum of Ancient Izumo," *Museums in the 21st Century: Concepts, Projects, Buildings*, New York: Prestel, pp. 44–49.

Cadwallader, Gary (2002) "Foreword," in Robin Noel Walker, *Shoukouken: A Late Medieval Daima Sukiya Style Japanese Tea-house*, New York: Routledge.

Canizaro, Vincent (ed.) (2007) *Architectural Regionalism: Collected Writings on Place, Identity, Modernity and Tradition*, New York: Princeton Architectural Press.

Castle, Rand (1971) *The Way of Tea*, Tokyo: Weatherhill.

Chamberlain, Basil Hall (1893) "Notes on Some Minor Japanese Religious Practices," *Journal of the Anthropological Institute of Great Britain and Ireland*, vol. 22, pp. 355–370.

Clammer, John (1995) *Difference and Modernity: Social Theory and Contemporary Japanese Society*, London: Kegan Paul International.

Clancey, Gregory (2006) *Earthquake Nation: The Cultural Politics of Japanese Seismicity, 1868–1930*, Berkeley, CA: University of California Press.

Clark, Clifford E. (1991) "House Furnishings as Cultural Evidence: The Promise and Peril of Material Cultural Studies," *American Quarterly*, vol. 43, no. 1 (March), pp. 73-81.

Clark, Scott (1994) *Japan: A View from the Bath*, Honolulu: University of Hawaii Press.

Coaldrake, William H. (1992) "Unno: Edo Period Post Town of the Central Japan Alps," *Asian Art*, vol. 5, no. 2 (Spring), pp. 9-29.

Coaldrake, William H. (2008) "Beyond Mimesis: Japanese Architectural Models at the Vienna Exhibition and 1910 Japan British Exhibition" in Cox, Rupert, ed. *The Culture of Copying in Japan: Critical and Historical Persepctives*, London: Routledge.

Colquhoun, Alan (1985) *Essays in Architectural Criticism*, Cambridge, MA: MIT Press.

Colquhoun, Alan (2007) "The Concept of Regionalism," in Canizaro, Vincent (ed.) *Architectural Regionalism: Collected Writings on Place, Identity, Modernity and Tradition*, New York: Princeton Architectural Press, pp. 147-155.

Converse, Julia Moore and Bermingham, Ann (2007) "Preface," in Helfrich, Kurt G. F. and Whitaker, William (eds.), *Crafting a Modern World: The Architecture and Design of Antonin and Noémi Raymond*, New York: Princeton Architectural Press.

Cook, Peter (1990) "Shonandai Symbols," *Architectural Review*, vol. 188, no. 1122 (August), pp. 30-35.

Crasemann Collins, Christiane (1987) "Le Corbusier's Maison Errazuriz: A Conflict of Fictive Cultures," *Harvard Architectural Review*, vol. 6, pp. 38-53.

Crisman, Phoebe (2007) "From Industry to Culture: Leftovers, Time and Material Transformation in Four Contemporary Museums," *Journal of Architecture*, vol. 12, no. 4 (September), pp. 405-421.

Daniell, Thomas (2000) "Kazuhiro Ishi'i: Meta-Architecture," *Archis*, November, pp. 58-63.

Daniell, Thomas (2001) "Back to Nature," *Archis*, March, pp. 33-34.

Dormer, Peter (ed.) (1997) *The Culture of Craft: Status and Future*, Manchester: Manchester University Press.

Finch, Paul (2006) "View," *Architectural Review*, vol. 220, no. 1317, p. 27.

Forty, Adrian (2004) *Words and Buildings: A Vocabulary of Modern Architecture*, London: Thames and Hudson.

Frampton, Kenneth (1978) *A New Wave of Japanese Architecture*, New York: Institute for Architecture and Urban Studies.

Frampton, Kenneth (1983) "Prospects for a Critical Regionalism," *Perspecta*, vol. 20, pp. 147-162.

Fridell, Wilbur M. (1973) *Japanese Shrine Mergers, 1906–1912: State Shinto Moves to the Grassroots*, Tokyo: Sophia University.

Fujie, Kazuko (2007) "*'Ki' no mitsudo – Kagu Dezain*" 「気」の密度–家具デザイン *[Density of Spirit: Furniture Design] Shinkenchiku* 新建築 [New Architecture], vol. 82, no. 6 (June) p. 83.

Fujimori, Terunobu (1998) *Fujimori Terunobu Yaban Gyarudo Kenchiku* 藤森照信:野蛮ギャルド建築 *a.k.a. Terunobu Fujimori: Y'Avant-garde Architecture*, Tokyo: Toto Shuppan.

Fujimori, Terunobu (2002) "*Kouki Korubyuje*" 後期コルビュジェ *a.k.a. "Le Corbusier after 1930's [sic],*" *X Knowledge Home*, vol. 2, "Le Corbusier as Primitive Design," (February) p. 22.

Fujimori, Terunobu (2006a) "Works Using Natural Materials," in Okabe, Miki and Koyama, Naomi (eds.), trans. Stan Anderson, Venice Biennale: 10th International Architecture Exhibition 2006/Japanese Pavilion, © 2006 Japan Foundation, p. 8.

Fujimori, Terunobu (2006b) "Fuku Akino Art Museum," in Okabe, Miki and Koyama, Naomi (eds.) trans. Stan Anderson, Venice Biennale: 10th International Architecture Exhibition 2006/Japanese Pavilion, © 2006 Japan Foundation, p. 12.

Fujimori, Terunobu (2006c) "Architecture of Terunobu Fujimori and ROJO," in Okabe, Miki and Koyama, Naomi (eds.) *Objects Collected by the ROJO Society 1970–2006*, trans. Stan Anderson, Venice Biennale: 10th International Architecture Exhibition 2006/Japanese Pavilion, © 2006 Japan Foundation, p. 7.

Fujimori, Terunobu (2006d) "*Fujimori Terunobu ni Tou*" 藤森照信に問う *[Ask Terunobu Fujimori] Home X Knowledge*, vol. 6, no. 1, Special Issue no. 7 "*The Fujimori*," (10 August), pp. 12-21, 81-85.

Fujimori, Terunobu (2006e) "*Hajimete no Onsen Kenchiku*" 初めての温泉建築 *[My First Hot Springs Building] Shinkenchiku* 新建築 [New Architecture], (January), p. 125.

Fujimori, Terunobu (2007) "The Tea Room: Architecture Writ Small," in Isozaki, Arata *et al.*, *The Contemporary Tea House: Japan's Top Architects Redefine Tradition*, Tokyo: Kodansha International.

Fujimori, Terunobu (2008) "How I Created My First Building (Aged 45)," *Il Giornale dell' Architettura*, (2 July), p. 12, available at: www.ilgiornaledellarchitettura.com.

Fujimori, Terunobu *et al.* (2005) *Fujimoriryuu Shizenn Souzai no T sukaikata* 藤森流自然素材の使い方」 [The Fujimori Way of Using Natural Materials], Tokyo: Shokokusha.

Fujimori, Terunobu and Ito, Toyo (2007) (Dialogue) "Nijuu Seiki Kenchiku no Wasuremono" ２０世紀建築の忘れ物 [Forgotten Architecture of the Twentieth Century], *Enkin Wochi Kochi* 遠近をちこち *[Perspectives Far and Near] a.k.a Wochi Kochi*, no. 15 (February/March), pp. 46–51.

Futagawa, Yoshio and Shin Takamatsu (2004) "*Dai Juuhachikai: Shingendaikenchiku wo Kangaeru 'O to X' Busshitsu Shikou 47 Kotohiraguu Purojekuto*" 第１８回：新現代建築を考える「０と*X New Contemporary Architecture Plus and Minus, No 18: "Experience in Materials No. 47, Kotohira Shrine Project"], GA (Global Architecture) Japan*, 70 (September), pp. 40-45.

Goulet, Patrice (1991) "Wild and Uncertain Times: Team Zoo's Savoir-Faire," in Speidel, Manfred, *Team Zoo: Buildings and Projects, 1970–1991*, New York: Rizzoli, pp. 22-25.

Grapard, Allan G. (1984) "Japan's Ignored Cultural Revolution: The Separation of Shinto and Buddhism Divinities in Meiji ('Shimbutsu Bunri') and a Case Study: Tounomine," *History of Religions*, vol. 23, no. 3 (February) pp. 240-265.

Greenhalgh, Paul (1997) "The Progress of Captain Ludd," in Dormer, Peter (ed.) *The Culture of Craft: Status and Future*, Manchester: Manchester University Press.

Grilli, Peter (1992) *Pleasures of the Japanese Bath*, Tokyo: Weatherhill.

Gutdeutsch, Gotz (1996) *Building in Wood: Construction and Details*, Basel: Birkhauser.

Hagenburg, Roland (2004) *14 Japanese Architects: Interviews by Roland Hagenburg*, Tokyo: Kashiwa Shobo.

Hamaguchi, Ryuichi (1956) "Note on the Expression of Sukiya Architecture," *Sinkenchiku*, English edition, vol. 31, no. 8, pp. 57-59.

Hara, Akio (1982) "Making the Ordinary Appealing," *Japan Architect*, no. 303 (July), p. 5.

Hara, Hiroshi and Ueda, Makoto 植田実 (1986) "*Conpe Yomigaetta*" こんぺ蘇った *[A Competition Revival] Kenchiku Bunka* 建築文化 [Architecture Culture], vol. 41, no. 474 (April), pp. 72-73.

Hardacre, Helen (1986) "Creating State Shinto: The Great Promulgation Campaign and the New Religions," *Journal of Japanese Studies*, vol. 12, no. 1 (Winter), pp. 29-63.

Hardacre, Helen and Adam L. Kern, eds. (1997) *New Directions in the Study of Meiji Japan*, London, New York and Koln: Brill.

Hasegawa, Itsuko *et al.* (2000) *Itsuko Hasegawa: Island Hopping, Crossover Architecture*, Rotterdam: Netherlands Architecture Institute.

Hasegawa Itsuko (1995) *Space Design (SD)* no. 374 "Itsuko Hasegawa, 1985-1995" (November).

Havens, Thomas R. H. (2006) *Radicals and Realists in the Japanese Non-Verbal Arts: The Avant-Garde Rejection of Modernism*, Honolulu: University of Hawaii Press.

Helfrich, Kurt G. F. (2006) "Antonin Raymond in America, 1938–49," in Helfrich, K.G.F. and Whitaker, W. (eds.) *Crafting a Modern World: The Architecture of Antonin and Noemi Raymond*, New York: Princeton Architectural Press, pp. 45-64.

Helfrich, Kurt G. F. and Whitaker, William (eds.) (2006) *Crafting a Modern World: The Architecture of Antonin and Noemi Raymond*, New York: Princeton Architectural Press.

Higuchi, Hiroyasu and Kusumi, Akira (1993) "*Tsuchi to Kurashi*" 土とくらし *a.k.a. "Expressing Earth," Kenchiku Bunka* 建築文化 [Architecture Culture], vol. 48, no. 557 (March), pp. 89-95.

Higuchi, Hiroyasu and Miyake, Riichi (1993) "Discovery of Places," *Kenchiku Bunka*建築文化 [Architecture Culture], (July), pp. 73-80.

Housekeeper (2007) *"Sekai ga Sonkei suru Nihonn no Kenchikuka Daitokushuu"* 世界が尊敬する日本の建築家大特集 a.k.a. "Architecture - Japan's New Mega Export", *Casa Brutus* vol. 85 (April) pp. 59-110.

Huyssen, Andrea (2006) "Nostalgia for Ruins," *Grey Room*, 23 (Spring), pp. 6-21.

Igarashi, Taro (2006) "Time-Bridging Architecture," in Okabe, Miki and Koyama, Naomi (eds.) trans. Stan Anderson, Venice Biennale: 10th International Architecture Exhibition 2006/Japanese Pavilion, © 2006 Japan Foundation, pp. 12-13.

Iijima, Youichi (1997) 飯島洋一 "*Toumei na Shi*" 透明な死 *a.k.a. "Transparent Death," Space Design (SD)*, no. 398, "Kengo Kuma, Digital Gardening," (November), pp. 88-95.

Imafuji, Akira 今藤啓 and *Kenchiku Toshi* [建築都市] Workshop (eds.) (2002) Taisha Kenchiku Jisho 大社建築事始」 [The Beginning of Taisha Architecture], Taishacho: Taishacho 21 Seki Bunkou.

Ingersoll, Richard (1991) "Context and Modernity: Delft, June 12–15, 1990," *Journal of Architectural Education*, vol. 44, no. 2 (February), pp. 124-125.

Ishii, Kazuhiro (1982) "*Hyougen Shugisha to Shite no Posuto-Metaborizumu*" 表現主義者としてのポスト・メタボリズム *[Advocates of Expression as Post-Metabolists], in* Suzuki, Horoyuki and Kazuhiro Ishii *Gendai Kenchikuka* 現代建築家 [Contemporary Architects], Tokyo: Shobunsha.

Ishii, Kazuhiro (1985a) *Sukiya no Shikou* 数奇屋の思考 [Thoughts on Sukiya], Tokyo: Kajima.

Ishii Kazuhiro (1985b) *Nihon Kenchiku no Saisei* 日本建築の再生 [The Rebirth of Japanese Architecture], Tokyo: Chuo Koran.

Ishii, Kazuhiro (1989a) "*Atarashii Jidai no Tabidachi*" 新しい時代の旅立ち *a.k.a. "The Sources of My Inspiration: In Response to Reyner Banham," Space Design (SD)*, no. 295, "Kazuhiro Ishii" (April) pp. 6-14.

Ishii, Kazuhiro (1989b) "*Sedaiteki Houhou no Shouka no Mairusuton*" 世代的方法の昇華のマイルストン [A Milestone that Sublimates the Methods of a Generation], *Kenchiku Bunka* 建築文化 [Architecture Culture], vol. 44, no. 515 (September), pp. 34-35.

Ishii, Kazuhiro (1992) "*Rekishi, Chihou, Mokuzou Chougen*" 歴史・地方・木造・重源 *[*History, Region, Wood Construction, the Monk Chogen], *Kenchiku Bunka* 建築文化 [Architecture Culture], vol. 47, no. 548 (June), pp. 182-186.

Ishii, Kazuhiro (1994a) "*Jiko Henkaku Jidai no Kenchiku 3 Rekishi*" 自己変革時代の建築*(3)*-歴史 [An Era of My Change 3, History] *Shinkenchiku* 新建築 [New Architecture], vol. 69, no. 8 (August), pp. 189–192.

Ishii, Kazuhiro (1994b) "Kazuhiro Ishii: Seiwa Bunraku Puppet Theater," *Architectural Design Profile* 107, "Japanese Architecture III", London: Academy Editions, p. 45.

Ishii, Kazuhiro (1997) *Kenchiku no Chikyuugaku* 建築の地球学 *a.k.a. The Geocosmology of Architecture*, Tokyo: Toto Shuppan.

Ishiyama, Osamu (1986) *Shokunin Kyouwakoku da yori: Izu Matsuzakimachi no Bouken* 職人共和国だより：伊豆松崎町の冒険 [From the Commonwealth of Craft: An Adventure at Izu's Matsuzaki Village], Tokyo: Shobunsha.

Ishiyama, Osamu (1987) "*Kenchiku ya Hashi ya Tokeito to Sekkei Shite Kita no de ha nai*" 建築や橋や時計塔と設計してきたのではない [It Is Not That the Result Was the Design of Architecture, a Bridge, or a Clock Tower], *Kenchiku Bunka* 建築文化 [Architecture Culture], vol. 42, no. 489 "Special Issue: Osamu Ishiyama: Exploration Toward Making Town" [*sic*] (July), pp. 106–107.

Ishiyama, Osamu (1999) *Ishiyama Osamu, Kangaeru, Ugoku, Kenchiku ga Kawaru: Hiroshima, Seikatsu, Ie, Komyunike-shon* 石山修武 考える, 動く, 建築が変わる:ひろしま、生活、家、コミュニケーション [Osamu Ishiyama, Think, Move, Architecture Changes: Hiroshima, Lifestyle, Houses, Communication], Tokyo: Toto Shuppan.

Ishiyama, Osamu (2008a) セルフ・ビルド a.k.a. *Self Build*, Tokyo: Kotsu Shinbun Sha.

Ishiyama, Osamu (2008b) "Interview with Osamu Ishiyama," in Noda, Natoshi and Mie Moriyasu (eds.), *Osamu Ishiyama: 12 Architectural Visions*, Tokyo: Kodansha, pp. 47-62.

Isozaki, Arata (1989) "Of City, Nation and Style," in Harootunian, H.D. and Maso Miyoshi (eds), *Postmodernism in Japan*, Durham, NC: Duke University Press, pp. 47-62.

Isozaki, Arata (1996) *The Island Nation Aesthetic*, London: Academy Editions Polemics.

Isozaki, Arata (2006) *Japan-ness in Architecture*, Cambridge, MA: MIT Press.

Isozaki, Arata *et al.* (2007) *The Contemporary Tea House: Japan's Top Architects Redefine a Tradition*, Tokyo: Kodansha International.

Ito, Nobuo (1956) "Traditionalism and Tradition," *Sinkenchiku*, English edition, vol. 31, no. 12 (December), p. 37.

Ito, Teiji (2003) "*Honden he Michibiku Takumi na Fuukei*" 本殿へ導くたくみな風景 [Ingenious Scenery Guides to the Main Shrine], *Shikoku Shinbun* 四国新聞 [Shikoku Newspaper] (21 September), available at: http://www.shikoku-np.co.jp/feature/kotohira/25/index.htm (accessed June 12, 2007).

Ito, Toyo (2007) "*Fujimori Kenchiku no Souzouroyku*" 藤森建築の想像力 [The Imaginative Power of Fujimori's Architecture] *Shinkenchiku* 新建築 [New Architecture], vol. 82, no. 6 (June), pp. 50-55.

Ito, Toyo with Kengo Kuma and Yoshio Futagawa (2006) "*Kenchiku 2006/2007: Soukatu to Tenbou*" 建築2006/2007: 総括と展望 [Architecture 2006/2007: Recap and Outlook], *GA (Global Architecture) Japan*, vol. 84 (January/February), pp. 92-103.

Ito, Toyo with Koji Taki (1994) "A Conversation with Toyo Ito," *El Croquis*, no. 71, "Toyo Ito: 1986–1995," pp. 16-31.

Ivy, Marilyn (1995) *Discourses of the Vanishing: Modernity, Phantasm, Japan*, Chicago: University of Chicago Press.

Iwabuchi, Koichi (2002) *Recentering Globalization: Popular Culture and Japanese Transnationalism*, Durham, NC: Duke University Press.

Iwaki, Ken'ichi. (2001) "The Logic of Visual Perception: Ueda Juzou," in Marra, Michael F., ed. and translator. *A History of Modern Japanese Aesthetics* Honolulu: University of Hawaii Press, pp. 285-317.

Jameson, Fredric (1991) *Postmodernism, or, The Cultural Logic of Late Capitalism*, Durham, NC: Duke University Press.

Jencks, Charles (2000) "Black Box, White Cube, Ersatz Cathedral, Shopping Mall and Renta-culture," *The Art Newspaper*, no. 109 (December), pp. 44-47.

Jones, Lindsay (2000) *The Hermeneutics of Sacred Architecture: Experience, Interpretation, Comparison*, Vol. 1, *Monumental Occasions: Reflections on the Eventfulness of Religious Architecture*, Cambridge, MA: Harvard University Press for the Harvard University Center for the Study of World Religions.

Karatani, Kojin (1994) "Japan as Museum: Okakura Tenshin and Ernest Fenollosa," in Munroe, Alexandria (ed.), *Japanese Art after 1945: Scream against the Sky*, New York: Harry N. Abrams, pp. 33–39.

Karatani, Kojin (2001) "Japan as Art Museum: Okakura Tenshin and Fenollosa," in Marra, Michael F. (ed. and trans.), *A History of Modern Japanese Aesthetics*, Honolulu: University of Hawaii Press, pp. 43-52.

Karatani, Kojin and Kohso, Sabu (1998) "Uses of Aesthetics: After Orientalism," *boundary*, vol. 25, no. 2, "Edward Said," (Summer), pp. 145-160.

Kawagoe, Noboru (1968) *Contemporary Japanese Architecture*, Tokyo: Kokusai Bunka Shinkokai.

Kelbaugh, Douglas S. (2002) *Repairing the American Metropolis: Common Place Revisited*, Seattle and London: University of Washington Press.

Kenchiku Bunka (1986) *'Fujisawashi 'Kasho' Shounandai Bunka Senta-' Puropo-zaru, Dezain, Conpetishon: nyuusen Happyou* 藤沢市「(仮称)湘南台文化センター」プロポーザル・デザイン・コンペティション：入選発表 [The (Provisionally Named) Shonandai Culture Center in Fujisawa City: A Presentation of Awarded Entries in the Proposal Design Competition], *Kenchiku Bunka* 建築文化 [Architecture Culture], vol. 41, no. 474 (April), pp. 53-71.

Kikuchi, Yuko (1997) "Hybridity and the Oriental Orientalism of 'Mingei' Theory," *Journal of Design History*, vol. 10, no. 4, "Craft, Culture and Identity," pp. 343-354.

Kikuchi, Yuko (2004) *Japanese Modernisation and Mingei Theory: Cultural Nationalism and Oriental Orientalism*, London and New York: RoutledgeCurzon.

Kishi, Waro (2000) "PROJECTed Realities: Waro Kishi vs. Ken Tadashi Oshima," *PROJECTed Realities*, Tokyo: Toto Shuppan, pp. 8-79.

Knabe, Christopher and Noennig, Joerg Rainer (eds.) (1999) *Shaking the Foundations: Japanese Architects in Dialogue*, Munich: Prestel.

Knight, John (1994) "Rural Revitalization in Japan: Spirit of the Village and Taste of the Country," *Asian Survey*, vol. 1, no. 7 (July), pp. 634–646.

Knight, John (1997) "A Tale of Two Forests: Reforestation Discourse in Japan and Beyond," *Journal of the Royal Anthropological Institute*, vol. 3, no. 4 (December), pp. 711–730.

Kohara, Takaharu (2007) "The Great Heisei Consolidation: A Critical Review," *Social Science Japan*, vol. 37, "Decentralization," (September), pp. 7–11.

Kondo, Yoshiki (2007) 近藤良樹 "*Kodai to Gendai wo Tunagu Fuukei no Kouchiku*" 古代と現代を繋ぐ風景の構築 [The Construction of Scenery That Unites Past and Present], *GA (Global Architecture) Japan*, no. 87 (July/August), p. 99.

Kotohiraguu Ofisharu Gaidobukku (2004) 金刀比羅宮オフィシャルガイドブック [Kotohira Shrine Official Guidebook], Kotohira: Kotohira Shrine Office.

Kotohira Shrine Office (2005) "*Chakuchaku to Susumu Shaden Zoun Shinchiku Oyobi Iten Kouji*" 着々と進む社殿ゾーン新築及び移転工事 [Step by Step, Shrine Zone and Transfer Progress], *Kotohira* ことひら no. 60, Kotohira: Kotohira Shrine Office, pp. 11-15.

Krieger, Alex (1993) "To Remain Modern, to Return to Sources, and to Employ Time," in-house publication, Harvard University Graduate School of Design (1–19 November).

Kuba, Toshiko (2007) "Plasterer Finds Creativity in Father's Footsteps," *Daily Yomiuri*, 4 October, p. 16.

Kuki, Shuzo (1997) *Reflections on Japanese Taste: The Structure of Iki*, trans. John Clark, Sydney: Powerhouse Publications.

Kultermann, Udo (1998) "Architecture as a Second Nature – a Feminine Discourse? The Work of Itsuko Hasegawa," *Marg*, vol. 50, issue 2, pp. 90-97.

Kuma, Kengo (1986) *Juutakuron* １０宅論. [A Theory of Ten Houses] Tokyo: Tousou Publishing.

Kuma, Kengo (1989a) "Tale of a Collision: Asia Versus the Sukiya Tea Ceremony Cottage," *Japan Architect*, no. 386 (June), p. 41.

Kuma, Kengo (1989b) "*Ooinaru shi shuuen*" 大いなる終焉 a.k.a. "Grand Denouement," *Space Design (SD)*, no. 295 (April), pp. 18-20.

Kuma, Kengo (1992) "*Mita koto ga nai no ni Natsukashii*" 見たことがないのに懐かしい [Nostalgia Like Nothing You've Ever Seen], *Jinchokan Moriya Historical Museum*, Tokyo: Architectural Riffle 001.

Kuma, Kengo (1997) "Digital Gardening," trans. Hiroshi Watanabe, *Space Design (SD)*, no. 398, "Digital Gardening: Kengo Kuma," (November), pp. 6-9.

Kuma, Kengo (2000) *Han Obujekuto: Kenchiku wo Tokashi* 反オブジェクト:建築を溶かし、砕く [Anti-Object: The Dissolution and Disintegration of Architecture], Tokyo: Chikuma Koubou.

Kuma, Kengo (2003) "*Voido he Henkan Sareru Soriddo*" ヴォイドへ変換されるソリッド [A Void Transformed into a Solid], *GA (Global Architecture) Japan*, vol. 65 (November/December), pp. 120-121.

Kuma, Kengo (2004a) *Materials, Structures, Details*, Berlin: Birkhauser Publishers.

Kuma, Kengo (2004b) "Murai Masanari Art Museum," *C3*, no. 243, p. 72.

Kuma, Kengo (2004c) *Makeru Kenchiku* 負ける建築 [Defeated Architecture], Tokyo: Iwanami Shoten.

Kuma, Kengo (2005a) "Introduction," in Botond Bognar, *Kengo Kuma: Selected Works*, New York: Princeton Architectural Press, pp. 14-17.

Kuma, Kengo (2005b) "*Ki wo Shiru, Kuma Kengo no Murai Masanari Kinen Bijutukan*" 木を知る:隈 研吾の村井正誠記念美術館 [He Knows Wood: Kengo Kuma's Masanari Murai Memorial Museum] Shitsunai 室内 [In the Room], no. 715/605 (May), pp. 58-61.

Kuma, Kengo (2005c) "*Wa Modern no Sumai sono Bi to Chie*" 和モダンの住まいその美と知恵 [Japan-flavored Modern Houses' Beauty and Wisdom] a.k.a. *Waraku*, (May), pp. 62-73.

Kuma, Kengo (2005d) "Weak Architecture" *GA (Global Architecture) Architect*, vol. 19, "Kengo Kuma" (September), pp. 8-15.

Kuma, Kengo (2006) "*Nihonn no Kenchikubi no Dentou to Gendaibi no Yuugou Santorii Bijutsukan*" 日本の建築美の伝統と現代美の融合サントリー美術館 [Japan's Architectural Beauty, Traditional and Today's, Melt into One at the Suntory Museum of Art], *Machi Gurashi* 街ぐらし [Urban Living], vol. 27 (Winter), pp. 72-73.

Kuma, Kengo (2007a) "Anti-Construction" (an Interview with TaeHee Lim), in *Kengo Kuma*, Seoul, Korea: C3, pp. 26–35.

Kuma, Kengo (2007b) "*Hyugatei kara Umi wo Nozomu*" 日向邸から海を臨む [From Hyuga Villa, Wanting the Sea], (2 March), lecture at the Watarium Museum in Tokyo.

Kuma, Kengo (2007c) "*Interiaka wo Unagasu Middotaun no Tokonoma*" インテリア化を促すミッドタウンの床の間 [Inciting Interiority in Midtown's *tokonoma*], *GA (Global Architecture) Japan*, no. 86 (May/June), pp. 42-43.

Kuma, Kengo (2007d) "*Hirareta Purosesu ga Machi wo Kaeru*" 開かれたプロセスが町を変える [Changing the Town through an Open Process], *Shinkenchiku* 新建築 [New Architecture], vol. 82, no. 3 (March), pp. 150-151.

Kuma, Kengo and Fujimori, Terunobu (2007) "*Taidan: Fujimori Terunobu, Kuma Kengo*" 対談：藤森照信、隈研吾 [Dialogue: Terunobu Fujimori, Kengo Kuma] *TOTO Tsuushin TOTO* 通信 [*TOTO News*], no. 478, "New Year," pp. 6-17.

Kuma, Kengo with Hiroshi Naito (2004) "Conversation between Hiroshi Naito and Kengo Kuma," in Kuma, Kengo, *Materials, Structures, Details*, Berlin: Birkhauser Publishers, pp. 58-67.

Kurita, Isamu (1983) "Revival of the [*sic*] Japanese Tradition," *Journal of Popular Culture*, vol. 17, no. 1, pp. 130-134.

Leatherbarrow, David and Mohsen Mostafavi (1992) "On Weathering: A New Surface out of the Tracks of Time," Daidalos no. 43, pp. 115-123.

Leatherbarrow, David and Mohsen Mostafavi (1993) *On Weathering: The Life of Buildings in Time*, Cambridge, Massachusetts: MIT Press.

Leatherbarrow, David and Mostafavi, Mohsen (1996) "Opacity," *AA Files*, 32 (Autumn), pp. 49–64.

Le Corbusier (1927) *Towards a New Architecture*, trans. F. Etchells, New York: Payson & Clarke.

Levine, Gregory P.A. (2005) *Daitokuji: The Visual Cultures of a Zen Monastery*, Seattle: University of Washington Press.

Lummis, C. Douglas (2007) "Ruth Benedict's Obituary for Japanese Culture", *Japan Focus*, (19 July), available at: http://www.japanfocus.org/products/details/2474 (accessed October 25, 2007).

Lynn, Greg (1997) "Pointillism," *Space Design (SD)*, no. 398, "Digital Gardening: Kengo Kuma", (November), pp. 46-47.

MacKeith, Peter (ed.) (2005) *Encounters: Juhani Pallasmaa, Architectural Essays*, Helsinki: Rakemmstietot.

Maki, Fumihiko (1973) "An Environmental Approach to Architecture" *Japan Architect*, vol. 48, no 3-195, "Fumihiko Maki and his Recent Works," (March), pp. 17-84.

Maki, Fumihiko (1975) "Japanese City Spaces and the Concept of *Oku*," *Japan Architect*, no. 265 (May), pp. 51-62.

Maki, Fumihiko (1985) "The Public Dimension in Contemporary Architecture," in Munroe, Alexandra (ed.), *Maki, Isozaki: New Public Architecture: Recent Projects by Fumihiko Maki and Arata Isozaki*, New York: Japan Society, pp. 16-19

Maki, Fumihiko (1986) "*Toukyou to iu Gendai*" 東京という現代 a.k.a. "The Present that is Tokyo," *Space Design (SD)*, no. 256 (January), pp. 140-141.

Maki, Fumihiko (1987) "To Offer Unforgettable Scenes: A Discussion with Fumihiko Maki," *Japan Architect*, no. 359, "Special Feature: Fumihiko Maki," (March), pp. 68-71.

Maki, Fumihiko (1988) "The Roof at Fujisawa," *Perspecta*, vol. 24, pp. 107-121.

Maki, Fumihiko (1993) "*Yobun*" 予文 a.k.a. "Complexity and Modernism," *Space Design (SD)*, no. 340, "Fumihiko Maki, 1987–1992," (January), pp. 6-7.

Maki, Fumihiko (2000a) *Selected Passages on the City and Architecture*, Tokyo: Maki and Associates.

Maki, Fumihiko (2000b) "Architecture and Communication," *Space Design (SD)*, no. 424 (January), pp. 6-7.

Maki, Fumihiko (2000c) "Kaze-no-Oka Crematorium," *Space Design (SD)*, no. 424 (January), pp. 44-53.

Maki, Fumihiko (2003) "Shimane Prefectural Museum of History and Folklore, Shimane, Japan," *GA (Global Architecture)*, Document no. 73 (April), pp. 94-97.

Maki, Fumihiko (2005) "Early Memories of Tokyo," *Tokyo From Vancouver*, Vancouver, British Columbia: University of British Columbia private printing, pp. 14-19.

Maki, Fumihiko (2005–2006) "Kunio Mayekawa and the Present," in *Kunio Mayekawa Retrospective*, Tokyo: The Exhibition Organizing Committee for Kunio Mayekawa Retrospective, pp. 248-249.

Maki, Fumihiko (2007) "*Maki Fumihiko (Taiwa) Basho-Jikan wo Yomitoite Arata no Kuukan wo Tsukuru*" 槇文彦(対話)場所・時間を読み解いて新たな空間をつくる [A Conversation with Fumihiko Maki: Making a New Space that Unfastens Place and Time], *GA (Global Architecture) Japan*, no. 87, (July/August), pp. 102-103.

Maki, Fumihiko and Hara, Hiroshi (1979) "*Taidan: Keikenteki, Ba no Kouzou, Sukima, Soshite Oku*" 対談:経験的、場の構造、すき間、そして奥 a.k.a. "Dialogue: Hiroshi Hara and Fumihiko Maki," *Space Design (SD)*, no. 177, "Special Issue: Fumihiko Maki," (June), pp. 4, 141-152.

Maki, Fumihiko and Kengo, Kuma (1997) "*Kenchiku no Toumeisei: Kenchiku to Kankyou no Arata na Kankei*" 建築の透明性:建築と環境の新たな関係』槇文彦+隈研吾 [Architecture and Transparency: Architecture and Environment in a New Relationship, A Dialogue between Fumihiko Maki and Kengo Kuma], *Space Design (SD)*, no. 398 (November), pp. 122-125.

Matsuda, Tetsuo (2006) "What is ROJO?" trans. Stan Anderson, in Okabe, Miki and Naomi Koyama (eds.), *Objects Collected by the ROJO Society 1970–2006*, Venice Biennale: 10th International Architecture Exhibition 2006/Japanese Pavilion, © 2006 Japan Foundation, p. 2.

Matsuo, Mitsuaki (2004) "The History of Izumo Grand Shrine and its Architecture," trans. T. Tsukitani and T. Shinagawa, Prefectural Institute for Ancient Culture, in *5th International Symposium of Asian Architecture in 2004*, available at: http://www2.pref.shimane.jp/kodai/about-kodai/matsuo.htm (accessed 1 May, 2005).

Matter, Fred S. (1989) "Critical Regionalism from a Desert Dweller's Perspective," *Arid Lands Newsletter*, no. 28 (Spring/Summer), available at: http://ag.Arizona.edu/OALS?ALN/aln28.matter.html (accessed on July 20, 2005).

McDermott, Hiroko T. (2006) "The Horyuji Treasures and Early Meiji Cultural Policy," *Monumenta Nipponica*, vol. 61, no. 3 (Autumn), pp. 339–374.

Metcalf, Bruce (1997) "Craft and Art, Culture and Biology," in Dormer, Peter (ed.), *The Culture of Craft: Status and Future*, Manchester: Manchester University Press. pp. 67-82

Meyers, Victoria (1999) "Space and the Perception of Time," *Journal of Architectural Education*, vol. 53, no. 2, pp. 91-95.

Miyake, Riichi (1993) "*Fuukei no Seisei*" 風景の生成 a.k.a. "Auto-Poietic Scenery," *Kenchiku Bunka* 建築文化 [Architecture Culture], vol. 48, no. 564 "*Aimaimoko* あいまいもく [Ambiguity]," (October) pp. 126-127.

Miyake, Riichi (2007) "*Kiro ni Tatsu Nihonn Kenchiku – 21 Seiki ni Muketa Kada*" 岐路に立つ日本建築--21世紀に向けた課 a.k.a. "Japanese Architecture at a Crossroads – Tasks for the 21st Century," *Japan Architect*, vol. 65, "Parallel Nippon," (Spring), pp. 8–15.

Montaner, Josep Maria (2003) *Museums for the 21st Century*, Barcelona: Editorial Gustavo Gili.

Moore, Charles (1978) "Impressions of Japanese Architecture," *Japan Architect*, no. 250 (February), pp. 5-6.

Munroe, Alexandra (ed.) (1985) *Maki, Isozaki. New Public Architecture: Recent Projects by Fumihiko Maki and Arata Isozaki*, New York: Japan Society.

Munroe, Alexandria (ed.) (1994) *Japanese Art after 1945: Scream against the Sky*, New York: Harry N. Abrams.

Naito, Hiroshi (1992) "*Ushinawareta Toki wo Motomete*" 失われた時を求めて [Hoping for a Lost Time], *Shinkenchiku* 新建築 [New Architecture], vol. 67, no. 11 (November), pp. 198-199.

Naito, Hiroshi (1993a) "*Riaru no Shozai*" リアルの所在 [Reality's Whereabouts], *Shinkenchiku* 新建築 [New Architecture], vol. 68, no. 4 (April), pp. 157-160.

Naito, Hiroshi (1993b) "*Umi no Hakubutsukan no Purosesu*" 海の博物館のプロセス [The Sea Folk Museum Process], *Space Design (SD)*, no. 343 (April), pp. 31-36.

Naito, Hiroshi (2002) "*Naitou Hiroshi no 42 no Shitsumon*" 内藤廣屁の42の質問 a.k.a. "42 Questions to Hiroshi Naito, Part II," *Japan Architect*, no. 46 "Hiroshi Naito," (Summer), pp. 118-121.

Naito, Hiroshi (2005) *Kenchiku no 'Sozai' wo Motomete* 建築の「素材」を求め [Wanting Architectural 'Materials'] in Taira, Kei'ichi (平良敬一), ed. *'Basho' no Fukken: Toshi to Kenchiku he no Shiza* 「場所」の復権：都市と建築への視座 [The Rehabilitation of Place: A Point of View on Cities and Architecture] Tokyo: Kenchiku Shiryou Kenkyuusha, pp. 125-142.

Naito, Hiroshi and Magnago Lampugnani, Vittorio (1996) "Dialogue with Vittorio Magnago Lampugnani [letters], *Kenchiku Bunka*, 建築文化 [Architecture Culture], vol. 51, no. 594 (April), pp. 88-97.

Nakayama, Hideyuki 中山英之 (2006) "*Futatabi Shiroku Nure! - Aomorikenritsu Bijutsukan ni Tsuite*" 再び、白く塗れ！—青森県立美術館について a.k.a. "Paint it White Again!: On the Aomori Museum," in Aoki, Jun with Noi Sawaragi and Hideyuki Nakayama, *Jun Aoki: Complete Works 2: Aomori Museum of Art*, Tokyo: INAX Publications, pp. 34-48.

Nitschke, Gunter (1993) *From Shinto to Ando: Studies in Architectural Anthropology*, London: Academy Group and Ernst & Sohn.

Noda, Natoshi and Mie Moriyasu, eds. (2008) *Osamu Ishiyama: 12 Architectural Visions*, Tokyo: Kodansha.

O'Doherty, Brian (1976) "Inside the White Cube: Notes on the Gallery Space," *Art Forum*, vol. 14, no. 7 (March), pp. 24–30, available at: http://www.societyofcontrol.com/whitecube/insidewc.htm.

Ogawa, Masataka (1987) 小川正隆. "*Murai Masanari: hito to Sakuhin*" 村井正誠：人と作品 [Masanari Murai: People and Things], in Tokoro, Akiyoshi (ed.), *Murai Masanari:Yusai, Sopyou, Hanga* 村井正誠：油彩、素描、版画 [Masanari Murai: Oil Paintings, Sketches, Prints], Tokyo: Galerie Tokoro, pp. 4–13.

Okabe, Miki and Koyama, Naomi (eds.) (2006) trans. Stan Anderson, Venice Biennale: 10th International Architecture Exhibition 2006/ Japanese Pavilion, © 2006 Japan Foundation.

Okagawa, Mitsugu (1995) 岡河貢, "*Koukyou Kenchiku no Shinjidai to Atarashii Modannizumu no Seimeiryoku no Yokan*", 公共建築の新時代と新しいモダニズムの生命力の予感 a.k.a. "The Era of New Public Architecture and Harbinger of Modernism's Vitality," trans. Hiroshi Asano, *Space Design (SD)*, no. 374, "Itsuko Hasegawa, 1985–1995," (November), pp. 24-25.

Okakura, Kakuzo (1964) *The Book of Tea*, New York: Dover.

Okamoto, Taro (1994) "What is Tradition?" in Munroe, Alexandria (ed.) *Japanese Art after 1945: Scream against the Sky*, New York: Harry N. Abrams, pp. 381-382.

Olin, Margaret (1986) "Self-Representation: Representation: Resemblance and Convention in Two Nineteenth-Century Theories of Architecture and the Decorative Arts," *Zeitschrift für Kunstgeschichte*, vol. 49, no. 3, pp. 376-397.

Oliver, Paul (1983) "Earth as a Building Material Today," *Oxford Art Journal*, vol. 5, no. 2 "Architecture," pp. 31-38.

Oshima, Ken Tadashi (2003) "Constructed Natures of Modern Architecture in Japan, 1920–1940," unpublished doctoral dissertation, Columbia University.

Oshinomi, Kunihide 押野見邦英, *et al.* (2001) "*Sozairyoku he no Kitai: Shinka Suru Kabehyougen 1*" 素材力への期待：進化する壁表現1 a.k.a. "Expectation of the Power Inherent in Materials: Expression of Evolving Walls," *Diteiru* ディテール [Detail], no. 149 (Summer), pp. 48-67.

Pallasmaa, Juhani (2000) "Hapticity and Time," *The Architectural Review*, vol. 207, no. 1239 (May), pp. 78-84.

Parent, Mary (1983) *The Roof in Japanese Buddhist Architecture*, Tokyo and New York: Weatherhill.

Pilgrim, Richard B. (1997) "The Artistic Way and the Religio-Aesthetic Tradition in Japan," *Philosophy East and West*, vol. 27, no. 3 (July), pp. 285-305.

Plutschow, Herbert (2003) *Rediscovering Rikyu: and the Beginnings of the Japanese Tea Ceremony*, Kent, UK: Global Oriental.

Pollock, Naomi (2006) "Masanari Murai Art Museum, Tokyo, Japan," *Architectural Record*, vol. 194, no. 1 (January), pp. 140-144.

Reynolds, Jonathan (1996) "Japan's Imperial Diet Building: Debate over Construction of a National Identity," *Art Journal*, vol. 55, no. 3,"Special issue. Japan 1868-1945: Art, Architecture, and National Identity" (Autumn, 1996) p. 38-47.

Reynolds, Jonathan (2001) "Ise Shrine and a Modernist Construction of Japanese Tradition," *The Art Bulletin*, vol. 83, no. 2 (June), pp. 316-341.

Ricouer, Paul (1961) "Universalization and National Cultures," in *History and Truth*, Evanston, IL: Northwestern University Press.

Ruskin, John (2006) "'The Nature of Gothic' (1851-3)," in Mallgrave, Harry Francis (ed.), *Architectural Theory*, Vol. 1: *An Anthology from Vitruvius to 1870*, Malden, MA: Blackwell.

Saito, Yuriko (1985) "Why Restore Works of Art?" *Journal of Aesthetics and Art Criticism*, vol. 44, no. 2 (Winter), pp. 141-151.

Saito, Yuriko (1997) "The Japanese Aesthetics of Imperfection and Insufficiency," *Journal of Aesthetics and Art Criticism*, vol. 55, no. 4 (Autumn), pp. 377-385.

Saito, Yuriko (1999) "Japanese Aesthetics of Packaging," *Journal of Aesthetics and Art Criticism*, vol. 57, no. 2, "Aesthetics and Popular Culture," (Spring), pp. 257-265.

Sawaragi, Noi (2006) "Strictly Provisional: the Aomori Museum of Art," trans. Alfred Birnbaum, in Aoki, Jun with Noi Sawaragi and Hideyuki Nakayama, *Jun Aoki: Complete Works 2: Aomori Museum of Art*, Tokyo: INAX Publications, pp. 18-33.

Shigemura, Tsutomu (1991) "Wakimachi Library," in Speidel, Manfred, *Team Zoo: Buildings and Projects, 1970–1991*, New York: Rizzoli, pp. 50-51.

Shirai, Sei'ichi (1956) "The Tradition of the Jomon Culture: On the Nirayama Mansion of the Egawa Family," *Sinkenchiku*, English edition, vol. 31, no. 8 (August), p. 4.

Slessor, Catherine (2000) *Concrete Regionalism: Antoine Predock, Tadao Ando, Wiel Arets, Ricardo Legorreta (4 x 4)*, New York: Thames and Hudson.

Smith, Charles Saumarez (1995) "Architecture and the Museum: The Seventh Reyner Banham Memorial Lecture," *Journal of Design History*, vol. 8, no. 4, pp. 243-256.

Sobin, Harris (2007) "From *L'Air Exact* to *L'Aérateur*: Ventilation and its Evolution in the Architectural Work of Le Corbusier," in *The Green Braid: Towards an Architecture of Ecology, Economy, and Equity*, London and New York: Routledge, pp. 140-152.

Sonoda, Minoru (2000) "Shinto and the Natural Environment," in Breen, John and Teeuwen, Mark (eds.), *Shinto in History: Ways of the Kami*, Honolulu: University of Hawaii Press, pp. 32-46.

Speidel, Manfred (1991) *Team Zoo: Buildings and Projects, 1970–1991*, New York: Rizzoli.

Stewart, David (1987) *The Making of a Modern Japanese Architecture: 1868 to the Present*, Tokyo: Kodansha International.

Sullivan, Lawrence E. (2000) "Foreword: Monumental Works and Eventful Occasions," in Jones, Lindsay, *The Hermeneutics of Sacred Architecture: Experience, Interpretation, Comparison. Vol. 1, Monumental Occasions: Reflections on the Eventfulness of Religious Architecture*, Cambridge, MA: Harvard University Press for the Harvard University Center for the Study of World Religions, pp. xi-xviii.

Sumner, Yuki (2006) "Box of Tricks," *Daily Telegraph*, 10 October.

Suzuki, Akira and Terada, Mariko (2006) *Archilab Orleans: Japan 2006. Nested in the City*, Orleans, France: HYX.

Suzuki, Hiroyuki (1996) "*Nihon Kenchiku no Genzai*" 日本建築の現在 [Japanese Architecture Today], *GA (Global Architecture)*, Document no. 47, "Japan '96," (May), pp. 6-13.

Suzuki, Hiroyuki (2000a) "Nature, Material, and Substance", *Japan Architect*, vol. 38, (Summer), p. 10.

Suzuki, Hiroyuki (2000b) "A Return to Materials: Hiroyuki Suzuki and Kengo Kuma," *Japan Architect*, vol. 38 (Summer), pp. 4-5.

Suzuki, Hiroyuki (2006) "*Takasugian no Chakai: Fujimori Ikkyuu Setsu Josetu*" 高過庵の茶会：藤森一休説序説 [Tea Meeting at Too Tall Teahouse: An Introduction to the Theories of "Ikkyu" Fujimori], in Fujimori, Terunobu "*Fujimori Terunobu ni Tou*" 藤森照信に問う [Ask Terunobu Fujimori], *Home X Knowledge*, vol. 6, no. 1, Special Issue no. 7 "*The Fujimori*," (10 August), pp. 89-91.

Suzuki, Ryoji (1987) "An 'Archipolitique' of Architecture," *Japan Architect*, no. 366 (October), p. 36.

Suzuki, Ryoji (1992) "Ryoji Suzuki: Kounji Temple, Tokyo," *Architectural Design*, vol. 62, no. 9–10 (September), pp. 72-73.

Suzuki, Ryoji (2004) "Ryoji Suzuki: Experience in Material #47: Project Konpira," *GA (Global Architecture)*, Document no. 81 (August), pp. 64-83.

Suzuki, Ryoji (2006) *Experience in Material No. 47: Project Konpira, July 2001–May 2004*, Osaka: acetate 007.

Suzuki, Ryoji (2007) "*Busshi Shikou 47 Kotohiragu Purojekuto*," 物資試行47金刀比羅宮プロジェクト a.k.a. "Experience in Material No. 47/ Project Konpira," *Japan Architect*, vol. 47 (Autumn), pp. 74-85.

Suzuki, Ryoji and Futagawa, Yoshio (2007) "*Dai24kai: Shingendai Kenchiku wo Kangaeru O to X: Santori-Bijutsukan*," 第２４回 新現代建築を考える0とX：サントリー美術館 [Thinking about New Contemporary Architecture No. 24: Suntory Museum of Art], *GA (Global Architecture) Japan*, vol. 86, (May/June), pp. 58-65.

Swenarton, Mark (1989) *Artisans and Architects: The Ruskinian Tradition in Architecture Thought*, New York: St. Martin's Press.

Takenaka-O'Brien, Akiko (2004) "The Aesthetics of Mass-Persuasion: War and Architectural Sites in Tokyo, 1868–1945," unpublished Ph.D. dissertation, Yale University.

Takeyama, Kiyoshi (1983) "Tadao Ando: Heir to a Tradition," *Perspecta*, vol. 20, pp. 163-180.

Taki, Koji (1991) "*Kenchiku no Koukyousei-Shakaisei: Shonandai Bunka Sentaa wo Megutte: Taki Koji X Hasegawa Itsuko*," 建築の公共性・社会性：湘南台文化センターをめぐって：多木浩二X長谷川逸子 [Public and Societal Character in Architecture: Koji Taki vs. Itsuko Hasegawa], *Space Design (SD)*, no. 316 (January), pp. 140–152.

Taki, Koji (1997) "A Conversation with Itsuko Hasegawa," in Scheou, Anne, *Itsuko Hasegawa: Recent Buildings and Projects/Réalisations et Projets Récents*, Basel: Birkhauser, pp. 13-20.

Tamamuro, Fumio (1997) "On the Suppression of Buddhism," in Hardacre, Helen and Kern, Adam L. (eds.), *New Directions in the Study of Meiji Japan*, New York: Brill, pp. 499-530.

Tanaka, Stefan (1993) *Japan's Orient: Rendering Pasts into History*, Berkeley, CA: University of California Press.

Tanaka, Stefan (2004) *New Times in Modern Japan*, Princeton, NJ: Princeton University Press.

Tanaka, Tomoaki 田中友章 (2003) "*Suzuki Ryoji Ron*" 鈴木了二論 a.k.a. "Ryoji Suzuki: A Portrait," *GA (Global Architecture)*, Houses, no. 73, "Japan V" (January), pp. 154-157.

Tange, Kenzo (1956) "The Architect in Japan," *Sinkenchiku*, English language edition (October), pp. 7-13.

Tange, Kenzo and Kawazoe, N. (1960) *Katsura: Tradition and Creation in Japanese Architecture*, New Haven, CT: Yale University Press.

Tashiro, Kaoru (2006) "*Fujimori Terunobu wo Shitte Imasu ka?*" 藤森照信を知っていますか? "Do You Know Terunobu Fujimori?" *Casa Brutus*, no. 81 (December), pp. 181-193.

Team Zoo and Atelier Mobile (1982) "Nago City Hall," *The Japan Architect*, no. 303 (July), pp. 7-17.

Thal, Sarah (2005) *Rearranging the Landscape of the Gods: The Politics of a Pilgrimage Site in Japan, 1573–1912*, Chicago: University of Chicago Press.

Thiel, Philip (1962) "City Hall at Kurashiki, Japan," *Architectural Review*, vol. 131, no. 780 (February), pp. 106-114.

Toh, Tadahiro (1978) "Nakagin Village Center: Cracks Pulling Space Apart," *The Japan Architect*, vol. 53, no. 2 /no. 250 (February), pp. 53-61.

Tomii, Reiko (2007) "*Geijutu* on their Minds: Memorable Words on Anti-Art," in Mereweather, Charles and Rika Iezumi (eds.), *Art, Anti-Art, Non-Art: Experimentations in the Public Sphere in Post-War Japan, 1950–1970*, Los Angeles: Getty Research Institute, pp. 35-62.

Totman, Conrad (1984) "Land Use Patterns and Afforestation in the Edo Period," *Monumenta Nipponica*, vol. 39, no. 1 (Spring), pp. 1-10.

Toy, Maggie (ed.) (1993) *Itsuko Hasegawa: Architectural Monographs no. 31*, London: A.D. and Ernst & Sohn.

Toyota, Motoi 豊田基 (2004) "*Dai 53 wa: Konpirasan ha Kyoju no Hoko (Chinju no Mori ha Shinkou to Tomo ni*" 第53話。こんぴらさんは巨樹の宝庫(鎮守の森は信仰と共に) [No. 53 in a series: Konpira is a Treasure House of Enormous Trees (The Garden of the God Chinju is at One with Faith)] *Shikoku Shinbun* 四国新聞 [Shikoku Newspaper], 18 April, 2004. Available at: http://www.shikoku-np.co.jp/feature/kotohira/53/index.htm (accessed 11 June, 2007).

Treib, Marc (1989) "The Making of a Modern Japanese Architecture: 1868 to the Present; The Architecture of Hiromi Fujii; Fumihiko Maki: An Aesthetics of Fragmentation" (Book review), *Journal of the Society of Architectural Historians*, vol. 48, no. 3 (September), pp. 304–307.

Ueda, Atsushi (1990) *The Inner Harmony of the Japanese House*, Tokyo: Kodansha.

Umbach, Maiken and Huppauf, Bernd (2005) "Introduction," in Umbach, Maiken and Huppauf, Bernd (eds.), *Vernacular Modernism: Heimat, Globalization, and the Built Environment*, Stanford, CA: Stanford University Press.

Usami, Keiji 宇佐美圭司 (1985) "*Asobi to Keitai*" 遊びと形態 a.k.a. "Play and Morphology," *Space Design (SD)*, no. 254, "Atelier Zo" (November), p. 95, available at: http://www.zoz.co.jp/libr_folder/usami_folder/index.html (accessed July 8, 2008).

Vlastos, Stephen (1998) "Tradition: Past/Present Culture and Modern Japanese History," in Vlastos, Stephen, ed. *Mirror of Modernity: Invented Traditions of Modern Japan*, Berkeley, Los Angeles, and London: University of California Press.

Walker, Robin Noel (2002) *Shoko-Ken: A Late Medieval Daime Sukiya Style Japanese Tea-house*, New York and London: Routledge.

Waraku (2003) "*Hosokawa Mutekatsuryuu, Chakai wo Nomu*", 細川無手勝流、茶会を飲む [Hosokawa's Guileless Style, Drinking Tea Ceremony], 和楽 a.k.a. *Waraku*, (July), pp. 132-157.

Watanabe, Hiroshi (1991) *Amazing Architecture from Japan*, Tokyo: Weatherhill.

Watanabe, Hitoshi and Emanuel, Muriel (eds.) (1994) *Contemporary Architects*, 3rd edn, New York: St. James Press/Gale Research International.

Wendelken, Cherie (2000) "Pan-Asianism and the Pure Japanese Thing: Japanese Identity and Architecture in the Late 1930s" *positions: east asia cultures critique*, vol. 8, no. 3, pp. 819–828, available at: http://muse.jhu.edu/journals/positions/v008/8.3wendelken.html.

Weston, Richard (1993) "Atelier Zo and the Ecology of Place," *Kenchiku Bunka* 建築文化 [Architecture Culture], vol. 48, no. 564, "*Aimaimoko*" あいまいもく [Ambiguity], (October), pp. 185-189, available at: http://www.zoz.co.jp/libr_folder/weston_folder/index.html (accessed July 8, 2008).

Wicks, Robert (2005) "The Idealization of Contingency in Traditional Japanese Aesthetics," *Journal of Aesthetic Education*, vol. 39, no. 3 (Fall), pp. 88–101.

Wigley, Mark (2000) "The Architectural Cult of Synchronization," *October*, vol. 94, "The Independent Group" (Autumn), pp. 31-61.

Wigley, Mark (2001) *White Walls, Designer Dresses*, Cambridge, MA: MIT Press.

Yatsuka, Hajime (1988) "An Architecture Floating on the Sea of Signs: Three Generations of Contemporary Japanese Architects," *Architectural Design*, vol. 58, no. 5/6, "Japanese Architecture", London: Academy Editions, pp. 7-13.

Yoshizaka, Takamasa and Atelier U. (1998) *DISCONT: Furenzoku Touitsutai* DISCONT–不連続統一体 [DISCONT: Discontinuous Continuity], Tokyo: Maruzen.

Zimmerman, L.L. (1962) "Marc Chagall: His Lessons for the Theater," *Educational Theater Journal*, vol. 4, no. 3 (October), pp. 203–205.

清水
大久保
山崎
松原
水上
宮下
阿久津
中島
川邊
志賀
よしこ
さきこ
伊東
竹内

Index

Numbers in italics refer to pages on which illustrations occur.

Material in footnotes and photo captions has not been indexed.

Photography and Drawing

I am grateful to the following individuals for permission to include their work in this book. Page numbers alone indicate all images on the page.

Unless noted below, all other photographs are by Dana Buntrock.

Ano, Daici 82; 83 (top); 86; 96 (top and bottom); 97; 98 (middle of page)

Aoki, Jun / Jun Aoki & Associates 212; 222

Asakawa, Satoshi (ZOOM, Inc.) 66 (top left)

Fujimori, Terunobu 51

Fujitsuka, Mitsumasa 66 (top, right); 67 (all); 71 (top left); 72 (all); 73; 78 (middle of page); 79 (top right and bottom right); 94; 95

Howard, LeRoy John 25 (right); 39; 50 (bottom left); 52; 69 (top and middle of page); 81 (middle of page); 96; 100 (top); 104; 106

IGA Projekt / Yoshiaki Irie 59 (plan at bottom); 60 (middle of page)

Kengo Kuma & Associates 75 (bottom); 83 (bottom); 103 (bottom); 107 (top), 111

Kojima, Hiroko (permission for use)

Ludquist, Björn 38 (top left and right); 42 (bottom); 43 (top left)

Maki, Fumihiko / Maki and Associates 191; 192 (top left)

Miyamoto, Ryuji 101 (middle of page, left and right)

Pintos Perez, Eduardo 62 (bottom)

Shuto, Katsugi and Daimaru Onsen 63

Suzuki, Ryoji / Ryoji Suzuki, Architect & Partners 165; 166 (top and middle of page); 176 (middle of page); 183; 184 (top left and right); 185 (top, left and center; middle of page); 186 (middle of page)

Tompkins, Erin M. 38 (bottom); 42 (bottom); 43 (top right and bottom); 55 (bottom right); 60 (top row, all photographs)

Toto Shuppan 13 (plan at top left and section at bottom)

Photo and Image Permissions

In addition, the following works are used with permission of the copyright holders of images portrayed. I am grateful for their willingness to allow these images to enrich this book.

Araki, Nobuyoshi / Nihonjin no Kao 218 (bottom)

©2010 Artists Rights Society (ARS), New York / ADAGP, Paris 217

IGA Projekt / Yoshiaki Irie 62 (bottom)

Kojima, Hiroko 224 (top, right)

Museums für Angewandte Kunst Frankfurt 111

Okamoto, Mitsuhiro 227 (right)

Every effort has been made to contact copyright-holders, but if there are any errors or omissions, please contact the publishers.